Fear and Loathing in World Football

Global Sport Cultures

Eds. Gary Armstrong, *Brunel University*, Richard Giulianotti, *University of Aberdeen*, and David Andrews, *The University of Memphis*

From the Olympics and the World Cup to eXtreme sports and kabbadi, the social significance of sport at both global and local levels has become increasingly clear in recent years. The contested nature of identity is widely addressed in the social sciences, but sport as a particularly revealing site of such contestation, in both industrializing and post-industrial nations, has been less fruitfully explored. Further, sport and sporting corporations are increasingly powerful players in the world economy. Sport is now central to the social and technological development of mass media, notably in telecommunications and digital television. It is also a crucial medium through which specific populations and political elites communicate and interact with each other on a global stage.

Berg Publishers are pleased to announce a new book series that will examine and evaluate the role of sport in the contemporary world. Truly global in scope, the series seeks to adopt a grounded, constructively critical stance towards prior work within sport studies and to answer such questions as:

- How are sports experienced and practiced at the everyday level within local settings?
- How do specific cultures construct and negotiate forms of social stratification (such as gender, class, ethnicity) within sporting contexts?
- What is the impact of mediation and corporate globalization upon local sports cultures?

Determinedly interdisciplinary, the series will nevertheless privilege anthropological, historical and sociological approaches, but will consider submissions from cultural studies, economics, geography, human kinetics, international relations, law, philosophy and political science. The series is particularly committed to research that draws upon primary source materials or ethnographic fieldwork.

GLOBAL SPORT CULTURES

Fear and Loathing in World Football

Edited by

Gary Armstrong and Richard Giulianotti

BERG

Oxford • New York

First published in 2001 by
Berg
Editorial Offices:
150 Cowley Road, Oxford OX4 1JJ, UK
838 Broadway, Third Floor, New York, NY 1003-4812 USA

Berg is the imprint of Oxford International Publishers Ltd.

Library of Congress Cataloging-in-Publication Data
A catalogue record for this book is available from the Library of Congress.

British Library Cataloguing-in Publication Data
A catalogue record for this book is available from the British Library.

ISBN 1 85973 458 8 (Cloth)
       1 85973 463 4 (Paper)

Typeset by JS Typesetting, Wellingborough, Northants.
Printed in the United Kingdom by Biddles Ltd, Kings Lynn.

Contents

Contents

Acknowledgements

Invaluable assistance in the completion of this book has been provided by the following people to whom we are greatly indebted: Gerry Finn, Andrew Blakie, Tony Mangan, Eduardo Archetti, Matti Goksoyr, Rosemary Harris and David Russell. Sincere thanks for their secretarial skills are due to Sally Scott, Alison Moir and Karen Kinnaird. For a meticulous proof reading we thank Keith Povey. Our thanks are especially due to those who commissioned and assisted in the production of this work at Berg publishing, particularly Kathryn Earle, Katie Joice, Sara Everett, and Paul Millicheap. Last but not least we thank our partners Hani Armstrong and Donna McGilvray for their patience and support throughout the duration of this work.

Notes on Contributors

Pablo Alabarces is Professor and Researcher at the University of Buernos Aires, Argentina. He is co-author of *Cuestión de Pelotas* (1996) and editor of *Deporte y Sociedad* (1998) and *Peligro de Gol* (2000). He is coordinating a working group of Latin American social scientists on sport and society.

Abdul Karim Alaug, a long-time al-Fatuah member and supporter, holds an M.A. in anthropology from Brown University. His thesis focused on the acculturation of Yemeni immigrants in Detroit, Michigan. He is completing *Women's Organization in the Republic of Yemen* for the doctoral degree in Women in Development at Tilburg University (Netherlands). He is on the faculty of the Empirical Research and Women's Studies Center, Sana'a University.

Gary Armstrong lectures in the Department of Sport Sciences at Brunel University, England. He has written *Football Hooligans: Knowing the Score* (1998), *Blade Runners: Lives in Football* (1998), and has co-edited (with Richard Giulianotti) *Entering The Field: New Perspectives on World Football* (1997) and *Football Cultures and Identities* (1999).

Frederic Augustin is a social worker and a former social science student at the University of Mauritius.

Alan Bairner is a Professor in Sports Studies at the University of Ulster at Jordanstown. He has written widely on sport, politics and society. He is co-author of *Sport, Sectarianism and Society in a Divided Ireland* (1993), and joint editor of *Sport in Divided Societies* (1997). His latest book is titled *Sport, Nationalism and Globalization: European and North American Perspectives* (2000). He follows the fortunes of Cliftonville FC.

Janos Bali lectures in Ethnological Studies at Budapest University, in the Department of Ethnography and Cultural Anthropology. He is particularly interested in the role that sport, and particularly football, plays in the symbolic construction of national identity. His other interests are Middle-East and European Peasantry and the transition from the traditional peasant economy into profit-orientated repoduction. He is currently working on his thesis titled, 'From Peasants into Agrarian Enterpreneurs: An Economic Anthropological Case Study in a North-Hungarian Raspberry-Producing Village'.

Carlton Brick is currently completing his doctorate on the discursive politics of contemporary football fandom at the University of Surrey, Roehampton. He has published widely on such issues as commodification and regulation within football. He is also a founding member of the football supporters civil rights campaign, *Libero* and is editor of the football fanzine, *Offence*. He currently lives in East London and, of course, supports Manchester United.

Ramiro Coelho is a research assistant at the University of Buenos Aires. He is currently undertaking an ethnographic study of the 'barras bravas' fandom phonomena in Buenos Aires football. Graduating in Communication Studies he subsequently worked in adult education.

Paul Dimeo lectures in Sport Studies at University College, Northampton. His doctoral research at the University of Strathclyde explored questions of racism, identity and ethnicity in Scottish football. Since then he has been researching various aspects of football in South Asia. He is currently co-editing (with Jim Mills) a special issue of the journal, *Soccer and Society*, to be published in 2001, also to be published as a book entitled, *Soccer and South Asia: Empire, Nation, Diaspora*.

Tim Edensor lectures in Cultural Studies at Staffordshire University. He has written *Tourists at the Taj* (1998). Recent work includes articles on walking in the countryside and in the city, and an edited book, *Reclaiming Stoke-on-Trent: Leisure, Space and Identity in the Potteries* (2000). He is currently working on a book titled *National Identities and Popular Culture*.

Mike Gerrard is a teaching assistant in the Department of Sociology at the University of Aberdeen, Scotland. As an undergraduate and postgraduate student he was based in the Department of Cultural History at the University of Aberdeen. His doctorate which was completed and awarded in 1998 examined religious movements.

Richard Giulianotti is a Senior Lecturer in Sociology at the University of Aberdeen. He is author of *Football: A Sociology of the Global Game* (1999), and co-editor of several books with Gary Armstrong including *Entering the Field. New Perspectives in World Football* (1997), and *Football Cultures and Identities* (1999). He is currently working on a monograph on sport, and a collection on football in Africa.

David Gould is a doctoral candidate in the Department of History at the University of Reading. His work is concerned with the nature of the relationship between organized sport and the Fascist government during Mussolini's period of rule in Italy. Several research trips to Italy have enabled him to follow present-day Italian football.

Roy Hay teaches sports history at Deakin University in Victoria, Australia. He is the author of books on social policy and has written articles on the social history of soccer. He is currently working with Dr Bill Murray on a history of Australian soccer. He is President of the Australian Society for Sports History and of the Victorian branch of the Australian Soccer Media Association.

Patrick Hazard, a graduate of social anthropology at University College London, is conducting postgraduate research into migrant identities in Turin, Italy.

Hans Hognestad is an anthropologist who conducted ethnographic field work with the supporters of Heart of Midlothian FC between 1992 and 1995. He spent three years subsequently working for UNESCO as a cultural attaché. He currently works as a lecturer at the Norwegian University for Physical Education and Sport.

Roger Magazine is Professor of Anthropology in the Department of Social and Political Sciences at the Universidad Iberoamericana in Mexico City, Mexico. A former Fulbright scholar, he received his doctorate in anthropology from Johns Hopkins University, USA in 1999. His dissertation was entitled *Stateless Contexts: Street Children and Soccer Fans in Mexico City.*

Jon P. Mitchell trained in Social Anthropology at Sussex and Edinburgh Universities and since 1997 has been lecturer in Social Anthropology in the School of Cultural and Community Studies, University of Sussex. His doctoral research was based in Malta, and covered issues of national and local identity, ritual and religion, history, memory and the public sphere. Since then he has published on issues as diverse as football, tourism and masculinity. He jointly edited (with Paul Clough, University of Malta) *Powers of Good and Evil: Commodity, Morality and Popular Belief* (2000), which explores the relationship between economic and religious change. His monograph *Ambivalent Europeans: Ritual, Memory and the Public Sphere* will be published in summer 2001.

Garry Robson is a research fellow in the Department of Sociology and Anthropology at the University of East London. He received his PhD in sociology from Goldsmiths College, University of London, in 1998. He is the author of *No One Likes Us, We Don't Care: The Myth and Reality of Millwall Fandom* (2000). He is currently working on a book on middle-class gentrification and the future of London.

Juan Sanguinetti is a research assistant at the University of Buenos Aires. Graduating in Communications , subsequent post–graduate research examined the nature of social assistance in poor neighbourhoods in Buenos Aires. His current employment involves ethnographic research into the 'barras bravas' of the Buenos Aires football clubs .

Peter Shirlow is a Senior Lecturer in Human Geography at the University of Ulster at Coleraine. His work on the political economy of Ireland has been published in the journals; *Antipode, Capital and Class, Political Geography, Space and Polity, Area and Recluse.* He is editor of *Development Ireland* (1995) and *Who Are the 'People'?* (1997). He follows the fortunes of Linfield FC.

Thomas B. Stevenson holds a PhD in anthropology from Wayne State University. He first went to Yemen in 1978 and has completed five fieldwork projects, the latest in 1998. The author of *Social Change in a Yemeni Highlands Town* (1985) and *Studies on Yemen: 1975–1990* (1994), he has published on sports, migration and family. He teaches at Ohio University's regional university and is an honorary member of al-Sha'b Ibb.

Bea Vidacs will complete her PhD in Anthropology at the CUNY Graduate Center in summer 2001. She carried out nineteen months of field research in Cameroon on the social and political significance of football; her research addresses both the issues of construction of national and ethnic identities and sport's role in legitimizing or challenging these conditions as they manifest themselves in the lives of Cameroonian football people.

John K. Walton is Professor of Social History at the University of Central Lancashire, Preston, UK. His interest in Basque football has grown out of an initial project on tourism and identities in San Sebastian and the Basque Country. He has also worked on, among other things; Lancashire, the social history of fish and chips and English seaside resorts, especially Blackpool. His most recent books are *Blackpool,* (1998), and *The British Seaside: Holidays and Resorts in the Twentieth Century* (2000).

Introduction Fear and Loathing: Introducing Global Football Oppositions

Gary Armstrong and Richard Giulianotti

The history of football is the story of rivalry and opposition. Indeed, the binary nature of football, involving rival teams and opposing identities, precedes the modern game of 'association football' (or 'soccer') and its codification in 1865. During the Middle Ages, the various European forms of 'football' were often violent affairs involving rival social groups (Magoun, 1938). Often, these games would be part of a folk carnival and so would dramatize opposing social identities, such as those between married and single men, masters versus apprentices, students against other youths, village against village, or young women against older women. Football games were brought into the English public schools during the mid-nineteenth century, serving to inculcate an idealized vision of muscular, Christian masculinity (Holt, 1989). In the process, the sporting contests dramatized rivalries between aggregates of young men, while dissipating the energetic conflicts between staff and pupils (Mangan, 1986; Russell, 1997).

With the establishment of football's modern rules, the game had a more rationalized, universalist framework. Accordingly, the game provided a ready background for the expression of deeper social and cultural antagonisms that were existent anywhere on earth. In Britain, rivalries between the old aristocratic football teams were quickly displaced by those between clubs formed in the new industrial conurbations. Typically, the strongest club rivalries grew up between neighbouring localities, due to larger crowds of opposing, working-class, male fans. These occasions were inevitably exploited by early football entrepreneurs, giving rise to a system of local, regional and national leagues (Mason, 1980). Public attention shifted increasingly beyond single games, towards winning tournaments during the course of the football season. Wealthier clubs exercised the privilege of their resources, thereby antagonizing the weaker opponents. The modern sport of football also came to dramatize senses of national difference and cultural opposition, as 'international' fixtures were played, beginning with the annual fixture between Scotland and England in 1872. A similar process occurred overseas, as the game spread through Europe, South America and other British trading centres. A strong rivalry continued to exist between local teams and the various patrician British clubs that had introduced and cultivated football in new lands.

The football world continues to be strongly flavoured by these senses of difference and rivalry. In their most extreme manifestation, the enactment of these rivalries through football can be linked closely to inter-communal violence, such as between Serbs and Croatians (in the former Yugoslavia or among *émigrés* in Australia), Catholics and Protestants (in Northern Ireland or Scotland), or Hondurans and Salvadoreans (as in the 'soccer war' of 1969).[1] In more prosaic form, the non-violent expression of 'hot' rivalry and opposition enlivens the football spectacle for both the participants (fans, players and match officials) and the fascinated, external observer. Hence, we have witnessed in recent years the rise of the sporting tourist, or to borrow from Baudelaire, the football flâneur, who combines a cosmopolitan stroll through European grounds and fixtures with a hint of the bohemian, in toying momentarily with the authenticity of local club cultures. Such cultural tourism is made attractive through the screen images afforded by the transnational transmission of football, and the financing of such coverage, which in turn relies on the safe but ecstatic representation of the game's public gatherings. Football's intense matches remain highly conducive to the game's controlling forces and their principle concern – the accumulation of capital – whether through gate receipts or, more importantly, television revenues.

This book is about the deep-seated senses of rivalry and opposition that emerge through football, primarily at club level. The collection builds upon the peregrinations of the journalist Simon Kuper (1994) to provide the first sustained, academic enquiry into the nature of football's rivalries and oppositions, specifically at club level. The book features sixteen chapters that explore the social and historical construction of football identities that pivot upon senses of opposition and difference. The contributions are drawn from throughout the football world, and centre specifically on the game in the UK (England, Scotland, Northern Ireland), the European continent (Italy, Hungary, the Basque region, Norway, Malta), Africa (Cameroon, Mauritius),

---

1. The two-week war was placed in some kind of perspective by the acerbic essayist P.J. O'Rourke (1989: 143) who noted that it had been predated by no fewer than 42 conflicts between Honduras and El Salvador since the mid-nineteenth century. See also Kapusinski (1992) for a journalist's account of the war.

the Middle East (Yemen), Central Asia (India), Latin America (Argentina, Mexico) and Australia. All of our contributors have undertaken substantial research into the football cultures on which they write. The articles draw upon anthropological, sociological and historical perspectives that are rooted in a qualitative methodological approach. The chapters are organized into four parts.

In Part I, entitled 'The Break-Up of Britain: Power and Defiance in Football Opposition', we examine four forms of cultural rivalry and opposition which surround football clubs in the UK. We begin with three chapters on UK football's richest national clubs. Carlton Brick provides a critical study of Manchester United, the world's richest club, drawing particular attention to the intense animosity that the club now generates from rival English clubs, but also detailing the divisions between local United fans and the 'middle-class day trippers' who are drawn primarily to the team's winning profile. Richard Giulianotti and Mike Gerrard examine the historical rivalries surrounding Glasgow Rangers, Scotland's richest club. Rangers' traditional anti-Catholicism, as expressed through the Old Firm rivalry with Glasgow Celtic, has tended to remain as intense rivalries have emerged with other Scottish clubs, notably Aberdeen. Latterly, Rangers' domestic dominance and financial potential has been thrown into stark relief by a struggle to compete with Europe's top clubs. This discussion of anti-Catholicism is extended through the chapter by Alan Bairner and Peter Shirlow, in their study of Linfield. As Northern Ireland's wealthiest club, Linfield have drawn strongly on their ties to anti-Catholic and Loyalist communities, yet Linfield's claim to pre-eminence as the Unionist club in the province generates animosity from rivals in both Protestant and Catholic communities. Nevertheless, within the Protestant community, there remains an over-arching antagonism to an imagined 'other': the defunct Catholic club, Belfast Celtic. Finally, Gary Robson's chapter on the small Millwall club from south-east London confirms that club rivalries are not all outgrowths of resistance to financially dominant forces. Since at least the early post-war period, Millwall have been typified as a club surrounded by a violent, regressively masculine, racist and neo-fascist fan culture. Robson's research, combining strong ethnography with rigorous anthropological insights, provides a potent challenge to these stereotypical assumptions.

From UK football we turn to Part II, entitled 'Fighting for Causes: Core Identities and Football Oppositions'. Here, we examine four non-Anglo-Saxon rivalries that develop issues initially raised within the Rangers and Linfield cases, and which centre upon sub-national and religious antagonisms. In all of these cases, violence has been one key resource in negotiating relations between the minority groups and the majority communities. Roy Hay discusses the importance of football clubs to the settlement of Croatian immigrants in Australia throughout the postwar period. These Croatian football clubs helped their members to integrate into Australian society, but also marked out and reproduced senses of Croat national identity prior to the formation of the Croatian nation-state. In the small island of Mauritius, as Tim Edensor and Frederic Augustin indicate, football is a key venue in which the ethnic tensions of this 'rainbow nation' may erupt. Edensor and Augustin discuss the violent circumstances surrounding the suspension of football in Mauritius in 1999; they take a critical, long-term view of how global football culture (such as support for English club teams) might serve to bring rival communities together, albeit temporarily. Paul Dimeo introduces his research findings from the football culture in India. Dimeo examines the communal politics that underpin football rivalries in Calcutta, notably involving Mohammedan Sporting Club and the Hindu East Bengal club arguing that football in the sub-continent thus possesses rather paradoxical properties, by serving to unify people while also dividing them. John Walton examines the complex dynamics surrounding the rivalries of Basque football clubs and, in doing so, challenges our popular assumptions about the homogeneity of Basque national identity, at least as far as these fractious forces are manifested via football.

In Part III, entitled 'Fragmentary Nationality: Civic Identities and Football Oppositions', we present five chapters that tease out the complexity of regional differences and political contests between club sides within the context of specific nation-states. Gary Armstrong and Jon Mitchell explore the football rivalries in Malta, noting that the reference points for such oppositions centre on local senses of patronage and class identity, though more recent antagonisms have emerged to reflect the modernization of the island. The interplay of traditional and modern social forces strongly informs three further chapters. In Norway, as Hans Hognestad notes, the rivalry of Viking Stavanger and the small Bryne club enacts a wider cultural tension between urban centres and rural locales. The latter, bucolic identity has been a dominant strand in Norwegian national identity, but Hognestad muses on its future in the context of the world's premier urban game. The next three chapters examine how football rivalries can be strongly influenced by formal politics. In Yemen, Thomas B. Stevenson and Abdul Karim Alaug discuss the rivalries involving clubs from the cities of Sana'a, Aden and Ibb. The authors note that inter-urban rivalries and violence have intensified in recent years, while a greater political symbolism is added to these contests through the widespread club affiliations of politicians and dignitaries. In Mexico, Roger Magazine discusses the widespread cultural opposition that the powerful América F.C. generates among opposing supporters. Magazine notes that Mexicans view the club's supporters with real scepticism; *Americanistas* are deemed to be merely displaying their ambition for upward mobility within a clientelistic society. Finally, Patrick Hazard and David Gould examine the position of the Juventus club in Italian football. They locate the rivalries surrounding the club at four levels: local derbies with Torino, relations with southern teams, rivalries rooted in local honour, and the emerging confrontation with Milan and its owner, Silvio Berlusconi, that is rooted in the televisual commodification of football. Hazard and Gould are critical of prior analyses of Italian football and society, which fail to consider the ideological complexities of fan symbolism.

In Part IV, 'The Others Abroad: Modernity and Identity in Club Rivalries', we conclude with case studies of football rivalries that are defined by relations abroad. In each of our three settings, the host nation undergoes strong cultural anxieties in its attempts to succeed while under perceived pressure to modernize its traditional beliefs and practices. Bea Vidacs discusses the case of Olympic Mvolyé in Cameroon – a club which, though relatively powerful and strongly unpopular with rival fans, appears to be unable to realise its potential. Vidacs situates her analysis within the broader historical and political contexts of imperialism, Westernization, traditional belief systems and science. Olympic are thus seen as particularly undermined by African uncertainty as to whether the 'white man's magic' is more potent and successful in football, than the indigenous variety. In Argentina, Pablo Alabarces, Ramiro Coelho and Juan Sanguinetti examine the historical clash between the traditional 'Latin' style of Argentinian sides, and the modern 'European' style embodied by the defensive, physical and highly successful club team of Estudiantes de La Plata, during the late 1960s. This opposition of styles came to be a metaphor for the Europe-style modernization of Argentinian football and the wider society; while the 'other' model proved temporarily successful in football at least, it was despised as a foreign cultural system. Finally, the chapter by Janos Bali discusses the Ferencváros–Ajax Amsterdam fixture in 1995 and the Dutch accusations of Hungarian racism and incivility towards their players. The furore, involving Hungary's most popular club, was understood locally in terms of the nation's uneasy, lowly position in Europe. And, as Bali points out, the Hungarians did point out the hypocritical aspect of these criticisms, given the record of the Dutch in their treatment of non-Western peoples and cultures.

Part I

The Break-Up of Britain: Power and Defiance in Football

Can't Live With Them. Can't Live Without Them: Reflections on Manchester United

Carlton Brick

'. . . if we didn't exist then they would have to invent us.'

(*United We Stand*, issue 77, January 1999)

This chapter is concerned with a phenomenon widely referred to as the 'ABU' (Anyone But United), forms of which have emerged as significant features of the consumption of contemporary English club football. I suggest that the 'othering' of Manchester United Football Club within the popular football imagination functions as means by which cultures of fandom seek to understand negotiate and relocate themselves within increasingly complex global contexts that now shape the domestic English game. Processes of 'othering' are a deeply embedded and, some would argue, an inevitable consequence of sport, particularly those of a highly competitive nature such as professional football (Brick, 2000). Within the context of English football this process is made all the more real by the historical and cultural centrality of the game as a producer of deeply intense and deeply felt identities at both national and local levels. It would be naive and inappropriate to argue that the 'othering' of a club such as Manchester United by rival supporters is a wholly new phenomenon. Nevertheless, the 'othering' of United has acquired a significance that transgresses the narrow jealousies and binary oppositions of what could be termed 'traditional' domestic fan rivalry. In particular, I outline and assess how significant formations of Manchester United fans have incorporated aspects of the 'othering' of their club. In turn, they use this to express the 'superiority' of their club, and themselves, over domestic rivals.[1]

---

1. This chapter draws on research with Manchester and non-Manchester-based groupings of United fans.

Going 'Glocal' In Manchester 16[2]

It is generally assumed that football and the football club provide a significant focal point upon which local identities can be constructed and expressed. Local ties are generally held to be integral to the function and expression of football fandom, providing the elements of 'authentic' allegiance, passion and rivalry. But the recent period has witnessed a profound problematization of these relationships and their assumed meanings. Giulianotti suggests that the process of problematization is exacerbated by football's increased tendency towards global complexity, whereby: 'Old boundaries between the local, the regional, the national and the global are routinely penetrated or collapsed' (1999: 24).

The footballing renaissance that has occurred at Manchester United over the last decade or so has coincided with the marked penetration of the structures and cultures of English football by global processes. The Premier League has become home to an ever-increasing number of overseas players, Chelsea becoming the first 'English' club to field a side comprised entirely of 'non-British' players in domestic competition, during the 1999–2000 season. England's 'traditional' cup and league competitions have undergone rapid transformation, having in effect been subsumed by the historical evolution of increasingly interconnected and interdependent networks of European and global competition. No longer simply trophies 'in their own right', the FA Cup, the Premier League, and to a lesser extent the League Cup, (known variously as the Milk Cup, the Coca Cola Cup, the Littlewoods Cup, the Rumbelows Cup, and the Worthington Cup according to its most recent sponsor) have become increasingly important to clubs as gateways to these expanding European and global networks.

The fracture of 'traditional' and localized patterns of supporter allegiance has been quite protracted since at least the 1960s. By the mid-1960s English league attendances had fallen to 27.6 million, compared to an all-time high of 41 million at the end of the 1940s (Walvin, 1975). This fall was not evenly distributed, though, as the period witnesses a polarization of support away from local towards bigger 'national' club sides. The relative affluence of the postwar period and the development of integrated and affordable transport networks facilitated greater geographical mobility and accessibility to 'non-local' teams. The increase in television ownership and the increasing centrality of sports coverage within broadcast schedules heightened this already manifest tendency away from the 'local'. As such, by the end of the 1960s, clubs such

2. M16 is the postal code for Manchester United's Old Trafford ground.

as Glasgow Celtic, Glasgow Rangers and Manchester United emerged not only as 'national' clubs, but, facilitated by success in European competition, as clubs with international reputations and fledgling global fan bases.

Manchester United currently has some 203 official supporters' branches, twenty-five of which are located overseas. In order to serve such a globally dispersed fan base the club has self-consciously sought to promote themselves as a global brand. The club already has an extensive retail and merchandising network throughout the UK and Ireland, and plans to open a further three merchandising megastores in Singapore, Kuala Lumpar and Dubai. Indeed, Sir Alex Ferguson has intimated that he would like to take up a role as the club's 'global ambassador' when he finally steps down as team manager. Furthermore, the club have also sought to relocate themselves within the emerging global structures of club competition. United were involved in initial talks concerning the Media Partners-backed European Super League (ESL) (the ESL proposal has for the time being come to nothing as FIFA have agreed to a substantial restructuring of the European Champions League format), and withdrew from the domestic FA Cup to participate in the inaugural FIFA World Club Championships in Brazil in January 2000.[3]

Paradoxically, as the boundaries between the local and the global become less fixed, as Giulianotti suggests, discourses championing the 'essentialist' centrality of 'traditional' local relationships to the cultures of English football have proliferated. Indeed, within populist critiques of the contemporary game 'essentialist' discourses of local 'authenticity' dominate, particularly with reference to Manchester United. In 1995 writer and biographer Hunter Davies presented a television broadcast on the terrestrial Channel 4. In the documentary *J' Accuse: Man United*, Davis accused the club of 'corrupting' and perverting' the course of English football, by '. . . cutting itself off from its cultural and geographical roots'. Davies reiterated these 'fears' in a broadsheet article:

---

3. The British Government's Minister for Sport Tony Banks (1997–9) had initially sanctioned United's exemption from the FA Cup, to allow them to play in the FIFA tournament which United had threatened to boycott in order to avoid fixture congestion. Banks' rationale was that United's involvement would boost England's bid to host the 2006 World Cup. Following Banks 'resignation' a few weeks after it was announced that United would not be playing in the FA Cup, the new Minister of Sport, Kate Hoey, pulled off a rather dramatic government U-turn, announcing: 'I think it's something that should not be happening. Manchester United should be playing in the F.A. Cup; I still hope it's something that will happen. I'm amazed that they have treated their supporters in what I would say was quite a shabby way' (*The Guardian*, 30 July 1999).

The non-Manchester-based fans buy most of the tat. Go to any home match, and you will hear as many Irish or Devon or Scandinavian accents as Lancashire . . . attracted by the glamour which the club skilfully manipulates. (*The Guardian*, 4 April 1995)[4]

Similar conceptualizations were expressed through populist media reactions to the attempted take-over of Manchester United, by the BSkyB satellite broadcaster, owned by the global media 'potentate' Rupert Murdoch. Writing in *The Guardian*, Jim White, sometimes spoof sports journalist, holiday programme broadcaster and Manchester United fan, argued that as a consequence of the proposed bid:

. . . they [Manchester United] may be the choice for everyone from soccer moms in the California valleys to the new Reds is China, no longer a football club but an international sporting brand. But the lad in Stretford, who like his father and grandad before him, has been going to Old Trafford all his life, will be left wondering what precisely it is that he supports. (*The Guardian*, 7 September 1998)

Davies and White share a number of significant tendencies regarding their conceptualizations of the global processes imagined to be at play here. The first is the pronounced tendency towards a 'mythologized' and ahistorical use of the concept 'local'. In his study of the leisure patterns of working-class cultures in Salford and Manchester during 1900 and 1939, social historian Andrew Davies draws explicit attention to the distinct lack of access to 'local' sporting institutions such as Manchester United Football Club. According to Davies the lack of access within local communities was predominantly manifest through forms of economic, geographical and gender exclusion (Davies, 1992: 38). So it is as likely to be the case that Jim White's 'Stretford lad's' father and grandfather didn't get to see United for one reason or another.

The second tendency Davies and White share relates to the processes of globalization. Both construct a false dichotomy between on the one hand 'the global', and on the other 'the local'. Such misconceptions suggest that the dynamic process at play is one of the confrontation and contestation of binary opposites, of the global versus the local, 'us versus them'. Both Davies and White construct very definite notions of who they consider the 'us' and the 'them' to be. The 'us', the local authentic fan; the 'them' the ersatz 'glo-bofan'. Within the rhetorics of anti-globalization, the theme of being under

4. In Hunter Davies's case the phrase 'those in glass houses shouldn't throw stones' comes to mind. Davies shifted his football allegiances from his native Carlisle United to the fashionable Tottenham Hotspur when he moved to London in the 1960s (see Davies, 1990). As for 'foreign' fans buying 'tat', Davies should think himself lucky that they do, as he has just recently penned the biography of the United striker Dwight Yorke. The publishers of such an esteemed tome? – none other than Manchester United.

threat of 'invasion' from outsiders and alien cultures is marked (Maguire, 1999). Such themes are again evident in populist critiques of Manchester United. *The Guardian's* chief football writer, David Lacey, employs this theme in a much more explicit and unmediated way than either Davis or White, drawing direct comparisons between the BSkyB attempt to buy Manchester United and the Second World War:

> For football followers the name Munich is heavy with tragedy.[5] To historians it is synonymous with sell-outs.[6] By accepting Rupert Murdoch's offer for Manchester United the Old Trafford board have effectively marked the 40th anniversary of the first in the spirit of the second. (*The Guardian Sport*, 10 September 1998)

Lacey's evocative manipulation of two distinct but emotive images of Munich to suggest that selling a football club is akin to 'selling-out' to the militarist expansionism of National Socialism is absurd to say the least. But, nonetheless, such conceptual themes are a significant feature of discourses concerning Manchester United.[7] This may be considered as nothing more than a rather clumsy and crude assertion of a middle-class British chauvinism. Such prejudices are, however, imbued with a certain footballing radical chic, given that the 'enemy' is no longer a 'foreign' nation-state but the rather more abstract and amorphous forces of global capital.

But whilst such conceptualizations are commonplace, they are inadequate as expressions of the processes at play. The process of globalization is a much more fluidly complex process than the simple contestation of binary opposites as suggested above, and as Robertson (1992) suggests it is a profoundly dynamic and creative process. Whilst it is undoubtably the case that contemporary processes of globalization threaten 'traditional' local identities, it also facilitates and influences a process whereby notions of the local are reconstructed and reasserted, often with increasing vigour. The oppositions between the global and the local are not mutually exclusive; rather, the process is one of 'glocalization' (Robertson, 1992). Furthermore, 'glocalization' is a key process in the formation and articulation of fan rivalries within English club football.

5. This is a reference to the 1958 Munich air crash which claimed the lives of eight members of the famous 'Busby Babes' Manchester United side. A further three members of United's staff, and eight journalists were among the other fatalities

6. This is a reference to British Prime Minister Neville Chamberlain's infamous 'Peace in our time' attempt at appeasement towards Adolph Hitler's Nazi Germany prior to the outbreak of the Second World War in 1939.

7. Similar comparisons between Murdoch and Nazi Germany are made within the club's unofficial fanzine culture (see *Red Issue*, 14, October 1998).

United Against United?

Following his sending-off against Argentina during the 1998 World Cup quarter-final, a sarong-clad effigy of David Beckham hung from a noose outside a London pub. On his return to domestic football the following August, Beckham became the non-United fans' wicked-witch, in being booed, hissed and abused at every turn. As a talented and influential player, Beckham is subject to greater abuse from rival fans than perhaps other lesser players might expect. Indeed, such abuse has undoubtedly been enhanced by his high-profile marriage to Victoria Adams of Spice Girl fame.[8] I would argue, however, that the abuse meted out to Beckham has less to do with these factors, than the fact that he plays for Manchester United. Paul Ince, Eric Cantona and Roy Keane have all featured prominently in Manchester United's rise to dominance during the 1990s, and have, for one reason or another, been subject to similar forms of 'othering' by rival supporters. Likewise, the post-World Cup 'othering' was a manifestation of an already significant feature of the ways in which contemporary English football is consumed.

Prior to the 1998 World Cup it had become *de rigueur* amongst followers of the English national side to abuse Manchester United players whilst playing for England (at the time of writing, United have eight current England internationals in their first team squad). Renditions of 'Stand up if you hate Man U' has become a noticeably audible chant at Premier League grounds, even when United aren't playing, particularly at televised games, with supposedly 'rival' sets of supporters singing in unison. Since the mid-1990s the chant has been repeated frequently at Wembley during England inter-nationals. The 'hate Man U' phenomenon has also been commodified in more directly consumable formats; a number of websites and books are devoted to the subject.[9] A popular weekly football magazine of the mid-1990s, *90 Minutes*, described itself as 'The Magazine For fans Who Hate Man United,' and produced car stickers to be given away free with the magazine which bore the legend 'Don't Follow Me Or Man United'. These complimentary gifts only accompanied copies of the magazine distributed outside of the Manchester area (*Red Issue*, no 4, November 1997). The writer Colin Shindler, a Manchester City supporter, gave his recently acclaimed autobiography the snappy title 'Manchester United Ruined My Life' (Shindler, 1998). The publishers were wise to the fact that with the words 'United' and 'Ruined' on

8. Formerly 'Posh Spice' in the best-selling pop group The Spice Girls, Victoria Beckham has now embarked on a career as solo artiste, fashion model, mother and TV chat-show host.

9. For examples visit http://www.ihatemanunited.com, a website that sells 'ihatemanunited' merchandising such as t-shirts and baseball caps.

the front cover it was likely to shift a few more units by tapping into the current anti-United *zeitgeist*, than perhaps a book simply about a Manchester City fan might otherwise have been. The appeal of the book lies not in a story of a fan growing up in a city with a historically deep, intense and specific football rivalry, but rather lies in its more general anti-United sentiment. Such generalized reorientations of inter-club fan rivalries are representative of a dramatic reconstruction of the meanings of 'local' and 'rivalry' within domestic English football.

In many respects Manchester United have become, at least at a rhetorical level, everybody's 'local rivals'.[10] This process exposes but also gives voice to a number of tensions manifest within the contemporary English game. Sociologist Anthony King (1998) suggests that the 'othering' of United by rival fans is an attempt to belittle United's achievements, cheapen them and make them less significant. For opposing groupings of fans, Manchester United is the 'inauthentic creation of global capital' (King, 1998: 17). The 'othering' of United operates as a means of displacing the powerlessness felt by fans both within the cultures of their own clubs and the cultures of football more generally, in the face of what seems to be the unchallengeable march of global capital and the rapid transformation of the game's everyday cultures. The irony here is that the process of 'inauthenticating' United, of making them less significant, results in the opposite. Manchester United become increasingly more significant and central within the popular football imagination, as a shared experience through which a number of problematics within English football are expressed.

A significant shared experience has been the use of the 'Stand up if you hate Man U' chant as a rallying cry in attempts by fan groupings to consciously contest the increasingly authoritarian and intrusive surveillance of the match-day experience (Brick, 1997). The 1990s have witnessed a pronounced effort

10. According to an opinion poll in the *Daily Telegraph* (22 May 1999) 86% of respondents claimed they would 'prefer' United to win the 1999 European Champions Cup Final, rather than the German side Bayern Munich. Whilst it is true that within the domestic sphere there is a tendency towards a significant 'othering' of United, it should also be noted that United's European Cup success provided a means through which aspects of a 'British-English' national identity could be expressed. The claim, however, that United's success in Europe was a success for English football was vigorously contested by some United fans claiming that those non-United fans who cheered the club's European success were '. . . the very worst kind of glory hunters. They don't like the team, but can't resist the opportunity to celebrate an "English" victory' (*UWS*, no. 82, 1999).

United have also become symbolic of a national identity at another level. On a royal visit to Malaysia in 1998, the Queen visited the Kuala Lumpur branch of the Manchester United Supporters Club, where she was photographed autographing a football emblazoned with the United club crest. The British tabloid newspaper the *Sun* referred to this moment as an 'amazing break with tradition' (23 September). This breach of royal protocol provides a vivid image of the 'old' Britannia being usurped by the 'new'.

on the part of the police, the football authorities, and the clubs themselves to discipline, regulate and criminalize particular expressions of the match-day carnivalesque. This has taken the form of the imposition of increasingly moralistic codes of conduct and etiquette (Brick, 2000). The introduction of the all-seated stadium has become, for many fans, the key symbol of this criminalization of the contemporary match-day experience, and has actively been resisted through sections of fans deliberately standing throughout games *en masse*. Within this context the significance of the 'Stand up if you hate Man U' is not so much about the 'othering' of Manchester United but the deliberate transgression and contestation by fans of what they perceive to be the unwelcome intrusions upon their relationships with the game and with each other by official forms of authority.

'24 Years' and Still Counting

For significant elements within the domestic United fan base the phenomenon of 'hating' United amongst 'rival' fan groupings has to a greater extent become something of a badge of honour. For many fans of United, their prestige and the prestige of the club is enhanced by virtue of the emphasis placed upon hating United. For these fans, hating United has become a means by which other clubs' fan groupings convince themselves that they and their clubs 'matter'. This is evident within United's Manchester-based fanzines, *United We Stand* (UWS) and *Red Issue* as the former stated in its editorial:

> Being hated in the way that Leeds are appeals to clubs like Chelsea. It would give them a feeling of importance. They would love to think that United fans are upset or even remotely interested in their results because of the reflected glory that that would bring. To be hated by United in the 90's is a very attractive proposition because it shows you are a threat and that what you do matters to the biggest club in the country. (*UWS*, no. 77, January 1999)

Since his return to club football after the 1998 World Cup David Beckham has been significantly 'othered' by opposing and rival fans. But for every form of abuse aimed at Beckham there came a resolute and vocal reply from United's match-going support:

> 'You can stick your fucking England up your arse' has been the best thing about the season so far. This increasingly popular song, along with the associated chant 'We all believe United are better than England' and even the odd cry for 'Argentina' is the sound of a growing republicanism amongst the Red Army. (*UWS*, no. 74, October 1998)

Although the reaction to Beckham's sending off has undoubtedly enhanced the 'anti-Englishness' of sections of United's support, it predates the 1998

World Cup and has been a significant feature by which United fans have 'relocated' themselves within the increasing inter-connectedness of club football at a European level:

> ... it's only Europe that offers a genuine release from the anti-climatic mundaneness that currently inspires an insipid Premiership. (*UWS*, issue 66, December 1997: 29, quoted in King, 1998: 13)

Williams has suggested that this 'pro-European' orientation of Manchester United supporters is representative of a '... search for ways of expressing a properly European cultural identity which both has strong regional resonances with United's north-west Manchester location but which also profoundly by-passes the nation' (Williams, 2000: 105). Whilst these observations throw up some interesting themes relating to regionalism and nationalism, they miss a key driving force behind United supporters' apparent 'pro-Eurpeaness'. The significance of United's 'non-Englishness', and 'pro-Europeanness', lies in the fact that it becomes a dominant form by which certain groupings of United fans are able to 'other' fans of their Premier League rivals. 'Are you England in disguise?' is a frequent United chant. Meant as an insult, suggesting that the team it is aimed at is as poor in ability and style as the national side. Such a chant was a particularly effective retort to West Ham fans' abuse of David Beckham during United's 4–1 victory at Old Trafford on 10 January 1999. During United's FA Cup fifth-round tie victory in February 1999 at home to first division Fulham – then managed by Kevin Keegan (Keegan was being promoted as the favourite to replace the recently departed Glenn Hoddle as England coach) – United fans began to chant 'Keegan for England' after United had taken a 1–0 lead. The television commentator interpreted the United fans' chant as evidence that Keegan was the popular choice for the job of England coach, oblivious to the ironic meanings within the chant. Far from being evidence of support for Keegan, it was an insult, a term of abuse with its embedded message of 'England's for losers'.

The fanzine *Red Issue* is particularly notable for its 'othering' of rival fans through associating them with being 'English'. This is expressed through a variety of entertainingly crude characterizations of 'southern' football support-ers in cartoons such as 'DWAIN DUVATT, COCKNEY TWAT' (*Red Issue*, no. 13, September 1998: 17). Duvatt is characterized as an inarticulate racist Londoner. He is rabidly anti-Manchester United and supports England. It is Duvatt's proposed 'Englishness' and its associated values that are considered alien to the United fan culture. A similar 'othering' occurs in the cartoon 'THE CHELSEA RENT BOYS' (*Red Issue*, no.21, April 1999: 5). A Chelsea fan is depicted as a swastika-tattooed skinhead in an England shirt, siege heiling whilst chanting 'Stand Ahp. . . If yer ayte Manyoo' (ibid.).

For some United fans support for the English national team has simply become another means of 'having a go' at United.[11] This in turn has facilitated an aggressive means by which United fans on the one hand express their superiority over rival fans, and also seek to 'other' rival fans through an association with a parochial and racially-oppressive form of 'Englishness'.

United's away matches in European competition also serve as a means of 'othering' and recasting fan rivalries. During United's recent European campaigns, particularly in the Champions League, symbols of domestic fan rivalries have been a prominent feature of how United fans present themselves. The 1999-2000 Champions League game away to Bordeaux was memorable because of the dominance of the chant 'Allo, Allo we are the Busby boys, and if you are a city[12] fan surrender or you'll die, we all follow United' (*UWS*, issue 91, April 2000). At the same game a sizeable banner with the legend 'JOE ROYALS FAT HEAD' (a reference to the current Manchester City team manager) was displayed prominently throughout the French city. A significant feature of United's European away support is the presence of a flag (a red, white and black tricolour) which has been a prominent feature since an away trip to Honved in Budapest in September 1993 (King, 1998: 15). The original flag bore the legend '17 years', a reference to the last time Manchester City won a major trophy (the League Cup in 1976). Each subsequent season the number of years has been changed to reflect the passing of time since Manchester City's last victory of note. As with other European away games, the flag was prominently displayed in the ground during the Bordeaux game, this time bearing the legend '24 Years'. Such is the deeply-embedded 'localism' of the meanings constructed around the flag that, allegedly, the national BBC Radio 5 match commentator (and long-time adversary of the United manager Alex Ferguson), Alan Green, was verbally perplexed as to its significance to either United fans or United's history (*Red Issue*, no. 32, April 2000).

The significant display of symbols of domestic rivalries by United fans in evidence at the 'Euro away' has markedly distinct features to the 'othering' of rival fans through an association with 'England'. For United's travelling supporters, European competition serves as a site for the reaffirmation of what

11. This is a sentiment shared by both Manchester and London-based United supporters. Indeed one prominent member of a grouping of London-based United fans considered England as 'just another team' and if they required the use of United players they should have to compete for them on the transfer market as any other team would have to.

12. It is the house style of *United We Stand* to consistently refer to Manchester City as 'city'. The use of lowercase in the spelling of 'city' demarcates them as the lesser Manchester club.

are consider as 'real' and meaningful rivalries – such as Manchester City, Liverpool and Leeds United.[13]

The rivalry with Liverpool has a basis in that the two cities contest the position of the major cultural- industrial centre of the North West of England. This has manifested itself through a football rivalry. Throughout the 1970s and 1980s Liverpool were by far the most successful team in England, but despite this success it was Manchester United who were generally perceived as the 'biggest' club in the country. United's crowds were consistently higher than Liverpool's, they generally spent more in the transfer market on 'big' names and were generally considered the more glamorous club. Liverpool fans felt aggrieved that, despite their success, they were still considered a lesser club than United. Likewise, United fans felt aggrieved that the tag of 'biggest club' meant naught in the trophy stakes when compared to Liverpool. For United fans, throughout the 1970 and 1980s, to beat Liverpool was often of far greater significance than beating Manchester City, as it is perhaps for today's Liverpool fans who possibly regard a victory over Manchester United as more significant than beating local rivals Everton.

The rivalry with Leeds United is interesting. Whilst there is an historical antagonism between the geographical regions of Lancashire (Manchester United) and Yorkshire (Leeds United), the rivalry between the two sets of fans is very much rooted in the cultures of contemporary football. When visiting Old Trafford, Leeds United fans have consistently been the most 'unpleasant', frequently singing the 'Munich Song' (a song that disrespects the Manchester United players that died as a result of the Munich air crash in 1958, and much hated by United's supporters). As a result, the 'aggro' between both sets of fans has been particularly fractious and violent. These tensions have been heightened more recently by Leeds beating Manchester United to the 1991–2 League Championship, and the transfer from Leeds to Manchester United of Eric Cantona during the 1992–3 season, a player who was to play a key role in Manchester United's dominance in the 1990s.

The depiction of these rivalries stands in stark contradistinction to the 'othering' of fans of other clubs. In comparison, to be 'othered' through an association with 'Englishess' such as the fans of clubs like Chelsea and West Ham, are considered inauthentic and ersatz rivalries, devoid of any real meaning. United fans tend to see them as the products of fans of 'insignificant' clubs in an attempt to elevate their clubs' standing through hating and wanting

13. According to fans interviewed that had travelled to Barcelona, anti-Liverpool chants and songs were a memorable feature of the carnivalesque that accompanied United's victory in the 1999 European Champions Cup, prior to, during and after the match itself.

to be hated by United.[14] But it should be noted that whilst United fans may consider these rivalries inauthentic, this does not mean that they are not important or any less fractious than a rivalry that may be considered as authentic. I argue above, that as a result of attempts by other fans to de-authenticate Manchester United, conversely United become more centrally important to how these fans see themselves and their own clubs. A similar process works itself out through the 'de-authenticating' by United fans of the rivalry with Chelsea and West Ham. The visit of these clubs to Old Trafford and the away visits to Upton Park and Stamford are for United's more hardcore support amongst the key highlights of the season.

Far from being a point of departure or rejection of domestic English football, the orientation towards European competition and the 'anti-Englishness' of sections of Manchester United supporters, is representative of a process of reconnection. The significant feature of this process is that what could be considered as 'traditional' and 'local' domestic rivalries are recast and made anew within a global context. Whilst the notions of supremacy constructed by the United fanzines and sections of United support are mediated through the club's consistent qualification for European competition throughout the 1990s, they are done for consumption by 'traditional' domestic fan rivals, '. . . with whom United fans have much more interaction' (King, 1998:14). Similar orientations and articulations are evident in other European fan cultures. In his study of club fandom in Turkey, Kozanoglu (1999) draws attention to the prominence amongst Galatasary supporters of the chant 'Do you still play in your mother's league? We are European, we play in the European League' (Kozanoglu, 1999: 121). Similarily with United, Galatasary fans enhance their own and their club's superiority over domestic rivals through the club's 'privileged' position within global footballing networks.

Conclusion

As I have touched upon above, there is a general tendency that suggests that global processes render what might be considered as 'traditional' rivalries irresolute if not obsolete, as clubs increasingly turn their attentions towards the lucrative European global spheres of competition. But whilst it is the case that global processes do indeed cut across and disrupt 'traditional' binary oppositions, they do not eradicate them, nor do they necessarily dilute them. To the contrary, as I hope I have illustrated, rivalries rather than disappearing are remade, recast and certainly in the case of Manchester United tend to be

---

14. The anti-England chants are particular favourites of a number of London-based United fans, who interact more regularly with a wider range of English club fans.

expressed in increasingly fractious ways. The significance of the 'anti-Man U' phenomenon lies in its cultural dominance as a means by which problematics within contemporary football are understood, evaluated, expressed and contested. Within the increasingly complex political and cultural inter-relationships between the local and the global, Manchester United assume the role of a kind of cultural interface whereby global processes are translated 'into a more local context' and are contested within the everyday context and meanings of domestic football (Armstrong and Giulianotti, 1997: 21). Through the 'othering' of United, notions of 'localism' and 'authenticity' are expressed, transgressed and recast anew. So it is perhaps fitting that the final word should go to the visceral *Red Issue*, the most forthright of United's unofficial fanzines:

We've all seen the rampant bitterness in English football in recent years, but this latest bout of moaning just takes the piss.[15] Selling the soul of the game, ramming more football down the throats of a sated public and sticking the prices out of all reality have all contributed to the storm clouds that have gathered. To turn around and blame the one success story for the greed, corruption and stupidity threatening the game, and for killing the magic of the Cup defies belief, even in that climate. The sad thing is, I suppose we should have expected nothing else. (no. 29, January 2000)

15. This is a reference to the critical reaction to United pulling out of the 2000 FA Cup to play in the FIFA World Team Cup.

2

Cruel Britannia? Glasgow Rangers, Scotland and 'Hot' Football Rivalries

Richard Giulianotti and Michael Gerrard

Glasgow Rangers are Scotland's most domestically successful and powerful club. By the summer of 2000, they had won an unparalleled forty-seven league championships, including twelve in the past fourteen seasons, though their European ambitions have been restricted to one trophy, the Cup-Winners' Cup, in 1972. Within Scotland, Rangers have the greatest share of club fans; recent successes ensure average home crowds of over 50,000 at Ibrox Stadium and the club has supporters' clubs all over the world, notably in the UK's former colonies. The majority shareholder is Rangers' Chairman David Murray, while other major investors have been the South African Dave King (£20 million) and the Bahamas-based billionaire Joe Lewis (25 per cent of equity since 1997). The accountants Deloitte and Touche had listed Rangers as the world's fourteenth richest club in 1996–7 with an annual turnover of £31.6 million, but the club slipped two positions to sixteenth place a season later (1997-8) with very moderate growth to £32.5 million.

In this chapter, we explore two general dimensions of Rangers' history and culture. First, we examine how specific, intense senses of rivalry and opposition have been central to Rangers' club identity. These features are most famously located in the traditional 'Old Firm' rivalry with Celtic, and Rangers' long history of anti-Catholicism. A more modern and potentially 'secular', football-centred rivalry grew up through the 1980s and 1990s in Rangers' relationship to Aberdeen. Second, we explore Rangers' standing within an international context. We focus on how their Scottish-Unionism impacts upon the Scotland–England rivalry, and examine Rangers' contemporary international position within the context of club football's continuing globalization.

'Fuck the Pope and the IRA': Rangers, Celtic and the History
of Scottish 'Sectarianism'

Rangers were founded in 1873 and, for most of the club's history, their identity
has been closely shaped through a rivalry with Celtic. In November 1887,
Celtic Football and Athletic Club was founded by Brother Walfrid, a Marist
and headmaster of the Sacred Heart School in the east end of Glasgow. The
new club's *raison d'être* centred on 'raising money to provide free meals for
poor Catholic children' (Smout, 1986: 153). Murray (1998: 33) claims that
there was a more sectarian, ideological imperative: Brother Walfrid was
'determined to keep the poor free from the temptations of Protestant soup
kitchens and to provide a leisure occupation that would save them from
apostasy'. For those exploring the roots of Scottish football sectarianism, the
forming of 'Catholic clubs', and Celtic's rapid success in winning four league
championships over 1893–8, become the seminal events through which
Rangers 'assumed a mantle of similar social and cultural significance . . . as
the home grown team to challenge most successfully and keenly "the Irishmen".
Home grown meant Protestant just as "Irish" was synonymous with Catholic'
(Walker, 1990: 138).

The view of Rangers as a *response*, as a sporting and social defence mechanism, to the rise of Celtic, permeates academic and journalistic accounts of
the Old Firm's origins. Bradley (in Paterson, 2000a) asserts that Rangers'
Protestant political and cultural identity 'would not have been possible without
the formation of Celtic'. Murray (1998: 33) states that Rangers were a 'saviour'
to Protestant Scots who deserted other teams to follow 'the one team capable
of putting the Irishmen back in their places'. Jamieson (1997: 108) suggests
that the Queens Park club might have represented the 'native communities',
but it remained staunchly amateur and eschewed the Scottish league; hence
the Govan team of Rangers set about 'putting the Catholic upstarts in their
place'. Murray (1984: 84–6) concludes, 'The real origin of sectarianism in
Scottish football lay in the very formation of the Celtic football club and
their unprecedented success.'

Finn has been the leading academic force to challenge these 'Creation Myths'
on football sectarianism. For him, Celtic's entry to the Scottish league reflected
the wider attempt by Irish-Scots to *participate* in Scottish society. Finn (1991:
92) argues that 'at no time could the club be categorized as sectarian in the
exclusive and aggressive sense of the term'; instead, Celtic reflected the 'dual
social identities' of their followers, as Irish-Scots. Brian Wilson, a minister in
Blair's Labour government and author of the club's official history, maintains
that Celtic's founders 'were very much against exclusivist Irish Catholicism.
They were very much outward looking in the Irish political context' (*Celtic*

Official History video 1988). Both Finn and Wilson note that the Irish-Scots community rejected the Gaelic Athletic Association's philosophy, in its protection of 'uniquely' Irish sports and ban on members playing 'foreign' sports (such as football). All commentators agree that Celtic never adopted a sectarian policy for the signature of players. In 1895 the Celtic board rejected an attempt to restrict the number of non-Catholics in the team to three; Murray (1998: 107) confirms that the issue was never again raised.

Murray (1998: 34) argues, 'there was nothing religious in the origins of Rangers, they were Protestant only in the sense that the vast majority of clubs in Scotland at that time were made up of Protestants.' Conversely, Finn (1991: 82; 1999) locates Rangers within a tradition of Scottish clubs, formed with distinct religious and political affiliations, and predating Irish-Scots clubs. For example, the 3rd Edinburgh Rifle Volunteers, Larkhall Royal Albert and Clydebank had strong Unionist, anti-Catholic identities before Celtic's foundation. Similarly, prior to 1888, Rangers had begun to openly develop a distinctive ideology based on the involvement of Sir John Ure Primrose who left the Liberal Party in 1886 over the issue of Irish Home Rule. Primrose was associated with the most virulent anti-Catholic and anti-Irish sentiments, and was openly allied with the Orange Order (Finn, 1991: 86). He was elected club patron in 1888 and chairman in 1912; in 1890 he publicly gave support to Freemasonry, 'on his own behalf and that of the Rangers club, a bond which remains to this day' (Finn, 1991: 87). Other prominent club members were involved in Freemasonry and Unionist politics.

Celtic's success helped to sharpen, rather than provoke or create, the Rangers identity. Paterson (2000a: 181) notes, 'Catholic players were being asked to leave the club in the early 1900s once their religion was determined'. 'Bad blood' was recorded between the two clubs as early as 1896, but management at both clubs 'arguably encouraged sectarianism and its accompanying violence as a crowd-puller' (Smout, 1986: 154). Football rivalry was part of a wider religio-ethnic tension in west-central Scotland before the Second World War. Rangers supporters were numerous in skilled working-class areas that had experienced Protestant–Catholic riots during the nineteenth century, and which were religiously hostile to Catholicism, partly due to fears of unemployment engendered by Irish immigration (Walker, 1990: 140). Harland & Wolf, a Belfast shipyard company, opened in Govan in 1912, attracting Ulster Protestant workers to Glasgow, thus strengthening the Irish dimensions of Scottish Unionism. Murray (1998: 34–5) observes, 'Like other giants of the heavy industries in Scotland the owners were happy to appoint foremen who favoured fellow Protestants when employment was scarce. It was about this time that Rangers' practice of not signing Catholics became a policy.'

The interwar period saw the formation of the Republic of Ireland; and an

> increase in sectarian content as Celtic began to fly the Irish free state flag at its matches and
> Rangers flaunted its Union Jacks and Orange supporters badges. The reply to 'get stuck into
> them Orange-Masonic bastards' was 'Kill the Fenian shite'. (Smout, 1986: 154)

Some militant Protestant political parties in Glasgow and Edinburgh gained seats at local elections during the 1930s. Bruce (1985: 104) argues that militant Protestantism in Scotland was marginalized after the war; hence, 'anti-Catholicism in Scotland is no longer a force . . . if Protestantism survives it will be in a "ghetto" in small isolated communities separated from the main culture' (ibid.: 247). More caustically, Nairn (2000: 244) claims that zealous anti-Catholicism is now 'the preserve of cranks and ideological gangsters in Scotland'. Hence, according to Jamieson (1997: 18), Rangers' general ideology was rejected by growing numbers, including the 'mass of decent Protestants', from the late 1950s onwards. Alternatively, Finn (1991, 1994a) argues that anti-Catholicism and other forms of intolerance towards minorities remained within Scottish civil society, with these sentiments partly crystallizing in the practices and discourses of Rangers officials and their supporters.

Until the late 1980s, Rangers appeared to intensify their anti-Catholic employment policy. In 1950, Laurie Blyth was signed on the grounds of his Protestant father, but the scouting system had not uncovered his mother's Catholicism. Blyth was released at the end of the 1950–1951 season without playing for the first team, the only Scottish Catholic signed by Rangers until 1989.[1] In July 1989, Scotland's best-selling newspaper revealed, under the headline 'I was Rangers' secret Catholic', that Don Kichenbrand, a 1950s Rangers forward who in his first season scored twenth-three goals in twenty-five games, had harboured 'a dark secret'. Signed on the basis that as a native South African he would have impeccable Calvinist roots, Kichenbrand also joined the Masons to hide his Catholicism. When rumours about Kichenbrand began to circulate, he was sold in 1958 to Sunderland. In the 1960s and 1970s, marrying even a lapsed Catholic was sufficient still to damage a promising career at Ibrox, as evidenced by Alex Ferguson, Graham Fyfe, Bobby Russell and Gordon Dalziel. Rangers' policy was also thought to have accounted for their failure to sign the goalkeeper Jim Leighton (who won 91 caps for Scotland, and played outstandingly for Aberdeen), and Kenny Dalglish (a boyhood Rangers fan who signed for Celtic, then Liverpool, and went on to win 100 caps for Scotland). Symbolically, Rangers also appointed Willie Allison as their Public Relations Officer. Allison was described by a prominent

---

1. Jamieson (1997: 115) observes, 'Blyth himself claimed that he was so demoralised by his treatment he gave up football'.

sports journalist, Alex Cameron, as 'about as bigoted as they come: the type who would have been in the Ku Klux Klan had he lived in America. He asked right away about my religion' (*Scotland on Sunday*, 30 January 2000). Rangers came to deny the existence of an 'official policy' on not signing Catholics, but the period of 1967–74 saw officials trying to defend their position. In 1967, the Vice-Chairman, Matt Taylor, stated that the ban 'is part of our tradition. To change now would lose us considerable support' (Jamieson, 1997: 117). Rangers Chairman, John Lawrence, confirmed in 1969, 'The policy of not signing Catholics has been with the club since it was formed'; and one board member, George Brown, remarked privately in 1972, 'We will not sign a Catholic, Rangers are the Protestant team and always will be.' In BBC interviews in 1985, the Chairman, John Paton, maintained, 'It's a case of signing the players good enough . . . Celtic are known as a Catholic club even when they play Protestants, so what's the difference' (*Only a Game*, BBCTV: 1986). Novelist William McIlvanney commented acidly, 'Perhaps the answer is the subtle difference between black and white' (ibid.).

Having been overshadowed by Celtic's European Cup-winning team of 1967 – assembled by a Protestant manager and comprising at least four Protestant players – Rangers could no longer rely upon playing success to deflect questions on club policies. The club's greatest achievement – winning the European Cup Winners' Cup in 1972 in Barcelona – was tarnished afterwards when their fans fought Franco's police in a full-scale riot. In response, the Rangers manager, Willie Waddell, announced a ten-point plan to eradicate hooliganism, recommending bans on alcohol at matches and on sectarian songs. The former suggestion was backed by the 1978 McElhone Report, and enacted through the Criminal Justice (Scotland) Act 1980. However, Waddell's brave point on sectarian songs was generally ignored by football officials, the police force and the supporters themselves. At this time, Rangers were embarked on an ambitious redevelopment of Ibrox, following the 1971 disaster at the ground in which sixty-six Rangers fans had perished and a further 145 had been injured. The new stands were effectively financed by the Rangers Pools and other marketing interests that had been established by David Hope, the club's enterprising business manager. According to Pawson (1973: 178–9), Hope was a lifelong Rangers fan, a 'perfectionist', 'an organiser of outstanding ability', and 'the driving force' behind an enterprise that far surpassed any equivalent at other UK clubs. Hope was set to become Rangers Chairman in 1973 and an exciting new era of expansion beckoned. But his elevation was blocked following a divisive board meeting at which it had been noted that he had married a Catholic forty-three years earlier (Finn, 1994a). Clearly, even the economic modernization of Rangers could be directly compromised by cultural traditions at this time.

Souness, 'Secular Unionism' and Scotland

By the mid-1980s, Rangers were in obvious decline: crowds even dipped below 7,000, and the team had fallen well behind Celtic and the 'New Firm' of Aberdeen and Dundee United. To break with managerial tradition, the Rangers board appointed the Sampdoria and former Liverpool player, Graeme Souness, as player-manager in 1986. Souness had no personal connections with Ibrox and, significantly at that time, was regarded in Scotland as an Anglo-Scot who had never played in the peculiar environment of the Scottish league. Nevertheless, the subsequent 'Souness revolution' saw Rangers dominate Scottish football and promised to usher in a secular, monetarist club culture. According to Jamieson (1997), Souness was a child of Thatcherism and New Right market logic, as demonstrated through his intention to buy the best players available, including Catholics. Yet Souness was not averse to exploiting Rangers' Scottish-Unionist traditions, most notably when signing numerous English players, and displaying pictures of the Queen to his team in the build-up to matches against Celtic (Finn, 1994b). Souness's *laissez-faire* conservatism was given a major fillip when David Murray bought control of Rangers in 1988. Murray was a high profile, self-made millionaire from Edinburgh, who accepts he may be seen as a 'fat Tory' by the public (*The Independent,* 26 January 2000). Nevertheless, Murray's 'publicity-minded cunning', according to the sports columnist Graham Spiers, has ensured Rangers may 'continue calling upon the Bacchic approval of the press' (*Scotland on Sunday*, 2 April 2000). However, as we shall see, even with Murray in tow, Souness encountered strong impediments to his stated secularist ambitions; he later reflected that, 'I'll never be comfortable with bigotry, and it will always be at Rangers' (*The Independent*, 14 October 1996). Souness left Ibrox in 1991 to take over as Liverpool manager. He was replaced at Rangers by his assistant, Walter Smith, who stepped down in 1998 to be succeeded by the former Netherlands manager, Dick Advocaat. During that period, Rangers' position in the rivalries and antagonisms within Scottish football underwent some changes, and it is to a discussion of these issues that we now turn.

Unionism, Catholicism and Cultural Intolerance

Since 1986, Rangers have publicly 'dropped' their ban on signing Catholic players, although critics have pointed towards evidence of a lingering anti-Catholicism. In 1989, after prolonged anticipation, Souness made Rangers' 'first' Catholic acquisition by signing the former Celtic player, Maurice Johnston, in highly controversial circumstances. The move was made more palatable to traditionalist fans by the 'snatching' of Johnston from an immanent signature for Celtic, a switch that had been assisted by his agent, the staunch Unionist and Rangers fan, Bill McMurdo. Subsequent media reports began to question the true extent of Johnston's Catholic background, and he was reported later to have aired anti-Catholic songs in pubs during Scotland's World Cup trip to Italy. In the mid-1990s, Walter Smith then signed a few players of Catholic extraction from southern Europe and Latin America. The new recruits were advised by the club to avoid blessing themselves in the Catholic manner during games for fear of antagonizing their own supporters.

Through the 1990s, Rangers players were reported in other incidents with a possible sectarian element, such as switching on the Christmas lights across the Loyalist Shankhill Road in Belfast (Andy Goram), and playing an imaginary flute in Orange Order-style before Celtic fans (Paul Gascoigne). SFA officials complained about the rowdy singing of anti-Catholic songs in the Rangers' dressing-room after one Cup Final victory. Most controversially, in May 1999, the flamboyant lawyer Donald Findlay QC, resigned as Vice-President of Rangers following press reports of his behaviour at an Ibrox celebration party to mark their victory over Celtic in the Scottish Cup Final. Findlay had been caught on film singing 'sectarian songs', notably 'The Sash'. He was fined £3,500 by the Faculty of Advocates for 'professional misconduct', an honorary degree at St Andrews University was withheld, and his season ticket at Ibrox stadium was removed but returned several months later. Findlay was described by *BBC News* as a 'well-known Conservative Party supporter' who had 'acted in some of Scotland's most high-profile criminal cases'. The report cited only two, separate cases: first, when Findlay had defended a man sentenced to life for murdering a Celtic fan; and second, when he had represented another man sentenced to ten years for attacking another Celtic fan.[2] In a television interview, Findlay drew a categorical distinction between physical violence and the singing of songs, adding somewhat paradoxically that he had considered the ultimate act of personal violence (suicide) when the story of his own songs first broke.

Ironically, in August 1999 in Northern Ireland, at the epicentre of ethno-religous division, renewed attempts were made by the authorities to halt sectarian singing after a friendly in Belfast against France. Findlay's behaviour acted as a serious counterweight to the apparent strategy of Rangers manager Dick Advocaat, who had signed the catholic player Neil McCann in 1998. Yet there are few signs of the disappearance of anti-Catholic songs and chants among Rangers fans, particularly at away matches that tend to be attended by the most committed supporters. (Findlay later complained that Rangers were hypocritical in accepting large sums of money from fans whom the club

---

2. *BBC News* (www.bbc.co.uk), 9 June 1999.

would then condemn for singing such songs). Towards the end of the 1999–2000 season, two further controversies emerged that questioned the club's stance on sectarianism. First, Kilmarnock FC elected to change their pre-match entertainment after visiting Rangers fans had appended sectarian lyrics to some tunes at previous fixtures. Second, prior to the Scottish Cup Final, Rangers encouraged their fans to wear a specially designed orange shirt to the match, an invitation accepted by tens of thousands, to the great benefit of the manufacturers, Nike. Murray dismissed any claims of a sectarian undertone to the shirt, but many rival fans and commentators were unconvinced (*The Scotsman*, 26 May 2000).

For some analysts, expressions of anti-Catholicism (such as through songs) are nothing more than residual elements of Rangers' cultural 'traditions'. It is further stated that there is no systematic anti-Catholicism in a secular Scotland, given interdenominational marriages, voting patterns or social mobility (cf. Bruce, 2000; Paterson, 2000b). For other analysts, this secularization thesis is founded on sketchy secondary evidence, while anti-Catholic discourses need to be located more critically within the context of racism, racial prejudice and ethnic intolerance.[3] In other sporting nations, religious intolerance and racial prejudice are issues that are addressed together.[4] In Scotland, in some contrast, the authorities have been willing, when requested, to confront racism against non-whites but reluctant to address more traditional forms of intolerance (Evans, 1999). Yet broadening the comparative remit of the study does allow us to address incidents that pivot on senses of deep-seated prejudice and intolerance. Since 1986, Rangers were instrumental in bringing non-white players into Scottish football, beginning with Mark Walters who suffered sustained racist abuse from rival fans, particularly against Celtic and Hearts. Latterly, Rangers have contributed to anti-racism publicity within football. However, some of this work was undone by an incident in December 1999, when the Rangers captain, the Italian Lorenzo Amoruso, was caught on camera mouthing a racist obscenity (in English) towards a Nigerian opponent, Victor Ikpeba, during a UEFA cup-tie against Borussia Dortmund. Following an initial denial and then apology by Amoruso, the club sought to mitigate the outburst by emphasizing the 'tense' and 'passionate' nature of the game. A few days later, *BBC Scotland News* reported that a Rangers fan of Asian extraction had experienced intimidating levels of racist abuse among fellow supporters, and blamed the club's failure to reprimand Amoruso as contributing to this problem. Rangers' chairman, David Murray, replied that 'this

3. See the collection edited by Devine (2000) which debates the status of Catholicism in Scotland.

4. For example, in Australian Rules Football, the governing body employs an officer to deal specifically with 'racial and religious vilification'.

was only one person who complained'; in relation to racist chanting among fans, he replied 'what do you expect me to do?'[5]

Problems relating to racism and other forms of deep social intolerance tend to be underresearched in Scotland, and are certainly not confined to one football club within Scottish society. However, as one of the UK's biggest clubs, Rangers' response stood in some contrast to the changing legal and institutional culture surrounding UK football. Fan racism has been a recurring concern for football's new institutional actors, such as the Kick It Out anti-racist movement, the government-appointed 'Football Taskforce', the small Football Supporters Association, and the Professional Footballers' Association. There are ample legal powers in Scotland and England to prosecute those guilty of racial abuse. Accordingly, top UK clubs are committed to a more effective public stance that is declaredly anti-racist. For their part, Rangers have recruited several non-white players, while Amoruso himself has contributed to anti-racism publicity. In seeking to expand from their traditional supporter base, the club certainly has the high profile to draw in new, non-white consumers. However, in terms of attendance profile, Rangers mirror other UK clubs in failing to draw in the large ethnic minority communities that often sit on their doorsteps due to demographic changes. Ibrox stadium itself sits in Govan, a part of Glasgow previously synonymous with shipyard employment and a working-class, Protestant identity, but which at the start of the new millennium contained the city's highest concentration of non-white, ethnic minorities. Some marketing personnel at Rangers foresee future initiatives at Ibrox to counteract all racism and bigotry, in order to attract the ethnic minorities in particular (*Sunday Post*, 16 April 2000). It is difficult, however, to envisage an imposition of change in the fan culture purely from above. While ethnic prejudices are usefully located within the analysis of wider social intolerance, we also need to situate the changes and continuities in Rangers' club culture within the context of recent structural changes in Scotland. In this sense, we need to consider the emergence of a strong regional rivalry between Rangers and Aberdeen from the mid-1980s, and the continuing English-Unionism among Rangers' directors and supporters relative to recent political developments in Scotland.

Secular Rivalries? Aberdeen, Rangers and variants of Scottish Identity

During the late 1980s, Aberdeen emerged as Rangers' strongest and, it is often reported, most bitter rivals. Prior to Souness's accession, Aberdeen had won the league championship three times in six years, and triumphed in two

5. *BBC News* (www.bbc.co.uk), 14 December 1999.

European competitions. Their success symbolized the contrasting post-industrial futures of Scotland's major regions. Throughout the 1980s, the West of Scotland struggled through socioeconomic decline, wrought by the Thatcher government's neo-liberal policies and the regional dependency on old industries such as mining and shipbuilding. Conversely, in Aberdeen and the wider north-east, the oil boom of the early 1970s had underpinned a broadening service sector, and greater wealth, security of employment and cultural self-confidence. Economic interdependencies with Europe and North America were much more prominent, and reflected in the Aberdeen football team's European aspirations, and the fan subcultures' embracing of a new supporter habitus. Correlatively, Aberdeen's players became Scottish football's highest earners, while Old Firm players were still considered club servants who should revel in temporary celebrity (Pawson, 1973: 176). Aberdeen's successes provided a community-based challenge to the large minority of Old Firm fans from north-east Scotland who followed the Glasgow teams primarily for reasons of instrumentality (football success) rather than biography (family migration from Glasgow). In a wider historical sense, Aberdeen's rise pointed towards more 'secular' possibilities within late modern, Scottish club football. The local football culture considers itself to be agnostic to questions of religious identity and Irish Home Rule. As early as the 1930s, some Glasgow-based football writers had contrasted the Old Firm's violent, sectarian fan cultures with rather romanticized portraits of Aberdonian self-restraint and civility (Crampsey, 1990: 64). Football thus comes to reflect senses of regional difference within Scotland that are often ignored in the UK or European context.[6]

Souness's multimillion pound side quickly seized the initiative from Aberdeen. Some early matches between the two sides were deemed 'classics' (notably the three league cup finals of 1987–9), but league games were notably violent and bitterly contested, with red cards, player injuries and ground vandalism subjects of broad sporting debate. Rangers players commented that Aberdeen matches had surpassed Old Firm derbies in the competitiveness and enmity among players and fans. After 1991 Aberdeen endured serious decline, but Rangers players and officials complained that Aberdeen still played exceptionally well against them. Latterly, some Celtic fans endeavoured to draw Aberdeen supporters into a symbolic anti-Rangers alliance, such as by chanting, 'Stand Up If You Hate Rangers'. Aberdeen fans have replied by chanting, 'We Hate Rangers More Than You'. While the verse is certainly

---

6. For example, the debates of the late 1980s on the 'Europe of the regions' tended to discuss Scotland as a relatively homogeneous cultural-national unit, analogous to regions like Catalonia, when, as the chapter by Walton in this volume indicates, such generalizations are often shown to be problematic (particularly by the nature of football rivalries).

intended to offend Celtic fans, it also expresses a critical realization, found elsewhere in Scottish club football, that the Old Firm have rediscovered their mutual financial interdependencies from which other clubs are categorically excluded. Celtic are a relatively equal partner in the Old Firm, in terms of playing team, annual budget, stadium and merchandise profile. Close links exist between the clubs' marketing and planning personnel, in planning joint business domestically and overseas.[7] Thus, for Aberdeen, what we have here is a metaphor for the structural changes within post-industrial Scotland through to the late 1990s. The Rangers' revival mirrored the emergence of Glasgow as a 'core' location for post-industrial services and flexible accumulation, such as in media, retailing, property investment, the arts and sport.[8] Conversely, in the north-east, there have been growing concerns that control over local cultural services and political representation has been annexed by the West.[9] In terms of football's globalization, and in the creation of post-industrial service sectors, Aberdeen appears to have been comparatively *dis*connected from European business in which it had previously hoped to compete.

A significant, wider reference point for the Rangers–Aberdeen rivalry has been the senses of diverging Scottish identity that the two clubs can be taken to represent. Aberdeen fans clearly identify with the dominant form of Scottish political and civil identity, with its senses of clear difference from England and Englishness. Conversely, Rangers' variant of English-Unionist identity has intensified since the mid-1980s. Graeme Souness signed top English players, including the England captain (and major Thatcher supporter) Terry Butcher. Rangers fans have extended their celebration of English-Unionist influence, wearing England football regalia and brandishing the English flag, the St George Cross, and singing songs such as 'God Save The Queen', 'Rule Britannia', 'Swing Lo' and 'Three Lions'.[10] Rangers club officials have also been very vocal in supporting the Conservative and Unionist Party in Scottish

7. In 1999, the clubs signed a £13 million joint sponsorship deal with telecommunications giant NTL; a proposed joint 'club shop' at Glasgow airport was shelved only because of high start-up costs.

8. It should be noted that, in the context of rapid restructuring, the new 'leisure-centred' service economy would precipitate illegal activities that reflect entrenched forms of social exclusion. For example, in 1999, Glasgow's illicit drug trade had an estimated annual turnover of £100 million, more than that of Rangers and Celtic combined; this figure excludes huge revenues from 'related services', notably prostitution and theft.

9. The takeover of Aberdeen-based radio and television stations by a Glasgow-based institution led the north-east press to complain that regional services were being superseded by outside interests. Using a striking football analogy, one local media employee claimed that it was 'as if Aberdeen Football Club was being run as a reserve team by David Murray at Ibrox' (*Aberdeen Independent*, 27 January 2000). Meanwhile, more populist elements in the north-east media have sought to portray the new Scottish Parliament as dominated by Glasgow–Edinburgh interest groups and cronyism.

politics. Yet such a political stance mirrors the club's anti-Catholic history in terms of its growing political marginality within Scotland. At the 1992 election, the Conservatives remained a rump in Scotland, winning only eleven of seventy-two seats; at the 1997 election, they were wiped out in Scotland. At the 1998 Scottish referendum on Home Rule, Donald Findlay played a leading role in the Conservative-led 'No' campaign, but Scots voted strongly for a devolved Scottish Parliament with tax-raising powers.

Within the strict context of Scottish football, the embrace of English signifiers by Rangers fans serves to present them as the fundamental 'others', and thus reflects the intensified opposition of many rival fans towards an increasingly powerful Rangers side. English signifiers serve to redouble the Rangers fans' traditional sense of embattlement, immortalized in one line of their songs ('No one likes us, we don't care'), and which parallels the sense of ethnic encirclement found among the more militant Protestant communities in Northern Ireland. But within the broader context of political devolution and cultural modernization, the references of Rangers fans to symbols of the old Britannia (the Empire, the Union Jack, seventeenth-century wars) appear increasingly kitsch. Opposing Scottish fans (except Celtic followers) have taken to singing 'Flower of Scotland', the *de facto* Scottish anthem, to challenge the apparent English-not-Scottish identity of Rangers. At one Aberdeen–Rangers fixture in January 1999, the local police intervened to stop Aberdeen's disc-jockey from playing the anthem over the PA system, following vandalism and strong booing by Rangers fans.

The English-Unionism of Rangers, and its confluence with football and wider identity questions, comes under closer scrutiny with regard to the national football team, which is the sporting symbol of Scotland. The England–Scotland fixture is the oldest in world football and, for the Scots particularly, was an important venue for the performance of cultural differences and nationalist rivalry. During the 1970s, the fixture acquired some stronger elements of anti-Englishness for Scots, as symbolized by the intensified booing of the official British national anthem, 'God Save The Queen'. For some political nationalists, this Scottish obsession with beating England and other teams served to vitiate any 'fairytales about independence' (Nairn, 2000: 197). The violence involving rival English and Scottish fans through the late 1980s led to the annual fixture being suspended after 1989. Certainly, Rangers fans

10. 'Rule Britannia' is a British imperialist standard associated with the music hall patriotism of the early 20th century. 'Swing Lo' is the unofficial anthem of the English rugby team, while 'Three Lions' was the English football team popular anthem for the 1996 European Championship, at which Scotland played England at Wembley. Networked supporter sub-cultures have sprung up between Rangers fans and their parallel entities in other parts of the UK. In particular, there are the so-called 'Blues Brothers' links with Chelsea fans in London and Linfield fans in Northern Ireland; respectively, these clubs have explicitly right-wing and Loyalist elements within their following.

were well-represented among the Tartan Army (Scotland's fans at matches); they also contributed significantly to its anti-English practices and discourses. However, for hard-core Scotland fans, there are obvious tensions between Rangers' English-Unionism and the Tartan Army's ritualized anti-Englishness. Symbolically, there has been a particular antagonism of hard-core followers to the wearing of Rangers colours at Scotland matches, notably overseas.

The debate here becomes most polarized when the nationalist pull of Scotland apparently contradicts the business interests and ideological frame-work of Rangers. When the national team played at Ibrox in the early 1990s, some non-Rangers fans were dissuaded from attending due to the match's location and the sizeable 'rent' being charged by Rangers. Through the late 1990s, some of Rangers' Scottish internationalists were scrutinized by supporters for being caught in a 'club versus country' conflict; attention centred on the players' presumed tendency to withdraw from the Scotland squad with 'injuries', but then play for their club soon afterwards. Tensions between the aspirations of dominant clubs and those of national teams are hardly specious to Scotland, as the chapter by Carlton Brick (Manchester United and England) most clearly illustrates. However, with the Old Firm, and most acutely with Rangers in respect of Scotland, that tension is considered to go beyond business interests. As the columnist and broadcaster, Stuart Cosgrove, has argued, 'Scotland is not a concept that Rangers are entirely comfortable with . . . at times it seems as if they are living in forced exile in a foreign country' (*Daily Record*, 3 March 2000).

These kinds of criticism were thrown into stark relief in November 1999 when Scotland were drawn against England in a two-leg qualifier for the Euro-pean Championships. Predictably, the draw excited immense interest throughout the two nations. As usual, the captain Colin Hendry was picked for the Scotland squad. After the 1998 World Cup, Hendry had signed for Rangers in a move that was partly intended to reaffirm Rangers' Scottish links, but he was rarely selected to play. Nevertheless, prior to the England fixture, Rangers' chairman David Murray warned the Scottish Football Association that he would be seeking compensation for injuries incurred by Colin Hendry while he had been captaining Scotland. Press reports at the time also focused on the possible 'burnout' of Rangers' young midfielder, Barry Ferguson, who was due to play for Scotland in both matches. For analysts such as Ian Bell, Scotland's leading political journalist, Murray's interventions suggested a 'certain arrogance', leaving the impression that he wanted to pick the national side to the benefit of Rangers rather than Scotland (*The Scotsman*, 11 November 1999).

Now there is certainly a sense in which the England–Scotland fixture, and relations between the two nations, have undergone some significant trans-formations. The fixture itself was a means to an end (qualification), rather than a competitive end in its own right, while the rival players were demonstrably inferior to many overseas stars at top UK clubs. Media discussions of the game were articulated through a rather 'conservationist' lexicon. In memory of times past, rival fans were furnished with a hologram of the old British antagonism. In Scotland, the old referents for anti-Englishness had been displaced by political devolution and a more autonomous Scottish civil society. (One could even argue that these political and civil expressions of Scottishness emerge *as a compensation for* the national team's failure to deliver the more important, football prizes). Conversely, the post-devolution English made greater use of this virtual event, adding a sporting edge to the belated, contemporary debates on the meaning of Englishness.

Never the less, this Rangers–Scotland debate inevitably points up the transnational business ambitions of the club, and how these may run counter to the national team and its attendant institutions. Murray's comments about possible injuries to one of his reserve players echo the publicized concerns of European superclubs regarding damage to their expensive assets while on national duty. Hence, the comments seem to be framed as discursive passports into such exalted company. The globalization of elite club football certainly provides the structural backdrop for this business vision, and it is to a discussion of Rangers' post-national, global possibilities that we now turn.

Beyond the 'Old Consumers'? Rangers, cultural identity and the contours of globalization

To discuss Rangers' position within the globalization of club football, we shall draw upon the work of Roland Robertson (1990, 1992). Specifically, we focus on three interrelated aspects of globalization that are suggested by Robertson. First, the migration of peoples generates forms of 'wilful nostalgia', the greater organization of cultural memories, and the nurturing of 'unique' collective identities. Robertson (1990) accepts Stauth and Turner's (1988) position that such nostalgia involves *inter alia* imagining the world in terms of historical decline and a loss of collective cohesion. Second, the 'universalization of particularism' establishes the grounds for cultural nostalgia through the organization of international and indeed global relations that centre on notions of particularized, national-societal difference. Third, the parallel process of 'particularization of universalism' allows the world to acquire a 'sociopolitical concreteness' in specific ways, such as through global time-zones that enable particular, national variations.

Rangers' historical and cultural identity helps to demonstrate the value of these typologies. 'Wilful nostalgia' has been expressed in two, spatially-centred ways. Within the UK, it has sought to reverse signs of decline by conserving magically the Empire and the Union, in song and in symbolism. In terms of the 'universalization of particularism', Rangers have long tapped into the Protestant Scot communities that emerged in the old Dominions throughout the late nineteenth and twentieth centuries. Importantly, these immigrants were relatively well-resourced within the host societies, and so support for Rangers became a key popular cultural space through which an imagined (and rather frozen and exclusionary) Protestant Scot community could be magically recovered (cf. Walker, 1990: 146; Boyle, 1994: 81). Additionally, the 'particularization of universalism' occurred in one significant way, through football's development into the 'global game'. But, the universal game was 'particularized' for Rangers fans through dominance of the Scottish league system, the 'traditional' club culture of Unionism and anti-Catholicism, and the associated rivalries with Celtic. The net result of these processes was to create a massive market comprising, what we term here, the 'old consumers', that is those Rangers fans who were socialized into the early wave of the club's modern commodification through until the late 1980s.

New processes of globalization now centre less on the imagining of traditional community ties, and more on fluid, cosmopolitan or neo-tribal forms of consumption. These transformations undoubtedly affect the marketing of global football identities. 'Wilful nostalgia' and the 'universalisation of particularism', as they currently stand, would otherwise artificially restrict consumers to those holding a specific association with the nation-state (Protestant Scots for Rangers) or, in football terms, with the club's 'traditions' (anti-Catholicism, Unionism for Rangers). Meanwhile, the 'particularization of universalism' is being revolutionized, in football terms, by the challenge to the 'particularist' primacy of the nation-state and its ordering principles (such as the Scottish league system). Player interests, transnational merchandising companies and the growth of club football, notably among the world's 'superclubs', are coming to reorder football's basic structures.

For Rangers, there are both opportunities and major problems within this new global context. More positively, constant league victories and European appearances (albeit brief) have enhanced Rangers' 'universal' profile. Rangers' long-term support, suffused with these 'old consumers', shows an inelastic demand for club products and services, providing a solid basis for growth (cf. Conn, 1997: 155). Rangers might still trade to that market on the 'wilful nostalgia' of club history and ethno-religious identity, but Celtic are perhaps better placed to expand here: there are far more people of Irish-Catholic extraction than Protestant Scot background. Similar problems exist in the 'universalization of particularism' *qua* Rangers' identity overseas. Rangers' British-Unionist baggage and symbolry is increasingly outmoded in a British state that badly needs reinvention (Nairn, 2000). Meanwhile, the residual anti-Catholicism contradicts the multicultural market imagery of football's major corporations (from FIFA through to Nike).

It is within the new 'particularization of universalism' that Rangers' longer-term prospects face crucial examination. The salient indices here are club growth and the structure of competitive frameworks. Economically, the Old Firm are untouchable in Scotland, but encounter faster-growing competitors elsewhere, especially England.[11] Rangers' top-twenty European status is threatened by future capitalization of clubs in Italy and Germany, while, in global terms, South American teams are pursuing legal changes to enable share-market entry. David Murray's spending on players has exacted a heavy toll on his parent company; Murray International Holdings (MII) lost £12.8 million in 1999, nearly all of it through Rangers, placing MIH fourth top in the 'loss leaders' of all Scottish companies (*Scottish Business Insider*, 17 January 2000). By the summer of 2000, Rangers' debts stood at around £48 million.

The kernel problem is Rangers' location in a semi-peripheral national league and its associated symbolic economy. Like other top clubs in smaller European nations (such as in Portugal, the Low Countries, Scandinavia), Rangers endure low domestic television income and a 'virtual curtain' of exclusion from the large national leagues in Germany, England, Spain and Italy (Giulianotti, 1999). For the year 2003, estimated television income for Barcelona, Manchester United and Scotland's Old Firm are £60 million, £35 million and around £4 million respectively (*Independent*, 1 March 2000). Top world professionals are reluctant to join a hugely wealthy but semi-peripheral club, hence Rangers pay inflated fees and salaries for players outwith the global elite.[12]

Three organizational solutions have been mooted recently: an enlarged European Superleague system involving up to eighty or more sides; an Atlantic or European League of top clubs from semi-peripheral nations; and possible entry of the Old Firm to the English league. All proposals envisage a likely continuation of Rangers' marketable rivalry wih Celtic. The European Superleague would ideally be approved by UEFA, but would still enable clubs from larger nations to continue in lucrative domestic tournaments, thereby debilitating Rangers' long-term competitiveness. Entry to the English league system would probably be strongly opposed by many other English clubs.

11. Turnover at English clubs expanded spectacularly in the late 1990s: Arsenal, from £27.1 million to £40.4 million; Liverpool, from £39.1 million to £45.5 million; Newcastle, from £41.1 million to £49.2 million; and Chelsea, from under £27 million to £47.5 million (*BBC News* [www.bbc.co.uk], 3 February 1999, 1 December 1999).

12. For example, we may list the Dutch players Van Bronckhorst and Mols (not Kluivert, Seerdorf or Bergkamp); the Chilean striker Rozenthal (not Salas or Zamorano); the Italian defenders Amoruso and Porrini (not Ferrara, Maldini, Cannavaro or Nesta); the Argentinian Amato (ex-Real Mallorca); the post-injury Kanchelskis.

Most likely, the much-discussed Atlantic or European league would deliver a potential television audience of over 50 million, and probably require secession from the Scottish league. The involvement of other Scottish clubs has been suggested. But with the distribution of television monies and league membership being calibrated according to prior wealth and viewing figures, there is little prospect of Scottish clubs outside the Old Firm mounting serious challenges within the new competition.

Towards New Fan Identities? A lack of 'cool' in the old 'hot' Rangers

Evidently, the cultural identities surrounding Rangers, and their antagonistic relationships to other identity constructs, have undergone some changes throughout the club's history. A useful way of explaining these changes is to employ the dichotomy of tradition and modernity. Within the business-orientated football world, as Taylor (1971) and Critcher (1979) long ago indicated, this opposition can be explained in terms of supporter identity as we move from *traditionalist* supporters (with communal ties to the community) through to *modern* consumers (whose consumption patterns constitute their means of club identification). However, this simple opposition perhaps does not allow for important internal gradations within football fandom. For example, surely fans who consume club products heavily and identify strongly with the club culture are categorically different, both to local-standing fans who have been priced out of attending games, and to fans who buy into supporting the club from afar. Moreover, there is no overnight, irreversible shift from a traditional fan base to a rampant consumer one.

To enable a more reality-congruent taxonomy to be advanced, we find it useful to introduce a further opposition. This additional binary, of *hot* and *cool*, thus refers to a supporter's cultural identification with the club, its historical values and its community of fellow fans. This opposition of hot-cold is a modified application of the binary that Turner (2000) uses to explain the sociology of body fashions and adornments. Hence, *hot, traditional* fans constitute fans who tend to have long-standing personal identification with, or community ties to the club, but make a relatively limited (or consciously no) consumer engagement with the club. *Hot, consumer* fans are those fans who spend significantly on the club, while retaining their strong sense of community membership with its history and ethos. *Cool, traditional* fans are those followers who spend little on football; they may identify with established club cultures, but have little personal attachment to any of these, since free-to-air television and other popular media are their main sources of fleeting football participation. Finally, we have the vast number of *cool, consumer* fans, a postmodern category which is targeted for football's brave new global world. They spend regularly on the game, particularly through subscription television or on merchandise. They develop relatively circumscribed club allegiances, beyond an ironic attachment to fashionable teams and celebrity players, but their market potential is enormous and greatly prized. As we argue here, it may be that Rangers' social history puts them in a particularly difficult position for attracting these supporters, relative to other prospective superclubs.

A long-standing, even intrinsic feature of Rangers' history has been its hot, traditional association with deep-seated anti-Catholicism, as a particular manifestation of Rangers' Scottish, Protestant and Unionist identity. What is striking here is the role of Rangers' cultural identity in countermanding the financial expansion of the club at important stages. In other words, Rangers have been successful generally in transforming the club's corporate culture from a traditional, wealthy institution centred on fans and playing, to a business that responds to consumers. But ideological residues have lingered, resistant to a cultural cooling, and often have threatened the club's pure business interests. Anti-Catholic recruitment policies robbed Rangers of potentially decisive personnel, most acutely during the 1970s and early 1980s when the club was embarked on major infrastructural investment programmes. These conflicts highlighted the contradictions behind Rangers' conversion of the hot traditionalist identity of its supporters into a hot form of consumer identity (such as by improving ground facilities and catering).

From the mid-1980s onwards, Rangers' English-Unionism became more prominent, increasingly among its hot consumer fans. This stance represented a counterpoint to the aggregated Scottish identity of rival teams outwith the Old Firm, just as Scottish political and civic autonomy was intensifying. But, like the Irish-Scottish identity of Celtic, Rangers' Scottish-Unionist identity served to point up the potential for diverse expressions of Scottishness. The core–periphery antagonism of Aberdeen and other clubs towards the Old Firm adds a regional inflection, again illustrating that the seemingly homogenous, new Scottish polity contains internal realms of difference and division. These other stances towards Scotland have proved conducive to the establishment of a Rangers identity that can ignore the constitutive interests of the Scottish football team or the Scottish football authorities. The construction of Rangers as a genuine, global club player (not merely a national one) is certainly viable in terms of starting wealth and market trends. But how might that modernization be vitiated by cultural baggage from the late-nineteenth century?

In terms of cultural reinvention and social representation, it is instructive to consider two sets of parallels faced by Rangers and the Blair political regime. First, in relation to the old emblems of 'Great Britain', some analysts posit that there is no possible future for the perishable symbols of the world's oldest modern state. According to Nairn (2000: 57–9), the Labour government under Blair (its landslide victory and ultra-modernist media patina notwithstanding) was merely a curator for the British state and its symbols. Nairn scoffs at Blair's conservationism, his lack of qualities and ineffible predilection for youthfulness and 'cool'. Certainly, New Labour's arrival in office was tied crassly to the envisioning (ultimately doomed) of a reinvented, 'cool britannia', culturally primed for the new millennium, featuring the greatest theme park (the risible London Dome), the greatest rock bands (the fragmenting Oasis or the onanistic Radiohead), and the greatest festival on earth (the 2006 World Cup Finals, given to Germany).[13] The social meaning of 'cool' is also redolent of a lack of 'hot' membership, and thus numerically unstable.

Second, and developing this point, the technically successful reinvention of Labour under Blair does shadow Rangers' uncertain pursuit of what we would dub here the cool consumers, that is those free of ideological or membership concerns. In sephological terms, the existing institution (Labour or Rangers) is detraditionalized to attract these cool voters or consumers. Traditionalists are encouraged to forfeit the old hot bonds of community (Labourism or anti-Catholicism) in return for cold, instrumental benefits (more votes or more victories). Modernizers argue that, however alienating the cool reincarnation may be, the old hot supporters or consumers will not desert the ship, since they have no obvious exit points into rival clubs or parties. Traditionalists point out that a cool, consumer attitude in politics or football gets you no guarantees of future loyalties, in support or finance. Yet unlike Blair's Labour, Murray's Rangers are still surrounded by far more regular gatherings of the hot elements, and their celebration of symbols and songs from an earlier age.

Rangers' proposed role in a European league of semi-peripheral nations might appear to suspend these potential conflicts, between British and global imagery, and between hot and cool forms of consumption. This kind of league would represent only a partial celebration of the globalization of club football, in terms of political economy and cultural identity. Rather than compete with Europe's real elite clubs, and thus turn the club into a global commodity sign, this European tournament would encourage Rangers to return to its established supporter base, to its 'hot consumer' group and its lingering strains of Scottish-Protestant, English-Unionist and anti-Catholic ideology. Certainly, Rangers still have to test the extent to which these hot consumers may finance

13. In the context of this failed mission of Brit reinvention, we may note the inference of a seminal commission report, launched by the Blair government, which concluded that 'Britishness is racially coded' – and thus incapable of redefinition (*The Guardian*, 11 October 2000).

future initiatives, such as more European fixtures or pay-per-view television. Nevertheless, as Graham Spiers and other sports journalists have noted, there must be limits to the hot consumers' demand for club products (*Scotland on Sunday*, 2 April 2000). As we have stated, the hot significations of these supporters (notably anti-Catholicism) may be considered off-putting to a global market of multicultural, transnational consumers. But there remains one market, in England, which has not been adequately tapped. There are millions of fans at dozens of English clubs who, in European competition, would support any other team than those English sides which dominate at home (especially Manchester United). In Rangers, these cool (television-fed) supporter groups may find a club to warm to, a club which retains English-Unionist connections and harbours a very strong supporter culture replete with British symbolism. Some English fan groups already proclaim warm Rangers' allegiances, and claim to have informal 'twinning' ties with hardcore Rangers followers. Most of these English followers might fall into the unusual category of cool traditional followers of Rangers. They develop a reversible interest in the club, initially through their apparent English connections; their support is sustained only by catching the club's regular victories on television, while there is very limited consumption of Rangers paraphernalia. It is within this cool market that Rangers might find the seeds of a possible warm consumer group, willing to ignore the question of cultural modernization at the UK's biggest 'British club'. But that must still be considered a 'second-best', relative to the cool, global ambitions that Rangers should have if they are to compete with the world's superclubs.

However, our final point here relates to the very nature of football rivalry that emerges through such a European league. The founding of a new league for the purposes of television might itself be blighted by this medium's logic of consumption. Television is a 'cool medium' belonging to 'cool times', with low intensities and affects, compared to the 'hot' public rituals of the past. In terms of a prospective European league, artificial, 'cool rivalries' emerge; matches are viewed through the distanced medium of subscription television or with analytical detachment from the stadiums' stands. For example, Rangers versus Sporting Lisbon (ironically in Celtic-style colours) has no underlying, hot antagonism, except for the professional rivalries between players or marketing machines. Such a virtual form of rivalry does appeal more obviously to the new, cold consumers, rather than to the old, hot consumers that still predominate at Rangers and many other European clubs. But in order to win their fair global share of cool consumers, and to join a global elite, Rangers may struggle harder than other top European clubs to jettison the hot social forces that have largely taken them this far.

3

Real and Imagined: Reflections on Football Rivalry in Northern Ireland

Alan Bairner and Peter Shirlow

The development of association football in Ireland was given initial impetus from the close relationships between people in the island's north-east corner and the British, most notably the Scots (Garnham, 1999). The city of Belfast dominated the early years, not only in Ulster but in Ireland as a whole. Although football first established itself within the working-class Protestant areas of Belfast, it soon acquired widespread popularity in the city's working-class Catholic communities. This occurred despite the foundation in 1884 of the Gaelic Athletic Association (GAA) with its express aim of diverting Irish nationalists from British pastimes. Gradually support for football spread to other towns in the north of Ireland and also to the south's urban localities, especially Dublin. By the 1900s, national competitions were being contested by teams from throughout Ireland. Nevertheless, most clubs affiliated to the Irish Football Association (IFA), which was established in Belfast in 1880, were located in the more industrialized north-east. The Irish League championship title did not leave Belfast until the 1951–2 season when it was won by Glenavon, a club from Lurgan, Co. Armagh. Long before that, the difficult political situation which culminated in partition had prompted Dublin-based clubs to leave the Irish League, thereafter joining the League of Ireland, based in Dublin and, at least until the arrival of Derry City to its ranks in 1985, consisting exclusively of clubs from the Irish Free State (subsequently the Republic of Ireland). Belfast clubs tended to dominate all major Irish League and Irish Football Association competitions throughout the twentieth century. Furthermore, although Glentoran has achieved some notable successes, these are eclipsed by the achievements of Linfield and, for a time, until its departure from the league in 1949, by Belfast Celtic (Brodie, 1980; Bairner, 1996)

In this chapter, we argue that two teams are more hated and feared than any others in the world of Irish League football. To be more precise, one team, a real team, Linfield, is the object of the most widespread hatred. The other, today only imagined but with a once proud history, Belfast Celtic, is arguably even more feared than Linfield. Just as Linfield is hated for football-related reasons but also as a consequence of both sectarian division and intra-community rivalry, so the fear of Belfast Celtic is rooted in sectarianism as well as in an internal struggle for the sporting soul of Irish nationalism.

Throughout the history of the Irish League, one club has stood head and shoulders above the rest in terms of success on the field of play and the degree of hatred from other football fans which it has inspired. The point is well made by Linfield's chronicler, local journalist Malcolm Brodie (1985: 1), who writes,

> There is no other football club in Ireland quite like Linfield. They are loved and hated. Loved by thousands of fans – some of whom have had their ashes scattered at Windsor Park while others were buried in their Linfield regalia. Hated down the years by the opposition with an implacable enmity, a fierce and relentless sporting rivalry has always existed between Linfield and all other teams.

Although Brodie's comments are generally accurate, he fails to point out that hatred for Linfield goes beyond the boundaries of conventional sporting rivalry. It is true that many reasons for their dislike are identical to those found throughout the football world. Linfield is undeniably the most successful club in Northern Ireland. The club has won forty-three league championships, with nearest rivals, Glentoran, lagging well behind with twenty-one titles. Similarly, Linfield have won the Irish Cup thirty-five times and Glentoran seventeen. In addition to unrivalled success on the field of play, Linfield is also the richest and most commercially viable club in Northern Ireland and arguably on the island of Ireland as a whole. Linfield are perceived to have a close relationship with the football establishment, with Northern Ireland playing home internationals at Linfield's Windsor Park for example. Match officials and the sports media are also regarded as being well-disposed to the club. For Linfield, then, read Manchester United, perhaps.

As we shall see, there are more specific reasons for the dislike of Linfield. These relate to the ethno-sectarian divide that has impacted so forcefully on Northern Ireland's socio-political and cultural development since the state's inception, and most notably since the late 1960s. Traditionally Linfield has presented itself as a Protestant club for Protestant people, pursuing, until recent years, a policy of denying employment to all but a very few Catholics either as players or in other capacities. For Linfield then, read Rangers, the Glasgow club which has a similar history of sectarian employment. This certainly goes some way towards explaining the attitude of most Catholics and also many Protestants towards Linfield just as unrivalled success is clearly a source of generalized hatred amongst all but Linfield fans themselves. It is too simplistic, however, to think in terms of football hatred in Northern Ireland being rooted only in either envy on the one hand or sectarian rivalry on the other. Closer analysis of the multiple reasons why specific groups hate Linfield and fear the return of Belfast Celtic offers a more nuanced reading not only of this specific topic but of Northern Irish society in general.

Two basic facts must be recognized about Northern Ireland before any adequate appraisal of the status of clubs in the eyes of the local football community can be fully understood. First, in many respects, the north of Ireland is little different from other places in terms of feelings of communal attachment. Thus, people love those places and objects, football clubs included, with which they are most familiar. Their fears and loathing are reserved for the unfamiliar, the other. Second, the less than universal characteristics of Northern Ireland are by no means confined to a single straightforward ethno-sectarian conflict. On many occasions, the collective other does consist of members of the opposing tradition. But intra-community rivalry which is also closely bound up with the history of the troubles should not be ignored. While sectarian division is a major factor in the relationship between certain fan groups, intra-community rivalry, for example, goes some considerable way towards explaining the hatred felt towards Linfield by fans of clubs such as Glentoran, Portadown and Glenavon. Even those relationships, therefore, can be linked to local themes as well as to the more universal reasons for football antipathy.

Football and the Politics of Identity

Without doubt the intensity of individual–team ties creates an arena within which the emotions of fear and loathing can be both produced and reproduced. However, as Giulianotti (1999: 63) observes, 'football's fan sub-cultures . . . display significant goegraphical and cultural differences between one another'. Thus, the ferocity of football-centred emotions is neither simple to explain nor static in volume or intent. Indeed, what fear and loathing might mean, within football, is contingent upon a range of socio-cultural, economic, political and gendered forces which are in many instances unique to specific nations, regions or places. Football provides a metaphorical space within which frustrations, hatreds, cultural contestation and fears which are non-sporting in origin are reworked and played out. In Northern Ireland, for example, football provides arenas and sites of habituation within which wider political, territorial and cultural contestation is disclosed and reconstructed. Sport in general provides a wider socio-political landscape within which cultural frag-mentation and discord are interwoven (see Sugden and Bairner, 1993, 1999).

Understanding the sociocultural model of fear which surrounds Linfield and Belfast Celtic helps to establish the relationship between communal devotion, social organizations and the broader emotions of cultural experience. Fear of a defined sociocultural 'other' is in many ways an integral part of fandom and the creation of loyalty to a chosen club. Moreover, fear and hatred within football in Northern Ireland is based upon support for wider mandatory values and norms which can serve the manipulative purposes of individuals and wider communities. Indeed, fear and hatred serve as vehicles for social control and communal obligation.

In this chapter, we do not merely argue that the fear and loathing of Linfield and Belfast Celtic are simply tied to the symbolic and real reproduction of inter-community division. We note also that the reproduction of hatred of such teams also reflects intra-community tensions and patterns of cultural fragmentation which are usually obscured behind more structured modes of ethno-sectarian conflict. As such we argue that football provides one of the few outlets within which intra-communal conflicts can be vocalized, defined and articulated.

Let's Look at Linfield

The detestation of Linfield is somewhat ironically placed on both axes of sectarian division. In its most common form it is predicated around Linfield's failure to employ Catholic players between the 1950s and mid-1980s, and the sectarian chanting and violence generated by the club's supporters. The sectarian nature of Linfield as a sporting institution and the wider role that the fans play in the reproduction of sectarian tension have provided a part-time club in a well-below average European league with a degree of visibility incompatible with either Linfield's playing ability or even with the average football fan's fascination with the game's trivia.

Linfield's employment practices came to light outside Northern Ireland in 1992 through the activities of the Irish National Caucus, a relatively influential Irish-American pressure group dedicated to challenging discrimination and cultural exclusion in Northern Ireland (Sugden and Bairner, 1993). Under the leadership of Fr. Sean McManus, the organization demanded that the Irish Football Association should sever its ties with Linfield or face difficulties in the event of the national team qualifying for the World Cup Finals in the United States. In March 1992, Coca Cola threatened to withdraw its support to IFA and later in the year, as a result of the adverse publicity surrounding Linfield, the club's sponsorship deal with Thorn-EMI was not renewed. Moral pressure on Linfield to review its traditional signing policy was by that stage considerable. Additionally but no less significantly, after a number of highly successful seasons, the club's playing performances had declined from its previous high standards. If Catholic players could help the cause, then, irrespective of ethical arguments, perhaps a new policy had to be considered. For different reasons, therefore, during the second half of the 1990s, Linfield signed a growing number of Catholic payers, albeit more of them coming from the Irish Republic or rural parts of the north of Ireland rather than from the nationalist districts of Belfast. As with Rangers in Scotland, however, changes in signing policy did not destroy Linfield's sectarian image. Indeed, fans have continued to sing Ulster loyalist songs, many of them offensive to and disparaging of Catholics, regardless (or conceivably as a response to) the presence of Catholics in their team.

In the past, the club also received significant media coverage due to rioting and hooliganism. The hooliganism of Linfield fans who visited Dundalk in 1979 for a preliminary round European Cup tie, after the Irish Republican Army's assassination of Lord Louis Mountbatten, together with other outbreaks of violence at Windsor Park and elsewhere during the 1970s and 1980s, have all been well-documented, especially in the local press (Brodie, 1985). However, these reports tell us little about why violence, hatred and fear surrounds Linfield. In particular, the wider interpretation of Linfield as a Protestant club also undermines other complex and intra-community reasons as to why it is synonymous with fear and hatred. Without doubt the club is associated within nationalist consciousness as the very embodiment of sect-arianism, anti-Catholicism and violent atavism. However, it is detested by other Protestant clubs due to the complex patterning and nature of intra-community division and devotion. Before returning to the issue of hatred located within the dialectics of sectarianism, therefore, this chapter highlights how wider processes of sociocultural domination and spatial division repro-duce fear and loathing around Linfield.

Given that the Irish league's support base is predominantly Protestant, it is peculiar that the comprehension of loathing and fear within football in Northern Ireland has customarily been dedicated to exploring and explaining the vinculum between Catholic and Protestant supporters. As stressed within this account, Linfield is synonymous with Protestant identity, tradition and metaphor. As a consequence it can be argued that those Protestant supporters of other clubs who also hate Linfield have an atavistic attitude towards the club which is linked in certain ways to patterns of cultural fragmentation within that Protestant community. The reality of this hate of Linfield among Protestants yet again emphasizes how sport provides an arena within which complex social processes which are usually concealed are patently visible.

Within an increasingly heterogeneous Protestant community Linfield is hated, somewhat ironically, for being both sectarian on the one hand and for diluting the foundations of its sectarianism on the other. Evidently, being the most Protestant-supported club has bred a mistrust of and cultural resistance to Linfield which is shared by significant sections of both Catholic and Protestant communities, albeit for different reasons. Although the detestation is constructed around multiple meanings and interpretations, there is no doubting that Linfield's status and actions have led to it being detested because of the representation of the club as a political entity.

Our reading of fear and hate recognizes that the imposition of negative and putative characteristics upon communities is not merely conditioned by simple stereotypical definitions of cultural discord between Catholics and Protestants. Instead, we argue for a more defined understanding of fear and hate which includes a discourse of intra-communal diversity and asperic rivalry. In this sense hating and being hated by fellow Protestants is for many fans a rational response which aids the fortification of group togetherness, on the one hand, and provides a rationale for group action, on the other (Bairner and Shirlow, 1999a, b).

Therefore, it can be argued that the 'Collective Self', for sections of Linfield support, shifts in relation to the nature of the opposition. When playing Cliftonville, for example, a club with a predominantly nationalist following, the 'Collective Self' of Linfield becomes subjectively defined in terms of 'Devotion' to what is imagined as a distinctly Protestant and anti-Catholic way of life. However, when playing Glentoran, the other half of the so-called 'Big Two' also based in Belfast and with a mainly although not exclusively Protestant support, the 'Collective Self' is subjectively defined by Linfield fans in terms of 'Devotion' to what is implied as a distinctly more Protestant and loyal way of life. It is this ability to shift between these ethnically defined and morally superior states of being which provokes hatred and animosity for Linfield across the sociocultural spectrum. When such airs of moral superiority are backed up with physical strength and mobilization of force, it is possible to not only determine but also explain why Linfield has become such a symbolic object of hate and revulsion (Bairner and Shirlow, 1999b).

Given that Linfield has the largest support base in the Irish league, and that when the team plays away from home Linfield fans tend to outnumber the home support, often by a considerable margin, it is obvious how the mobilization of this support base can create a sense of 'menace' among other teams' supporters. The volume of support, and its potential for serious physical threat towards rival fans, means that the fear Linfield generates among others leads to a sense of loathing which is produced and reworked through animosity and identifiable defence strategies. In many ways the legend of Linfield as the self-superior, violent, brutal and menacing 'other' for all football clubs in the Irish League operates with such force that fear and hate, as illustrated below, are built up through a peculiar but real and adopted value system. At the same time, the 'threat' of Linfield is based not only on the ability of this team to constantly win trophies and to dominate the football landscape, but in the experience and reality of lines of division and communal conflict (Bairner and Shirlow, 1999b).

'Gerry Adams is your MP!': Linfield versus Glentoran

The most intense rivalry in contemporary Irish league football is that between Linfield and Glentoran. Although Glentoran has Catholic supporters, its support is largely drawn from the Protestant population of east Belfast. Games between the two sides have frequently been marred by fighting amongst fans and other incidents such as missiles being thrown on to the field of play. Violent relations between the two clubs have escalated in recent years to include attacks on players socializing in what are deemed to be the respective heartlands of each club.

The rivalry between the two clubs has intensified for two main reasons. First, the demise of Belfast Celtic meant that Glentoran emerged as the obvious rival to Linfield because of its enhanced ability to win trophies and the fact that it was the only remaining club in Belfast which was capable of mobilizing a similar support base. Second, the backdrop of conflict has thrown up a desire by supporters of both clubs to claim the title of being not only following the most successful club, but also being the most devoted and loyal Protestant set of fans. However, the intra-communal tensions created by this rivalry are intensely complex. The fact that Glentoran has had Catholic players through-out most of its history has produced two distinct reactions. First, some Glentoran fans criticize Linfield for manifest sectarianism, thereby facilitating a negative but nevertheless valid categorization of their main rivals. For those Linfield fans who are less sectarian than their counterparts there is a tendency to feel a sense of guilt and shame concerning sectarian practices within their own club. Thus, the Glentoran supporters' anti-sectarianism, whether genuine or merely strategic, has consistently represented a trump card in verbal contests between the two sets of fans giving added piquancy to the palpable sense of mutual loathing. This particular instrument of contestation centred around self-proclaimed decency provides a sense of moral superiority among certain Glentoran supporters. Given that fandom is based to a significant extent upon the eulogization of the club, the ability of the 'collective other' to deconstruct a club to a sectarian and politically unacceptable level is a key weapon in the reproductive cycle of animosity and atavism.

Second, a sectarian section of Linfield's support used to castigate Glentoran for failing to field exclusively Protestant teams. This was clearly indicated in the place-centred narrative of the song 'There's a chapel on the Newtownards Road for all you Fenian bastards'. The fact that there is a Catholic church relatively close to Glentoran's ground, the Oval, was thus linked by Linfield supporters to the club's non-sectarian employment policy in a crude attempt to question Glentoran's loyalty to the Protestant people. In addition, the capacity to cast up the reality of Glentoran having Catholic supporters, some from the immediate vicinity of its ground, as well as players provided many Linfield fans with a feeling of communal purity. In this sense hatred of Glentoran focused upon a perception that the club was, in cultural terms, perverse and disloyal, as it openly interacted at various levels with the 'Catholic Other'. For those Glentoran fans who present themselves as Protestant loyalists, the reality of supporters of their most hated team being in a position to castigate them in terms of their loyalty to Glentoran further added to a sense of loathing and mistrust.

In due course what was most feared by many Linfield fans and then became a reality, namely the signing of Catholic players, provided an opportunity for the more sectarian elements within Glentoran's support to gain revenge by mocking the loyalist pretensions of Linfield's support base. Sectarian Glentoran fans have been given a chance to reproduce allegations of communal purity formerly levelled against them at times with renewed vigour. Another example of questioning communal devotion by way of terracing rhetoric came about as a result of the election of Gerry Adams, president of Sinn Fein, as MP for West Belfast. Since the Shankill Road, an iconic space in terms of loyalist discourse and home to many Linfield supporters (or 'Bluemen'), was at that time part of the West Belfast electoral constituency, some Glentoran fans chose to taunt their equally loyalist adversaries by singing 'Gerry Adams is your MP'. This did not simply play upon the reality of political representation. It is also significant that the area around Windsor Park was becoming increasingly more likely to be peopled by Catholics than was the case for the Oval's immediate environs. As a consequence, Linfield's claim to a territorialized Protestant place in the form of Windsor Park and of true devotion to the Protestant cause was called into question.

It is worth noting that Linfield fans have found ways of reestablishing their loyalist status relative to Glentoran. Since the latter signed Tim McCann from Cliftonville, a Belfast club with a mainly nationalist following, some Bluemen have chosen to sing 'You've got a Provo on your team' during 'Big Two' games.

This claim, linking McCann to the Provisional Irish Republican Army, the ultimate enemy within, has no basis in fact but represents an attempt by some Linfield fans to transcend the humiliation which they felt when their club started to sign Catholics. Now the terracing rhetoric implies that whilst Linfield's Catholics are acceptable members of the community, honorary Protestants by virtue of playing for the Blues, Glentoran employ Catholics who are true outsiders thereby typifying a club whose history is one of collaboration with the collective other. Consistently, language is used in this way to prolong and, if anything, to heighten the bitter rivalry between the two clubs and their supporters.

The importance of these material, residual and topophilic relationships and their expressive meaning is evident in other relationships between Glentoran and Linfield. The rivalry between the clubs is firmly rooted in other realities; over a number of years, violence between fans has been a factor in the reproduction of mistrust; and the fact that Linfield's ground is heavily subsidised by the IFA has led to obvious tensions. For Linfield fans, however, the reality of Glentoran supporters damaging seating at Windsor Park is interpreted as an attack not only on Linfield but also the national team and, by implication, the Northern Irish community, whether real or imagined . A common quip among Linfield supporters when such incidents occur is that 'you would expect that sort of behaviour from Fenians but not Prods'. Yet again the question of loyalty is addressed in terms of relative moral superiority.

Another factor in the hatred between the clubs is intra-community rivalry within loyalist paramilitarism. Although organizations such as the Ulster Defence Association (UDA) and the Ulster Volunteer Force (UVF) may provide the appearance of homogeneity and certainly seem indistinguishable from one another to the outside world, it is clear that the command structure of loyalist groups is based upon distinct localities. Furthermore, the fact that such groups are constructed around localities means that violence between them and over football in particular is not uncommon. It is not unusual for loyalist paramilitaries to state, whether truthfully or not, that they hate Glentoran or Linfield more than they abhor Catholics. As such the rivalry between Linfield and Glentoran permits other tensions and violent masculinities to be expressed and reworked.

In many ways it is possible to conclude that the rivalry that exists will continue to exacerbate animosities which are already firmly established within subjective and, at times, introspective iconographies and landscapes of past and present hatreds and fears. In many ways the rivalry extends far beyond the fear of losing in derby matches or being ridiculed by opposition fans. Instead, it reflects the complexity of cultural confrontations which have been influenced by the violent brutalization of society. Fear in many ways mirrors wider paranoias, concerns over cultural collapse and the evaporation of communal devotion due to wider sociopolitical and cultural changes.

Linfield and the 'others'

During periods in the 1980s and early 1990s, Portadown and Glenavon emerged as teams capable of successfully challenging the domination by Glentoran and Linfield of domestic competitions. Given that these clubs are based in Co. Armagh and are derby rivals, it was not surprising that the media began to refer to them as the mid-Ulster 'big two'. The willing acceptance of this title by Glenavon and Portadown fans reflected not merely a desire to gain recognition but also to celebrate the pleasure gained when rural clubs dare to challenge the success of the Belfast-based clubs. In this type of relationship, the detestation of Linfield is based, therefore, upon urban–rural divisions at least as much as on the standard reasons why people hate that particular club.

A visit by Linfield to any of the other clubs in the Irish League, most of which are located in rural towns, often produces a sense of fear which over time has given way to loathing. Undoubtedly, such visits present a financial lifeline to many clubs in the shape of gate receipts and other forms of revenues that are generated. However, on the downside Linfield fans have a reputation for violence and are known to look down on their rural counterparts. In many instances the Bluemen ridicule smaller clubs because of their inadequate facilities, codes of practice and inability to win trophies. In this sense, Linfield closely resembles dominant clubs in other countries. In terms of the social stereotyping of entire communities, Linfield fans are seen as the ' fast-talking wide boys' and 'lumpen scum' of the city. In contrast, the towns such as Bally-mena, Coleraine, Portadown and Lurgan are regarded by city fans as unsophist-icated backwaters whose residents speak in dialects which are deemed peculiar and humorous. In this sense rivalry is based upon distinctions, common throughout all societies, between urban and less urban lifestyles. In addition, however, Linfield was traditionally regarded as having a sectarian support which was offensive to the sensibilities of less sectarian supporters of rural teams just as it was to certain elements of the Glentoran following.

However, as with the attitudes of Glentoran fans towards Linfield, the hatred of Linfield which is felt by followers of clubs like Portadown and Glenavon is partly based on alternate sectarian readings. Thus, among less sectarian supporters of clubs outside of Belfast, Linfield is seen as the violent and vile representation of an extreme sectarianism which is thought to be peculiar to city life. As a result Linfield has come to constitute a rough and vulgar version of city-based loyalism. However, in recent years this pattern of rejecting Linfield because of its sectarian connotations has been inverted in curious ways.

Without doubt a more fanatical and fundamentalist strain of Ulster loyalism has grown in towns such as Portadown and Lurgan since the mid-1990s. In particular, internal loyalist divisions which have come about through the creation of paramilitary groups including the Loyalist Volunteer Force (LVF) and the Red Hand Defenders which reject the support given by the UDA and the UVF to the peace process, has had an impact on relations between fans of Irish League teams. The LVF, in particular, emerging as it did in Portadown under the leadership of Billy Wright, a former UVF commander in the area who was later murdered by republicans whilst serving a sentence in the Maze Prison, quickly attracted at least vocal support from fans of the local club as well as nearby Glenavon. For them a visit from Linfield was now seen in terms of a new set of intra-communal relationships. Linfield could no longer be regarded as the true sporting embodiment of Ulster loyalism. Just as the UDA and the UVF had handed over the mantle of 'true defenders' to the LVF, so the right of Linfield fans to present themselves as the real loyalists had been conceded to the supporters of the mid-Ulster teams. More recently the UVF appears to have reestablished its control in Portadown and, given the fact that football grounds in Northern Ireland as elsewhere are useful sites for public displays of political affiliations, it is perhaps no coincidence that a social club adjoining Shamrock Park, home of the local football team, was chosen on 27 December 1999 as the venue for a violent attack on LVF members who had been released from the Maze on parole. It is doubtful, however, that altered power relationships between loyalist groups in mid-Ulster will lessen the animosity of Portadown and Glenavon fans towards Linfield in the foreseeable future.

It is notable that with the exception of Glentoran supporters, fans of visiting teams, Glenavon and Portadown included, are reluctant to attend matches at Windsor Park. This occurs for a range of reasons, but undoubtedly for some the fear of attack is a major factor. For others, Belfast in general is imagined as a place to be avoided due to a history of violence. However, the main reason why supporters do not attend what may well be one of the biggest games their club plays in any given season, is an unwillingness to contribute financially to Linfield by way of admission costs and additional spending. In this instance, the detestation of Linfield's control of football and the more obnoxious elements of its support precludes significant numbers of fans from participating in games at Windsor Park. Ironically this also impacts upon attendance figures for games involving Northern Ireland. Many of the self-proclaimed Ulster loyalist fans of teams like Glenavon and Portadown are willing to renege on their responsibilities towards the 'national' team for the simple reason that the home games are played at Windsor Park and, therefore, directly and indirectly benefit the hated Linfield. Few nationalist football fans attend Northern Ireland games at Windsor Park either, but for reasons additional to those which are cited by Protestants who happen to dislike Linfield. Many of the factors already discussed have a bearing on nationalist hatred of Linfield; for Catholics, however, the fear and the hatred are even more intimately bound up with the most visible aspects of ongoing political conflict.

Sectarianism and Irish League Football

Although large numbers of Catholics play and watch football in the north of Ireland, the dominant character of the game at the senior level has tended to be both Protestant and unionist as well as hegemonically masculine (Bairner, 1999). There are a number of factors that account for the unionist or loyalist ambience at the overwhelming majority of Irish League grounds. First, the early history of the game was such that it was initially adopted by Protestants. Although Catholics quickly developed an enthusiasm for what was to become the global game, their participation was to some extent curtailed as a consequence of the pressure applied by the GAA, by certain members of the clergy and by many nationalist politicians to eschew 'foreign' games and play Gaelic football and hurling instead. Second, unlike most other sports in Ireland, the organization of football has followed the constitutional contours established by partition. The IFA, the Irish League and the Northern Ireland national team are all symbolic representations of the existence of a Northern Ireland state, a concept which most northern nationalists have at the very least viewed with suspicion and, in many instances, regarded with outright hostility.

Perhaps not surprisingly, therefore, most IFA and Irish League administrators have come from the unionist community. As with the overwhelmingly Protestant presence at Northern Ireland games, this can be explained in part as the result of nationalist abstentionism. What should not be ignored, however, is the degree to which protectionism rooted in sectarianism has served to dissuade nationalists from deeper involvement with the governing bodies. In turn this has helped to produce a third element in the development of unionist hegemony over Northern Irish football. Sectarian chants and songs are to be heard at most Irish League grounds, particularly when the visiting team is Cliftonville, the only club with a reasonably large nationalist following. Little or nothing has been done by the football authorities to bring this practice to an end. For nationalists, at least, this suggests a degree of complicity in a campaign to make Irish League football inhospitable to Catholics. Further evidence is adduced from the fact that both Derry City and Belfast Celtic, clubs well-supported by nationalists, were obliged to leave the league and Cliftonville itself has faced countless difficulties in more recent years at the hands of rival fans, the police and officialdom in general. All of this must be set against a background of football's widespread popularity amongst nationalists evidenced by the fact that most senior clubs have more Catholic than Protestant players. In addition large numbers of Catholic fans travel to Britain each weekend to support either Celtic in Scotland or a number of English teams, most notably Arsenal, Everton, Liverpool, Manchester United and Tottenham Hotspur. The Falls Road, the main artery of nationalist west Belfast, is the location of two pubs dedicated to football clubs – The Red Devil (Manchester United) and The Celtic Bar ((Glasgow) Celtic). All things considered, therefore, the game in Northern Ireland is neither exclusively Protestant nor unionist; it only feels that way sometimes, particularly to nationalists.

The View from Solitude

The rivalry between fans of Cliftonville and Linfield is largely defined in terms of sectarian division. The rules of standard hatred also apply. But even some of those are felt in particular ways by Cliftonville fans given that most of them belong to the nationalist tradition (O'Hanlon, 1997). Thus, Linfield's relationship with the IFA is seen in more conspiratorial terms than would be the case for supporters of 'Protestant' clubs. Linfield and the IFA are seen by the more paranoid elements of the Cliftonville supporters as Ulster unionism at play. This analysis has been at least partially confirmed by events, not least the fact that for almost thirty years Cliftonville were prevented from playing their 'home' games against Linfield at their own ground, Solitude. Instead, both league and cup matches were moved to Windsor Park. As a result a situation which gave Linfield one, and after league reconstruction, two extra home games was allowed to persist despite its manifest iniquity. Of particular concern to Cliftonville fans was the fact that the decision to favour Linfield in this way was sanctioned by the IFA which, in turn, was acting on the basis of public-order advice given by the Royal Ulster Constabulary (RUC), itself a hated police force, regarded as sectarian and suspected intermittently by nationalists of collusion with the more extreme forms of loyalism.

For Cliftonville fans, therefore, and also for the smaller numbers of nationalists who support Omagh Town and Newry Town, the customary reasons for football rivalry and hatred are augmented by factors linked to the politics of ethnic division. Linfield and its fans are viewed as elements of a unionist power structure, other contributors to which include the IFA, the

RUC, the Orange Order, the loyalist paramilitaries, sections of the media and the various unionist political parties. In a context of ethno-sectarian conflict, hating the other team takes on connotations which are far less common in more stable societies.

The fact that Cliftonville supporters today can be presented as the fans most likely to hate Linfield for reasons rooted in sectarian conflict itself provides interesting insights into the patterns of fear and loathing in Northern Irish football. Until the mid-1970s the club itself had no sectarian connotations. Only Solitude's location in north Belfast and the fact that the other Belfast teams (Belfast Celtic and Distillery) which had earlier received nationalist support but for different reasons no longer did so, conspired to attract a growing and increasingly almost exclusively nationalist following to Cliftonville. Distillery had been forced to leave its Belfast home during the height of the troubles and eventually settled in a largely Protestant area on the outskirts of the city. But the real vacuum in terms of nationalist involvement in football in the north of Ireland resulted from Belfast Celtic's departure from the Irish League in 1949.

In the final section of this chapter, we argue that Cliftonville has never so fully entered into the realm of unionist demonology as to assume a hate status equivalent to that of Linfield in the eyes of nationalists. This is partly because Cliftonville has been unable to develop its support base, largely because it plays in north Belfast whilst the largest nationalist population area is to the west of the city, but also because it has been traditionally so unsuccessful on the field of play. An important additional factor, however, is that English (and Scottish) football operate in an unlikely alliance with Gaelic games to offer nationalists major sporting alternatives. A resurgent Belfast Celtic on the other hand would be an entirely different matter. For that reason we suggest that a club which no longer exists can still create feelings of fear and loathing amongst Protestant fans and, in addition, prompt feelings of unease if not outright fear in the minds of Gaelic games enthusiasts who would recognize in Belfast Celtic a genuine threat, unlike that posed by Cliftonville, to their aspirations to promote sporting purity within the city's nationalist population.

Bring on the Celtic!

There is no denying that during the fifty-eight years of its existence, Belfast Celtic posed a major threat to Linfield's supremacy. The Irish Cup was won eight times and, more significantly, Celtic won the league championship on fourteen occasions, including four successive titles from 1926 to 1929 and six between 1936 and 1948 with war interrupting the sequence. The 'Big Two' during the interwar years consisted of Linfield and Belfast Celtic with

Glentoran winning only three league titles in a period when the Blues won six and Celtic ten, including a triumph in 1940. To add to its illustrious history, shortly before the club left the league, it defeated the Scottish national team during a visit to the United States. Even for those who never saw Celtic play but who have an interest in Irish League football the achievements of the west Belfast club are known, savoured and, in some cases, feared. Indeed, there are many who would argue that Irish League football has never had the same hold on the popular imagination since the departure of Celtic and the termination of the Big Two rivalry, for which Linfield–Glentoran games offer a poor substitute.

Belfast Celtic was never a sectarian club in the sense of employing only Catholics or even having an exclusively Catholic support. It is undeniable, however, that it was the team most favoured by football fans in nationalist west Belfast. As Coyle (1999: 10) observes, '. . . although the numbers who can claim to have seen its players in action may be in steady decline, its former players grown old, its enormous achievements have passed down through family generations and into the folklore of catholic nationalist West Belfast'. The story of those achievements has been told many times as, indeed, have the claims that the demise of Celtic was the result of a unionist conspiracy within Northern Ireland's football establishment (Tuohy, 1978; Kennedy, 1989; Coyle, 1999). Yet the truth about why Celtic left the Irish League in 1949 may never be known. What is certain is that while fans of others clubs would welcome the return of senior football to west Belfast for the excitement that such a development would generate in a domestic scene which is in serious danger of becoming moribund, all of them, even Linfield fans buoyed up by continuing success, would fear the potential of such a club. For the time being, however, it would appear that a potent combination of fear and hatred originating from very different sources continue to make this an unlikely scenario.

Half-hearted attempts are made from time to time to revive Belfast Celtic (Coyle, 1999). More realistic, however, have been the long-term aspirations of another west Belfast club to assume its predecessor's mantle. According to Coyle (1999: 122), 'if initiatives to rekindle Belfast Celtic fail to ignite, the ambition of ever seeing a team kit of green and white hoops playing in the Irish League again may have to rest with junior side Donegal Celtic which is situated in the Suffolk area of west Belfast'. Coyle notes, however, that the club's ambitions have been obstructed in recent years by certain controversial incidents. For example, an Irish Cup game against Linfield at Windsor Park was marred by serious crowd trouble. Coyle omits to mention that the decision to play the game at Linfield's ground was taken by the IFA on police advice, thereby fuelling fears of an establishment conspiracy aimed at thwarting the ambitions of nationalists involved in Irish League football. It has also been suggested by west Belfast football fans that further progress by Donegal Celtic has been made virtually impossible due to the fact that any further advances would mean playing in the Irish League B Division, which currently includes the RUC team, members of which would be unwilling to fulfil fixtures in a staunchly nationalist area.

Arguably, however, the endeavours of Donegal Celtic have also been undermined in recent years by other, less likely, forces than Linfield and its perceived allies, the IFA and the RUC. In 1998, the club was drawn to play against the RUC in a semi-final tie in the Steel & Sons Cup, Northern Ireland's most prestigious knock-out competition for junior clubs. There was a widespread feeling amongst nationalist football fans that this provided an ideal opportunity to get back at a traditional enemy. Gradually, however, pressure from relatives of people injured or killed by the police began to affect the mood surrounding the game. Sinn Féin added to the expressions of disquiet by supporting the views of those relatives and arguing that Donegal Celtic's participation in this match would be an insult to the thousands of local people who regard the RUC as a discredited and wholly unacceptable police force. In the end, the club's officials agreed to withdraw from the competition not least because some of the players, for whatever reasons, decided that they would be unable to take part in the event of the fixture going ahead.

There is no doubt that certain people used Donegal Celtic in this instance for political purposes. The issue was turned into a publicity exercise by opponents of the RUC. It is possible, however, that a sporting agenda albeit one with distinct political connotations was also at work. Despite west Belfast's long-standing enthusiasm for football, there are some nationalists in the area and beyond who would argue that a 'foreign' sport should not be pursued, particularly if this is to the detriment of Gaelic games. This is not to imply that Gaelic games are without their supporters in west Belfast. In fact, Gaelic clubs flourish throughout the area, not least as places of entertainment. The problem for some advocates of nationalist purity, however, resides in the fact that Gaelic games are unable to oust football from its dominant position. Often, indeed, people congregate in Gaelic clubs simply to watch televised soccer games, involving Celtic, which may be suggestive of some degree of cultural resistance, or English Premiership sides which appears more like a form of accommodation if not outright betrayal in the eyes of the purists.

Given these exclusivist nationalist attitudes towards Donegal Celtic in particular and association football in general, we conclude that there are more than Linfield fans, the supporters of other Irish League clubs, the IFA and the RUC who actually fear the imagined Belfast Celtic. As with attitudes towards

Linfield itself, we discover that whilst ethno-sectarianism is a key factor, it should not be allowed to obscure the significant impact of intra-community rivalry within Northern Irish social life. Protestant fans would undeniably hate a revitalized Belfast Celtic. They might even come to fear it given the likelihood that the new club would be almost certain to enjoy considerable success on the field of play. But the custodians of Irish sporting purity would also fear and perhaps even hate the return of a team which would possess massive potential to engage the passions of nationalist people by virtue of playing a 'foreign' game.

Conclusion

There is no denying that, in Northern Ireland, Linfield is the most hated football club in the eyes of all but its own supporters. There are generalized reasons for this phenomenon which are rooted in the vagaries of the game itself. As one would anticipate, however, Linfield is also hated for reasons that are more directly linked to Northern Ireland's most visible source of social division and conflict. We have argued, however, that it is important to recognize the degree to which intra-community rivalry, so often overlooked in analyses of the region, is also an important factor in creating enmity towards Linfield amongst Protestant and even loyalist fans of other clubs.

Similarly we have argued that the idea of Belfast Celtic is sufficient to provoke feelings of hatred and fear amongst Protestant football fans, and, in part, the reasons are located within ethno-sectarian contestation. Nevertheless, we also believe that there are those within the nationalist community who would also fear the return of a club which, in their opinion, would lack authenticity. As with Linfield, therefore, while sectarian divisions are responsible for a large part of the negativity which would surround the return of senior football to west Belfast, intra-community conflict is also an important factor with implications extending well beyond the world of sport. It is a truism, therefore, but one that is worthy of repetition, that sport in Northern Ireland is in a very real sense a microcosm of the wider society. Furthermore, sport demonstrates that society is far more complex than many conventional academic readings might have us believe. In life as in football the 'Big Two' match may well be the one that is played out between Real Belfast and Belfast Imagined.

4

The Lion Roars: Myth, Identity and Millwall Fandom

Garry Robson

Millwall's in a corner of London where time stands still even if they do have a plush new ground. The streets and people remain the same and Cold Blow Lane was a wicked place full of nutters, and the New Den may look flash but it's full of the same old faces standing in the background waiting patiently . . . we're putting ourselves on the edge and when you're in south east London it's a fucking long way to the bottom if you get thrown off . . . through streets they know like the back of their hands. This gives them the advantage because you could get lost for days in the blocks, houses, empty yards. There's no colour in the buildings, bricks identical and wasteland overgrown, rows of broken walls and broken wire, smashed glass and rusted metal, dull new houses . . . It's fucking eerie this place. Full of decaying dockers in flat caps bombed and left to rot under a collapsed London.

John King (1996: 225–7)

The word *Millwall* has become one of the most evocative in contemporary Britain. It functions as a condensed symbol, widely and indiscriminately used to express ideas and feelings about an entire sphere of activity and experience well beyond the compass of its original meaning. It has become a metaphoric byword for, amongst other things, violent mob thuggery, unreconstructed masculinity, dark and impenetrable urban culture and working-class 'fascism'.[1] The metaphoric power of the word derives, of course, from the archetypal

---

1. Links between Millwall and far-right political activists are minimal and opportunistic rather than organic (Back et al., 1996). The idea that Millwall fans are inherently fascistic is a persistent element of their myth. This notion is based partly on what were real connections between a minority of fans and the National Front in the late 1970s (Robson, 2000), and more generally on liberal-left anxieties about politically unfocused expressions of white, working-class masculine vitality. The customary renunciation of the body in leftist intellectual culture (Hoberman, 1984) is an important factor here. It is also worth noting the presence of a significant number of black fans – the 'Millwall Blackskins' – at the core of the club's hooligan formation (see Robson, 1999, for a fuller discussion of the complex matters of race and the metaphysics of belonging).

status of the 'Millwall supporter' as the defining and emblematic 'Football Hooligan'. The archetypal status of the Millwall fan is a vexed and complex one, in which myth and reality have perhaps become so closely intertwined that even some of those most closely involved are unsure as to where the one might end and the other begin. It is a story of violence and mayhem both real and apocryphal, of particular and localized patterns of masculine culture, and of the ways in which popular representations of that culture meet with subcultural self-definition in a dialectics of identity. It is also about a cultural struggle for the right to *embody* that identity. It is in this struggle that the 'Millwall fan', considered as an archetype, has his central appeal. The nature of this appeal differs across constituencies of interest, two of which are of particular significance. The first of these is the generalized realm of popular media representations, in which the appearance of the Millwall fan signifies a complex nexus of social anxieties. Second is the sphere of football subculture, in which he excites a curious mixture of fear, loathing and desire. What follows is an account of the development and workings of the Millwall myth in each of these areas.

How the Myth Developed

'DON'T DO IT, CHUMS'

DON'T ever invade the playing pitch – keep your seats and places on the terraces – keep off the grass.

DON'T throw soil, cinders, clinkers, stones, bricks, bottles, cups, fireworks or other kinds of explosives, apples, oranges, etc. on the playing pitch during or after the match.

DON'T barrack, utter filthy abuse, or cause any physical violence to the referee and his linesman inside or outside the Den.

DON'T barrack, utter filthy abuse, or molest in any manner players of the visiting team.

DON'T barrack, utter filthy abuse, or molest in any manner the players of the Millwall Football Club.

DON'T assemble in small or large numbers in the streets adjacent to the Den.

DON'T deface or remove Warning Notices which are posted within the Den.

(Warning Notice issued by Millwall F.C. 1949–50 Season and
displayed outside the Den stadium, South East London)

Foul language, missile throwing, vandalism, large street 'assemblies' and occasional violence. These are, of course, the staple activities of what came, from the mid-1960s on, to be known as Football Hooliganism. By 1949 Millwall's

'Lion's Den' was, in fact, already well-established as a site of proto-hooligan activity, and had been so since the early decades of the century (Murray, 1988). Millwall Athletic Football Club, one of the first in London, was founded in 1885 by workers at Morton's preserve factory on the Isle of Dogs on the north of the Thames in east London. The majority of the founders were of Scottish origin, and chose blue as their colour and the Lion Rampant as their emblem.[2] Like many of its early northern counterparts, Millwall was closely identified with particular proletarian occupational groups, in this case with the docks. It was not until 1910, following a succession of ground changes as support expanded, that the club relocated to the Den south of the river at New Cross. As anticipated, the bulk of support for the club was soon derived from south of the river, from Bermondsey, Rotherhithe and Deptford – a very similar sociodemographic constituency of Dockland support to that previously obtaining on the Island. The social origins of the club's support at this time, then, were firmly located in the proletarian masculinism of the period and area, providing a highly specific social context for the formation of the identity and culture of the club and the development of its supporting traditions. Millwall fans have thus been characterized by an extreme and voluble raucousness, sufficiently distinctive to have been consistently noted as such by a long succession of observers since the 1920s.

Though Millwall fans were clearly far from being alone in their capacity for unbridled fervour in the early days, from the 1920s on their reputation for intemperate passion and occasional violence came to be expressed in terms of the now familiar and historically continuous theme of *intimidation*. In 1920, following a fractious encounter in which the visiting Newport County FC goalkeeper was pelted with missiles before being 'flattened' by a 'useful right hook' (Murray, 1988: 83), the Den was closed by the FA for the first time. It has since been closed as a consequence of crowd disturbances on six occasions, a statistic without precedent in the annals of football disorder. The Den had therefore entered into the realm of myth long before phenomenon of 'Football Hooliganism' found stable definition and currency in the 1960s. And Millwall fans were central in the development of the latter as a consequence of their activities being picked up at key moments in the development

2. William of Scotland chose the 'red lion rampant' as his heraldic cognizance in the 12th century, since which time it has symbolized the visceral pride and martial defiance of the Scots. It has performed a similar symbolic function at Millwall since the club's inception, though for the last three decades a more popular representation of the lion among fans has it leaping, aggressively and frontally, at the beholder. For the 1999–2000 season Millwall returned, for use on its livery, to the more stylized and less confrontational lion of tradition. This was part of the club's ongoing attempt to distance itself from the more aggressive tendencies of its fans and to repair its public image. The decision has not, on the whole, been welcomed by the body of Millwall fans.

of the media (and sociological) narratives which frame our understanding of the phenomenon (Robson, 2000). Though the folkloric reputation of Millwall and its fans persisted throughout the early and mid-1970s, two events in 1977 and 1978 led to the Den becoming constituted as the defining and emblematic 'spiritual home of football hooliganism' (*Match of the Seventies*, BBC1, 3 September 1996).

When in 1977 the makers of BBC1's *Panorama* decided to contribute in 1977 to the flurry of media concern and fascination with hooliganism, the reputation of Millwall fans made them an obvious choice as exemplifying subjects. In choosing to frame and interpret the general phenomenon of football hooliganism through the particular culture of a (numerically modest) aggressive Millwall fandom at a time when public concern and interest was at its earliest peak, the programme-makers fixed and mythologized the association between the two in perpetuity. The anxious furore generated by the programme was matched by its reception in the less well-publicized, informal sphere of hooligan culture: Millwall fans became both a symbol of everything that was wrong with the country in the late, state-of-the-nation 1970s, *and* the ultimate icons in football subculture. 'Harry the Dog', the fiercest Millwall 'nutter' of them all, made for fantastic television: a combination of high-intensity violence and a cinematically thuggish demeanour meant that he quickly acquired a genuinely symbolic status. The defining populist image of embodied Millwall fandom had arrived, and it stayed. Few who saw Harry's one-man assault on the Bristol Rovers 'end' have forgotten it (Murray, 1988: 243).

The framework of definition and interpretation of all matters relating to Millwall set up by the programme has been employed in automatic, shorthand and symbolic ways ever since. A consequent sense of embittered injustice and a defensive wariness of outside opinion are amongst the primary characteristics of Millwall fan culture. With the reporting of disorder at the following year's FA Cup sixth-round game against Ipswich (Murray, ibid.: 245; Ball, 1986: 188),[3] the pattern was set. Fighting in the crowd on that occasion led to the

---

3. In fact the violence was more in the nature of a massacre than a battle. The game took place when Millwall's fearsome reputation was at its peak. Very few teams took travelling supporters to the Den, and lack of crowd segregation meant that such fans would invariably be required to fight their way out again. A large number of Ipswich fans were untypically present due to the importance of the game, but were ill-equipped to defend themselves against a Millwall horde enraged by both their temerity in attending and Ipswich's humiliating superiority on the field (Millwall lost the game 1–6). Murray, Millwall's historian, regards the disorder as 'the most savage scenes ever witnessed at the Den', and notes the significance of the 'disquieting yet almost inevitable irony that the BBC cameras should be back again, this time recording for *Match of the Day* but also, as it turned out, for the main news bulletins' (1988: 245). Ball, referring to the same incident, describes 'the most violent, hostile atmosphere I have ever experienced inside a football ground' (1986: 190). Though a good deal of fantastical media coverage has been generated around it, the actual propensity for violence of Millwall's 'firm' is no myth.

first closure of the Den since 1949, and probably definitively strengthened a universal association of Millwall with violent mayhem. The following year saw an extremely high-profile game at West Ham, when Millwall were again at the very centre of an apparent worsening of the general situation at a match which:

> produced what, up until that time, was the most comprehensive and sophisticated show of force for dealing with spectators at an English Football League match. All told, more than 500 police officers took part. (Dunning *et al.*, 1988: 178)

1977–8, then, were the years in which public perceptions of Millwall had become sufficiently fixed and widely disseminated to constitute the *Millwall Fan* as a more or less stable referential symbol (Turner, 1967).

Serious disorder attending a fifth-round Cup tie at Luton in March 1985 extended and solidified the reputation of Millwall fans still further, to the extent that 'the name Millwall had become synonymous with everything that was bad in football and society' (Murray, 1988: 269). Again, Millwall symbolized an apparently worsening situation, in a period which saw the reputation of the game reach its nadir. Crucially captured by television cameras, the event was a focus of national attention, significant enough to stimulate House of Commons debate and lead to the creation of Margaret Thatcher's 'Soccer War Cabinet'. The Luton riot is widely considered to be the symbolic watershed in the postwar history of the game and the battle against hooliganism (Dunning *et al.*, 1988: 246, 1992: 129; Campbell and Shields, 1993: 123; Murray, 1988: 269). In the public consciousness the Millwall fan thus became not merely further associated with, but incontrovertibly *representative of* boorishness, thuggery and violent mayhem.

Millwall fans therefore found themselves in the late 1980s carrying a heavy mythological and symbolic burden which the club itself has found difficult to overcome. The development of groundbreaking community initiatives in the late 1980s (Williams, 1991: 182; Bale, 1993: 174; Campbell and Shields, 1993: 122) and successive attempts to improve the image and status of Millwall had only a limited impact on public perceptions, and evaporate altogether when a powerful media archetype underpinning the structure of received understanding becomes operational. I do not define the status of Millwall as *archetypal* for simple effect. Rather, I want to suggest that archetypes perform an important and particular role in the context of ritualized news production which operate according to a principle of 'eternal recurrence' (cf. Rock, 1973).

Garry Robson

The Social Function of the Millwall Myth

The overall context of this principle of eternal recurrence is the role of media institutions in the maintenance and consolidation of a definition of social reality premised upon a paradigm of national 'consensus' (Hall *et al.*, 1986: 55), and cognitive maps of meaning organized around the primacy of liberal individualistic conceptions of subjectivity and expression. One low-level but continual characteristic of mainstream media production – leaving aside periodic, high-profile 'moral panics' – is the recurring validation of these conceptions in an ongoing confirmation of the primacy of the manners of social being derived from them.

The Millwall archetype – though it is always waiting to be operationalized in its literal, folk-devil sense as circumstances arise – has by now transcended and outlived its role in the framing of specific, conjunctural panics. It is used rather as an important symbolic marker in the recurring and ritualized media narratives relating to social order and the illegitimacy of particular cultural and moral forms.

Millwall has been critical in this process, for it allows a number of incipiently transgressive themes situated on the major boundaries of 'consensual calm' (Hall *et al.,* ibid.: 66) – crime, violence and volatile collective culture in the context of a working-class area within minutes of the metropolitan centre – to become conflated and condensed into a unitary, exemplifying symbol. This status as a primary symbol expressive of these themes underpins the archetypal nature of the Millwall fan, and has generated the unique burden associated with that fandom.

The negotiation of this burden, of this dialectic of ascribed and experienced identity, is at the heart of Millwallism. Few other social groupings – of any description – have had to come to terms with and absorb into their cultural forms so particular and widespread a body of 'knowledge' and opinion about themselves. The Millwall archetype, arising as it has out of a complex interplay of culture and representation, constitutes the Millwall fan as a primarily symbolic being. His reputation *always* precedes him, and an awareness of this special, iconic status saturates the sharply self-aware expressive cultural forms generated by Millwall fans, and clearly underpins the emergence of the anthem *No one likes us* during the 1980s.[4]

4. At Millwall this somewhat paradoxical anthem, sung to the tune of Rod Stewart's 1970s hit 'Sailing', developed as both an aggrieved response to the media hysteria surrounding the club and a celebration of notoriety. It is the fan-collective's impassioned *cri de coeur*, and since the mid-1980s football grounds around England have been heard proclaiming:

No one likes us, no one likes us, no one likes us, We don't care

We are Millwall, super Millwall, we are Millwall, from the Den

A public, dialogical engagement with reputation and myth is therefore central to the way in which fans constitute themselves as a collective. Millwallism, in this sense, contains both the classical ingredients of passionate, local-patriotic English football-supporting and something which passes beyond them: those collective responses to the reformulation of 'Millwall' as a highly charged and ubiquitous symbol in the cultural politics of the public sphere.

This idea of Millwall as a media symbol is particularly important in the context of contemporary developments in the expansion of football into new markets, in a post-1990 climate in which football would appear to be shedding its working-class iconography and associations at an unprecedented rate (Armstrong, 1998; Giulianotti, 1999). Though the tensions generated in fan cultures by the progressive commercialization of the game are at least as old as the sociology of football itself (Taylor, 1971; Critcher, 1979), the game appears genuinely poised on the brink of a definitive and stable breakthrough into middle-class markets as it enters the new millenium. This is the context into which Millwall, with all its unruly, counter-bourgeois and market-unfriendly baggage, is routinely inserted in symbolic contrast to the prevailing wind of progressive change held to be blowing through the game – even in periods of calm when Millwall fans are not in the news.[5] The routine and widely disseminated circulation of this archetype in a variety of contexts has been a feature of both broadcast and printed news-production, documentary and entertainment programming and sociological analysis itself.

These developments have, at one level, transformed Millwall from a modest leisure institution to a highly charged and richly connotative symbol independent of the club and its supporters.

Millwallism's Social Sources

The bewildering size and variety of London has historically generated a social patchwork of intensively localist culture and sentiment, and a series of highly

---

5. Three references to Millwall, collected at random in October-November 1996 from radio, television and newsprint, illustrate this. On 17 October, Radio Four's *Today* programme focused on Millwall–in connection with an anti-racist initiative at Newcastle – as part of a generalized discussion of race and football. No other club was involved, Millwall clearly being defined as exemplary in any such discussion. A short interview with a south-London accented fan was contemptuously undermined and mimicked by the show's presenter. On 5 November the Channel 4 comedy show *Drop the Dead Donkey* featured the assertion that it was as difficult for the office lothario to control his genetic predisposition towards promiscuity as it was to control Millwall fans on holiday in Benidorm. Here the Millwall fan represents not only football hooliganism, but unreconstructed, atavistic British masculinity itself. On 10 November, the *Observer* newspaper, in a report on the Bristol City vs Millwall match the previous day, could not resist a reference to the 'brutality' of Millwall fans even though the trouble-free game itself provided absolutely no context for it. It appears that neither moral panics nor ostensible 'newsworthiness' are preconditions of the continual circulation of these ways of framing and representing the club. Readers with access to British media productions might like to collect examples of this phenomenon for themselves.

differentiated social spaces within the city. By the nineteenth century, urban sociologist Richard Sennett observes, London was a conglomeration of 'class-homogenous, disconnected spaces' (1994: 322). Extreme localist identifications in the context of a vast and ultimately unfathomable metropolitan whole thus became a primary characteristic of the historical development of London's working-class communities, differentiating them from their provincial counterparts. It is little wonder, given this variety and diffusion of communities and of the obscurely folk-taxonomic ways of interpreting and representing them, that so much of London tends to be missing from its social history. This is most acutely true of south-east London, an area which remains chronically under-historicized. This is primarily due to the fact that socio-historic accounts of London invariably revolve around the easily juxtapositionary cognitive scheme of West-East. These apparently obvious and reassuring polarizations, between rich and poor, grandeur and squalor, light and dark, and order and chaos become translated into contrastive analyses of relationships between west and east London (Walkowitz, 1992). South London is marginalized in this conceptual framework by its location on the other side, its separation marked symbolically, as well as spatially, by the River Thames. The effect of this separation has led to its demarcation as an obscure and unknown space, a region of darkness nestling, in the case of Southwark, hard by the very heart of the metropolis itself. And when it does appear in social histories of London at all, it tends to do so as a shadowy realm of crime, disreputability and 'incipient decay' (Ash, 1971: 39).

South-east London therefore enjoys a specific position in those folk-taxonomic schema which so characterize life in the city. And its close association with crime and plebeian entrepeneurialism (Robson, 1997), in themselves central themes in historical relations between the metropolitan classes, marks it out as an especially significant site in the ongoing dialectics of class and culture, of social identities embodied and ascribed. This particular tradition and iconography, from medieval criminal quarter and pleasure ground to pick-pocket Fagin and the definitive Dickensian criminal warren at Jacob's Island in Bermondsey, from the original nineteenth century 'Hooligan' to the first 'Teddy Boys' (Pearson, 1983; Rook, 1899), from classical gangland enclave[6] to home of the archetypal football thug at Millwall, marks south-east London out as a very particular and historically significant place.

Contemporary accounts of the area are usually informed by these historical themes, which are invariably used to support an iconography of working-

---

6. A considerable literature has grown up around this phenomenon in recent years. Differing accounts – from both within and without – can be found in Fraser (1994), Hogg *et al.*, (1988), Kelland (1993), Morton (1994) and Richardson (1992).

class-gangsterish masculinism. This specifically understood urban ecology is the context for that south-east London gangland which has produced some of Britain's most notorious criminals. I would stress here that assessing the accuracy or otherwise of these claims is not of primary importance. What is significant is the way in which so many accounts of the area, and particularly of its darkly conceived masculine subcultures, revolve around the manipulation of a particular and consistent repertoire of symbolic meanings and identifications.

Millwall and some South-East London Archetypes

The historical formations of class cultures in London have sedimented a powerful strain of combative local sensibility in the city's working-class populations. Local-patriotic and masculinist structures of feeling suffuse the interactive everyday life of the city, and are nowhere more firmly rooted – and articulated – than in south-east London. Elaborations of Millwallism are invariably situated in these broader networks of understanding, sentiment and attribution, and fans will often articulate the two as coterminous. Terry, a Millwall fan in his late-twenties, exemplifies this tendency:

> Like, when you go to certain parts, when you go north London, east London, 'ave a look round and you think 'nah, I wouldn't like to live over 'ere, its not home'. In south-east London they're on a different wavelength, they really are, from like, up North, or even on the other side of the river. Its like, we got *common sense* an' they aint, that's 'ow it really is. Its really 'ard to explain – but its there. There aint no gettin' away from it. An' they say all about the gangsters an' all that from south London, most of 'em live in south London, or in the suburbs, like, of Kent, like Welling, which is still in south-east London.

There is much that is implicit in Terry's statement about the defining characteristic of south London people as having 'common-sense'. The reference is to the characteristics implicit in a particular structure of feeling and to qualities which are not necessarily held in the sphere of articulate reflection. Terry has a powerful sense of the uniqueness of his cultural background which may be very difficult to put into words. It does not derive from a fully programmatic and detailed system of classification but is rather located in the sphere of experience, of a commonly held and tacit sense of specific and embodied forms of cultural capital. This does not mean that these identifications do not find public articulation – as they clearly do in moments of cultural or violent conflict between sets of fans – but that they are experienced most powerfully as constitutive elements of the self rather than as explicit themes awaiting cognitive deliberation.

Terry's invocation of the south London gangster tradition is, in this context, a metaphorical clue to the substantive content of this distinctive sphere of 'common sense'. Terry is a law-abiding family man, who, in all likelihood, will never come close to committing a serious crime. But this does not prevent him from emblematically summoning up the gangster as the representative of a particular strain of south-east London masculinity. The *traditional* gangster thus continues to function in the broader culture as an ambiguously folk-heroic ideal type. He is, first and foremost, personally inviolable and answers, in the main, to nobody. He is materially successful and able to provide the best for himself and his family. He has a deeply rooted sense of tradition and moral code – and, though he might be a 'complete *bastard*' – he looks after his own. Moreover his capacity for violence is matched by his guile, his practical intelligence and his metropolitan social alertness – his 'common sense'. He has, in an important sense, triumphed (whether materially or gesturally) over the apparent limitations of his class origins. He is his own man and *no one fucks with him* lightly. He is, ultimately, a force to be reckoned with. For he is potent, resourceful, sharp and experienced.

These themes are understood and are being implicitly drawn on by Terry as a specific kind of masculine aura, as characteristic of himself and his peers. It is for these reasons that the archetype of the gangster continues to resonate powerfully at Millwall amongst an overwhelmingly law-abiding interpretative community. And these interconnected themes of specific patterns of culture, of masculine autonomy but collective identification, are routinely spatialized by Millwall fans in connecting the character of the club with the culture of the area. Mick, a fan in his late-thirties, makes this explicit:

> I sometimes think the big estates, the redevelopment, was a conscious attempt to try an' break it all up, move the people around, break up the culture of the area. But there you're into social policy. . .I don't think the area will ever change. Even the yuppies, they won't last. They all bought their houses in Dockhead, but they'll move out of the area, they'll go. You'll never change the area, I mean, Bermondsey, Deptford, you won't change 'em. Its like, the Bonamy Estate – before they knocked that down there was more armed robbers and villains coming from there than any other part of London.

The cult of villainy in south-east London is no myth, and is but the spectac-ularized extreme of a pattern of culture which the area has bequeathed to its sons. The drive towards personal autonomy is strong here, and it is derived from a long history of independent trading, competitive individualism and hostility towards institutional modernity into which the working-class corporatism of the provincial cities made only marginal impact (Johnson, 1968; McMullan, 1984; Robson, 1997). This has generated, amongst the populations from which Millwall fans have been drawn, a particular variety of masculine culture characterized by an embodied dispositions towards fierce local pride, metropolitan supremacism, personal inviolability and volatile truculence. Sedimented into the habitus of 'working-class' masculinity in south-east London, these very real dispositions and patterns of behaviour have had an impact on the development and distinctive flavour of Millwallism. In the football context, the general attitude underpinned by these characteristics is one in which opponents in hooligan and ritual contests are usually constituted as a *joke*. The very real violence still occasionally unleashed by Millwall's hooligan formations[7] should be set in this context, for it is based on a deeply held conviction that Millwall possess a unique kind of metropolitan toughness which cannot be matched by any of their potential adversaries. This attitude is summed up in the motto *we fear no foe wherever we go*. A minority of fans are as active in violent conflicts as they ever were, and for 'big' games and old vendettas (against, for example, West Ham or Chelsea, Cardiff City or Birmingham City) Milllwall can mobilize one of the most formidable 'firms' in England.

Though very real in themselves, these ongoing martial tendencies have been amplified and given a heightened performative edge among Millwall's hooligan formations by the recurring pervasiveness of the myth. It is in this sense that the cultural politics of identity around the club are dialectical. It is the power of this dialectic which allows Millwall fan culture to flourish however obscurely the team is situated in the football league, and ensures that a game against Millwall always carries, if not glamour, then a certain extra charge for the followers of opposing teams.

Fear and Loathing on the Old Kent Road

One of the most significant developments in the late-1980s 'renaissance' in football culture (Redhead, 1991, 1993; Williams and Wagg, 1991) was the emergence of the 'fanzine' phenomenon. While it is certainly the case that fanzines played a critical role in processes of cultural contestation (Jary *et al.*, 1991: 581), they have had an equally significant role as textual forums for

7. After a relatively quiet period on the 'hooligan front' in the mid-1990s, as fans struggled to come to terms with a change of stadium, its effects on the identity of the club and a long period in the football doldrums (Robson, 2000), there are clear signs that Millwall's hooligan formations have renewed themselves. Fresh blood in the form of younger recruits and the continuing presence of older hands have combined in the last two to three seasons to form a considerable 'away firm', albeit for 'major' games. The best illustration of this was the game at Manchester City in 1998–9, when a large Millwall contingent travelled north with the intention of 'teaching the Mancs a lesson'. This followed a series of exchanges (many of them on the internet) in which City fans were held to have offended Millwall's sense of honour by issuing challenges to 'come up and have a taste of what you gave us down there (in south London)'. Media coverage presented this game as a return to the bad old days, complete with a concerted attack on the home 'end', a rarity indeed in the strictly segregated and controlled environment of contemporary grounds. See Johnson (1999) for a full account.

the circulation of the kind of dialogical subculture previously maintained orally in English football. As repositories of the kinds of humour, lore and apocrypha with which fans have always framed their participation, fanzines represented something new in the culture of the game: fixed, stable and documentary channels of communication *between,* as well as within, clubs. This enables us to look at some of the understandings and imagery by means of which ideas about and experiences of Millwall are conveyed by other sets of fans.

One of the annual staples of fanzine practice is of course the pre-season preview of the prospects for the coming campaign. These usually include a guide to those grounds to be visited, and to the kinds of (primarily alchoholic) entertainments and adventures to be had in their environs. The August 1996 issue of Rotherham's *Moulin Rouge* asks:

> Millwall – Why us? I mean why? I'm crappin' miself already about the New Den visit. They'll be rightly upset about being 2nd division fare after they thought they'd be premier poseurs. Rotherham town reduced to a moonscape, life as we know it altered forever?

This humourous, mock-apocalyptic style, is absolutely typical of fanzine correspondents as they contemplate their impending doom in south-east London, and fanzine culture is saturated with examples. What is perhaps most interesting in accounts of these games is the invariable focus on Millwall's iconic urban context. *Forest Forever* (Nottingham Forest) wonders:

> How can four clubs, all located within five miles of each other geographically be so socially distant from each other? Unassuming Charlton, Wombling Wimbledon, Suburban Crystal Palace and then savage, nasty, malicious Millwall. I'd read and seen all about the problems Millwall have with their fans but nah, I thought, hooliganism's on the wane isn't it ? Perhaps it is, generally, but it's alive and well and truly kicking in Deptford and Peckham.

Arsenal's *The Gooner* (Febuary 1994) is more strident still. The report relates, like the foregoing, to a highly charged and important fixture. The correspondent has been intimidated, and clearly regarded himself to have been in real danger. This is beyond dispute – there was very real 'trouble' after this game. What is interesting for present purposes is the language and imagery used to convey the experience:

> I hope you all made it back in one piece from The Den on 10th January after our FA Cup 3rd round victory over Millwall. Wasn't the atmosphere horrendous? They can build as many new grounds as they like but the supporters will never change. And what about those Dickensian surroundings with water dripping from the dank viaducts? . . . Getting away from the ground after the match was like being on manoeuvres in some enemy infested

outpost of Vietnam ... And by the way Mick McCarthy, we're not *supposed* to be a Premiership team, we are and have been for 75 years, which is 73 years longer than your shabby underworld outfit. Good riddance and so long.

These kinds of ways of writing about Millwall and its environs, with its fused imageries of urban decay and sense of Dickensian obscurity and danger are not confined to the sphere of fanzines. In the burgeoning field of football-related literature, one highly specialized genre is the memoirs of the reformed hooligan. This trend, originating in the late 1980s (Allan, 1989; Ward, 1989), is characterized by a widespread dissemination of the subcultural staples around which so much of fanzine culture revolves: a carousel of reputation and myth, claim and counterclaim, tall tales and journalistic despatches from the front line. Millwall tends to feature largely in these accounts, the legendary status of its fans of the 1970s secure. As Colin Ward reminisces:

> The word 'Millwall' sent shivers down my spine; the hardest fans in the land. They had once taken the Everton end in an FA Cup tie. Everyone knows dockers are tough . . . when it [the whistle] blew we shot out of the exit towards our car. Every street looked the same: bleak and uncompromising. At every alleyway we passed we were fearful that Millwall fans who knew the area would emerge. (Ward, 1989: 29)

Ward later declares that, while it was one thing to defend your 'end' against attack, 'it is quite another mixing it on the streets against Millwall' (ibid.: 95). The iconic status afforded Millwall fans in these matters is clearly apparent, and subsequent contributions to the genre have continued the trend (King, 1996; Francis and Walsh, 1997; King and Knight, 1999).

These accounts reveal a very solid – indeed invariable – core of themes and images: the mythical status of Millwall fans' exploits and adventures, especially in the 1970s; a darkling urban iconography in which danger lurks around every corner; and the association of a legendary toughness and capacity for violence with particular occupational and cultural groupings such as dockers and gangsters. They have received their most explicit and forceful articulation in one of the additions to the hooligan-memoir genre (King, 1996). In this ostensibly fictionalized account of a Millwall–Chelsea game at the New Den, the Chelsea-supporting narrator crystallizes many of the prevailing understandings of Millwall in their rawest form. Chelsea's 'boys' have come to south-east London to test themselves against the might of Millwall's 'firm'. Millwall–Chelsea games, like those against West Ham, have been characterized by high levels of violence over the years, as the respective firms fight for supremacy of the capital. As the Chelsea firm enters the environs of the New Den the narrator describes, from his west London perspective, a very different city:

We're building up for Millwall and it's going to be nasty, yet we respect Millwall somehow, deep down, though we'd never say as much, knowing New Cross and Peckham are the arseholes of London . . . As far back as our memories go Millwall have always been mad. Something special, mental, off their heads. They've got their reputation and they deserve it, raised on docker history spanning the century. A hundred years of kicking the fuck out of anyone who strays too far down the Old Kent Road. (1996: 225)

In this London, it is clear, myth and reality cannot easily be separated. And yet this fearful contempt for the area and for Millwall fans is clearly fused with an attraction based on Millwall's status as the hooligan's historical benchmark, as the place where one can be most proud of 'getting a result' – or at least saying one has been and survived. It would appear that English football subculture's pet hate-objects are, ironically, also its most desired. This desire is rooted in the potency of myth as well as in south-east London's undoubted capacity to act as a venue for those interested in serious violence. Millwall fans revel in the mystique and anti-charisma of generations of football lore and, beyond that, of many more generations of a people historically situated as the obscure and implicitly counter-bourgeois 'other' of one of the great metropolises of liberal-individualist modernity. It may be that this surviving repository of pre-modern sensibilities, of embodied cultural dispositions which do not speak their own name, owes its continuing fascination to social sources deeper than those of which the contestants of hooligan dramas and circulation wars are fully aware.

Part II

Fighting for Causes: Core Identities and Football Oppositions

5

'Those Bloody Croatians': Croatian Soccer Teams, Ethnicity and Violence in Australia, 1950–99

Roy Hay

When I first arrived from Scotland in Geelong in 1977 and resumed an amateur soccer career with Deakin University, I was quickly informed that the Croatian team, North Geelong, was different.[1] Games against it always carried an undercurrent of hostility, and a 'history', even though Deakin was a completely new team. 'Those bloody Croatians', I was told, wanted to win at all costs. North was selfish and clannish; its players would resort to violence to obtain a result. The club was political and always shoving its ethnicity in your face. Members of other clubs recounted stories of battles involving North Geelong and its predecessor Croatia, which had played in Geelong in the 1950s before returning to its origins in Melbourne. If North won a local tournament its supporters would not stay and socialize at the match venue but would return to their own club to celebrate. Outsiders were not welcomed at the club; meetings were conducted in Croatian. Referees or linesmen from the Croatian community who gave decisions against the club would be ostracized. One Dutch migrant who played for Croatia and who did not take part in an all-in brawl during a local derby was hauled before the club committee and told, 'You play for Croatia, you fight for Croatia'.[2] My colleague Bill Murray, born in Scotland and raised in Adelaide, confirmed some of this from experience, adding that Croatians were particularly nasty because they spat on referees. Mosely (1994a) and Hughson (1996) have produced highly critical, academic studies of Croatian clubs and their members' behaviour.

1. Geelong is a conurbation of about 200,000 people about 50 miles south-west of Melbourne in Victoria, Australia.
2. Chris van Beek, personal communication, August 2000. Needless to say, he left the club immediately.

This litany of criticism aimed at the Croatian club struck me as excessive and, increasingly, at variance with my experiences. Certainly Croatians played hard to win. There was a clannishness about the Croatians, but no worse than that among the Scots or the English, or the Macedonians, Greeks, Italians or Hungarians who all had clubs in Geelong. Off the field the Croatians were marvellous company, friendly, passionate and interesting people, although the youngsters could be rude, offensive, chauvinistic, prepared to cheat and violent on occasion. Gangs of Croatian youths were not a pretty sight (Warren, 1995), and very prickly. At the Australian Indoor Soccer championships in Canberra I congratulated a group of young Victorian Croatians who had just won the under-18 title. 'Well done, you guys', I said. One seized me by the throat, 'Who are you calling Yugos?', he demanded. Just the problem of the author's Scottish accent, or an indication of a basic insecurity among Croatian youth?

People from the geographical area of modern Croatia have a much longer history of migration to Australia than most researchers realise. Several hundred arrived during the 1850s gold rushes; a steady stream of sailors and seamen jumped ship thereafter. Until well after the Second World War these migrants were not classified as Croatians. Sutalo (1999b) has traced over four hundred migrants from before the end of the nineteenth century that seem to have blended into Australian society (cf. Jupp, 1988). Their sporting activities included cricket and Australian Rules football but not, it seems, soccer. In the late-nineteenth century and between the World Wars there was a substantial settlement in Western Australia and around Broken Hill, in the far west of New South Wales (Tkalcevic, 1988: 17). The Alagich family, who have a strong influence in Australian soccer, settled in Broken Hill and Marin Alagich is credited with founding the first Croatian soccer team in Australia in Sydney in 1945 (Murphy, 1993: 186–91).

Thereafter, Croatian migration to Australia accelerated rapidly as groups of displaced persons arrived from camps in Europe; some political refugees followed, then a wave of more economically motivated arrivals (Hay, 1998). Many migrants in the 1950s were young, unattached males attracted to Australia by its accessibility and relative cheapness compared to the United States and Canada. Drawn overwhelmingly from working-class or peasant stock, they were regarded by Australians as a new manual-labour force and expected to settle in outback and rural areas after a period in reception camps.

In practice, the majority gravitated quickly to urban centres. Major employers like Ford and International Harvester in Geelong and Melbourne offered unskilled work, while builders like Branko Filippi in Adelaide took arrivals on as labourers. Filippi acted as a fairly draconian, surrogate father to many, to ensure these youngsters remained good advertisements for Croatian identity in Australia. He may have obtained some cheap labour in return, but he is still highly regarded within the community. Joe Radojevic, secretary of Geelong's Croatia club in the 1950s, visited incoming ships in the company of a Slovenian priest to recruit Croatian soccer players, bringing around 350 to the club in his own estimation. Frank Burin, a Croatia club official in the 1960s, worked for the Australian Commonwealth employment service placing many young Croatians in labouring jobs at Ford in Geelong. Soon immigrant numbers permitted the formation of soccer teams, the preferred sport, along with handball and bocce, for the majority of young Croatians. There were few other organizations for young Croatians, predominantly Catholic and anti-Communist, in the early 1950s. The Catholic church in Australia had catered for generations of Irish migrants, but appeared rather liberal and alien to the newcomers. Though the church in Croatia helped sponsor and process migrants, only gradually did Croatian priests acquire local influence. When they did the links between the Church and the soccer clubs remained strong, in part because that is where the young men were located.

Soccer clubs were formed in most capital cities and many smaller urban centres. The Adelaide Croatia club began in 1952, the Melbourne one in 1953 and Sydney followed in 1957 (Mosely, 1995: 65). Geelong had a Croatian team in 1954 and the Melbourne Croatia team temporarily moved there (Hay, forthcoming). The motives for founding these clubs varied. Groups of young migrants might gather for social games and then form a club to play league fixtures; later, fathers formed clubs so that their sons could play. The church and political groups also claimed responsibility for club formation.

Mosely (1994a: 35–6) is quite explicit about Croatian use of soccer for political purposes:

> More than any other group in Australia the Croats used soccer for political means . . . Convinced of perceived injustice, the Croats gave voice to their antagonism to Tito's Jugoslavia and backed it up with centuries old feuding, particularly with the Serbs and Orthodox church. For good measure, elements of the old Ustashi regularly surfaced, complete with pictures of the butcher himself, Dr Ante Pavelic, that hung in clubrooms. Not all Croats were fascists, far from it, and the Ustashi old guard did not control Sydney Croatia. However the same element, perhaps through fear, was tolerated on match day, resided in the club and dwelt in the community in general.[3]

3. Mosely does make excellent use of arguments about differences between British and Continental styles to explain incidents between British-Australian sides and European-derived ones. According to Andrew Moore (1995), Ustashi 'was an ultra-nationalist terrorist organisation which had supported the collaborationist "Independent Croatian State" of 1941 led by Ante Pavelic'.

Aside from its overtones of guilt by association, this interpretation reflects that of the Labour left in Australia, though Moore (1995) points out it was not simply a figment of left-wing imagination. As we will see below, it is not enough to outline the characteristics of the immigrant community, the existing 'host community' and its politics need to be examined and explained as well.[4]

Mosely (1994b) emphasizes the social psychology of the immediate postwar migrants, stressing the anger and vindictiveness of the 'displaced person's mentality'. People who had seen their homelands destroyed and their families oppressed, their political and social rights trampled upon, were likely to harbour grudges and resort to violent means of settling conflicts, including sporting ones, when these often carried the symbols of the former place of residence and allegiance. In the case of the Croatians when this was added to by the political opposition to communist and Serbian dominated Jugoslavia, then the circumstances were propitious for the triggering of conflict.

Before swallowing these explanations, it is worth addressing environmental concerns. In the immediate postwar decades there was a serious lack of facilities for the game, venues were poor and ill-equipped, and there was little demarcation between players and crowds, except at Olympic Park and the Melbourne Showgrounds. Demand outstripped the available venues. Between 1948 and 1958 the number of senior teams in Victoria rose from twenty-eight to sixty-eight, with equivalent growth in reserve grades and juniors (*Soccer News* (*SN*), 1 May 1948: 2–3; *VASFA Handbook*, 1958). Demand grew even more rapidly in New South Wales.

Soccer-related violence occurred in the early postwar years and the new immigrants were seen as the main cause. The format for reporting such violence was set as early as 1950. Symptomatically, J.O. Wilshaw's columns in the *Sporting Globe* appeared under such headlines as 'New Arrivals in Fisticuff Soccer', 'Foreign Element Causing Trouble', and 'Demonstrations a Blot on Soccer'. Wilshaw went on to say:

> The whole question of these new Australians being allowed to form National clubs should be the subject of special investigation and although one does not advocate a boycott of these recent arrivals from the playing fields it certainly would be much better if they were assimilated into the ranks of teams mainly of British stock and thus become better 'mixers' instead of keeping to themselves and in some cases endeavouring to settle political differences on the football field. (*Sporting Globe* (*SG*), 12 April 1950: 13)

According to Dettre and Schwab, however, many immigrants were refused access to Anglo clubs and so were forced to form their own organizations and

---

4. I have reservations about using the terms 'immigrant' and 'host' after reading Finn (1999).

then were damned for doing so.[5] The focus on soccer violence was very quickly directed at so-called Jugoslavs. Wilshaw again, under the headline 'Will soccer "incidents" never cease?' reported that 'On successive Saturdays referees have been assaulted and in each case a Jugoslav player has been involved' (*SG*, 27 August 1952: 15; 24 September 1952: 15). For the press, it was a case of Jugoslavs versus the rest, not one of troubles between Croatians and Serbians. A Croatian team did not exist in Victoria at this time.

As I have argued elsewhere, concern with soccer-related violence did have an evidential basis, but was shaped more strongly by the cultural attitudes of the early 1950s (Hay, 1994). Australia was in the grip of the Cold War and trying to establish an identity in the post-war world. Subsequent events thus tended to be linked to a predetermined pattern. Thus, in explaining soccer-related violence we need to go beyond wartime and post-war European politics, and to look instead at the peculiar features of the host society and its interpreters (Hay, 1992: 367–8).

If politics is key, then major clashes in Victoria would be expected when Croatian and Jugoslav (Serbian) teams were in opposition. The record has not been systematically examined in Victoria, though Mosely (1994a, b) has carried out a good study of New South Wales.[6] Croatia and JUST (Jugoslav United Soccer Team), representing the Croatian and Serbian communities respectively, played together in Victorian Amateur Soccer Football Association competitions from 1954-5 until 1962, and in Victorian Soccer Federation competitions from 1962 until 1984, when they joined the National Soccer League. Croatia and JUST met thirty-four times in league competitions from 1960 to 1972, and 1984 to 1989. Even when they were in different leagues, the clubs often met in knock-out competitions or private tournaments like the Laidlaw World Cup, specifically set up for the different national groups. JUST was much more successful in the earlier periods, winning the VSF State League four times between 1962 and 1973 to Croatia's single triumph in 1968, when it swept all before it in Australia not just Victoria. In the 1980s, Croatia was on the rise and JUST dropped out of the National Soccer League at the end of 1989 never to return. Croatia went on to win successive National League titles in 1995–6.

JUST was formed in March 1950 by Ivan Kuketz, then Vice-President of the Brighton club where many Jugoslav players were registered. Kuketz was

---

5. Schwab in conversation at Olympic Park on 23 February 1993, and Schwab, 'Will we embrace soccer at last?', *Sunday Age*, 28 February 1993: 12–13. For a contemporary statement to that effect, see 'National groups endanger assimilation' in the *Geelong Advertiser*, 4 July 1955.

6. There is a little information in Procter and Lynch (1995).

assisted by Harold Holt, then Minister for Immigration in the Menzies Liberal Government, in recruiting good players from Victorian and New South Wales migrant centres. Kuketz and John Ivanovic were the driving forces behind the new club which won Division Three South in 1950, Division Two in 1951 and finished third in Division One in 1952 and 1953. It was league champion in 1957, the last year of the old First Division, and became a founder member of the State League in 1958, first winning the championship in 1963. In 1960, JUST represented Victoria in the Ampol Cup Finals in Sydney and won the championship by a point from Hellenic of Queensland.

A couple of weeks after its Ampol Cup triumph, JUST was involved in a violent match with George Cross (a Maltese club) at Olympic Park which resulted in George Cross being banned from playing at Melbourne's main soccer venue (*SN*, 23 April 1960: 4, 8–9). Four Maltese appeared in Richmond Court on assault charges and all were fined (*SN*, 28 May 1960: 5). Milosevic, a JUST Reserves player, was banned for life for attacking the referee (*SN*, 14 May 1960: 1).

The first fixture between a Croatian and a Serbian (Jugoslav) team at top league level in Victoria occurred after Croatia amalgamated with Preston in early 1960. Preston and JUST met on 28 May 1960 at Preston, with JUST winning 2–0; there were no press reports of crowd trouble (*Age*, 30 May 1960: 19; *SN*, 4 June 1960). They met again at JUST on 20 August in a 2–2 draw, again with no reported trouble (*Age*, 22 August 1960: 21; *SN*, 27 August 1960). Preston was then relegated, but won the Division One South and returned to the State League as Croat-Preston in 1962.

In 1962, JUST beat Croat-Preston 1–0 at Schintler Reserve on 7 April. 'In a torrid game referee Emil Hecht had to use all his tact and strength to prevent an all-in brawl', according to the *Age* report (9 April 1962: 9). Croat wing-half Zerjav was suspended for five weeks for kicking (*SN*, 19 April 1962: 8), but no crowd trouble was reported. For the second match on 30 June at Elsternwick Park, Croat was coached by ex-JUST captain Peter Vidovic, who had played with Hajduk and spent four years in Nazi prison camps (*SN*, 1 April 1950: 8). Croat also re-signed former player Romel Bomahac, and flew him down from Darwin for the fixture, indicating how seriously the Croatians took the encounter. Bomahac added 'bite to his team's display', according to Alex Barr in the *Age* (2 July 1962: 15). The match finished 1–1 and no trouble was reported.

Alex Barr predicted a 'needle match', rooted in style rather than politics, when Croatia clashed with JUST at Maribyrnong on 13 April 1963 (*Age*, 13 April 1963: 18). A 3–3 draw resulted with no report of trouble on or off the field (*Age*, 15 April 1963: 12). On Easter Monday, Croatia played league leader

George Cross and despite a sending off and a dressing-room argument at half time, which saw Croatia reduced to nine men for the second half, a creditable draw was earned (*Age*, 16 April 1963: 15). In the return match JUST hammered Croatia 6–0 but again there was no trouble reported (*Age*, 1 July 1963: 17). Croatia was relegated so the teams met only on cup business in 1964.

Croatia returned to the State League in 1965, and from then until 1972 the team played regularly against JUST, often at Olympic Park and before crowds of up to 3,000. The matches were typically competitive, and includes both 'incidents' between players as well as high skill levels. Yet throughout this period there were no reports of crowd trouble at these matches.[7] However, in 1972 Croatia were expelled from the Victorian Soccer Federation. The incident which provoked the expulsion might easily but misleadingly be categorized as a simple case of ethnic violence, involving a crowd invasion and an attack on the referee at a match between Croatia and Hakoah (a club supported by Melbourne's Jewish community). The story is in fact far more complex and is dealt with at length elsewhere (Hay, 1998a, b). A leading referee, Fred Hutchison, recalled that other clubs had been expelled before, and that the penalty was appropriate in the light of Croatia's regular involvement in trouble.[8] While the case could be made that Croatia was treated with disproportionate severity, Schwab and Mackenzie's claim that everything had gone smoothly until the Hakoah match does not stand up (*Soccer Action* (*SA*), 19 October 1983: 8–9).

Earlier in the season, there had been politically inspired incidents after the Ampol Cup Final between Croatia and JUST. These incidents had led to the unprecedented VSF decision to have Croatia–JUST league matches played behind closed doors at venues unknown to players until 24 hours before the game (*Age*, 22 April 1972: 27). Both clubs appealed successfully, leading to the resignation of the VSF Chairman, John Gorton, who was reinstated a week later (*Age*, 3 May 1972: 24). The VSF ordered the two clubs to change their names to those of their home districts. JUST protested that it was now known as Footscray JUST (*Age*, 26 April 1972: back page), leaving Croatia in a difficult position.

We shall probably never know for certain whether political pressure was behind Croatia's expulsion. It is, however, hard to accept that the three expulsions

---

7. For example, see the following issues of the *Age*: 10 May 1965: 24; 2 August 1965: 21; 12 April 1966: 18; 16 April 1966: 18; 10 July 1967: 19; 22 April 1968: 18; 18 August 1968: 26; 19 May 1969: 20; 13 March 1971: 26; 9 August 1971: 29. See also *Sporting Globe*: 9 March 1966: 12; 14 March 1966: 18; 9 July 1966: 17; 8 April 1967: 16; 11 April 1970: 6.

8. Interview with Fred Hutchison.

of Croatian clubs from Victorian football (North Geelong were expelled from the Provisional League and the Ballarat and Geelong District League) were just a series of coincidences. The events occurred while a conservative government controlled the Federal and State legislatures. The election of Gough Whitlam's Labour government did not occur until December 1972, dramatically changing the political landscape in Australia. Overnight, the Croatians went from fellow travellers of the right and a bastion of anti-communism, to being former fascists and terrorists against a friendly socialist Jugoslavian government. A series of fire bombings occurred in Australia and a tiny group of Croatians from Australia engaged in an ill-planned and ill-conceived 'invasion' of Jugoslavia to stir a rebellion against the Tito regime.

Cain (1994: 205) argues that the Australian Security and Intelligence Organization (ASIO) and the conservative government under Menzies had been tolerant of Croatian terrorism. He suggests that the ASIO used the Croatian Ustashi to observe tactics and operations in Australia of Jugoslav intelligence in Australia. Seith (1986: 94–7) mentions the possible role of Jugoslav agent provocateurs in much of the violence that occurred, while from the left Coxsedge, Coldicutt and Harant (1982: 43–59) have published substantial evidence of the activities of Croatian political groups. Hall (1978: 81–98) identifies links between the Soviet Union and the Croatian Revolutionary Brotherhood (HRB) which were picked up in Canada and Australia and passed on to the CIA by ASIO infiltrators. There was a split in Australia between the States and Federal Police forces, who were closer to the actual offences and hence more aggressive and less sympathetic to the Croatians, and ASIO. The police raided the home of Jure Maric, a leader of the Croatian Revolutionary Brotherhood (HRB), who was implicated in the abortive invasion. Hall (1978: 97) states that Croatian 'extremists' were 'probably the most spied upon group in Australia' at that time.

It may be that this murky picture will not clear even when the relevant documents are released. There were Croatians and Jugoslavs (Serbians) who were prepared to use violence for political ends in Australia. Agents provocateurs on both sides, and possibly in the Australian intelligence community, connived at or fomented violent incidents. Political groups were tolerated and sometimes financially supported by other community organizations including soccer clubs, particularly during the 'homeland war' of the early 1990s (Moore 1995: 112). But at most times the soccer clubs tried to keep political activity to the minimum possible without losing credibility in the broader community. Some individuals involved with soccer clubs made huge sacrifices for their countries, including putting their own lives on the line by returning to take part in the struggle in a variety of capacities. Many others made extraordinary financial contributions and still felt that more should have been done. For a society in which there has long been a stable and accepted monopoly of violence by the state it is hard to agree that there can be a legitimate use of political violence in a nationalist struggle, as witnessed in the reaction of Australians to events in South Africa, East Timor and the Balkans.[9]

The VSL expulsion of Croatia was shattering for the Croatian community. Many people severed their football involvement and some never returned. Others were equally determined to keep the community identity to the fore and continued to hold meetings every Tuesday, though the club no longer competed. Croatian old-boys teams played social soccer against local teams (*Osvit*, 19 December 1973: 22). Subsequently, however, those involved returned to soccer through Essendon Lions which was gradually taken over by the Croatian community. Essendon Lions evolved into Essendon Croatia and then Melbourne Croatia, then Melbourne CSC and now the Melbourne Knights, back-to-back champions in the National League in the mid-1990s.

The Croatian Soccer Association of Australia was founded in 1974 during this period of expulsion, and has organized a national Croatian tournament since 1975. More than thirty clubs have been affiliated and the Association has convened overseas tours. Mosely (1997: 166) observes:

> The idea of a national association and national tournament stemmed from North American examples. Signs of communal unity fostered through the CSAA were evident in 1977. Adelaide Croatia, the oldest Croatian soccer club in Australia (1952) led a move to form a super club whereby the resources of all clubs would be pooled. The club was meant to represent the Croatian national community in the then recently formed Philips (national) Soccer League (PSL). Logistics were always going to be a problem but the Australian Soccer Federation's hierarchy proved an even greater burden. In an effort to Australianise the PSL, the Australian Soccer Federation banned clubs unwilling to forgo their ethnic names and symbols. No Croatian club, existing or proposed, entered the league until the ban was lifted for the 1984 season.

Mosely's argument about ethnic names will not stand up. The National Soccer League included JUST, Juventus, Hakoah, Marconi, Alexander, Budapest, two clubs called Hellas (West Adelaide and South Melbourne) and Olympic in its first season in 1977. 'The agreement reached in 1975 to exclude ethnic or nationalistic names disappeared pretty quickly' (*The Un-official beginners*

---

9. There is a formidable literature on the subject. See, for example, Hocking (1997), Crown (1986), Cuvalo (1990), Tanner (1997).

guide to the History of the Australian National Soccer League, 1999: 1). Croatia could not have been barred on that score. In fact with the possible exception of the Adelaide club none of the Croatian teams in the other capital cities were in a position to claim a national league place on playing merit or status. In Melbourne, Essendon Lions were in the Metropolitan League, not the State League, and their promotion did not occur until 1977 when gaps emerged in the State League thanks to the promotion of four Victorian teams to the NSL. Lions did have good crowd support, but no overwhelming case for inclusion.

From 1972 until 1984, Croatian and Serbian clubs did not meet in Victorian soccer league competitions, though in 1977 a leading player, Billy Vojtek, received threats from people connected with Essendon Lions for giving a record by the pop group Sherbet to the visiting Red Star Belgrade team (*SA*, 7 August 1985: 2). In 1984, following the splitting of the National Soccer League into two Conferences and its expansion to 24 clubs, Melbourne Croatia joined the League. It met JUST on 13 May at Schintler Reserve in Melbourne before around 5,000 fans, the match finishing 0–0. Afterwards, the JUST canteen was fire bombed, the press box windows were smashed and the ground's electricity was cut. Damage was estimated at $47,000. Melbourne Croatia dissociated itself from the violence, club official Frank Burin stating, 'Those who caused the trouble at the ground were mainly teenagers not associated with our club, and we deplore their action. Those who caused the violence should be dealt with by the law' (*SA*, 16 May 1984: 1). The return match on 16 September was won 3–1 by Croatia with no reported trouble (*Age*, 17 September 1985: 25). On the field, Brogan of Croatia was sent off for verbally abusing the linesman (*SA*, 19 September 1984: 7).

In 1985 the big story was the non-appearance of overseas star Eddie Krncevic, who had been billed to turn out for Croatia for the second meeting of the clubs, and the sending-off of Luka Bonacic of JUST and Drago Deankovic of Croatia. The first meeting of 1986 at Olympic Park before 7,000 fans led Schwab to report,

> A loud unruly group of teenage Croatia supporters marred the match. They shouted obscene slogans incessantly and after chanting 'There's gonna be a riot' during the last quarter-hour, charged towards the JUST spectators in the opposite stand. Police stopped them and later led away at least a dozen. There was at least one arrest. Melbourne Croatia president Joe Sigur pleaded with the most vocal group, but he too was abused. (*Age*, 21 April 1986: 33)

By now, European soccer hooliganism, particularly that in the United Kingdom, was at its height, and a strong copy-cat element appeared to exist among adolescent Croatians. But Schwab's report for *Soccer Action* has a significant detail missing from his *Age* column. The ex-JUST player Bonacic scored for

Croatia, 'then ran towards the JUST supporters in the far stand and made a provocative gesture similar to the one over which Eli Ohana was sent off during Israel's World Cup match against Australia last year' (*SA*, 23 April 1986: 6). The second match was fiercely contested and won 3–0 by JUST but no crowd trouble was reported (*Age*, 14 July 1986: 27; *SA*, 16 July 1986: 7).

The match between JUST and Sydney Croatia at Schintler Reserve on 10 May 1987 saw Croatians abusing and spitting on JUST fans, players and officials at half-time. 'Fighting broke out after the game. Police made 24 arrests' (*Age*, 11 May 1987: 33). Schwab went on 'It is regrettable that Sydney Croatia and Melbourne Croatia are burdened by supporters who continually harm the image of two progressive and respectable clubs. But even they could not detract from the finest match of the season so far: a tribute to skill, imagination and panache.' At this game the young Melbourne-based Croatians could have free rein since their own club was not involved. By the time of the match with Melbourne Croatia the following week at Olympic Park, 'A strong police presence and the vigilance of Melbourne Croatia officials prevented any possible repeat of the crowd violence during the JUST–Sydney Croatia match the previous week. A group of young Croatia supporters, however, kept up a constant barrage of verbal abuse aimed at the JUST players'. Nevertheless JUST was preparing to sign Drago Deankovic, the former Melbourne Croatia star who had spent some time playing with Osijek in the Jugoslavian first division. In Sydney, the second meeting between Sydney Croatia and JUST resulted in another riot:

> Croatia officials did their best to handle the disgraceful behaviour that came from part of the terraces, and particularly from behind the goals. Once again Soccer is facing a crisis – in this case as a carry over of the warfare that began in the first round fracas in Melbourne. Visiting goalkeeper Zoran Nikitovic summed it up. 'I was pelted with rocks, bottles, cans and fruit and even umbrellas. I have never seen the like of it in 350 games here and overseas. We came here for Soccer and not politics', he said. At one stage, when Ante Rumora was dismissed for persistent misconduct, a few people raided the field only to be chased off by security guards.
>
> There was no shortage of security. Had not Croatia seen to that then the NSL would have been investigating a riot – and I don't mean maybe. To play the game as it stood involved a horde of police with nine wagons and squad cars, plainclothes men in the crowd, private security guards, club attendants and later the tactical response group. (Keith Gilmour, *Australian Soccer Weekly* (*ASW*), 2 September 1987: 9)

For the second match in 1987 between Melbourne Croatia and JUST, the NSL arranged a double-header at Olympic Park with Juventus playing Sydney Croatia and JUST taking on Melbourne Croatia. A 3,000 crowd appeared despite traffic difficulties but no goals were scored, no crowd trouble reported and the game was described as boring (*Age*, 7 September 1987: 37; *ASW*, 9 September 1987: 9).

The matches between Melbourne Croatia and JUST in 1988 seem to have passed without incident (*ASW*, 30 March 1988: 5; 29 June 1988: 5; *Age*, 27 June 1988: 31). In 1989 the last round of the season saw JUST relegated when beaten 2–0 by Croatia, again without violence. Greg Blake mentioned 'brutality' on the pitch but said we were 'spared the unthinkable', and noted that all the players of JUST congratulated each of their Croatian counterparts at the end of the game (*Age*, 23 January 1989: 27; 17 July 1989: 31; *ASW*, 25 January 1989: 5–6; 19 July 1989: 6).

Soccer reports in papers like the *Age*, *Soccer Action*, *Soccer News*, *Australian Soccer Weekly* and *Sporting Globe* cannot be relied on totally for evidence of violent behaviour associated with games. While they tend to mention serious on-field incidents they may not report violence among spectators unless it affects the game. For example, the 1963 matches between Croatia and JUST appear to have passed without major incident, but two years later *Soccer News* reported that Tony Kovac had stood down as President of JUST and referred to his controversial past:

> In October 1963, he clashed with referee Lewis Stafrace during the Australia Cup game between JUST and Slavia at Olympic Park. At this time Kovach was chairman of the State League Management Committee. He was also involved in an incident at Olympic Park with a *Soccer News* reporter following the 'bloodbath' match between Croatia and JUST. (*SN*, 18 November 1965: 1)

Nevertheless, the absence of reported violence in league matches between Croatia and JUST in Victoria in the 1960s places the onus on those who would contend that violence was a regular accompaniment of matches between these two communities. This detailed research may be regarded as too empirical by sociologists, but it is the necessary first step before grounded theoretical analysis can proceed. It shows that there was violence between the Croatian and Serbian communities around soccer matches, but at a low level in the 1960s, and higher in the 1980s when the focus was on the national league. But still, despite tension, most matches passed off peacefully at times when there were serious incidents taking place away from the game in Australia and Jugoslavia, particularly in 1972. Indeed it could be argued that the soccer clubs were not so much the focus of violence, but rather oases where non-violent exchanges between opposed political groups were possible. This case needs to be thoroughly investigated, not dismissed out of hand. The soccer clubs on both sides of the divide tried hard to maintain a qualified independence of politics, though it could never be total. They tried hard to control violence within their own support and appealed to the authorities for support when it got out of hand. And they had some success. Some explanations of behaviour may be more prosaic. Many Croatians seldom went to Croatian games at Serbian-Jugoslav venues because that would be putting money in the pockets of the enemy, and vice versa. Given the imbalance of numbers between rival fans, incidents would be less likely to occur, unless some agent provocateur stirred up the supporter groups.

In the more recent past, and after clashes at National League level between Croatia and JUST had ceased, Hughson (1996) conducted an ethnographic study of the Sydney Croatian Bad Blue Boys (BBB), modelled on their counterparts in Zagreb who followed Dinamo Zagreb, renamed Croatia Zagreb by President Tudjmann.[10] The original BBB were the subject of some fascinating analysis by Furio Radin, Minister for Italian minorities in the Croatian Parliament, as they formed a key part of Croatian identity and the independence movement, and later became a focus of democratic opposition to Tudjmann (Hay, 1996: 10–12). Hughson argued that the young Croatians in Australia, who formed the BBB, clung to an image of their heritage from which they believed their parents were diverging and sought to use many symbols of the Pavelic era to construct their image of Croatia. In doing so they adopted the hooligan style and some of its substance, thus contributing to violence around Croatian games in the 1990s. When Sydney Croatia changed its name to Sydney United, the large 'U' symbol could be interpreted by the BBB as standing for the Ustashi.

The evidential basis for Hughson's study is inevitably tiny. Crowd attendances for Sydney Croatia, CSC and United at the time of his research averaged well under 5,000, probably nearer half that; the BBB were never more than a tenth of that, the total group and fellow travellers being less than 250, and Hughson dealt with only a tiny proportion of this group. He came and went as a sociologist, and his evidence applies to a brief period of three to four years in the early 1990s. A problem of his ethnographic approach is that it deals only with contemporary events: the past cannot be interrogated ethnographically. Hence there is inevitably a truncated vision in the accounts of Hughson reinforced by the lack of historical understanding of the 'neotribes' studied.[11]

10. Croatia reverted to Dinamo after the death of Tudjmann. See also Hughson (1997, 1999).
11. Terminology used by Hughson (1999), following Gary Armstrong.

Croatian clubs for all their reputation for chauvinism and fascist tendencies have regularly used non-Croatian players over the years: Scots, Aborigines (like Charlie Perkins, who rose to become Head of the Aboriginal and Torres Straits Islanders Commission in Canberra), Caribbean Englishmen including Frances Awaratife, and Africans like the Ghanaian Ransford Banini and Nigerian Toyin Abbas. Indeed, in Western Australia there have been claims that too many non-Croatians were used (Jones and Moore ,1994).

Though Croatians and Serbian clubs did not meet in the highest league after 1989, in lower leagues clubs continued to face each other. There has been some violence in Victoria since 1989, and matches were played behind closed doors during the 'homeland war'. Many others passed off without incident, but echoes of old discontents still rumble on. On 13 May 2000, during a match between Fitzroy City (with strong Serbian connections) and North Geelong (predominantly Croatian) in Division Two of the VSL, there were chants of 'Croatia' when North was doing well, and 'Serbia' when Fitzroy took the lead, which it held till the end. There was some more pointed verbal abuse and in the second half a police van arrived and drove around the ground parking very visibly opposite the clubhouse and stand. At one point the crowd in front of the press box, predominantly Serbian, began rude chanting and some moved in the direction of the North supporters behind the coach's box at the far end of the stand.

The North Geelong coach, whose parents are English, phoned me after-wards. He stated that a long-time North supporter, a committee man and a club and league secretary, had told him during the game to substitute a player who he claimed was going for the man not the ball. The coach ignored the request. A former club president, and still a major figure in the community, made the same demand. The player's brother overheard the argument and engaged in a verbal joust with the ex-president. It was this which sparked off the visiting supporters. It is not clear whether the club members' objection was based on tactical consideration or the ethics of the game, or whether they feared that the player's behaviour would spark trouble. But certainly this was not simply a Croatian versus Serbian incident. Hence, what looks from the outside like a clear case of ethnic politics leading to violence is actually something more complex and subtle. Understanding that is the first step, and only the first step, in coming to terms with the relationships between soccer and the various groups which play the game in Australia.

6

Football, Ethnicity and Identity in Mauritius: Soccer in a Rainbow Nation

Tim Edensor and Frederic Augustin

On 23 May 1999, on the final day of the football season, two teams played a match which would decide the Mauritian Premier League title. The Scouts, reigning champions, and traditionally the standard-bearers of the Muslim community, needed to draw to retain the championship. Their opponents, Fire Brigade, customarily drawing their support from the Creole community, required a victory to snatch the title. Midway through the second half, the Scouts scored but to the chagrin of their fans the goal was disallowed. In the 89th minute Fire Brigade scored, Scouts subsequently had another goal ruled out, and the former were proclaimed champions. Sensing injustice, the Scouts fans rioted, assaulted the referee, and destroyed 345 seats, numerous wash-basins, toilets, windows, the electronic scoreboard and a surveillance camera, at a cost of approximately three million rupees (£80,000). More seriously, the disorder spread to the capital city, Port Louis, where seven people were killed in an arson attack on L'Amicale Casino, close to the important Jumma Mosque. Although the attack was popularly viewed as an opportunistic assault by religious zealots upon what they regarded as a sinful site of gambling and prostitution, or alternatively, an attempt by a gang to eradicate a rival faction's drug business, the government acted firmly. This latest event in a long sequence of violent incidents connected with football, was the spur for an outright suspension of league football pending a radical overhaul of the game's organization (*Le Mauricien*, 24 May 1999; *5Plus Dimanche*, 30 May 1999).

This chapter aims to show how semi-professional football in Mauritius is a site of ethnic, communal performance and contestation, ensuring that the game is riven with rivalries which articulate wider, entrenched social divisions. Although since independence in 1968 attempts have been made to create a sense of national inclusiveness, ethnicity remains the first and foremost

constituent of Mauritian identity. Ethnicity here refers to the 'social reproduction of basic classificatory differences between self-defined categories of
people' (Eriksen, 1998: 49). Wishful thinking has ensured that Mauritius,
economically dependent on tourism and inward investment, has been
conceived and broadcast as a rainbow nation, an idealized example of unity
in diversity. Such delusions have been rudely shattered by the extensive riots
that broke out across the island in March 1999, resulting in loss of life, great
economic destruction and an increasingly fragile social and political order in
which tensions between ethnic groups have been exacerbated, and presently
simmer below the calm surface of everyday life. In this context, it is no surprise
that football, as a public occasion for expressing communal identity, has been
banned following the disturbances.

With its history of slavery and bonded labour to work on its sugar
plantations, Mauritius is home to various ethnic groups, usually described as
African Creole, Franco-Mauritian, coloured (usually 'mixed race' descendants
of Creole and Franco lineage), Chinese, and three major Indian groups –
Hindu, Tamil and Muslim. In the 1991 census, the 1.2 million population
consisted of 51 per cent Hindu (including Tamils), 17 per cent Muslim, 27
per cent general population (principally Creoles and Coloured), 3 per cent
Chinese, and 1 per cent Franco-Mauritian. Ethnic identity is expressed through
the mobilization of symbolic and practical resources. In party politics and
social life there is a continual jostling for position, but ethnic and communal
identification is expressed in quotidian rituals and unreflexive knowledge,
across multiple sites and in cultural forms and activities. It is thus as much
embedded in everyday life as in political organization, kinship networks and
official organizations.

Ethnicity is more spectacularly expressed and played out in popular culture:
popular histories, language, lifestyle, the wearing of clothes and the consumption and playing of music are wielded by communal groups as markers
of identity. Whilst there are certainly points of intersection, arenas for compromise and negotiation, even spaces where distinctions are temporary dissolved,
boundaries are frequently drawn, particularly during public practices such as
marches, religious festivals and sporting contests. But identity is inevitably
internally and externally contested. It is also contextual and ongoing, and
people can occupy contradictory positions, perhaps increasingly so. Accordingly, in order to achieve stability in the face of change, leaders of groups
often attempt to fix the symbolic importance of cultural resources to broadcast
a definitive representation. This has been the case, as we shall see, with the
ways in which football has been used to express communal identity through
support for ethnically identified teams. But this boundary-drawing also constructs ideas about 'others', and football officials, referees, journalists, trainers

and players have their ethnic allegiance identified and frequently called into question.

What we want to do is firstly look at the communal origins of Mauritian football and the clubs that persist in ethnic allegiance; secondly, we will explore the problems that have resulted from this; and, thirdly, we will look at the current policy of regionalization which aims to reorganize football along non-communal lines. Finally, we will suggest that despite this bleak picture of division and conflict, football is paradoxically an activity which can unify Mauritians, a common denominator, although this shared enthusiasm for the game is not expressed through club football.

Historical Background: Imperial Games

Football was imported into Mauritius by British colonialists, and played in English-run schools and by visiting sailors. Franco-Mauritians, descendants of the French colonizers usurped by the British, but who continue to own most large sugar plantations, established social and sporting clubs in the 1920s and 1930s and organized fixtures against each other. Football was regarded as a social activity played by gentlemen. These white teams were gradually supplemented by other occupationally and communally-based clubs from Creole, coloured, Chinese, Muslim, Hindu and Tamil communities. In 1952, the Mauritian Football Federation formed and inaugurated the First Division, initially including the Muslim Scouts, the non-communal Police, the Dodos (Franco-Mauritian), Fire Brigade (Creole) and the Hounds (coloured). The Hindu Cadets, Racing Club (coloured) and the Tamil Cadets would later gain promotion to the First Division. Thus club football, from its origins and after the inception of the League, was largely organized along communal lines.

Communal pressures at family, community and club level engendered a widespread assumption that young players would join clubs of their own ethnic affiliation, and in any case, that teams would reject players from other communities. A Coloured ex-player who reported to us that he had broached these guidelines by choosing to play for Fire Brigade rather than Racing Club, the team which he should have 'naturally' chosen, thus associating with Creole rather than 'coloured' team-mates, spoke of the reproaches from his family and community. The organization of football and the constitution of clubs remained unchanged until 1982, a communal focus which was responsible for a number of violent incidents between opposing supporters. Tension at matches was having a disastrous effect on attendances, as well as threatening public order. Football was suspended in 1956, 1964, 1969 and 1975 following disturbances in games between Fire Brigade and the Dodos, Hindu Cadets and Muslim Scouts, and Muslim Scouts and Racing Club.

To start with, the exclusively white Dodo team became increasingly subject to crowd abuse. The Dodo Club was founded in 1928 as a sporting and leisure club and remains an exclusive haven for Franco-Mauritians, who play a range of sports and socialize amidst verdant and well-equipped grounds in Curepipe. The club's bars, function rooms and restaurant are bedecked with sporting trophies and photographs of old teams, redolent of colonial times. Tim Edensor enquired about the possibility of his joining the club and was told that there was no problem– with a proviso: 'I hope you don't mind me asking, is your wife European?', a code for white. The Dodos left the league in 1978 after becoming a focus for discontent against Franco-Mauritians, but also, some argue, because they were aware of imminent legislation to decommunalize football. The club had stressed, 'the day we open our doors to blacks we are finished'. Like Racing Club, they did not want members of other communities to belong to the social club which they represented. Moreover, the Dodos believe Mauritian football has declined since they left, reasoning that 'football is not only about strength but also about organization and intelligence', a thinly veiled deployment of popular racist notions about the ethnic distribution of mental and physical attributes.

Such invective was directed not only against the Franco-Mauritian and coloured clubs, but also persisted in matches between rival clubs, notably the Hindu Cadets versus Muslim Scouts fixtures. Accordingly, in 1982 and after several thwarted attempts, it was decreed by the Football Association and the Ministry of Sport that football must be decommunalized. Communal names were disallowed and teams were required to be ethnically mixed rather than contain members of one community. Most clubs agreed with these policies and instituted them. The Tamil cadets became Sunrise Flaq United, the Muslim Scouts became Scouts, and the Hindu Cadets likewise erased their religious appellation. Moreover, players from other communities were drafted into teams. However, the ownership of Fire Brigade, Scouts and Cadets remained exclusively Creole, Muslim and Hindu respectively. More importantly, their communal fan base endured despite the mixed teams. Only the other team amongst the 'big four', Sunrise, made more extensive efforts to decommunalize, establishing a more professional ethos and higher standard of play to attract a more diverse fan base, and they have been partially successful.

However, even prior to decommunalization – and certainly since then – the vast majority of players in the Premier League have been Creoles. Whereas particular teams used to feature players from particular communities, Hindu, Chinese, Tamil and Muslim players are increasingly rare. Thus the teams recognized as Tamil (Sunrise) Muslim (Scouts) and Hindu (Cadets) include few players from their communities. This has reinforced racist ideas about the distribution of distinct ethnic qualities: for instance, that Creoles are predisposed to athleticism and strength, whereas Hindus tend towards responsibility, study and are more family-oriented. In fact, these trends signify social exclusion and economic marginalization, where the educational progression (see Bunwaree, forthcoming), unemployment rates, occupational profiles and political involvement of Creoles are inferior to those Mauritians of Indian and Chinese descent. Accordingly, their predominance in semi-professional football provides common-sense evidence to support stereotypical notions about why Creole economic, political and educational under-achievement persists: Creoles are good at sport but not academically inclined, and work less hard, putting greater emphasis on pleasure.

Hindus, Muslims and Tamils continue to play for local teams but increasingly place greater stress on fulfilling educational and career aspirations, relegating football to a less status-oriented activity. Yet despite the prevalence of Creole players in the league, Sunrise, Scouts and Cadets continue to be communally and ethnically identified. Nevertheless, it has been expressed to us by several fans that many Cadets and Scouts followers are deserting their teams since they can no longer identify with teams comprising mainly Creole players.

The Persistence of Communal Violence and Football

Since 1982, most of the teams that have played in the Premier League have been regionally-based, but, nevertheless, rivalries between Sunrise, Scouts, Cadets and Fire Brigade have only intensified, perhaps mirroring wider ethnic tensions throughout the island. There have been a catalogue of incidents – at least twenty-three cases of violence between 1985 and 1999 – including assaults on rival fans, damage to stadia, battles with the police, assaults on referees, players and officials, and pitch invasions. The most notorious include the following, selected to trace some of the contours of communal fan culture:

1. *Scouts versus Fuel Youth, November 1987.* The referee abandoned the game for fear of spectator violence, and was beaten by Scouts fans who also damaged the stadium. This led to the Scouts being ordered to play behind closed doors. In 1990, a game between the same clubs again provoked riots and the ransacking of the stadium, triggered off once more by a refereeing decision. Like the incident which opens this chapter, anger at a perceived history of refereeing bias against Scouts is believed to symbolize the allegedly systematic mistreatment of Muslims in Mauritius. According to the same logic, Scouts fans argue that their treatment by the police mirrors wider political and legal injustices towards Muslims.

According to this metaphorical thinking, teams represent particular communities, and authority figures associated with the game – whether the referee, police, stadium officials or football administrators – have their impartiality continually called into question. Their decisions and policies become subsumed into wider political discourses concerning official favouritism or discrimination against particular communities.

2. *Sunrise versus Zamalek (of Egypt) March 1996.* This notorious incident occurred during and after an African Club Champions Cup match. A full stadium of 20,000 fans included about 500 Zamelek supporters – apparently Scouts fans – wearing their red shirts and scarves and carrying flags of Egypt and other Islamic nations, as well as banners supporting the Hamas group. These fans, widely attacked in the media and physically assaulted at the game, were avowedly supporting their 'frères Musulmans' rather than joining in the patriotic support of a Mauritian team. After the game there was a large riot in Plaine Verte, a Muslim area of Port Louis, where damage to vehicles and buildings and attacks on the police were widely reported, leading to a commission of enquiry. It was a similar story the previous year when the Mauritian under-23 football team was playing against its Egyptian counterpart. The national team was constantly booed throughout the game whereas the away team received fervent support. These (Scouts) fans justified their anti-patriotic sentiments by arguing that there were no Muslims playing for Mauritius. The pre-match routine of many Scouts fans is to gather in the symbolic Muslim space, Khadafi Square, in Plaine Verte, a space in which pro-Muslim slogans are daubed and draped, as was the case in the Bosnian conflict and the Gulf War. A Mauritian nation-building project is thwarted by such religious and ethnic allegiances; and football is an important outlet for the proclamation of these identities.

3. *Cadets versus Maurice Espoir, November 1993.* Although they are most notorious, the Scouts fans are not alone in using football as an arena of communal contestation. Cadets were formed to include the nation's most promising youngsters, a symbolic role which contributed to the behaviour of Cadets fans on this occasion. The Cadets fans unfurled a large banner announcing 'Happy Diwali' (the game coincided with the Hindu festival) whereupon stadium and Football Association officials decided that it must be removed on the grounds that football should be free of communal performances. This was the cue for a large-scale riot causing damage amounting to three million rupees, principally, the fans asserted, because they were unhappy with 'anti-Hindu policies'. A prominent idea is that, since 1982, successive (non-Hindu) ministers of sport have acted communally to favour other sections of the community. It is frequently

assumed by all Mauritians that politics is concerned with doing favours for one's ethnic group or caste, that ministerial policies and decisions are based on advancing these aims and not reached objectively. For instance, many Cadets fans argue that sports scholarship schemes have favoured coloured and Creole youths. Whether this is true or not, it indicates how difficult it is to make administrative decisions that are beyond suspicion – and football is not innoculated against such scepticism. Prior to the tragic incidents of May 1999, there were calls to recommunalize football, principally from Cadets fans and officials, who argued that the dwindling number of Hindu players meant that support for their club was likely to ebb away if there were none in their team. Accordingly, plans were devised to develop island-wide coaching schemes to develop Hindu talent, and to organize training sessions which would fit in with Hindu aspirations concerning education and family life.

4. *Fire Brigade versus Sunrise, 1994*. The peculiarly symbolic, communal nature of football is exemplified by the response of fans to their teams when they perform badly, irrespective of whether they have had a successful run of results. Already proclaimed league champions, Fire Brigade faced rivals Sunrise on the final day of the season. The irrelevant nature of the game perhaps contributed to a 5–2 defeat for the Creole team. After the game, many fans boycotted the championship parade such was their sense of humiliation after this poor display, burned their team shirts and scarves and vowed never to support the team again. The fact that the fixture was against particularly despised rivals added insult to the feeling that the team had let the community down. This incident, and similar examples of spectator bitterness towards their own teams, seem to go beyond the usual range of supporter dissatisfaction.

5. Finally, the idea that players' communal identity continues to be relevant in terms of the team for which they play persists amongst fans. For instance, in the aforementioned game of 23 May 1999, Fire Brigade fans confronted the wives and girlfriends of the Scouts' Creole players. One partner, sporting a Scouts cap, was interrogated by a fan of Fire Brigade about how she could wear such headgear: she was a Creole, Catholic, a churchgoer, rather than an attendee at the mosque. Such accusations firmly associate fanship with community and faith.

Besides the events identified above, football fan cultures are saturated with communal identifications and sectarian antagonisms towards other teams. Clothing, banners and other items refer symbolically to teams and imply bounded collective identities. Fans' songs celebrate their team along with wider communal virtues, and occasionally direct racist chants against opposing teams and their supporters. Indeed, amongst fans, ethnic slurs are routine, with Hindus described as 'malbars', Muslims as 'lascars', and Creoles as 'Mozambiken', all derogatory labels. Nevertheless, to label all fans as violent or excessively partisan would be misleading. Whilst a small survey we carried out identified well-established support for teams on a communal basis, few fans engage in violence, indeed they either move away or try to deter fellow fans from such behaviour. Moreover, most fans agree that the referee ought to be beyond attack, and, crucially, a majority show a preference for regionalization and an end to communalism in football, despite their ethnic allegiances.

Regionalization

It was only in 1955 that the George V Stadium in Curepipe was built to accommodate growing numbers of spectators and to stage big games. Since then, the Anjalay Stadium has been built in the north of the island to accommodate Premier League fixtures, finals and international fixtures. However, until the cessation of football, Premier League games were played at only three stadiums. Consequently, for the best-supported clubs – those clubs with an ethnic basis – there is no sense of belonging to a particular place, no distinction between home and away fixtures, and hence no 'topophilia' (Bale, 1982), no sensual and emotional attachment to a stadium. Since these largest clubs are ethnically rather than regionally based, support is drawn from all over the island rather than from specific regions.

Following the disorders cited above, it has finally been decided by the government (with cross-party support) and the Mauritian Football Association that football must be thoroughly regionalized in order to vanquish the scourge of communalism. All football teams must belong to a region or urban centre, and must form a team of which 75 per cent should reside in that area. It is intended that facilities will be distributed amongst municipalities to develop this regional basis for sport, and committees will be established in all thirteen regions to sponsor local teams, provide training facilities and build the necessary infrastructure. The cost implied by this development will be considerable, given the necessary infrastructure and the need for each region to have its own stadium to inculcate a sense of regional belonging. Accordingly, fans are cynical about the possibilities of such a development, although private sponsorship of clubs has been mooted. Questions have also been asked about the unevenness of regions, notably in terms of population and resources. Initially, many regions may find themselves with a weak side, whilst others will be able to draw on a large pool of talented players, creating an imbalanced championship dominated by one or two teams. Moreover, promising players forced to play for a poor region may fail to nurture their talent.

Although widely welcomed, several team managers and fans strongly object to the discontinuity in the historical constitution of their clubs. Tradition and history are fundamental constituents of club identity, reverently referred to and used by fans. The creation of entirely new teams and the erasure of those clubs with strong traditions will be difficult to achieve. Furthermore, most Mauritians identify with an ethnic group before they identify with their region or nation. Many fans believe that regionalization will take a generation to work, for communal allegiances will not easily disappear, and this delay will cause the quality of Mauritian football to decline.

More seriously, clubs already appear to be reconstituting themselves on an ethnic basis as former owners and administrators attempt to find ways around the identification of clubs with ethnicity. Most clearly, this has been the case with the residence rules. For instance, the president of Vacoas-Phoenix – the former boss of Fire Brigade – has found places to stay in the area for the former players of the now defunct Creole team. It is also rumoured that some of the former leaders and players of the Scouts will become Association Port Louis 2000, Sunrise have become Olympic Moka and the Cadets club has formed a team in the town of Quatre Bornes. Since these new clubs can be readily identified as new incarnations of previously ethnically-based teams, under the same ownership, management and with many of the same players, it seems unlikely that regional assignations will prevail. Indeed, the only games played since the interregnum have been a specially arranged millennium game between Vacoas-Phoenix (Fire Brigade) and Olympic Moka (Sunrise), and an African *Coupe des Clubs Champions* game, between the former and a team from Seychelles. Vacoas-Phoenix fans were almost entirely Creole, descending on these two matches from all parts of the country singing the old songs and wearing Fire Brigade shirts.

This jockeying to reconstitute clubs has also had the effect of causing clubs to try to relocate in ethnically identified regions. For instance, Vacoas Phoenix have considered leaving Vacoas and merging with a smaller club, Pointe-aux-Sables, to form the Port Louis Red Star Mates. This has provoked opposition since the region of Point-aux-Sables has a large Creole population which will consolidate a communal attachment to the team. Because of these manoeuvres, the government has been reluctant to give the go-ahead to a new season and, as of May 2000, football has remained in a state of inertia.

Other Football Allegiances

Although Mauritian football acts as a focus for the communal performance of difference, in other contexts it is a common denominator, an occasion and a practice which brings Mauritians together irrespective of ethnic identification.

Firstly, we will look at the potential of the national side as a focus for common identification. In 1955, two national teams were selected to compete against a visiting team from Natal, South Africa, a white-only team and a team comprising players from other communities. Yet although this crude racial segregation is a thing of the past, it still seems difficult for Mauritians to unite in support for the national team.

Although the idea that Mauritius is a shining example of a society where communities live and work side by side is often hyped, the reality is that over thirty years since independence, the project of nation-building has been uneven with communal identification persistently saturating everyday culture as well as political life. In this context, the national team has been presented as a common symbol which all Mauritians can support. As mentioned earlier, the problems of divergent communal representation within the national squad can cause problems. Given that Creole players predominate at the national level – for instance in the latest squad, all twenty players were Creoles (by contrast, the 1975 national team included nine Hindus) – many Hindus and Tamils complain that they cannot support a national side that contains none of 'their' players. However, in a recent African Nations' Cup match against South Africa, support was much stronger than usual, and the national anthem resounded around a packed stadium. The limits of this potentially unifying locus is revealed by a recent fiasco which saw Mauritius being drawn against Egypt in the qualifying rounds of the 2002 World Cup. Due to the fear of communal disturbance – primarily because of concerns that Muslim Mauritians would again support their fellow Muslims – the government, proffering a host of reasons, ranging from the estimated cost of policing the game to the unprepared condition of the team and the certainty of defeat, ruled that both legs of the tie must be played in Egypt. Nevertheless, the more encouraging support for the team in recent years, partly due to their improved record in international fixtures, does offer a promise of a more unified spectatorship.

A more evident form of unified support is revealed in the almost fanatical support for English teams. The long association with English football extends to the Mauritian FA's original affiliation to the English Football Association. Manchester United, Liverpool and Arsenal are followed by legions of supporters that greatly outnumber the followers of Mauritian clubs. Walls and buildings throughout the island are sprayed with slogans proclaiming the feats of these teams, club magazines are sold in most newspaper outlets, and most of their games are broadcast live on the national television station. Mauritian club and even national fixtures are routinely postponed if they clash with these televised games, and parliament occasionally retires early if there is a big game on television. Coverage of football in the back pages of newspapers relegates local sporting affairs to a few paragraphs, if at all, while news about the English Premier League dominates column inches and headlines. But, crucially, the highly partisan support for these clubs is not communally-based, and membership of the large supporters clubs has no basis in ethnicity, but solely on enthusiasm for the team. Thus whilst bitter rivalries ensue between, for instance, Manchester United and Liverpool fans, these are not tainted with communal hatred. Here, unlike at Mauritian fixtures, football offers a shared interest, a focus for national discussion that constitutes a common denominator in national cultural life.

Conclusion

The legacy of football violence includes the destruction of buses, stadia and other buildings, the burning of sugar-cane fields, injury and death, and the banning of Mauritians' favourite sport. It has also contributed to increasing communal mistrust. The supranational identifications, ethnic tensions, convictions about communally-based injustice, fear of others and crude stereotyping widely present in Mauritian life – but largely confined to intra-communal and private discussion – are played out in Mauritian stadia. In the setting of league football, the game itself and the performative actions of fans provide a dramatic stage, an outlet for bigotry and zealotry, allowing 'an engagement absent elsewhere in life' (Armstrong and Giulianotti, 1997: 5), particularly where it may provide an arena for the disenfranchised to make their voices heard.

Football has been described as a 'mock battle' between the representatives of two communities (Dunning, Murphy and Williams, 1988: 240), as a realm in which communal honour is defended and identity inclusively and exclusively (re)constructed. Janet Lever (1983) argues that, as ritual conflict, football competition can deflect and contain antagonisms, thus contributing to social cohesion and sustaining pluralistic societies, However, Bromberger (1993) has countered by asserting that such antagonisms are rarely so confined and are apt to break out of conventional boundaries. In Mauritian football, it seems that the ethnic performances and ascriptions enunciated by fans via the drama of the game burst out of the normal processes of epistemological negotiation between (members of) communal groups that typify most social transactions. Eriksen maintains that this negotiation is partly facilitated by a shared symbolic system (Eriksen, 1998: 55) based on the circulation of common stereotypes whereby similar ethnic attributes are accorded positive or negative value according to whether one is describing one's own community or another group. This shared system of meaning via stereotypes is certainly prevalent at football matches but, in this context, its effects seem not to be as benign as Eriksen suggests. Given the currently strained relationships between communities following the riots of 1999, the excessively communal attachments and actions of football fans appear to threaten public order, and might spill out into a wider public arena. Therefore it is unsurprising that football has been suspended pending reorganization.

The decommunalization of football through the regionalization of sport is a utopian move, but one which rather sidesteps the present realities of communal division and performance in Mauritius which extend across social and political fields and are entrenched in popular culture. As a politician has pertinently remarked, 'What kind of decommunalization of sport is being discussed when inside the assembly, in the government or the opposition, communalism is well sustained'. To single out sport whilst ignoring communalism and exclusion in politics, economy, education and work is to utilize the game as a platform for symbolic gestures which further efface the communal tensions within the country and sustain the 'rainbow nation' myth.

Nevertheless, as we have shown, potentially through support for the national team and definitely through enthusiasm for English clubs, football has the capacity to unite Mauritians as well as divide them. It is a common denominator, constituting a field in which 'similarities and shared horizons, or platforms for discourse and interaction, are actively sought' (Eriksen, 1998: 18). This highlights the flexibility of football as a practice loaded with contesting symbols, ideals and identities. At one level, football sustains ethnically entrenched views. In Mauritius, ethnic identity is produced and reproduced in different fields, from local contexts such as the household, locality and workplace, to national fields including the economic and political systems, bureaucracy and the media. Yet in all these fields, the uses to which ethnicity is put, and the ways in which it is formulated, is in continual flux and subject to a multitude of classificatory attempts to define cultural differences. Thus ethnicity must be conceived as relational and contextual rather than fixed – although communalists on all sides aim to pin down their own ethnicity and that of others. This ethnic fluidity is increased by the globalizing tendencies which circulate money, ideas, images, people, commodities and technologies (Appadurai, 1990), and Mauritius has little hope of isolating itself from such processes. It is partly the threat posed by the decentring forces of globalization that inspires communal football fans to seek recourse in clubs that promise a fixing of identity, a sense of 'terra firma' in this unending globalizing flux (Robins, 1991). However, the increasing popularity of English football – as a globalizing phenomenon – means that parochial communalism cannot readily be transferred into support for English teams. It would be an imperialist move to see the embrace of English football to the exclusion of the domestic product as the only way forward. Perhaps future generations will adopt regional teams as their own, for evidence from fans suggests that excessive communal attachments to Mauritian clubs are the preserve of a minority of fans. Moreover, like ethnicity, football teams are surely condensation symbols, multi-interpretable entities that attract a wide range of supporters who follow different cultural patterns of fanship, and, accordingly, their symbolic value is liable to be contested amongst fans.

7

'Team Loyalty Splits the City into Two': Football, Ethnicity and Rivalry in Calcutta[1]

Paul Dimeo

The ethnic polarisation that underlines the rivalry between East Bengal and Mohun Bagan in Calcutta is best mirrored in the annual league encounter . . . football remains a unique phenomenon, one that binds and divides the city. While almost all are together in their love for the sport, team loyalty splits the city into two. One need not be a student of sociology to seize the palpable partisanship surrounding the two teams. Such an intense association merits violence . . .

(*Amitabha Das Sharma,* Sportstar, 22 September 1998)

Football has the capacity to unite communities, produce and reproduce identities, maintain and shape social formations, and to create identities of a specific nature that draw upon wider social issues in diverse and sometimes contradictory ways. These identities are 'carved out both in relation and in contrast to a series of others' (Goksøyr and Hognestad, 1999: 207) because football is 'about social differentiation' (Armstrong and Young, 1999: 179). Football clubs must always represent some sort of difference without which 'there would be no significance to this match between two opposed teams' (Finn and Giulianotti, 1999: 8). This study of football rivalries in India opens up a new area of inquiry within the sociology of sport. Indian sporting culture is largely viewed as revolving around cricket, but football has had a significant impact in specific areas such as Goa, Punjab, Kerala and – the focus of this essay – Calcutta, the capital of West Bengal state. The analysis therefore aims to offer fresh insights, not only into football culture, but also into modern Indian society.

1. I extend my appreciation to Sharda Ugra, Amitabha Das Sharma, Arnab Ghosh and Sanchita Sen who helped me research this chapter.

Potent rivalries have been at the heart of Indian football since the indigenous people began emulating the sports of the British colonizers. The game, once adopted, has always represented social difference. Whilst one major faultline in Indian society was that of colonial versus subjugated, the British Empire from 1905 began losing ground to nationalists. By the 1930s the nationalist movement became increasingly fractured by religious communalism. After the nation won its Independence in 1947, and British India was partitioned, immigration from the fledgling Muslim nations created new communities and divisions. Awareness of football's place within these historical processes is central to understanding the way in which it has been shaped by – and has shaped – political, religious, and ethnic identities.

The central focus of analysis is the rivalry evident in Calcutta concerning two clubs, East Bengal and Mohun Bagan. The former represents those people – known as 'Bangals' – who migrated from the former East Bengal region, now Bangladesh, into West Bengal after Indian Independence and Partition in 1947. Mohun Bagan is the team of the indigenous West Bengalis, who are known as 'Ghotis'. This is a football rivalry of an intensity to match any other, which captivates the city's 11 million inhabitants. Like other contests based on ethnic relations, this has tradition and significance far beyond the game itself.

Rivalries under the Raj: colonial, national and communal

Until 1905 the Bengal presidency was undivided, though stratified by class, caste, religion and education, which especially differentiated the urban elite from the rural peasantry. In that year Bengal was partitioned into West and East by the British Viceroy, Lord Curzon, much to the displeasure of the Bengalis. While the British claimed the move was due to administrative concerns, Bengalis saw it as a duplicitous strategy of divide and rule; an attempt to undermine the threat from educated, middle-class Bengalis who were demanding active roles in government administration. Their demands for equality and political autonomy were proving difficult to suppress. The response to the partition in Bengal was mass protest, unification in dissent, and the first eruption of nationalist power in India (Wolpert, 1997). Violent attacks on prominent colonialists were common, newspapers criticized colonial injustices, and the British responded with force. From the moment of partition began 'an escalating dialectic of repression and resistance' (Budd, 1997: 85), eventually leading to Independence in 1947. However, the aggressive nature of the Bengali nationalist movement during the first decades of the century stood in contrast to the non-violent approach that Gandhi took in the 1940s.

Around the turn of the century, football was controlled by the British. The game was multifunctional; as it was seen as a way of promoting discipline and fitness among soldiers, providing a sociable activity for European civilians, encouraging the incorporation of local elites, and promoting Anglophilia in the ranks of the Indian youth. Teams from the British Army and resident European colonialists dominated the tournaments they established in Calcutta. The prestigious competitions – especially the Calcutta League and the Indian Football Association (IFA) Shield – were the exclusive property of Europeans. Entry was officially restricted to just one Indian team in the League's First Division and one in the Shield. Nevertheless, some Bengali clubs began to challenge the on-field authority of the British, just as off the field their compatriots were the challenging political authority of the Raj (the British Indian government). The most successful and prestigious Bengali club of this period, Mohun Bagan (established in 1889), provided an epic moment for Indian football and nationalism when their bootless heroes defeated the East Yorkshire Regiment 2–1 – with two goals in the last five minutes – to take the IFA Shield in July 1911 (Mookerjee, 1989; Mason, 1990; Nandy, 1990). This victory proved an important historical moment of nationalist, political and racial significance (Mason 1990).[2]

The match drew a crowd of up to 100,000 who acknowledged the victory with 'wild excitement' (Mookerjee, 1989: 151). A similarly excited press did not pass up the opportunity to point out that the team had by proxy proved the Bengalis worth as a 'race'. The celebrations confirmed the sport's social function: 'The IFA Shield match in which Mohun Bagan beat the *gora sahibs* established football as part of Bengali culture' (*Telegraph*, 29 July 1997). Significantly, the conditions for the establishment of football in Bengal were the opposing forces of division and cohesion, as Bengalis became unified in their opposition to the British colonial 'other'. However, there was no simple dichotomy that pitched colonizer against colonized: each group had its own internal differentiations that were expressed in the profile of their football clubs. The predominant British concern was class; there were separate teams

2. In other societies football was used as an opportunity to resist colonial power (Armstrong and Giulianotti, 1999). Such forms of resistance often coexisted with colonial hegemony and patronage, and Mason (1990) argues that Mohun Bagan's victory 'reinforced admiration' for the British. Certainly, the game was played using British rules and the spirit of cultural imperialism inherent in the public school games ethic. However, Indians continue to celebrate the 1911 win as a victory for 'nascent nationalism' (Mookerjee, 1989). As Budd has argued of physical fitness in India during the same period: 'Like other implements of colonial rule such as military equipment and transportation technology, it was not considered inherently or uniquely Western, but as separate from its user, and capable of serving any master. The cultivation of physical strength thus offered the attractive promise that the British might be beaten at their own game' (1997: 85).

for jute workers, soldiers, tradesmen, educationalists, government officers and upper-class civilians. The Indian teams signified differences of religion, caste, region and heritage.

In the same year as this historic footballing victory, nationalists won their political battle over partition, the first major breakthrough since the Indian Mutiny of 1857. In 1911 the British conceded defeat and rescinded Curzon's 1905 edict. In retaliation the capital of British India was shifted from Calcutta to Delhi. The nationalists of Delhi and Bombay were less inclined towards agitation, more collaborative in their politics, and took cricket as their sport of choice.

After 1911, Indian teams gradually forced their way into the upper echelons of football. From 1914 to 1925, two Indian teams were permitted to play in the First Division of the Calcutta League. Indeed, it was the East Bengal Club (established in 1921) which agitated for equality in the local football scene. The club made an inauspicious start, struggling to gain promotion from the Second Division, and even after qualifying for promotion in 1924 they were not allowed to move up since two Indian clubs were already positioned in the First Division. They challenged the Indian FA over this 'colour bar' and overturned its discriminatory function.[3]

The rivalry between East Bengal and Mohun Bagan was established on the occasion of their first meeting, in 1925, which much to the surprise of all concerned saw the newcomers triumph 1–0. At this stage the former represented a fairly small community of East Bengali exiles who had moved to Calcutta for reasons of business and work. Players from this region were content to play for any club, including Mohun Bagan, since East Bengal were neither a prominent team nor representative of political or ethnic distinction.

It was, however, another team that eventually routed the British and added further to the significance of football rivalries. Mohammedan Sporting Club had been established in 1891 by 'a band of Mohammedan [Muslim] football enthusiasts' (De Mello, 1959: 192) but by the late 1920s were languishing in the Second Division almost bankrupt.[4] Their fortunes turned in 1931 when

3. The Indian newspapers of the period labelled this official discrimination a 'colour bar' (*Amrita Bazar Patrika*, 22 April 1925), while the later writer, Mookerjee (1989), referred to it as the 'black law'. Its function, to exclude Indian teams from equal competition, was essentially racist. Curiously, however, some European clubs realized the inequity of the system and supported East Bengal by threatening withdrawal. Other colonialists were not so enlightened, arguing that no such 'colour bar' existed since two Indian teams already played in the top league (*The Englishman*, 5 July 1924).

4. The club was first promoted to the Second Division in 1926. They survived relegation on the last day in 1928 by beating St Xavier's. In 1929 only the withdrawal of a British Army team prevented their relegation, and in 1930 only an administrative dispute kept them in the Second Division (*Forward*, 6 July 1934). Their sudden turnaround was indeed remarkable after a history of mediocrity.

S.A. Aziz took over as secretary. He was a man of vision, determined to raise the club's standards, and began by making 'an appeal to the leading Muslim footballers all over India to rally under the colours of black and white' (Mookerjee, 1989: 155). He established the club as essentially a national Muslim team, and attained consequential success. In 1933 promotion to the First Division was achieved; the Second Division was won after a close race with Bhowanipore FC.

While the slow withdrawal of British Army teams (reflecting the gradual reduction in British military presence) opened up opportunities for Indian teams, Mohammedan Sporting were an excellent and influential team during the years leading up to Independence. They shocked Indian football by winning the League Championship in 1934, the first Indian club to achieve this distinction, and were roundly praised. The newly elected nationalist Mayor of Calcutta, Nalini Ranjan Sarkar called the occasion a 'great unifier . . . a matter of pleasure and gratification to all citizens' (*Amrita Bazar Patrika*, 1 August 1934). Such was his enthusiasm that he spent 1,000 rupees on a lavish civic reception for the players and management. By contrast, a mass rally held the previous week in Calcutta for Mahatma Gandhi only warranted 10 rupees from the Mayor's purse (*Forward*, 12 July 1934).

While Mohun Bagan still receive plaudits from historians for their IFA Shield success of 1911 (see for example Mason, 1990), Mohammedan Sporting's achievements were greater. They went on to win the League every season between 1934 and 1938, and became the first Indian team to win the Shield and League double in 1936 by triumphing over that bastion of Britishness, the Calcutta FC, in the Shield final (De Mello, 1959; Mookerjee, 1989; Nandy, 1990). Only an administrative dispute in 1939 disrupted their run of successes.[5] After the interruptions of the Second World War and Indian Independence the club won the 1948 League Championship. Mohammedan Sporting's success focused Muslim pride, confidence and sense of community throughout the subcontinent. They prompted nationalist unity among Indians, especially after a series of vital wins over Calcutta FC, but their representation of Muslims proved divisive: 'with each victory, a communal wedge was driven deeper into Calcutta football if not into Calcutta society' (Nandy, 1990: 318). Religious communalism was the most prominent political issue of this period, and eventually led to the partition of the subcontinent along religious lines when Independence was achieved in 1947.

The Indian historian Sarunjan Das has described the events leading up to Independence:

5. The dispute was over mismanagement by the IFA. Some clubs, including Mohammedan Sporting briefly created their own league, but the matter was resolved within a season.

Starting in August 1946 India suffered an unprecedented wave of communal violence for nearly a year. The form, extent and immediate cause of individual riots differed, but inflamed communal passion was a common factor, and the outbreaks were all intimately connected with developments in institutional politics centering on the Pakistan movement. So the term Partition Riots can be used to describe all these outbreaks. The process started with the Calcutta outbreak of 16 August 1946, was continued in Bihar and at Noakhali, and ended in the Punjab carnage of March 1947. These riots convinced the overwhelming majority of Hindus and Muslims that the partition of the subcontinent was inevitable. (1993: 161)

In the weeks prior to 16 August, the atmosphere in Calcutta was charged with communal malevolence. Despite undervaluing the political potential within football, Das realized that the Muslim club provided an opportunity for populist mobilization:

Already during pre-riot days there were instances of self-mobilization along communal lines over trivial issues. For example, reverses suffered by the Mohammedan Sporting Club in football matches enraged Muslim feelings which were expressed in sporadic violence against the Hindus. (1993: 170)

The club fostered a feeling of Muslim cohesion, and of communal division, in the formative years of the Pakistan movement. It focused political mobilization at a populist level in 1946, and has been directly linked to the developing communal violence that climaxed on 16 August. As with the events of 1911, football rivalries took on a relevance beyond the field of play.

After Independence, Bengal was once again partitioned along the border used to such ill-effect in 1905. East Pakistan was created in East Bengal, and won its independence struggle to become Bangladesh in 1971. West Pakistan, which divided the Punjab in 1947, became known simply as Pakistan. In the Indian part of Bengal, now known as West Bengal, football rivalries shifted focus from colonial, national and communal issues to the ethnic, regional divisions resulting from partition and migration.

Ghotis and Bangals: migration, regionalism, ethnicity

In the aftermath of India's partition, refugee immigration from East Pakistan into Calcutta became an enormous social problem. Indeed, violence as a consequence of migration characterized Partition as a whole, 14 million people moved between nations resulting in communal clashes in the Punjab and Bengal that left over 600,000 dead (Samaddar, 1999: 69). West Bengal was flooded by millions of Hindu immigrants who fled the Muslim nation; the pinnacle of this influx coming in 1950 when almost one million people arrived. During their early years the refugees were forced to sleep in the streets, their poverty determining their position as an underclass: 'until 1956 there were nearly five hundred refugee families permanently encamped upon the platforms of Sealdah Station in the middle of the city' (Moorhouse, 1998: 292–3).

There then followed a steady flow of refugees arriving into West Bengal, averaging 300 a day; between 1946 and 1970 over four million refugees entered West Bengal from East Pakistan (Sarcar, 1971: 55). Just after the 1971 Bangladesh Independence, immigration peaked at around 2,000 a day (Moorhouse, 1998). Yet, many of these people, particularly the first wave of migrants (1946–69) were middle-class, having been landowners or business-men. They had education and experience to offer West Bengal, but their lack of economic capital overshadowed everything else in the minds of the indigenous population. Despite their ethnic similarity to West Bengalis – in language, religion and values – and despite sharing a common oppositional 'other' (the Muslim community), small differences of culture were exaggerated and suspicion greeted these incomers. At the same time, like all migrants, East Bengalis created a community for themselves, homogenizing an otherwise heterogeneous group on the basis of shared experience as migrants and the shared memories of 'home' (Bose, 1997: 76). The regional identities internal to Bengal before 1947 had hardened into more profound ethnic and political identities based on new contingencies:

> Ethnic boundaries were certainly present in Bengal in the pre-partition times. The partition not merely legitimised these boundaries, it made the question of how these boundaries melt or harden a critical one. (Samaddar, 1997: 108)

Before partition, East Bengal and Mohun Bagan had a friendly relationship, and the Mohun Bagan club had become India's most prominent after its historic IFA Shield success. Mohammedan Sporting had been prominent in the 1930s and 1940s, with East Bengal gradually joining these two to create the legendary 'Big Three' with their first League win in 1942. Just as Moham-medan Sporting was established as a focal point for Muslim players and supporters, East Bengal served the same function for East Bengalis. The main difference at this time was that while Mohammedan Sporting's rivalry with several Hindu clubs prompted serious communal violence, the two most successful Hindu clubs were on friendly terms. They shared a ground with Mohun Bagan and, until the cataclysmic political changes of 1947, the two clubs saw each other as siblings. After the 1942 League triumph, Mohun Bagan hosted a celebratory tea party for their 'younger brothers' (*Amrita Bazar Patrika*, 27 July 1942).

These football identities were diverse, multilayered, and subject to change according to wider social developments: East Bengali players had featured in Mohun Bagan's successes, not least in 1911 when seven of the eleven were from that region. Hindu clubs cooperated in opposition to Muslim clubs, and in opposition to the last remnants of competitive British clubs. Yet, an exhibition match in 1942 between the 'Bengalees' – a term referring to West Bengalis – and the Rest, took players' individual ethnicity as relevant: the Rest including Muslims, Europeans and East Bengalis. Football identities have always been structured in a way coherent to those familiar with local cultural differences. Muslims and Hindus unified in their opposition to the British before 1947, and unified again in opposition to other states in the national Santosh Trophy after Independence. Yet, internally, the communal divisions were clear as, by 1947, were the ethnic divisions based on migration and memory.

The friendly rivalry of previous years took on greater meaning as social changes altered the complexion of football culture in Calcutta. The new arrivals adopted the East Bengal football club as a symbol of their presence and aspirations, as well as an emotional identification of their origin and dislocation. The club became a manifestation of memory and identity, not obviously expressed through other cultural practices, and which would become diluted with time. In a situation where similarities are more obvious than differences, football rivalry was a place where individuals could express differences hardly visible in everyday life. In Calcutta, the clubs offered an opportunity for oppositional confrontation when few, if any, others existed. Bose outlines the Bangal–Ghoti difference as 'a sharp contrast', 'separateness and distinctiveness' and a 'distinct identity', but struggles to find any more stable, salient or explicit expression for Bangal differentiation than their football club:

> it is not uncommon to find a distinct identity among the people originally from East Bengal, in terms of dialect, culinary culture, rites and rituals, even in the support of a particular sporting club. (1997: 80)

Of these opportunities for East Bengal difference to surface, only the football club is a permanent monument where the communal 'self' can be defined against the Ghoti 'other'.

This shift from sibling competitiveness to starkly defined rivalry was almost immediate after Partition: when the rivals met in the 1947 IFA Shield final, the Mohun Bagan fans expressed their resentment against these refugees through violence, causing the match to be abandoned (*Telegraph*, 29 July 1997). The rivalry heightened as East Bengalis used the club to represent their identity: 'the one source of hope, pride and victory lay in the triumphs of the Club named after their abandoned homeland' (Nandy, 1990: 319). Or, as veteran journalist Arnab Ghosh put it:

> The East Bengali people found affinity with this club. They got their identity with this club. All those down-trodden people, who had no money, and who left everything, their landed properties, their home, etc. etc. They started identifying themselves with the East Bengal club because of their defeat in the social life, and the social structure; they wanted to see something rosy. These people basically love to come to the Maidan to see East Bengal because *they made themselves one with this club.* And if East Bengal become victorious they feel themselves at least they have established something. (Interview, November 1998 emphasis added)

The paradox of passion: triumph and tradegy

Mohun Bagan and East Bengal came to dominate football in Calcutta and in India; the Europeans had left for home, and Mohammedan Sporting descended from their heady heights as a consequence of Muslim migration from India. This post-Independence period brought prosperity to the game in India. The 1948 Olympics in London saw the national team miss two penalties in a closely fought 2–1 defeat by France, and in the 1952 Helsinki Olympics they were unfortunate to meet the powerful Yugoslavs who trumped the Indians 10–1. Fourth place was a creditable finish in the 1956 Melbourne Olympics. Closer to home India won the football tournament of the first Asian Games in 1951, held in Delhi, a success they repeated in 1962. This period also brought a phase of modernization: the All-India Football Federation, established in 1937, began organizing national competitions; bare-footed play was banned in 1952; the time period for matches was increased from 50 to 70 minutes, and eventually to 90 minutes; defensive tactics became more sophisticated as teams moved from the two-back system, to the three-back, and eventually to the four-back in the mid-1960s (Nandy, 1990: 319; see also Giulianotti, 1999). Many Indians reflect upon these halcyon days as the pinnacle of their country's football achievements.[6]

Central to the great achievements of Indian football was the East Bengal–Mohun Bagan enmity. Rupak Saha, of the *Ananda Bazar Patrika*, described this as 'the driving force of Bengali football'; while PK Banerjee, the great hero of the Indian national team who has managed both East Bengal and Mohun Bagan during the past three decades, explained that the matches were 'a big affair in Bengali society' (interview, November 1998). In the 1960s, as

---

6. It was recently argued that a 'quarter of a century has passed since the time that the rest of the world so much as acknowledged that India played football' (da Lima Leitao, 1997: 1).

East Bengals' manager, he would find over 2,000 people turn out to watch his training sessions. This enthralling power which football had, and still has, encapsulates social groups who would not otherwise become involved: 'The rivalry is so infectious that non-Bengalis living in the state are tempted to pick their favourite teams according to their closeness to a Bangal or a Ghoti family' (*Business Standard*, 19 July 1997). The Calcutta League has been dominated by these teams: since 1949 East Bengal have won it twenty-two times, Mohun Bagan have taken it twenty-three times.

During this period the rivalry intensified. Politically, these were tense days since the response to Bangladeshi immigration after 1971 had been especially virulent. Violent clashes occurred during vital matches between the clubs, at times drawing in the players and management as well as supporters. For instance, the celebrations of East Bengal's sixth League Championships in a row (1970 to 1975) were disrupted by Mohun Bagan fans who set the East Bengal 'tent' on fire.[7] This was far from an isolated incident. Simmering tension surrounded every match between the clubs, frequently prompting violence and confrontation. Fans' commitment to their club was taken to extraordinary lengths, sometimes tragic, as in the case of one young Mohun Bagan fan who killed himself in the hope of bringing good luck to his club and halting East Bengal's run of League championships.[8]

Further tragedy resulted from rioting at a match at Eden Gardens on 16 August 1980, causing the death of sixteen young men. A review of one newspaper's coverage[9] reveals the level of emotional commitment and manifest conflict when the teams met, despite the fact that the match itself was essentially meaningless. The result determined which team played the runners-up of the other group, and so had the easier draw for the following round. Trouble began around 2.45 p.m., when supporters of the rival teams waiting to purchase tickets 'started brickbatting each other'. The fans taunted each other by snatching and 'defiling' their opponents' flags, and the police 'had a tough time restoring order', on several occasions having to wade in with their lathis flying 'to disperse and disengage the warring groups working themselves up to a frenzy'. Fourteen minutes into the second half the East Bengal right-back, Dilip Palit, harshly challenged the Mohun Bagan winger, Bidesh Bose.

---

7. The 'tent' is a pavilion, usually a wooden construction next to the ground where players and club members meet, and where the club's offices are located. Most clubs have their ground and 'tent' on the Maidan, where other sporting and social clubs also have 'tents' for members' use. There is a tradition in Calcutta of retiring to one's club 'tent' after work to socialize. Bengalis have a term for this, *adda*, which means gossip.

8. Thanks to the journalist Novy Kapadia for this information.

9. *Hindustan Standard* (23 August 1980).

The referee, Sudhin Chaterjee, awarded a free-kick to Mohun Bagan, while Bose retaliated by kicking Palit. Both players were dismissed and the referee, instead of resuming the game with a free-kick, decided (no doubt due to the confusion) to restart with a dropped ball.

Immediately after the incident with Palit and Bose, agitated Mohun Bagan supporters 'shouted abuses and threw missiles' at the East Bengal fans. The latter replied in kind, and there followed 'another spell of brickbatting and yelling'. Further clashes ensued in response to on-field events, especially the referee's decision to drop the ball. A 'free for all' resulted, and in the western section where East Bengal fans occupied three-quarters of the stand, the minority Mohun Bagan fans 'were steadily losing ground'. Since the missiles which had been carried into the ground were exhausted, Mohun Bagan fans found 'replenishment' by 'pounding the concrete seats with shoes and rods'. The resultant hail of concrete missiles caused spectators to swarm towards the exits, which they unfortunately found locked:

Play continued even when the imprisoned spectators shouted for help and for water. But nobody responded. The police who were sitting at the base of the stadium on the ground, seemed absorbed in the match. When the police who had remained passive almost all through stormed the gallery swinging lathis, after the final whistle, the spectators started running in panic, knocking each other in the melee. A regular stampede was on. Some of those who had collected near the gates turned back and ran for the lower tiers of the stands hoping to escape to the ground. That was not easy. There was a ten foot drop to the lower tier concrete benches. Undeterred many took the plunge; some failed to survive the fall. The streams of people cascading through the narrow gates knocked down some who were trampled. The Mohun Bagan supporters being in a minority were more in panic. Amidst the confusion the survivors started bringing the dead to the Club House. First a teenage boy-dead. Then another. One by one ten bodies – all without life – were placed on the floor of the Club House. The wounded and the dead covered the whole floor. The tragedy slowly sank into the consciousness of a benumbed public (*Hindustan Standard, 23 August 1980)*.

This was a tragedy indeed, the result of numerous factors specific to the day in question – police inaction, corrupt ticket sales, insufficient safety procedures, the violence of the players – but fundamentally the result of a deeply-felt rivalry.

Oppositional identities, ambivalence and liminality

The tragedy of 1980 was the most manifest example of distinction and opposition; identities were sharply contrasted and individuals were prepared to risk their bodies for this conflict. P.K. Banerjee spoke of 'a vast difference in culture and attitude' (interview, November 1998), but the question is how these differences are defined when Bangals and Ghotis speak the same language, are largely Hindus, and co-exist as Bengalis. The football clubs are an opportunity for fans to identify explicitly with one group or another, resulting in stereotypes of fan behaviour that adds another dimension to knowledge of 'self' and 'other'.

According to N. Mohan Padmanabhan, Deputy Chief of the News Bureau of the *Hindu* newspaper:

> It is divided on everything. Eating habits, the way they speak, the *lingua franca*, sometimes even the way they dress. And appearance too. To the casual observer it may seem pretty odd: how can appearance be different if they're all from the same soil? But appearance, I think differs. For example, the Mohun Bagan supporter will consider himself better educated, better off financially, of better origins and social standing. And the East Bengali typically hardier, obviously the more violent, quick to temper and not so fortunate as far as social moorings are concerned. (Interview, November 1998)

East Bengal fans are considered more violent and passionate, rougher and ruder. Rupak Saha compared them to Argentinian fans, 'very aggressive, bubbling with enthusiasm . . . all the time they will dance', and ready to 'start a fight if they don't like any of the referee's decisions'; whereas Mohun Bagan fans are said to be like Brazilians, 'very sober, very calm, with proper dress and all that', their fandom expressed through 'good flags', 'drums' and 'colour-ful dress'. Thus football culture involves articulating social stereotypes rooted in the history of migration and prejudice. Indeed, a recent derby match prompted the following reflections on the relationship of fandom, ethnic difference and rivalry:

> The cultural divide between the people hailing from East Bengal [now Bangladesh], and the naturalised residents of West Bengal was manifested once again despite their cohabitation for decades in the city. Every East Bengal–Mohun Bagan match is a reflection of this divide. The 'Bangals' from East Bengal are accused by the 'Ghotis' [traditional Calcuttans] of lacking in refinement and the Ghotis, who are traditionally Mohun Bagan supporters are, on the other hand, freely accused of having a narrow focus and sticky lifestyle. (*Business Standard*, 19 July 1997)

However, beyond stereotypes there is a complexity with suggests distinction is not the full story. During the first decades of Independence the social boundaries between groups were recognizable and clear; for instance, inter-marriage was frowned upon. By the 1980s, though, identity markers were becoming less distinct. The memory of East Bengal as 'home' was the preserve of a fading generation of migrants, their sons and daughters more at home in

West Bengal. Intergroup relationships became more common, dialects less pronounced, and cultural traditions passed away. There are cases of fans with East Bengali parents supporting Mohun Bagan. Thus, a liminal, in-between space developed that contravened the polarity of previous years.

The response to the 1980 tragedy contributed to the ambivalence high-lighting both the limits to football conflicts and the sport's capacity to unite: 16 August is Football Lovers' Day. It is a day on which the IFA joins with the Association of Voluntary Blood Donors to set up a blood donation camp at Eden Gardens. Since 1981 this camp annually attracts numerous donors, is promoted by various officials and celebrities, and forms a considerable emotional moment for the West Bengali public – in 1998 there were 929 donors (*Telegraph*, 17 August 1998). It is an opportunity for collective mourn-ing, for grief, and yet for renewal and togetherness. The public giving of blood and life to mourn death, the presence of unity and love in the ritual perform-ance of remembrance. It is the realization that football as drama has its limits, that the seriousness of death breaches the unwritten laws of conflict within football cultures.

The rivalry also faced a series of pressures. Football's increasing commercial-ization during this period resulted in clubs abandoning loyalties in the pursuit of success; the ties of ethnicity with respect to playing staff became increasingly irrelevant. Moreover, the awareness of higher international standards led to anxiety over the poor quality of local football. This came to the fore in 1977 when Mohun Bagan invited the US club New York Cosmos to play in Calcutta; an event established in the folklore of Indian football as the great Brazilian Pelé graced Eden Gardens (Nandy, 1990).[10] Consciousness of Indian football's weaknesses was strengthened with the first live broadcast of the World Cup in 1982, since when Bengalis have been more likely to choose their foot-ball heroes from the international stage (*Telegraph*, 5 October 1996).[11] At the same time, Indian cricket proves a strong attraction, especially due to its inter-national successes.

The effect of these changes on the oppositional identities of football has been an apparent softening of divisions and conflicts, compounded by the ambivalence of subsequent generations. But the potency of this rivalry remains; this derby match attracts larger crowds than any other football competition – 130,000 attended a Federation Cup match in 1997 – and any cricket match

10. A photograph of this event assumes as much prominence in Mohun Bagan's 'tent' as pictures of their own achievements: the 1911 victory; a national postage stamp issued in their honour; other team photographs of league and Shield successes.

11. Indians choose from the pantheon of great players, but seem to prefer stylish attackers such as the Argentinian Gabriel Batistuta, Brazil's Ronaldo and England's Michael Owen.

except a major international test. It continues to dominate Calcuttan sport, and it still generates a football culture based on difference. Violence can still be found among the crowd, highlighting the continued emotional pull of these teams. These social differences are necessary for Indian football, without them the matches would essentially be pointless, and the economic viability of Indian football as a whole would be in doubt. Amitabha Das Sharma (*Sportstar*, 22 September 1998) captured the apparent contradictions with football cultures. Cooperation and togetherness are necessary for the expression of 'ethnic polarization': the rivalry '*binds* and *divides* the city'. Without agreement there would be no game, without difference the game would have no meaning.

The past informs the present: historical rivalries contained similar patterns of division and cohesion. Internal divisions of religion and ethnicity were overcome to unify Indian communities against European football teams. After Independence, club allegiances would be forgotten for inter-state and international competitions. Football identities can be complex and seemingly malleable, but they are always part of structured and hierarchical social relations. Rivalries have always been at the heart of Indian football whatever the broader social and political context to which they refer.

8

Basque Football Rivalries in the Twentieth Century

John Walton

The rivalry between Real Sociedad of San Sebastian and Athletic Bilbao, representing the capitals of the most populous and industrial of Spain's Basque provinces, is fervent and deep-rooted; but from its beginnings in the early twentieth century it has been complicated by a consciousness of Basque brotherhood which has, from time to time, brought the teams and their supporters together in displays of solidarity in response both to external pressures (above all from the Madrid government) and to internal conflicts (especially, since the 1970s, those involving the definition of attitudes towards the terrorist activities of the violent nationalist movement ETA and its associated political wings). The best analogy is that of the family at war within itself, which is at the same time capable of presenting a belligerent united front against outsiders and of composing a public face of unity, for particular purposes and when the occasion demands.[1]

In my early days in San Sebastian I was led so far astray by the local media's rhetorical expressions of amity between Real and Athletic in pursuit of greater pan-Basque enterprises, and by the sight of fans of both teams fraternizing before a local derby and marching with the common goal of protesting against the kidnapping of an industrialist by ETA, as to refer in affectionate tones to Athletic's stadium as 'la Catedral' in the first draft of a joint·article with a colleague who was a member of 'la Real'. His friendly rebuke at this transgression was immediate. No gratuitous supportive reference to Athletic could

1. This chapter follows on from recent work I have published on football, tourism and Basque identities, especially Walton (1998, 1999, 2000). I should like to thank the History Department, University of Central Lancashire, for covering the travel expenses for a research visit to the Basque Country in June 1999. Luis Castells provided (as always) essential conversational and bibliographical insights, and Ander Delgado eased my path in the Biblioteca de la Diputacion in Bilbao (a very hospitable research environment) and at the Lejona campus of the Universidad del Pais Vasco.

survive for an instant in an article dealing with the Basque Country. Whatever the rhetoric of Basque brotherhood, when the chips were down this had become an eternal rivalry, sustained by endless banter within (among so many other places) a University of the Basque Country history department which contained supporters of Real, Athletic and indeed Alaves of Vitoria. It was not to be trifled with. This has turned out to be a deep-rooted theme.

It is almost reassuring to find that other visiting academics have been blown off course in similar ways, and that their assumptions have found their way into print. The anthropologist Jeremy MacClancy's work on Athletic Bilbao and Basque identity is a case in point. His Bilbao-based fieldwork led him to state that Athletic was not only 'seen as *the* team of the Vizcayans' (Bilbao's province), but also 'in national contests, as *the* team of the Basques' (1996: 183). This view is held by some in Bilbao, and it is easy to see how MacClancy encountered it. Jose Manuel Alonso, introducing a popular centenary history of Athletic, identifies the club firmly with city and province, but goes further:

> Athletic is a football club which takes its identity from the people and the environment in which it develops: *the Basque people* and Bilbao . . . Bilbao from the beginning of this century, including a little earlier (1898), identified itself with Athletic de Bilbao, although to be fairer we should say that Vizcaya province did so, including all the Basque Country. (Alonso, 1998: 7, my emphasis)

This is not a position which would be shared in the other 'core' Basque provinces within Spain, Guipuzcoa and Alava, and nor would it hold in Navarra. It is emphatically a view from Bilbao and Vizcaya, as any spectator at Real Sociedad's ground who has heard whistles from the crowd at announcements of Athletic's goals, or cheers at those of their opponents, would be well aware (Leguineche *et al.*, 1998: 93).[2] Even within Vizcaya, there might be reactions against Athletic, as the journalist Santiago Segurola (one of a trio of Athletic fans whose well-informed and brilliantly-contextualized conversations form the most impressive of the recent centenary celebration books) admitted: 'At times reactions against Athletic occurred. I decided not to go back to Lasesarre, Baracaldo's ground [an industrial town in Bilbao's immediate hinterland], one day when quite a lot of people applauded a goal which had been scored against Athletic . . . the people really celebrated when it appeared on the scoreboard. I never went again' (Leguineche, 1998: 117).[3] MacClancy's work has its uses, despite his obvious lack of grip on football and its institutions (for example,

2. In my case, this happened most recently at the Real Sociedad–Espanyol game on 13 June 1999.
3. Interestingly, Segurola is native of Baracaldo.

he confuses the Spanish league championship with the Cup, and identifies Manchester United with a particular 'suburb'); but it has to be read with caution. His account needs to be set in the wider context of the complexities of Basque local and provincial identities, which cross-cut the 'national' one in interesting and changing ways; and we need especially to take account of the rivalry between San Sebastian and Bilbao, Real Sociedad and Athletic Bilbao, for supremacy within the Basque Country and beyond. An excellent recent study of football and Basque nationalism by Patxo Unzueta will help us here (Unzueta, 1999: 147–67).[4]

This rivalry is presented as a strong theme in the introduction to the standard club history of Real Sociedad, where struggles between the clubs in their early years, sometimes involving violence on and off the pitch and skulduggery in the manipulation of rules and organizations in pursuit of championships, are highlighted (Josemaritarra, 1980: 11). Significantly, it is less prominent in the much more extensive array of historical writings on Athletic Bilbao, prompted especially by the club's centenary in 1998, which tend to present it as the embodiment of Basque footballing identity and the focus of the ultimate loyalties of Basque football supporters, at least in the Spanish provinces of this nation without a state. For the upholders of this perspective it can seem highly significant that Athletic played its first matches in the year that Sabino Arana's Partido Nacionalista Vasco fought its first election campaigns (Unzueta, 1999: 149). The notion that there should be one unified Basque Country with shared political system, language, myths and consciousness did indeed develop in step with the rise of football, which became increasingly acceptable to most nationalists because it was compatible with prescribed core Basque values associated with manliness and strength, and because its English roots were much more acceptable than hispanicizing cultural influences, epitomized in bullfighting, which might dilute Basque identities and assimilate them into Spanish ones. Football came to be seen as a valuable distraction from such influences, which was capable of developing a distinctively Basque playing style and could be assimilated into the preferred Basque culture. There were some enduring reservations among nationalists, especially where football seemed likely to challenge the hegemony of 'traditional' Basque sports; and the generally positive attitudes which developed among nationalists tended to boost the notion that Athletic should be the flagship Basque club, located as it was in the cradle of formal Basque nationalist politics, which happened also to be the cradle of Basque football, and counting as it did prominent middle-class nationalists among its directorate, while at

---

4. Football has been neglected in most academic studies of Basque nationalism, such as Mees (1992).

the same time laying claim to uniting all strata of local politics and economic interests, providing a focal point of common identity to transcend other kinds of divisions in just the same way that Basque racial identity was supposed to do.[5]

This hegemonic vision of Basque nationalism failed consistently to take account of the divisions within the Basque Country, especially the ways in which provincial and local loyalties cut across attachment to the idea of a Basque nation. The journalists who discussed Athletic's history in 1998 thought that the assertion of provincial identities and stereotypes had been greatly stimulated since the mid-1980s by jokes about '*guiputxis* y vizcainos' (people from guipuzcoa and vizcaya regions) which were promoted in the press, and used football as a stimulant for provincial rivalries rather than vice versa; but, as they pointed out, this rekindled old tensions rather than initiating them (Leguineche *et al.*, 1998: 95–6). The province as the basis for place-identity among Basques has deep historical roots. Luis Castells has argued, building on Jon Juaristi, that this kind of attachment was reinforced from the 1880s with the development of a nostalgic literature which celebrated inherited provincial traditions, both reinforcing emergent Basque nationalism and leaving important fissures and fault-lines within it (Castells and Walton, 1998: 72). Such traditions took firm root, and football helped to perpetuate them: a survey in 1976 found that 50 per cent of Basque people identified themselves primarily in terms of their province, while only one in six thought of themselves first as Basques, and 30 per cent gave their first loyalty to the locality (Unzueta, 1999: 162–3). As this last statistic suggests, there were also rivalries within the provinces: for example, in the early decades of the twentieth century both Athletic and Real Sociedad had nearby rivals for provincial supremacy, and Real was enduringly resented in nearby industrial towns like Renteria as a team of 'senoritos', 'young masters' who laid claim to effortless superiority, as befitted its middle-class roots in a cosmopolitan tourist resort (Leguineche *et al.*, 1998: 117).

Nevertheless, Real and Athletic came to be the standard-bearers of provincial identity; but they developed in significantly different ways. Athletic came to take pride in a policy of only signing Basque players, coupling this with its status as a members' democracy to lay claim to a special unifying role in city, province and beyond, pulling its supporters together in a shared loyalty which transcended class or politics (despite the enduring identification with Basque nationalism). But local pride in what has become a unique policy among top-flight clubs tends to gloss over changing definitions of Basque identity.

5. Unzueta (1999) is the best way into this, but see also Juaristi (1987, 1994).

In the early days English players, and indeed English professionals, played alongside the locals, generating serious controversy in 1911 when Real Sociedad made successful protests. The Basque-only policy took hold subsequently, although it is not clear exactly when it became formalized as such: two suggested dates are 1919 and 1927 (MacClancy, 1996: 183; Unzueta, 1999: 153).[6] The sons of Basque parents, born elsewhere, might find their way into the team, and attitudes have become more flexible over the last generation. It helped to have passed through another Basque side on the way to Athletic, and the informal relaxation of criteria has coincided with a militant nationalist recognition that all who earn their bread in the Basque Country and recognize its distinctive language and culture are entitled to join the nationalist political camp. But the pride remains, however shifting and uncertain the definitions might be; and arguments in favour of abandoning Basque exclusiveness during a difficult period on the field in the mid-1990s soon faded away. This recruitment policy is a keystone of Athletic's claim to be the premier Basque side and the footballing flagship of the Basque nation; and it is coupled with claims about the players' proximity to the fans, and their virtuous, hard-working qualities. These ideas surface in the current version of Athletic's club anthem, which stresses the players' and fans' identification with the villages, green meadows and oak trees of the Basque Country, and their Basque virtues of honesty, loyalty and strength, alongside the more local attachments to Bilbao and Vizcaya. The Basque language of the song is much more complex than that of Real, also in Basque, which is a simple invocation of the youth of Donostia (the Basque version of San Sebastian) and Guipuzcoa (the provincial emblem of which is displayed at the ground), with a limited vocabulary and no complex constructions, and without the wider pretensions of Athletic. This may reflect a closer historic proximity of Athletic to political nationalism (MacClancy, 1996: 184–5; Unzueta, 1999: 152–4).[7]

But the contrast with Real Sociedad is not as sharp as might appear. As with Athletic, the club had espoused a robust English style of play, compatible with approved Basque virtues, from its earliest days; and its directors identified with Basque culture if not with the full-scale nationalist project which was more influential at Athletic. Moreover, after using a few English players, a Swiss and a Frenchman before the First World War, Real went from the late 1910s to the late 1980s with only a handful of foreign players, including nearly thirty years between the departure of the Swede Simonsson and the

---

6. Duke and Crolley (1996: 29) provide a useful but slightly oversimplified version of the differing recruitment policies of Real and Athletic.

7. See also the *Himnos* of Real and Athletic taken from the clubs' websites.

arrival of the legendary John Aldridge. Aldridge himself was acutely conscious of being the first foreign import for many years, and his autobiography recounts stories of hostile graffiti and individual unpleasantness, while emphasizing that these were isolated incidents. The change of policy, which brought eighteen other foreign players to San Sebastian in a decade, was precipitated by Athletic's decision to attract players away from its Basque competitors; but signings from the rest of Spain were still off limits, and when at the end of the 1994–5 season a completely Basque team drew with Espanyol of Barcelona the local newspaper was full of pride. Real Sociedad, too, retained a strongly Basque ethos which helped to fuel the internecine rivalry, especially in opposition to Athletic's pretensions to special status (Walton, 1999; *El Diario Vasco,* June 1995; Aldridge with Jawad, 1999: chapter 6).

The rivalry between the clubs has ebbed and flowed since the first match between Athletic and a San Sebastian team in 1905. In 1908 there were discussions about entering a combined Bilbao-San Sebastian team for the national championships, but this came to nothing, and fierce competition soon became the norm. It reached an early climax in the years between 1911 and 1918 when the clubs were consistently the leading contenders for the Basque regional championship. Already in June 1909 a match between San Sebastian's Club Ciclista (a close antecedent of Real) and Athletic drew criticisms of crowd behaviour from Bilbao sources: not only was the pitch too small and a wilderness of sand, grass and potholes, favouring the home side, but the crowd lacked consideration for the visitors and 'went so far as to utter some rather annoying words'. In November the words were harder, and the crowd more partisan, especially when the Athletic team left the field in protest against a goal which they claimed to be offside. The view from Bilbao was that the spectators had belied San Sebastian's reputation for courtesy, affability and hospitality, and Athletic placed an announcement in the Bilbao press lamenting the 'demonstrations of hatred' from a minority in the crowd. A Madrid newspaper referred to the 'duel between two cities'. The return match was postponed (Unzueta, 1999: 163; Terrachet, 1998: 55–7; Saiz Valdivielso *et al.*, 1998: 32).

Hostilities continued, and a year later a nationalist commentator from Bilbao at a championship match between the cities' teams, again in San Sebastian, was eager to praise the virile Basque enthusiasm for competitive sport, and the way in which it could promote both Basque and local pride, depending on who the opponents were; but he was also dismayed by the 'inappropriate' attitude of some of the spectators, describing those hostile to the visitors as non-Basque-speaking, foreigners and 'latinizers', who were undermining the ideal of a strong Basque sporting brotherhood.[8] Then came Real's protest over Athletic's English professionals, dismissed as sour grapes in Bilbao because Real's signings had failed to arrive, which in turn produced a schism in the national federation as Athletic were deprived of their championship and then reinstated. This practice of fighting footballing battles by other means brought bitter harvests between 1916 and 1918, when the conflict reached its height (Josemaritarra, 1980: 11; Unzueta, 1999: 154).[9]

The crisis was precipitated by Athletic's 4–0 victory over Real at San Mames in a regional championship match at the start of 1916, after an extended conflict over Athletic's opposition to the registration of a Real player who had spent time in Madrid had embittered relations during 1915 (Mateos, 1921: 678–80). The San Sebastian journalist Milon de Crotona blamed the defeat on the intimidating atmosphere in San Mames (with whistles, hooters and a crowd of over 6,000 behaving more like bullfight enthusiasts than cool, level-headed men of the North), and on the 'brutal' play of Athletic, assisted by the collusion of the referee. Visiting spectators were threatened in a style more befitting a bullfight than a football match (in other words, in a very unBasque way) (*El Pueblo Vasco*, 10, 12 January 1916). Characteristically, the Bilbao perspective was that the crowd had been perfectly well-behaved; and journalistic rhetoric and hyperbole was to add salt to the controversies throughout (Terrachet, 1998: 87). As the regional championship ended with the teams level on points, a play-off had to be organized; and as neither team would now play on the other's ground, the Northern Football Federation had to adjudicate. The extended controversy on how to find a neutral ground and referee dragged on for weeks in the press, complicated by Real's insistence on going beyond the Basque provinces, and with accusations of undue influence, conspiracy and counter-conspiracy on both sides. The Civil Governor of Guipuzcoa intervened to prevent the match from being played in his province, as football became a major public order issue; and the sport's national governing body, whose powers were still uncertain, strove ineffectually to intervene. Eventually the Northern Federation prescribed the Arenas ground, in a Bilbao suburb, and a referee from Vizcaya province who was described in San Sebastian as 'Athletic's best player'. The upshot was that Real refused to go to Arenas and were deemed to have forfeited the match. They were then suspended,

---

8. See the article by 'Blue-bird' entitled 'San Sebastian – Bilbao: Campeonato de Foot-ball', in *Bizkaitarra* (26 March 1910). Unzueta (1999: 157–8) has a useful commentary. MacClancy (1996: 190–1) ascribes this article to Sabino Arana, the founding father of Basque nationalism; but Arana must have been using a ghost-writer, as he died seven years previously.

9. Compare, for example, Barcelona's complaints of unfair discrimination against the club by officialdom and referees at this time and subsequently (Duke and Crolley, 1996: 27).

and did not play Athletic again until October 1917 (*El Pueblo Vasco*, 10 February to 28 March 1916).

Worst of all was the sequence of events in February 1918. The match between Real and Athletic at Atocha on 17 February coincided with one between Arenas and Real Union of Irun, the results of which would decide whether the regional championship went to Athletic or Real Union, whose ground was a few miles to the north of San Sebastian. Several hundred Athletic fans travelled from Bilbao, and many Real Union fans augmented the crowd. After a very tough match with many injuries and disputed decisions, a collision between an Athletic forward and a Real defender brought the crowd on to the field, led by the defender's brother, and the Bilbao players had to be rescued by the police after being attacked with sticks and stones. The score was left at 2–2 with seven minutes to go, which affected the championship outcome; and arguments began about how to distribute blame, and whether and where to replay the match. All the existing grievances were exacerbated: there were disputes over the legitimacy of the Northern Federation's decisions (which were governed by the Vizcayan majority, and always seemed to favour Athletic), the quality of referees, and the allocation of responsibility for crowd control. Real sought to excuse the pitch invasion because of the provocative behaviour of Athletic players and supporters. In the end, the issue became a contest between the Northern Federation and the national governing body. The former sought to impose a replay, under its own conditions, and to impose severe penalties on Real and one of its players; but the latter, after some vacillation, intervened to declare both the contenders champions and divide the Northern Federation into two, keeping Guipuzcoa province separate from Vizcaya. This was received angrily in Bilbao, but it did reflect the way in which the rivalries between the provincial capitals had extended to the wider provinces, and the San Sebastian press celebrated the good relations between Real and their Irun neighbours. There was no sense at all of a united Basque Country here: the provincial attachments were dominant (*El Pueblo Vasco*, 16 February to 13 May 1918).

These events were soon sanitized, and the clubs entered into an era of more friendly rivalry in the 1920s. Journalistic rhetoric was softened. When, in 1921, Athletic received the accolade of a special celebratory supplement in the Bilbao cultural review *Hermes*, the chairman assured his readers that the San Mames crowd showed 'the most exquisite correctness of behaviour, the most sincere impartiality'; and Ramon de Belausteguigoitia, himself a player, emphasized courtesy to opponents, respect for referees' decisions and vigorous discipline as among the game's virtues. He admitted that in earlier times play had perhaps been too violent, with referees too inexperienced to observe what was going on, so that games had sometimes become battlefields with players wounded by serious foul play (*Hermes*, 1921: 662, 666–9). This was the burden of much complaint about Athletic during the 1910s, especially from Real; and these reflections are doubly interesting. Players, crowds and administrative systems had matured, and rivalries were becoming less raw, although there was plenty of evidence of crowd trouble in other matches during the 1920s, including stone-throwing directed by a small number of Real fans at the Barcelona party when an important match was called off at the last minute at the end of 1928. Earlier in the year the teams' Spanish Cup contests had been violent encounters, and a Basque-Catalan rivalry seems to have over-shadowed the Real-Athletic contest at this time. Football violence was close to the surface throughout Spain at this time; a cartoon from the period shows a 'friendly match' with banner offering 'Fraternal greetings to the visiting team', and fighting in progress all over the field and among the crowd. A history of Cultural de Durango, a Vizcayan team, over the 1920s and 1930s takes accounts of pitched battles between players and supporters in its stride. Nevertheless, tempers seem to have cooled quite quickly between Real and Athletic.[10]

The easier atmosphere may have been helped, eventually, by the widening gap between the teams. When the Spanish League replaced the old champion-ship system of a knock-out competition between regional champions in 1929, both teams entered the First Division; but Athletic continued to be much more successful on the field, and in 1935 Donostia (Real's name under the Second Republic between 1931 and 1936) were relegated during one of Athletic's most triumphant periods. Real then had a chequered career until the early 1960s, and the rivalry probably gathered momentum again when they were regularly competing against Athletic on equal terms. But this requires further research. What is clear is that interesting patterns of rivalry, again within a broader context of Basque politics and provincial rivalry, have reemerged over the last generation.

The revived tensions were much in evidence for the Basque derby of April 1999 between Real and Athletic. This happened to take place on *Aberri Eguna*, the Basque national day, at a time when the main Basque nationalist party, the PNV, was moving towards a cautious reconciliation with ETA and its supporters in spite of a recent reversion to regular street violence by youth groups associated with the latter, wielding Molotov cocktails against rival

---

10. See Josemaritarra (1980: 78); *El Pueblo Vasco* (1–4 January 1929); Burns (1999); Zavala (1990: 90, 112).

parties and public installations. There was talk of the two teams displaying an *ikurrina*, the Basque national flag (invented by Sabino Arana, the founder of the modern nationalist movement), on the pitch before the game, putting 'brotherhood before fratricide', as had happened on a famous previous occasion in 1976. Then, the flag, whose public display was still illegal (though only just: it was to be legalized within six weeks), represented Basque national aspirations against Franco's Spanish nationalist project (and recent executions of Basque militants) in the shaky beginnings of what turned out to be the transition to democracy after the dictator's death (Unzueta, 1999: 164). Now, it was a matter of affirming Basque unity against internal divisions, as well as in face of a right-wing Madrid government of the Thatcherite Partido Popular, which was firm in its opposition to further extensions of Basque autonomy, and fiercely combative against terrorists who had recently targeted its own local politicians for assassination. But the flag nearly failed to appear. The *El Pais* reporter at the match describes the sequence of events (*El Pais*, 5 April 1999):

> The controversy was set up. The relations between the fans on both sides have worsened steadily and the decision to carry out the anonymous proposal fell on the players. Both dressing-rooms said yes. But a few minutes before kick-off, the Athletic team took the field alone. False alarm. After a few dashes around the field, they returned to the tunnel and came back on the pitch with the *ikurrina* in company with Real Sociedad. All a set of diplomatic paraphernalia, a kind of display of national brotherhood with a minor revolt before the show of fraternity.

The complexities of the relationship are well-illustrated here. The tensions between brotherhood and rivalry had moved on from the emotive moment on 5 December 1976, at Real's intimate, atmospheric old Atocha stadium when the flag was unfurled under very different political circumstances: an occasion which the *ikurrina* display in 1999 consciously sought to emulate. This has rightly been emphasized as a defining moment, even though unofficial *ikurrinas* had been waved within the crowd at Athletic's San Mames stadium since the 1960s. MacClancy's account, the most accessible version in English, is seriously flawed: he thinks Atocha was 'the main stadium of Madrid', which would have changed the frame of reference beyond recognition, and that the match was a cup final rather than an ordinary league match; and he gets Real Sociedad's full name wrong. The chapter is littered with such errors, which make it harder to take other aspects of it on trust (MacClancy, 1996: 193). Here as elsewhere, the talismanic character of the event has been asserted rather than explored, and detailed contemporary press coverage reveals rich strata of potential interpretation.

It is clear from the report in *El Diario Vasco*, the San Sebastian and Guipuzcoa newspaper, that the 'derby' of 5 December 1976 came at a time when relations between the clubs had been good, with established traditions to mark the brotherly nature of the Basque rivalry. Advance comment stressed that although this was 'the sort of game that strikes sparks because of regional rivalry and the teams' positions in the league table', it would unfold 'in the best spirit of good neighbourliness and the highest level of sportsmanship'. The atmosphere would combine throat lozenges, cigar smoke, scarves and rosettes with the Basque music of 'txistu y tamboril' (flute and small drum), and before the game the teams would pose together for the cameras 'in brotherhood as is now traditional' and both would pay their respects to the player whose benefit match this was, Real's long-serving Jose Agustin Aranzabal, 'Gaztelu' (*El Diario Vasco*, 5 December 1976).[11] The report on the match itself combined two strands: the relationship between sport and politics as events (and flags) unfolded, and the course, outcome and consequences of the match in its own right. The main sports-page headline was 'Atocha was an exciting demonstration, and not just of football', followed by the result (an overwhelming 5–0 victory for Real), and then a summary of the *ikurrina* affair. Jorge Reizabal's account stressed the special atmosphere, 'one to remember always', with flags in team colours and 'numerous *ikurrinas*'. Partisan shouts for the teams alternated with political slogans demanding freedom for nationalist prisoners and an amnesty; and there was a banner with the legend (in Basque) 'Presoak kalera' (Prisoners to the street). In this setting (*El Diario Vasco*, 7 December 1976):[12]

> The teams . . . burst on to the pitch, as is now their habit, in two parallel files. At their head went Cortabarria [Real] and Iribar [Athletic]. Between the files Uranga followed them, in his street clothes, as he was not going to play. The 'bearded one' of Guetaria unfolded an *ikurrina*, which the two players who were leading their teams immediately lifted up. The noise, already deafening, became a full-scale clamour. The players lined up on either side of the flag. And next they formed their usual group (for photographs) with the *ikurrina* on the ground in front of them.

The match report which followed highlighted the political dimensions as more important even than the remarkable result: they gave the day its historic character:

11. 'Gaztelu' means castle or fortress in Basque.

12. The reference to Uranga as 'the bearded one ('el bizardun') of Guetaria' is part of an enduring tradition of referring to footballers by nickname and village of origin in match reports, thereby highlighting their place in Basque emotional topography.

The old stadium lived through . . . the most exciting day of its life and in that excitement the victorious *guipuzcoanos* were united with the defeated *vizcainos* . . . because the Basque people, or a highly representative part of it, demonstrated without any kind of manipulation and shouted until hoarse about their most urgent demands. Because football presented its true and most expansive image as a socio-political entity, thanks above all to the admirable decision of a few footballers, who showed themselves to be first and foremost sons of their people, brothers of those who cheer them on from the stands, and not idols from some Olympus . . . the *ikurrinas* which came out in the stands went in brotherly union with the one provided by those who had renounced their status as idols to take on a true leadership [*caudillaje*], which was automatically assumed as democratic . . . This was the game that gave a pretext for that grandiose Basque festival which was celebrated around it. Forward with the people! Rise up, lads! [*!Aupa gizonak, jeiki mutil!*]

This looks remarkably outspoken for its time; and the word *caudillaje* evokes Franco's title as *caudillo de Espana* and advances the alternative legitimacy of this footballing democracy of the Basque nation. The ringing Basque exhortations at the end are still more remarkable, although Real's chairman had been using Basque in some club publications since 1972. Even more so, admittedly, was the silence on the issue elsewhere in the paper: the columnist 'Sirimiri' wrote about the result and the need to make improvements at the fruit-market end of the stadium, but ignored the *ikurrina*, which vanished from subsequent issues (ibid.; Duke and Crolley, 1996: 37).[13] It would be interesting to set the reporting of this event in the context of the evolution of journalistic representations of Basque nationalist imagery and aspirations during the post-Franco transition to democracy; but that is another project.

But we should not ignore the match itself. There was plenty to be said about it, as Real inflicted a defeat of novel dimensions on their old rivals. 'Sirimiri' praised the sporting spirit in which Athletic took their defeat, but it was impossible to suppress occasional outbreaks of gloating, and the newspaper's sports cartoonist made hay, depicting the Athletic lion taking punishment in various undignified postures. The day was understood as a footballing triumph over the old Basque enemy as well as a festival of unity behind the flag for the whole Basque people.

The affair of the *ikurrina* was, moreover, an initiative by certain players, rather than by the clubs themselves. Nor was it as free from manipulation as Reizabal claimed in the heat of the moment: Uranga, who brought the flag on to the pitch, was later to work closely with Herri Batasuna, the political wing of ETA, as a lawyer; and Iribar, the Athletic goalkeeper, was also to be

---

13. 'Sirimiri' is a characteristic Basque country drizzle, light but penetrating, not (as MacClancy has it) 'a local wind' (MacClancy, 1996: 189).

linked with the violent side of nationalism (MacClancy, 1996: 193; Unzueta, 1999: 164; Duke and Crolley, 1996: 38). This was no spontaneous gesture: it was done for purposes and in a context which go deeper than the excited newspaper rhetoric. But it was unofficial: Athletic's directorate was to resist flying the flag for a few months after it became unambiguously legal in 1977. The people concerned were out of step with changing times, however, and were ousted by the members at the next elections. This is a reminder that the imagined communities which clubs represent can and do sustain themselves in opposition to the current management, as did Athletic's Basque identities throughout the Franco years (when even the name was hispanicized), until (at this point in the summer of 1977) the club's democratic membership structure was able to reassert its demands (Leguineche *et al.*, 1998: 99–100; MacClancy,1996: 192).

Even at this apparent peak of brotherhood in 1976, at a point when political imperatives were powerful enough to transcend intra-Basque rivalries, the collaboration may not have been as spontaneous as it looked, and the result of the game itself was far from passing unnoticed. The mid-1980s and 1990s saw a reversion to higher levels of open conflict between Real and Athletic. In the late 1980s Athletic's chairman, Pedro Aurtenetxe, 'gave his opinion that the Basque country could not sustain two teams in the First Division, announcing that he intended to sign Real's rising stars'. He began with Real's defender Loren, who subsequently returned; but the declaration of war had been made, and other players followed, most recently the striker Joseba Etxebarria whose signing was regarded by Real fans as unethical. Hostility was stirred by journalistic rhetoric, as in the 1910s (though with less virulence), and there were 'sarcastic comments' from Real's chairman Uranga. In November 1998 there was a confrontation at Real's ground between the socialist mayor of San Sebastian and the chairman of Athletic. Hence, perhaps, the difficulties surrounding the attempt to revive the magic of the *ikurrina* in 1999. But there was more to it. In the mid-1970s most Basque opinion could be mobilized behind a broad post-Franco nationalist project; by the late 1990s the political divisions which had developed over the past generation made it impossible to use the flag in the relatively uncomplicated way which had been possible in December 1976. And the strength of the province as a basis of identity had if anything increased, perhaps reinforced by the developing polemics around football. The rivalry remained 'asymmetrical': Real cared more about it than Athletic, which was more concerned with confronting the Madrid teams which represented an external enemy. But there is no doubt that the tensions have revived in recent years, and are mutual (Leguineche *et al.*, 1998: 93–7; Unzueta, 1999: 163–4, 167).

Alongside the rivalries, however, can be found hints at collusion between the clubs to help each other when the outcome of a match matters greatly to one, at a dead point of the season for the other. Leguineche and his colleagues talk of such occasions. Segurola introduced the theme, referring directly to 'another controversial matter . . . that of institutional agreements between Real and Athletic'. Discussion focused on Athletic's second league championship under Javier Clemente's management, which depended on the outcome of a derby match, which Athletic needed to win. After an unexpected equalizing goal in the later stages, Real's goalkeeper, who normally cleared the ball with a powerful kick upfield, began to throw it out with unerring inaccuracy, regularly finding the Athletic forward Dani; while when the winning goal went in 'it seemed as if he had a sudden attack of lumbago'. Patxo Unzueta expressed the hope that no-one from San Sebastian would read the book; but on the other hand Real's second championship victory, which depended on a similar fixture with the roles reversed, was also put under the microscope. On this occasion Real were winning 2–0 when, with ten minutes left, Sarabia of Athletic not only scored but also hurried urgently back to the centre-circle with the ball, to the visible dismay and puzzlement of the Real players. 'Then Goiko(etxea) went up to Sarabia, gave him a friendly shake by the neck, said something in his ear and after that they strolled around quietly in midfield. The contest was over' (Leguineche *et al.*, 1998: 107–8). Stories or fears of such pacts are commonplace at the end of every Spanish football season, and in 1999 the *El Pais* reporter at an end-of-season Basque derby between Real Sociedad and recently-promoted Alaves of Vitoria was forthright in his comments. Alaves needed to win to stand a chance of avoiding the relegation play-offs, while Real's season was dead. Eventually Alaves won quite comfortably, and the other key result went their way (*El Pais*, 21 June 1999):

> Alaves had a lot of things to be grateful for . . . To Real, for being a good neighbour. The San Sebastian team applied no more pressure than they should have . . . De Pedro even made his excuses for scoring a spectacular goal . . . [and at the end] Real, who did not want to make enemies in Vitoria, limited themselves to cross-field passing and waited until Alaves could finally breathe peacefully.

There was, however, no tradition of fierce rivalry between these clubs, which had seldom played at the same level, as compared with the Real–Athletic relationship; and the comments on the championship deciders of the late 1970s and early 1980s offer another reminder of the tensions between rivalry and neighbourliness which punctuate this relationship. Ultimately, on a national stage when nothing else was at stake, there are strong hints that Basque fraternity was capable of suspending the normally conflictual relationship between the clubs, however unofficially. Like many features of this relationship, the capacity for such relaxations to take place has ebbed and flowed, and we have seen that it would be much less likely in the 1990s. But for there to be any evidence of it at all, however inferential and unofficial (and wrath from on high would undoubtedly descend if it were any stronger), the relationship must be inflected and cross-cut with occasionally powerful wider loyalties, to an extent which is unusual elsewhere. We have seen that the enduring contest between Athletic and Real Sociedad has been complex and fluctuating in its nature and in what it expresses; and there would clearly be room for a much longer and fuller account of it, taking the wider context of Basque politics and culture systematically into account. This is a very important example of a relationship between sport and the politics and culture of imagined communities; and it contrasts interestingly with Cataluna, where Barcelona developed into the unchallenged standard-bearer of Catalan identity, despite a role-reversal from its cosmopolitan origins, to an extent that Athletic was unable to match (Colome, 1999a, b). Perhaps its story should be written by someone from a point of neutral ground within the Basque Country, at a safe distance from either capital and province, but sensitive to all the nuances involved. It would certainly be a very worthwhile project.

Part III

Fragmentary Nationality: Civic Identities and Football Oppositions

9

Players, Patrons and Politicians: Oppositional Cultures in Maltese Football

Gary Armstrong and Jon P. Mitchell*

Valletta City – one of the most successful teams in Malta, with some of the most loyal and partisan fans on the island. The team unites a city that is otherwise split by rivalries: between the members of its two main parishes and devotees of their respective patron saints; between members of the two main brass band clubs that play at the saints' annual feasts; between inhabitants of the three 'barrio' areas-each with its own reputation for the production of uncompromising tough-guys; between canvassers and body-guards of local political candidates; between voters and partisans of Malta's two main political parties. [Research Notes]

Apart from two significant details, Malta itself is Valletta writ large. Despite being a small nation – with a population of around 400,000 and a surface area of only 122 square miles – Malta is also politically polarized and is characterized by powerful local chauvinism. Despite a unifying Roman Catholicism, many of its villages – and even parishes – are divided along the lines of patron saints' cults and their associated organizations: brass band clubs and *festa* (feast) associations (see Boissevain, 1995).

In contrast to Valletta, however, these divisions of the national populace are not mitigated by unified support of the Maltese national team. If anything, support for Malta increases tensions and divisions largely because – again in contrast to Valletta – they are resolutely unsuccessful. They have one of the worst records in international football over the past 10 years – a situation that has caused considerable soul-searching amongst the Maltese, who have

* The authors would like to thank the following for their help, patience and insight in researching this chapter. Without Carmel Baldacchino, Lewis Portelli, Victor Cassar, Joe Grech, Tony Pace, Joe Debattista, Paul Clough and the students of the Anthropology of Football course at the Institute of Mediterranean Studies, Malta, this chapter would never have been written.

placed the issue high on both the sporting and political agendas (see Armstrong and Mitchell, 1999). The old adage that football unites people across other boundaries and cleavages, then, is only partially true for Maltese football, which just as often reinforces other conflicts, inspiring fear and loathing.

The Maltese Premier League provides fuel for ecstatic carnivals of celebration and opposition that run along the fault-lines of Maltese society. Disorder both on and off the pitch has been a constant feature of the footballing scene since the game arrived there in the late-nineteenth century. Football is an obsession for a huge percentage of the population and games both domestic and those televised from Italy and England can be the cause of wedding dates and times being moved, political rallies being rescheduled and Parliamentary sittings being delayed. It is no surprise, given this degree of support for the game, that passions run high.

Producing Difference in a Small Nation State

In his now classic account of nationalism, Benedict Anderson argued that national identity works by promoting an 'imagined community' that unifies the spatially, temporally and often culturally-diverse populations that fall within the boundary of any one state, inspiring a 'deep horizontal comradeship' among them (1983: 16). This community is imagined, he tells us, because members of a nation will never know most of their fellow nationals. Whilst this is true of larger nations – and even probably true of smaller nations such as Malta – there is an important difference between the model of 'imagined community' as it applies to nations such as France or Italy, and its characteristics in smaller nations such as Malta. In the case of the latter, although people may never meet all their compatriots, they can nevertheless envisage doing so, and frequently do. The rhetoric of the small nation is that 'we all know each other'.

The community of Malta, then, is thought of as less imagined than that of larger nations. Indeed, there are more practical reasons why the Maltese community is less imagined than those of Anderson's model. His argument hinges on the development of the public sphere, and particularly the role of print capitalism in its development. Broadly speaking, his argument is that print capitalism – and the massification of print media – enabled people to think of themselves as being part of a wider community, through the mass dissemination of national ideology. The experience of sitting down to read a national newspaper, and knowing that thousands, at times millions, of other people are also sitting down to read the same newspaper at the same time is, for Anderson, a significant cognitive leap that lends itself to imagining the nation as a community.

Like other larger nations, Malta also has a well-developed print public sphere, not to mention an equally vibrant and expanding electronic media (see Chircop, 1994). The difference, however, is that this public sphere is less attenuated than that in larger nations (see Mitchell forthcoming, chapter 1). Rather than distant personalities who one only knows through mass media, public figures in Malta are more intimately known. They might be neighbours, friends, patrons – people with whom one can develop, or at least envisage developing, personal relationships. Likewise, the people about whom media articles are written – the Maltese populace – are actual or potential neighbours rather than conceptual or imagined members of a shared community. Unlike other larger nations, then, the community of Maltese nationhood is based on a recognition that a genuine personal knowledge of many, if not all, of one's compatriots is at least theoretically possible. This is an important consideration, for it raises questions about the relationship between similarity and difference, unity and diversity within the Maltese nation.

As a number of scholars have observed, Anderson among them, the nation-states of Europe began life initially as political units which were then charged with the task of producing cultural unity – states which produced nations, rather than vice versa (see also Calhoun, 1997; Eriksen, 1993; Gellner, 1983; Hobsbawm, 1990; McCrone, 1998). As D'Azelio is famously alleged to have stated after the unification of Italy in 1870, 'We have made Italy. Now we must make Italians' (cited in Calhoun, 1997). This clearly rails against received wisdom about the nature of nations, and indeed against the rhetoric of nations themselves which tend to regard themselves as eternal, primordial units with deep historical roots. It also– more importantly for our argument here – assumes a kind of logic whereby the unity of the nation is premised on a prior disunity; homogeneity is premised on a prior heterogeneity.

As in other nation-states, the initial moves to unify the nation were primarily urban and elite in their origins. However, rather than a singular elite uniting a diverse rural or semi-rural populace, Malta saw the process of nation-building – and the period during the late 1800s when the idea of nationhood came to the fore – dividing the elite, and consequently the wider populace, between two models of nationhood (see Frendo, 1979). On the one hand a pro-Italian, pro-Church movement emerged that stressed Malta's cultural and historical links with Italy and campaigned for the cessation of British Imperial rule. Malta was a British colony from 1800 to 1964. On the other hand, a more Anglophilic group developed that saw Malta's historical and cultural roots in pan-Mediterranean societies, including those that preceded the Roman empire. This side saw Malta's future within the British Empire. These two opposed movements eventually crystallized into the main political parties of twentieth-century Malta – the Nationalist Party and the Malta Labour Party – who maintained their respective Italianate and Mediterraneanist foci. Rather than uniting a divided society, then, and producing (imagined) homogeneity out of a heterogeneous reality, the development of Maltese nationhood worked in the opposite direction. It produced division and heterogeneity from a position which – given the intimate nature of Maltese public life – might be argued to have been more homogeneous. It produced imagined disunity out of genuine community.

This disunity persisted throughout the twentieth century in vehement – at times violent – struggles between the Nationalist and Labour movements (see Frendo, 1989; Hull, 1993; Koster, 1984). It mapped onto other fault-lines within Maltese society-between places, patron saints and band clubs – contributing to the antagonism and competition between them. It also, almost inevitably, became reflected in football antagonisms. Football at times sustains or even intensifies this political division, and with it the other fault-lines of Maltese society. At times, however, it also mitigates the competition, papering over certain cracks, but in so doing revealing others. In Valletta, for example, it unites opposing parishes and patron saints' supporters, each of which are associated with one or other of the main political parties. In so doing, however, it produces new rifts between Valletta and other Maltese towns, villages and neighbourhoods.

Idioms of Antagonism

A number of analysts of nationalism and national identity have pointed to the central role of ritual in the production and dissemination of the nation, and the promotion of imagined community (Connerton, 1989; Kertzer, 1988; Lane, 1981). By bringing the population together in symbolic activity, the nation is reinforced. But ritual also plays a part in disunity. As Gerd Baumann (1992) has argued, we should be aware that ritual activity is not always self-focused, but can also be aimed at communicating messages to 'others' – to opponents.

In such a small island with its dense network of personal relationships, there has developed an ethos of communicating with 'others' that applies to national politics and local religious feasts, and transfers itself well to football. The word *tmieghek* is used to describe this idiom, best translated as both the pleasure of rubbing the nose of the defeated further in to the dirt, and how victory is not as important as the chance it offers to denigrate your opponent. It is both a metaphorical and an actually realized state, which describes the well-established manifestations of ritualized denigration of defeated opponents. For example, in politics the 1998 election victory of the Nationalists saw three days of celebration for the victors who drove in cavalcades up to 100 in number, both rejoicing with fellow voters and more importantly abusing the populace of districts that were renowned Labour strongholds. This kind of manifestation is built into the structure of patrons' feasts – the day following the feast day is known as *xalata*, and involves an evacuation of the parish on buses and trucks that tour the island, visiting beaches and taunting the inhabitants of the places they pass through. Most popular with people from the south of Malta, which is known as the heartland of Labour Party support, the *xalata* will select its route carefully to allow maximum abuse to be showered on the citizens of the Nationalist north.

This process is repeated after sporting – particularly footballing – victories, which see noisy and lengthy carcades processing through the streets of the vanquished opponent. Following an early 1990s championship triumph, Valletta fans organized a funeral procession through the streets of their deposed neighbours and rivals Floriana. A 10-foot coffin draped in the green and white Floriana colours was paraded around the streets, to the consternation of local Floriana fans. Such is the texture of footballing *tmieghek*.

In the football ground itself, the taunts and insults are also often couched in a religious idiom. Thus, as further illustrated below, the football terraces appropriate the tunes of the band marches played during feast processions and add their own lyrics which include religious insults and boasts. For those who want to annoy rivals, the most common method is to insult the saint that is associated with the town. Hence Valletta supporters' shouts of 'Hello! Fuck Saint Publius' antagonize the residents of Floriana, who do not appreciate the slur on their patron saint. Insults then move beyond the saint to its statue, which is held in the Church throughout the year and taken out in procession during the annual feast (see Mitchell, 1998: 78–80, forthcoming: chapter 8). The quality of the statue is considered a sign of the wealth and respectability of a parish, so statue-based *tmieghek* focuses on the materials the statue are made of: 'Bronze and Iron? Saint Gajetan – Chicken Wire!'.

These political and religious idioms are complemented by the internationally more familiar gynaecological referents. These include 'F'ghoxx ommok' (fuck your mother) and 'Hudu zobb f'ghoxx ommok' (up your mothers vagina). Insults can be directed personally at a specific player which may have a very personal message or even make reference to his family members. It is not uncommon for a player so taunted to visit the home of the accuser who, having been identified by rival supporters and his whereabouts located, will usually have the error of his ways pointed out to him.

Football and Politics

Football loyalty lends itself well to the intransigent political divide wherein politicians preach to the converted rather than pursue potential converts. The mass public disorder that the game has engendered over the decades parallels the political process which venerates mass rallies. The central ethos is the show of symbolic might – noise and numbers matter on a small island. Such manifestations have surrounded politics for over 100 years, with football and religious *festi* matching the partisanship of the mass political meeting. Initially anti-colonial, mass political demonstrations crystallized opposition around cultural – and particuarly linguistic – development in the 1920s and 1930s during the so-called 'Language Question': was Malta to be seen as Italian by culture and language, or as a Mediterranean colony, with the Maltese vernacular and English developed as the national languages? (see Hull, 1993). Following the Second World War, and in the lead-up to Independence, Maltese politics was dominated by Church–State conflicts, and particularly the virulent anti-clericalism of Dom Mintoff, leader of the Malta Labour Party.

Mintoff's rise marked the emergence of a new type of political elite in Malta, displacing both an established Anglo-aristocracy and an Italianate elite of lawyers, priests and land-owners (see Boissevain, 1977). An Oxford-educated architect, he was a great rhetorician, an astute politician and a charismatic rabble-rouser (see Boissevain, 1994). From the 1960s to the 1980s he dominated the political scene, and he is said by his opponents to have instigated several outbreaks of mob violence. In 1979 a rampaging Labour crowd burnt down the printing press of the pro-Nationalist *Times of Malta*. In 1983, the Archbishop's Curia was ransacked following a period of acute tension between the Church and the Labour Party government of the time. Although the political scene had largely calmed down by the 1990s, Mintoff still exerted power enough to bring down the Labour Government of 1996–8.

Although not politically instrumental in such a direct way, and certainly not even rumoured to be responsible for civil disorder, football itself has developed a cadre of influential 'big men' such as Mintoff. Often themselves politicians, such figures find the status of presidential office in the football clubs useful in garnering political support, and political office helpful in pursuing the interests of the football club. For example, Lorry Sant, who was Labour's Minister for Sport and Public Works in the 1980s, used this position to help develop the Corradino stadium for his local Paola club, Hibernians, and employ four of the Hibs team on sinecures with his government depart-ment. In later years, Minister of Finance and Nationalist MP for Sliema, George Bonello-Dupuis, was instrumental in developing the Sliema club's artificial turf pitch and new training ground. Even achievements on the sporting field reflect on the status of footballing 'big men', many of whom have personal fortunes that they are prepared to spend in pursuit of a success that can translate directly into political office. In the past, presidents of brass band clubs or *festa* associations were involved in politics. Today it is football-club presidents. As recently as two years ago the president of Valletta City, Joe Caruana-Curran, stood as an Independent candidate at the local council elections, winning a Valletta seat by an enormous margin. The fact that the election came shortly after Valletta's third successive League Championship for the team was no coincidence.

The fact that football and politics are intertwined in Malta comes as no real surprise to those familiar with the country, in which there is an element of politics in everything. The nature of the relationship has moved in the same way as politics itself – with the emergence of entrepreneurial 'super-patrons' (Boissevain, 1995: 154) as the figureheads of political allegiance. This allegiance is also localized, however, giving added texture to the antagonism between different local teams. Localization also entails a linkage to band clubs and saints' feasts, and it is often through idioms of religious competition that football competition is manifest. Such competition is as old in Malta as the game of football itself. With this background, the rest of this chapter will now focus on specific rivalries in the Maltese game, and how such fear and loathing both reflect and are reflected in the local, political and parochial cleavages of Maltese society.

Early Antagonisms: St Georges and Floriana

The first football club that could be said to represent a village was St Georges of Cospicua. A one-time affluent dockside district, Cospicua housed military barracks and visiting warships, which influenced the local middle class to emulate the foreigners and form a team. Consisting entirely of Maltese players, they acted as a *de facto* national team when playing the selections from the British services personnel during the early years of the twentieth century (see Baldacchino, 1989). The British had their own League from which they excluded the Maltese unless the locals were in the Armed Forces, but the Cassar Cup, an annual fixture, pitted the Champions and runners-up from the Military leagues against their equivalent from the Maltese League – established in 1910. For the Maltese, a footballing victory over their colonial overlords was considered very important, and for this reason such matches produced widespread public disorder.

As well their rivalry with the British Services teams, St Georges developed an early opposition to Floriana – another dockyard area. They played the first official match in Malta in 1894, St Georges won 1–0. It was not until 1900 that the teams met again, for a wager of five pounds and ten shillings – a small fortune at the time. The St George's victory provoked another challenge match which was played eight years later and ended in a 1–1 draw. The replay took four years to arrange and Floriana won 1–0. Whilst Floriana went on to achieve great success in local football, St Georges virtually disappeared from the scene. Their one league championship was achieved in a year when Floriana did not compete. After a League and Cup double in 1917, St Georges managed only three Cup wins in the next twenty years. Extensive bomb damage courtesy of the Axis forces during the Second World War saw many Cospicua residents evacuate, never to return. Today, St Georges are a Division Three side with a small following drawn from a district renowned for its devout Labour voting electorate, its cheap housing and endemic drug use amongst its disaffected youth. For Floriana, a new and longer-lasting opponent than St Georges was to appear, who went by the name of Sliema Wanderers.

Mummy's Boys and the Irish: Sliema–Floriana Rivalry

The first fixture of the newly-established football league in 1910 featured Sliema and Floriana in front of a crowd of 5,000. The event was a shambles. A disputed goal saw the Sliema team walk off the pitch, and the match abandoned. Following weeks of argument the game was replayed, producing a Floriana victory. The latter went on to win the first-ever championship and thereby sowed the seeds of rivalry with Sliema for the next fifty years. The two did not have matters all to themselves, however .The title twice went to Hamrun, once to Valletta and once each to St Georges and the Kings-Own Maltese Regiment. However, two teams dominated. The years 1920–40 saw eleven championships go to Sliema and nine to Floriana. Games between the two sides were memorable for the levels of disorder on and off the pitch, as Malta's foremost football historian explains:

> It soon became customary for the players to leave the field for the least provocation, or for the supporters to invade the ground whenever they fancied. (Baldacchino, 1995)

The week that decided the first championship in 1912 coincided with the feast of St Publius, the patron saint of Floriana. The fans of 'the Greens' – Floriana's green and white striped kit stems from a match against soldiers from the Royal Irish Fusiliers regiment, after which the teams swapped shirts; the club retained the colours to this day – took this as a sign of Divine approval.

With a total of ninety-five trophies in their history, Floriana are Malta's most successful football club, followed closely by Sliema. The Sliema–Floriana rivalry became known as the 'Old Firm', alluding to the Celtic–Rangers antagonism in Glasgow. Unlike Glasgow, the Maltese rivalry did not reflect a denominational conflict. All the players and fans were Roman Catholic and in 1950 a fixture between Sliema and Floriana saw the first-ever attendance at a match by the Maltese Archbishop. The apparent religious unity, however, did not mask deep-seated local and parochial rivalry that ran along the fault-lines caused by attachment to particular patron saints. The Archbishop witnessed a brawl on the pitch that spread to the terraces and ended with the game being abandoned. Six years later the same fixture saw the authorities use the attendant fire engines' hosepipes in an attempt to extinguish the brawling on the terraces.

At times the Old Firm games attracted crowds of more than 20,000 to the national stadium located in Gzira. Both teams drew draw support from beyond their locality – in Floriana's case from the villages of Zebbug, Siggiewi and Kirkop. Sliema attracted fans from Qormi and Mellieha. The rivalry affected players both on and off the pitch. Transfers between the two clubs were unheard of – the first did not take place until 1970. International fixtures saw rival fans, whilst ostensibly supporting their national team, abusing players selected from their deadly rivals. The abuse spilled over into daily life, and at least one Sliema player felt the need to lower his head whilst travelling through Floriana on the bus, in an attempt to remain inconspicuous and thereby avoid a potentially hostile response from the locals.

At another level, the rivalry took on both pictorial and poetic forms. Cartoons and posters were drawn and displayed that denigrated rivals. During the games both sets of fans had renditions of *Il-Gigolet*, sung to the tune of *La Danza delle Libellule*, taken from the operetta Gigolette. The words reveal an awareness of social-class antagonism that fuelled the Sliema–Floriana conflict and, as in other parts of the Mediterranean, this manifest itself in the derogation of elite masculinity (see Mitchell, 1996; Pitt-Rivers, 1961). The fans and team from Sliema, an area regarded as solidly bourgeois, were berated by the Florianese, who regarded them as feminine and effete when compared to their own proletarian masculinity. *Il-Gigolet* went as follows:

The match has started, it has barely begun, what skill!
When the ball . . . bum . . . bum . . . was struck with skill,
Here *tal-mama* [mummy's boys] started to cry
And all the young men could not hold back their tears.

Here one has to see the Sliema supporters
Pulling their hair as they left for home, crying
For Floriana have broken 'the shilling'[1] in two
It was bad luck that against us you emerged as losers
The Irish are always as strong as iron

1. Like the other references in this song, 'the shilling' refers to Sliema's association with wealth.

Come what may, good or bad
So go and find some wounded
And take them with you to Ghar-id-Dud [a fashionable Sliema promenade]
Or take him home where it is better there
Fools! Go and hide from the public.

The Sliema response made equal use of locality, landmarks and ideas of fair play. Their version argued the following:

The match has started and already a goal has been scored
The ball has passed between the two posts
Already the sullen look is upon their faces
You have hidden the coffins you brought with you at Pietà [a cemetery between Floriana and the national Stadium]
So cheer up you boys *tal-gazaza* [baby's dummy]
Because a fiasco has occurred in Floriana
They have lost the cup as well as their wallets
We have the right to shout . . . Goal! Goal! Goal!
The *qaghqa* [circular bread[2]] has surely been broken, truly broken
They have lost their honour
If you play us fairly, you will never beat us.

And you will die of sorrow
Pity! What Floriana has been reduced to
The whole team finished and dead. The coffins thrown away
You have gone into hiding
Fools! Go and bury yourselves, all of you.

The references in the Floriana version need some explaining. Throughout Malta, Sliema provokes a derogatory response from just about everyone not born or resident there. They are popularly known as *tal-pépé* – which means 'snooty' or 'stuck up' and has a number of different connotations. It derives from *tal-Papa*, meaning 'of the Pope', but also has phallic connotations: *pépé* is sometimes used to refer to the penis. The Sliemese – Slimiz – then, are both too closely associated with religious authority, and therefore somewhat unworldy and naïve, and sexually and morally suspect. As *tal-mama*, they are 'mummy's boys' – as *tal-pépé* they are, behind their respectability, depraved. As one Floriana commentator put it: 'Fur coat, no knickers – that's the Slimiz'. Together, *tal-mama* and *tal-pépé* also signal the use of the terms 'mama' and 'papa' to refer to parents, rather than the colloquial 'ma' and 'pa'. In doing so,

2. A reference to Floriana's association with grain – the town houses large granaries built by the Knights of St John who occupied the islands from 1530 to 1798.

they also signal the Slimiz preference for speaking English rather than Maltese – and often an elite and rather antiquated English. Historically there was a logic to this, as Sliema had a high rate of mixed Maltese–British marriages and was therefore an important centre of support for the pro-British Constitutional Party.[3] The links with Britain, however, were also reflected in football.

Sliema Wanderers, founded in 1909, was an amalgam of three existing teams. The newly-formed club grew at the same time as the district it represented. A one time sparsely populated fishing village became the preferred summer bathing resort for the Maltese middle class and the residence of many a colonial family. The young men who were to play in the early Sliema teams were often drawn from British families who were from both military and civilian backgrounds .The latter were often referred to as 'Exiles', a name given themselves by employees of the Eastern Telephone Company. These and military personnel would 'guest' for Sliema, in defiance of an unwritten agreement that Maltese teams would play only Maltese players. Sliema were therefore renowned for the use of foreigners, and the success they enjoyed was attributed by opponents to their unwillingness to abide by the agreement. Sliema had the further advantage of being geographically close to the national stadium at Gzira, where all matches were played until 1980. Sliema teams of various decades were often to be found training at the stadium with the blessing of Meme Scicluna, a local entrepreneur and Sliema fan who rented the stadium from the owners and effectively ran the football League fixtures. Furthermore, the working-class district in which the ground is located was the breeding ground of dozens of footballers who would train with and be signed up by Sliema. As a consequence, Sliema were never considered a team which produced or displayed local-born talent, but rather were associated with the mercenary 'Exiles' and the neighbouring Gzira proletariat.

As such, Sliema were associated with a colonial ethos – not only in their links with the British but also in their *de facto* proprietorship of Gzira and its inhabitants. The middle class has been significant in the club's history, whose biggest benefactor was Joe Gasan, a car importer and owner of the first-ever fleet of buses. Today his son is a director of the club. Former club presidents have included local entrepreneurs and Nationalist politicians; since the 1970s the town has become staunchly Nationalist. The notary and former cabinet minister George Bonello-Dupuis was President for twenty-five years between

---

3. The Constitutional Party came to the fore during the 'Language Question', campaigning for the recognition of English as the national language and arguing more broadly for the maintenance of British imperial rule – and British culture. The party dissolved in 1946, and the Sliema élites became gradually associated with the Italianate Nationalists.

1970 and 1998. He was vehemently opposed to Dom Mintoff's Labour government of 1971 to 1987.

Although associated with the Nationalist bourgeoisie, Sliema is not exclusively middle-class. Some of its most devoted football fans are drawn from a working-class district known as 'Lazy Corner', which also houses the supporters-club bar. In comparison to their rivals, the Sliema fans are well-behaved. They do not go out of their way to antagonize or provoke, and so ignored the Floriana fans in their cavalcades who for decades would annually drive past the Sliema Wanderers social club taunting their long-standing opponents after a victory.

The watch-word of Floriana is unity. Not fragmented by the divisions of other Maltese towns and villages, Floriana consists of one parish, with one patron – St Publius – one *festa* committee and one band club. Many believe such unity of purpose goes some way towards accounting for the town's footballing success. In conversation with football historians and long-term residents recurring themes appeared which stressed the significance of local political wisdom, entrepreneurial ability and the presence of the military parade ground. These factors combined to produce a very successful football club. With its gardens, harbour views and open spaces Floriana was and remains an attractive place to live. The British military housed both barracks and administrative offices there, and the parade ground they built was for decades the largest regular playing surface on the island. When not used for military purposes the same space was taken over by local youths who would emulate the game played by the colonists. Following the granting of Independence in 1964 and departure of the British military in 1979, the parade ground was renamed the Independence Arena and has since become the official training ground of Floriana FC. The religious affiliation remains strong despite a severe test of belief when a championship decider in 1995 saw Floriana lose to Hibs on the feast of St Publius. They have never since played on the day of the feast.

Amidst this apparent unity, however, was a *de facto* socio-geographical division within Floriana. One district named the Balzonetta housed the cafes, bars and strip-joints that served the off-duty military personnel. The other half of town – which actually housed the barracks – was considered more refined. Balzonetta was characterized by a concentration of astute, capable and forward-thinking entrepreneurs, who were able to transfer their business skills to football.

In the 1950s the football team won the championship four times in a row, a feat only equalled by Valletta forty years later. For Floriana fans, the achievement was a moral victory attained in the absence of political favours. Their town has never produced a Prime Minister or indeed a Minister in any government who could have been the source of patronage. In the absence of any rich patron the club survives as a top team by virtue of an excellent youth set-up which saw them win the under-16 championship five times in six years between 1994–2000, and the under-18 title in consecutive years from 1997–2000.

The Lions Rampant: Floriana–Valletta Rivalry

Unlike their Sliema rivals, Floriana had a reputation for antagonism that coloured not only football fixtures. A notable incident occurred in Floriana in 1922 when a gang of locals awaited the return from the stadium of Valletta fans following their Cup Final victory. A trolley bus containing the most vociferous Valletta fans was pulled off its rails in the ambush, overturned and stoned. A number of serious injuries were sustained, and the police began a policy of re-routing Valletta fans to avoid their ever having to travel along the main street of Floriana. The fans have been subject to this procedure ever since.

The Floriana–Sliema rivalry was both preceded and succeed by that of Floriana–Valletta. This antagonism between two towns only half a mile apart continues to this day, even though Birkirkara have to a certain extent superceded Floriana as Valletta's *bête noire.* Floriana cannot compete with Valletta in terms of the number of fans they attract, but have proven to be a thorn in the side of their near-neighbours on the pitch. Thus in the 1990s, Floriana fans could gloat: 'They beat us every four years' and 'They hate to win the championship without beating us'.

Although Floriana fans boast that they are more astute than those from Valletta, they know that when it comes to a fight, they are weaker. They also know that football-related violence has a long and venerable tradition. As a consequence, even to this day the football club committee requests the presence of police officers at all fixtures, including under-16 games, because of the unpredictability and volatility of touch-line parents.

Whilst Valletta can trace its origins as a football club to 1904, it was only in post-war decades that they came to the fore as a footballing force. Founded by residents emulating the servicemen found in the Valletta barracks and no doubt inspired by envy of the nearby Floriana team, Valletta soon found success, winning the double in 1945. This success was largely a product of a team consisting of ex-servicemen and former Sliema players allowed to play in the absence of transfer regulations and restrictions. Funded mainly from the fund-raising efforts of their many and fanatical fans, Valletta remained a strong team throughout the 1950s. Until the 1960s Valletta were in the shadows of Floriana, but a change of committee brought success in the 1970s and raised the profile of the club to become the biggest on the island.

Without a doubt the most passionate fans on the island are those that follow the 'white lions', better known these days as the 'Citizens' or *tas-City*. When away from football, the people of Valletta – known as *Il-Beltin* (of the city) – are locked in intra-city rivalries between two main parishes, St Paul's and St Dominic's and their respective feasts; two main neighbourhoods, *L-Arcipierku* and the *Due Balli*; two brass band clubs, La Valette and Kings Own – all of which map onto a party political division between Nationalist partisans and Labour Party supporters. Football, however, brings the *Beltin* together.

Valletta fans are masters of *tmieghek*. Not content with winning championship after championship, they use every opportunity to remind their rivals of their superiority. Every Valletta victory over Floriana requires a provocative carcade through the streets of the vanquished town, with horns blown and fireworks thrown from the moving vehicles. More subtle provocation comes as the result of Floriana's government housing projects being used to re-house Valletta residents, who repay their new hosts by playing the club's anthemic cassette collection 'Forza Valletta City' at high volume. Fans of Valletta have used the most joyful of non-footballing occasions to annoy their neighbours. In 1998, the Carnival Grande Defilé[4] held in St Anne's Square in Floriana occurred a mere two days after the confirmation of Valletta retaining the championship. The National Festivities Committee commissioned a brass band to play at the occasion which did so without incident until, when in proximity to the supporters-club bar of Floriana, the band maestro, who happened to be a fanatical fan of Valletta, ordered the band to strike up a rendition of 'Forza Valletta City'. In the ensuing mass brawl the band were supported by Valletta people present in their capacity as Carnival organizers. A dozen arrests were made.

From a prewar population of 24,000, the peninsula that is Valletta today is home to 9,000 proud and parochial citizens. The depopulation is due to a combination of those evacuating during the Second World War, never to return, and decades of slum clearance and housing development. Inhabitants of *L-Arcipierku,* the *Due Balli* and the *Mandragg* – low-lying and low-status neighbourhoods – regard themselves as 'tough-guys' with a kind of 'diamond in the rough' ethos (see Mitchell, 1998). The long-standing association of Valletta with the docks, visiting sailors , the willingness of the locals to act as ships' chandlers and merchants, and the presence for 100 years of a red-light

---

4. This parade is held every year to mark Carnival, and involves a procession of state-sponsored floats organized and built primarily by people from Valletta and Floriana.

district serving the British forces known affectionately to them as 'the gut' has stigmatized the Valletta residents in the eyes of their detractors as a people who would do anything for money, including acting as pimps and selling their bodies. The association with prostitution and high-density multiple-occupancy housing schemes provides a rich vein of ribald mocking from Valletta's footballing opponents. Generations of rivals have asked *Min hu Missierkom il-Beltin? –* 'Who is your father, people of Valletta?' The inevitable response is either *Missierna hexa l'ommkom –* 'Our father is fucking your mother' – or cheering each touch of the ball by a Valletta player with the acclaim, *Jien Missierkom –* 'I'm your father'.

The Valletta fans' propensity to disorder and violence resulted in them referring to themselves in the 1960s and 1970s as *tal-Palestina –* the Palestinians. Rival fans chanted *tal-Palestina ghal gol-latrina –* 'Palestine is a toilet', indicating what much of the islands' population thinks of the capital city and its residents. The tough reputation enjoyed by the fans of Valletta permits them to promenade around most of the island in their gloating, but the place they enjoy annoying most is Floriana, with insults to St Publius abounding. Contestation also focuses on the clubs' emblems, because both teams claim the rights over the symbol of the Lion Rampant.[5] Both club badges feature the emblem. St Anne's Square in Floriana is home to a statue of a lion which the locals are very proud of, and, inevitably, Valletta fans deface the lion on the occasion of their championship victories. Six Valletta men were arrested and charged with indecent exposure after urinating on it in 1999 as part of the victory celebrations.

Hibs and Hamrun: Football and Polititcs

Hibernians of Paola emerged as a footballing force in the 1970s under the patronage of Lorry Sant (see above). An important industrial district, Paola suffers from its proximity to Malta's largest burial ground and is home to Malta's largest correctional facility. Inevitably, rivals focus on these features, suggesting that Hibs players and fans should either lock themselves away or retreat, as corpses, to the cemetery. Joining the League after the war, Hibs had by 1968 become the main rivals to the then dominant Sliema. A first championship victory in 1959 saw them join Floriana as Malta's first-ever representatives in European competition.

---

5. This symbolic conflict relates not only to football, but has a much older provenance, stemming from the rival claims made by Valletta and Floriana inhabitants to the patronage, respectively, of Knights' Grand Master Jean Parisot de La Valette and Manoel de Vilhena. Both had the lion rampant on their heraldic shield.

Precisely when the club were formed is a grey area. The Constitutional Club in the town had a team in 1922 which won the Amateur League Championship in 1932 and then applied to join the Maltese Football Association (MFA) as a full League member. However, because they were considered to represent a political party they were refused. A name change followed – to Hibernians; although nobody is certain why this name was chosen. This stronghold of the Labour vote has produced a club which at various times has won the affections of many Maltese tired of the Floriana–Sliema dominance. Despite often gallant performances Hibs were unable to win trophies in their early days due in no small part to the shenanigans of the MFA council, which mainly consisted of the well-to-do patrons of the Old Firm who took it for granted that footballing success was the preserve of their teams alone. In the 1930's when a Championship looked likely for Hibs, the MFA interrupted the League programme to play the Cassar Cup, thus spoiling their chances. Even when they finished top of the League, Hibs lost out one year to Floriana who were accorded a special status and given the title. In 1933, Hibs ended the season on equal points with Sliema, so a League decider was arranged by the MFA but the date chosen coincided with Hibs best player being posted overseas with his army regiment. Their request for a change of date was refused so Hibs refused to play the match thereby awarding the title to Sliema. The fight of Hibs against these political and personal odds provoked widespread sympathy for them amongst the footballing neutrals.

What did not provoke widespread sympathy was the patronage they were to receive from the Labour Party in the early and mid-1980s. In response, the fans of Hibs became renowned for their sympathies to the Labour Party cause. At times of heightened political tension the Hibs following would include contingents of young men from the southern village of Zejtun. Famed for the toughness of its young men the village is infamous in Maltese political history for an occasion when the inhabitants attacked a Nationalist rally in 1986. Not only was the rally routed but the Nationalist leader was days later prevented by force from entering the village church to attend a wedding. In the absence of any decent village team, the Zejtun enforcers attached themselves to Hibs – the nearest big club and the one with the most obvious Labour sympathies. Fighting the Nationalist-sympathizing Valletta fans was considered the duty of the Hibs fans, and in the political and masculine mythologies that exist the men of Zejtun are the only ones who scare Valletta. The latter have never taken a carcade into Zejtun.

A new force in Maltese football appeared in the early 1980s in the shape of Hamrun Spartans. Between 1983 and 1991 the club won twenty-three trophies thereby achieving more in nine years than the previous fifty. Their victories were witnessed by a vociferous and often violent following, particularly when the opposition were Valletta. Like that of Hibs, the success of the Spartans is attributable in no small part to political patronage and individual entreprenuership. A changeable electorate saw the former Nationalist club president replaced in the 1970s by a man with Labour sympathies. In 1984 the Labour government donated land to the club for them to build their own stadium, which they began in 1988. By that date, the Labour government had been replaced by the Nationalists, and the new regime gave more land – not this time to Hamrun Spartans but to Hamrun Liberty Sports Club. Adjacent to the Labour-sponsored Spartans ground, Liberty built a club which now houses basketball, the local variety of bowls known as bocci, and an amateur football club. This symbolic war of politics-by-sporting-patronage is not untypical, and demonstrates starkly the relationship between political cleavages and football rivalries.

The footballing success of the Spartans owed everything to the political abilities of Victor Tedesco, a local to Hamrun who stood for election in the 1980s and who, despite not being elected, was influential in Labour circles. With a personal fortune made from business interests in the oilfields of Libya and Saudi Arabia he was able to finance the purchase of three foreign players who were to prove instrumental in the club's success. This success provoked the envy of other clubs.

Hamrun gained a reputation for deceit, particularly after their 1982 championship. It was widely believed that Hibs had the best team that year, followed closely by Sliema, but every time Hibs and Sliema played Hamrun they underperformed, assisted, it was thought, by financial incentives emanating from within the victorious club. Having made the club successful, Tedesco led the club into financial straits in 1998 having borrowed Lm250,000 (*c.* £400,000) from a loan company which he was unable to repay. As a consequence, the club was unable to repay transfer fees and the MFA forbade them from buying any more players. Tedesco's successor, Joseph Zammit was then expected to act as saviour, particularly as he was personal secretary to a Labour Party minister. Unfortunately, two months after Zammit became president the Labour government were voted out of office and he was out of a job – both for the Labour Party and for Spartans. His successor was in the hot seat only months before suffering serious injuries in a road accident. Thus for all their attempts to join the big boys of Maltese football, Hamrun never really succeeded and were regarded by their opponents as somewhat naïve and pretentious in their ambitions.

The team and fans received chants which likened their attempts to be a big club as cow-like – *tal baqra* – by use of a wonderful metaphor which one fan explained: 'Cows are sincere but gullible. Their big eyes make them see things bigger than they actually are'. The same rivals would delight in accusing the Hamrun fans of being *tal-werwer,* which translates as 'trouble-makers' and *tas-sikkina* – 'knife-carriers'. As one native of Hamrun explained: 'Until the mid-1940s the stereotypical opinion was that Hamrun men all worked in the docks and in their spare time gambled and fought each other'.

Although united behind a single patron saint, Hamrun is divided between two brass band clubs that frequently fight during *festa.* At one time Tedesco held a role in local issues that transcended football and could sustain a relative peace, but a brass band dispute in 1987 was proceeded by two years of violent feuding. In this intense local hostility Tedesco mediated between the clubs, which were divided primarily along political loyalties. Significantly, he was the only individual that both parties agreed to accept as a mediator. With his demise the tensions reemerged and by the late 1990s the conflict had become so severe at *festa* time that the parish priest was forced to cancel band marches to preserve the peace. Although under the guidance of figures such as Tedesco football can act as a unifying force, its long-term role in mitigating such conflict is limited.

Citizens and Stripes: the 1990s Encounters

The fans and players of Birkirkara have become accustomed to being told – particularly by Valletta fans – to shove their new-found money up their arses. The nouveau riche *arrivestes* that are The Stripes – because of their kit – also suffer the occasional cacophony of moo-ing noises in homage to their part-sponsorship by the MacDonalds hamburger empire. As they have become a force in Maltese football, Birkirkara have become the most disliked team on the island. The reasons for this lie in ideas about the morality of success, and particularly the role of money.

Football clubs had existed in Birkirkara since 1919, but its distance from British service establishments explains the late development of the game. For decades the district housed people who were predominantly employed in agricultural production and it was, and remains, a stronghold of Nationalist politics, housing the Nationalist's Party's Prime Ministerial residence since 1987. It was businessmen sympathetic to the Nationalist cause that made them the force that they have become. With lofty ideas of how to gain a much longed-for championship – finally achieved in April 2000, after 50 years – Birkirkara broke with many Maltese footballing traditions in their five-year two-horse race with Valletta. This competition saw both clubs turn professional – openly in the case of Birkirkara and *de facto* in the case of Valletta, whose president's businesses provide sinecured employment for his star players.

Considered for decades a yo-yo club of little footballing consequence, a business deal in 1995 resulted in Birkirkara becoming major competitors who are able to pay the best wages in local football and recruit whoever they want. Their success is therefore regarded as having been bought, rather than fought for. Their sponsorship has assisted in the purchase of numerous international players, including an attempt to sign the son of Libya's Colonel Gaddafi. This is not without political significance, as Malta's southern neighbour is almost universally regarded with suspicion. Attempts by Mintoff to woo the Colonel during the 1980s troubled even the Labour faithful, who were unhappy with being associated with the Arab Mediterranean – his Nationalist opponents even more so. Birkirkara's deal with the younger Gaddaffi fell through, thus depriving the world the spectacle of seeing one of the Colonel's kin wearing MacDonalds-sponsored kit. It is irony indeed that one of the west's most vigorous critics should have come so close to a family connection with one of its most powerful corporations.

Birkirkara's sponsorship deal has provoked widespread hostility. The club had leased a building in a prime spot on the town's high-street during the Labour government of 1971-87. The lease was granted on the understanding that its sole use would be as a sporting club. However, the site was considered perfect by the expanding MacDonalds burger empire who negotiated to lease the building's ground floor from the club for Lm20,000 per annum. The MacDonalds logo was also placed on the team shirts, which happened to match the corporation's colour scheme of red and yellow. Many in the game argued that the property should not have been rented for financial gain, and resented the injection of funds into the up-and-coming team, which could now buy itself success.

The story of the club's development reaaly began in the 1960s when a small club was formed on the outskirts of Sliema in a district known as St Andrews. Here the Sliema Sports Association took part in amateur and youth competitions and proved to be very successful. When the British military left the district in 1979 the area was redeveloped and populated by the Maltese. A new club was formed after the name of the district and in the late 1980s the club were accepted by the MFA. Sponsored by Luxol the St Andrews side found themselves in the Premier League by 1991. However, their proximity to Sliema and relative newness meant they had no following. A proposal to amalgamate with Sliema came to nothing when the latter refused to have the name Luxol added to their name. The same idea, however, appealed to Birkirkara who took on the joint name in 1993. Funded by two well-known millionaires the club paid good wages and soon attracted good players.

Forced as a consequence of the amalgamation to begin life in Division Three, they were in the Premier League three seasons later. This arrangement saw, for the first time in Maltese footballing history, the merging of two districts. Keen to maintain this novelty, the club developed a management structure different to everyone else, and operate as a limited company with 600 shareholders and with two committees-one for football, the other for business. They have a club chairman, not a president. With the wages they offer, the rest of the Maltese footballing world consider them a team of mercenaries and the board avaricious for success to the point of having no qualms about buying victory when the need arises. In 1997, one player received wages of Lm1400 per month plus a free apartment and school fees for his children. Such an income was considered preposterous by the fans and committees of other clubs and provoked a variety of rumours as to where the funding came from.

A pleasant place to live, Birkirkara is, with a population of 27,000, the largest village in Malta. Attractive to young couples seeking refuge from the constraints of their parent's village traditions Birkirkara is also a destination for the aspiring middle class. It also at one time housed a poor district known as *il-Laqxija* – the left-overs – and with it developed the insulting metaphor of *il-karkura tax-xitan* – 'the slippers the devil left behind' when departing in haste at what he saw. This district was demolished and rebuilt in the 1970s by the Labour government who, in an attempt to alter the voting ratio, packed it with their own supporters drawn from the south of the island. Such newcomers are not considered the true people of Birkirkara.

Home to six churches, the largest of which is St Helens, Birkirkara was at one time infamous for its intra-*festa* hostilities. As the success of the football team has grown, however, this conflict has abated, and Birkirkara appears united behind its team. They have a core following of some 3,000 fans, which can be doubled for a big game, and in the past few years have been the only fans to offer a dialogue with those of Valletta. The latter point out that as a proportion of the total population of 27,000, 3,000 is not particularly impressive – particularly in comparison to the levels of Valletta support drawn from the city's population of 9,000. Such negotiations are not polite and see mutual insults traded every game, with the occasional street brawl ensuing en route. As a consequence the police routinely block all access to the high-street of Birkirkara on match days, to avoid football-related disorder.

Maltese football fans, like those the world over, are quick to grumble and willing to insult. Their rivalries are channeled into a tradition of *tmieghek* that sees the mocking of a vanquished opponent as more significant than victory itself, and regularly leads to carnivalesque parody and violent confront-ation. Such confrontation often takes on a religious form, but also coincides with the other fault-lines of Maltese society: class-based and party political. As with politics itself, football is often dominated by significant patrons, who are both financial and political backers of a club, and can make the difference between success and failure.

The role of such financiers is to fund club developments and sign expensive players, but there are often accusations that money also buys success through match-fixing (see Armstrong and Mitchell, 1999). These rumours and their consequent conflicts are as old as football in Malta. By the 1920s a series of significant scandals led the MFA to act. At that time it was permitted for any team to represent a local district, which led to a proliferation of teams who vied for the attention of local fans, competing against each other to command their support. In Sliema and Valletta, for example, three or four separate teams might be entered in the league to represent the town, which inevitably increased intra-local conflict, but also led to a series of accusations of bribery and match-fixing. The MFA responded to this situation by setting up the District Representation System, in which only one team could represent a single named district. As a result, teams were amalgamated, but conflict was not abated. Rather, it was displaced, and the best-laid plans of the MFA to reduce antagonism at an intra-local level merely transposed it to the inter-local. Where once the fans of Sliema, for example, argued amongst themselves, now they argued with Valletta, Floriana and Hamrun – and the accusations of match-fixing continued.

As are evident from the examples given here, the rivalries and conflicts in Maltese football are era-specific, with particular polarities emerging at particular times. In some cases, the rivalries serve to unite the population of a village or town – mitigating the conflicts that can be caused by politics, *festa* or the band clubs. In other cases, they fail to do so, adding fuel to already-stoked fires. In all cases, however, the idioms of antagonism are drawn from a repertoire of symbols associated with patron saints, local history, social status and political allegiance. In all cases, such idioms are chosen with care to inflict maximum symbolic damage and in the spirit of the gloating tradition of *tmieghek*. In all cases it is as important to have one's rivals lose as to win oneself.

10

Viking and Farmer Armies: The Stavanger–Bryne Norwegian Football Rivalry

Hans Hognestad

The Danish author Carsten Jensen noted that Norway is one of the few places in the world where you have to leave the city to get to the centre. Jensen's insight suggests that the heart and soul of Norway's national identity are found outwith the urban areas. It was not until the mid-nineteenth century, and after the rest of Europe, that Norway underwent industrialization and urbanization. Tord Larsen, a Norwegian anthropologist, has argued in an article entitled 'Bønder i by'n' (Peasants in town) that urbanity continues to be alien to the dominant narratives surrounding Norwegian national identity. The fragmentation associated with modern urban lifestyles is still flatly denied, hence 'the strategies which maintain a rural ideal in an urban context are moving the rural community into the city' (Larsen, 1984). Rural community life maintains its position as a vehicle for national virtues in Norwegian public discourses. Urbanization and 'the escape from rural districts' is still strongly regarded as an undesirable development by leading politicians, both right and left wing, and throughout the postwar era various Norwegian governments have tried hard to sustain isolated, rural communities by funding local industry and improving public infrastructures.

It is perhaps unsurprising to find that a rivalry between two football teams centred around metaphorical antagonisms between 'peasants and townies' has evolved in Norway. Viking FK from Stavanger, a town of around 100,000 inhabitants on the south-west coast, are a club with long traditions and significant domestic success since the 1950s. Bryne FK, their local rivals, and the focus of ethnographic attention here, illustrate the little village team that progresses to threaten the competitive hegemony of the older team from the nearest town. However, it was not until 1975, when Bryne were first promoted to the Premier Division, that the rivalry escalated via derby matches until Bryne were relegated thirteen years later. After eleven years in Division One, Bryne were again promoted in the autumn of 1999, revitalizing the opportunities to recapture the intense rivalry of the 1970s and 1980s. Unlike the stereotypical association of such clubs and their supporters with peasantry in other parts of the football world, Bryne's links to rurality are not excessive. In pre-professional times, Gabriel Høyland whilst the team captain and local icon during the 1970s and 1980s, and also worked as a farmer (a job that he retains). Then, Viking fans directed the chant, with an element of truth, 'Smell of cowhouse!' at Bryne supporters. Some Bryne fans did indeed arrive straight from milking cows to watch evening games. Yet, during the 1980s Bryne developed the image of a modern, exemplary little club, with clichés about the well-run farms at Jæren, the home district of Bryne, providing metaphorical references for this progress. In a preview of the 2000 season Norway's biggest selling national tabloid paper, *Verdens Gang*, presented Bryne under the heading 'Farmers' Army, tractors and Brøyt', the latter being a company at Bryne producing agricultural excavators. The preview concluded 'Bryne will never be a sexy team', proclaiming furthermore that their attitude is 'as sober and down-to-earth as the stonefences characteristic of Jæen.'[1]

Norwegian football: a rural success story?

As a sport and a cultural form football originally developed out of industrialization. Whilst the game had its origins in the middle classes, clubs soon proliferated within working-class communities and became integral parts of the urban life of inner-city locations (Armstrong and Giulianotti, 1997, 1999; Holt, 1989; Russell, 1997). As a spectator sport the world over the game is played in stadiums, usually located in or near densely populated areas. But this is not the case in Norway, where the best Norwegian teams hail from small towns and rural districts. Most contemporary Norwegian stars, such as Solskjær, Johnsen (Man. United), Berg, Østenstad (Blackburn Rovers), Flo (Chelsea and Glasgow Rangers), Mykland (1860 München), Bakke (Leeds United), and Iversen and Leonardsen (Tottenham Hotspur), were born in sparsely populated areas and have played a central part in the international progress that Norwegian football has enjoyed since the early 1990s. Dan Eggen, currently at Alaves in Spain, was the only player in Norway's Euro 2000 squad who began at an Oslo club. Two of the most successful clubs in Norway, Rosenborg of Trondheim and Molde, are both peripheral to the most densely

---

1. www.vg.no-pub-vgart.hbs?artid=9052198

populated areas of Oslo and Bergen.[2] Ironically, clubs from Oslo, the capital city with a population of around half a million, struggle to survive in the top division and to attract a large and loyal support. In the 2000 season Vålerenga was the only Oslo club in the premiership. Rosenborg, by far the best league team since the early 1990s onwards, come from Trondheim, a University town of around 150,000 people located in a sparsely populated district in central Norway, around 500 km north of Oslo. The other Champions League team in 1999–2000 were Molde, who come from an isolated fishing town of around 30,000 people on the north-west coast. In recent years the town has become more famous for its annual international jazz festival. Arguably the best-supported team in Norway, Brann, hails from Bergen, the second largest city with a population of around 250,000.

The expression of rivalries in world football is regularly fuelled by local antagonisms and contrasting social identities. Characterized by an often playful negativity from the stands, opposing sides are generally constructed in terms of a stereotypical otherness during matches (Armstrong, 1998; Archetti, 1999; Hognestad, 1995). Metaphors taken from life in the countryside may be applied towards opposing teams and their fans, to debase them as rural perverts in accordance with very rough geo-sociological maps. Hence in Scotland, supporters of Aberdeen are labelled 'sheepshaggers', despite the fact that most of their fans live in a relatively large and prosperous city. The same goes for some teams from Yorkshire and Derbyshire in English football. In football as in many other urban social dramas, rural lifestyles continue to appear as a theme for mockery and caricature (Hognestad, 1995).

In contrast to these emphases on rivalry and conflict, the Norwegian game has been more influenced by the ideals of a national sports movement committed to unification and consensus (cf. Goksøyr, Andersen and Asdal, 1996). Positive support for teams has dominated supporter practices in the Norwegian league, rather than the dynamic negativity witnessed in leagues elsewhere in the world (cf. Goksøyr and Hognestad, 1999). However, more recently, the caricature of rural lifestyles has become more central to the vocal repertoire of numerous supporter groups in Norway, which might be interpreted as a metaphor for urban prejudice towards the perceived 'backwardness' of rural people. Football terraces thus represent liberated spaces for expressing opinions about the intellectual level of people from the rural districts and rural teams, in contrast to what is deemed politically correct in Norwegian society. Opposing fans regularly subject each other to chants of 'for en gjeng med bønder' (what a bunch of farmers) to ridicule the vocal backing that is

2. As a whole, Norway is a vast and sparsely-populated country. Oslo is actually nearer Rome than Hammerfest, the northernmost town of Norway and, indeed, the world.

given to rival teams. Members of *Klanen* (The Clan),[3] fans of Vålerenga, have been major protagonists in this development since the mid-1990s, and proudly chant 'øl og vold og skamslåtte bønder' (Beer and violence and manhandled peasants) as their adopted song.[4] However, among the emerging supporter-cultures even in rural surroundings, farmer-related metaphors are currently applied in chants as a dominant, if not always imaginative, means of criticizing the smaller and more rural others.

Leaving village rivalries

Founded in 1926, Bryne FK is perhaps most famous for kick-starting the entrepreneurial career of Rune Hauge. A now notorious player agent, Hauge was Bryne's marketing director in 1984, when Norway's football industry was undergoing rapid professionalization.[5] Alf Inge Håland, currently at Manchester City, is probably Bryne's most famous player export. Operating as a small company with turnover of NOK 14 million (*c.* £1 million) for the 2000 season, Bryne are nonetheless a fairly successful club, with a Norwegian Cup Final victory over Brann in 1987 and two league runners-up medals for 1980 and 1982.

This is a noteworthy history considering that Bryne is an industrial village of 5,500 people, located twenty-five miles south of Stavanger. Bryne evolved as a centre of the Jæren district after the Stavanger–Egersund railroad was built in 1878. Jaeren is a rural district south of Stavanger, of around 100,000 inhabitants. Bryne is partly considered as a suburb to Stavanger, but also as a labour resource for the numerous factories in or near the village. Close links to modern farming are evidenced by the numerous factories specializing in agricultural products. Before modern technology enabled local farmers to cultivate the characteristically rich but stony earth, Jæren was a poor district. New technology introduced after the war helped Jæren to prosper through efficient industrial production and profitable farming methods.

---

3. 'Klanen', adopted as a name by Vålerenga fans in 1981, is inspired by the Scottish clan system and its structuring around notions of family strength.

4. This song has been performed everywhere by Vålerenga fans including a ludicrous rendition in Norwegian at Stamford Bridge, the home of the London club Chelsea, during the first leg of the quarter finals of the European Cup Winners' Cup tie in March 1999!

5. Hauge has directly or indirectly represented the bulk of Norwegian footballers who have ended up with a contract for a club in the English leagues since the early 1990s. A famous incident dates back to 1991 which involved the then manger of Arsenal, George Graham. Graham was sacked by Arsenal in 1994 for having received illicit money to the sum of £300,000 from Hauge in connection with the transfer of Norwegian player Pål Lydersen to Arsenal. Hauge was blacklisted by FIFA for a while and was later charged with a number of business crimes both in Norway and in England. No jury found him guilty.

One major company occupying a factory plant just outside Bryne is Brøyt, known nationwide for its innovative development in agricultural excavators. Brøyt sponsored Bryne in the mid-1970s, thereby underlining the club's close links to the agricultural industry. In the decisive promotion match in 1975 against Vard Haugesund, a local journalist from Haugesund associated Bryne's 1–0 win on a particularly muddy pitch with the cultivation of new land:

> . . . they appeared in tracksuits with 'BRØYT' painted on their backs, as if to make it quite clear that they were some sort of personified ploughs . . . Eventually 'The Brøyts' ploughed up the pitch to such an extent that it would have been possible to grow both Kerrs Pink and Pimpernell potatoes in the northern goal. (*Haugesunds Avis*, October 1975, author's translation)

The farming connection is a token of pride among supporters and people involved with the club, thereby inverting its association with backwardness to become a symbol of strength and determination. When Bryne beat Brann in the 1987 Norwegian Cup Final, the travelling contingent of 5,000 Bryne fans carried sheep-bells, and created an unprecedented noise and atmosphere inside the national stadium. A ram named Victory was brought in and presented to the team afterwards by a fan working at the agricultural school near Oslo. A picture of the team's captain, Lars Gaute Bø, riding the ram in the dressing room, was famously printed in the national press the next day.

By contrast, Viking of Stavanger, founded in 1899, are the biggest and most successful club in Rogaland, a county within the Jæren district, having won eight league championships and the Norwegian Cup four times. In the 1930s several Viking players figured in Norway's successful teams in the 1936 Berlin Olympics and the World Cup in France in 1938. When Bryne were promoted in 1975, Viking had just completed a fourth successive league championship. Their home ground, Stavanger stadiun, is close to the town centre, underlining the central position of the football club in Stavanger's modern history. It is the fourth largest town in Norway, its economic dependency on the fishing industries has been replaced since the 1960s by income from North Sea oil. Despite their city associations, Viking attract support from across the region, including Bryne's neighbouring villages.

For most of their history, Bryne and Viking have been in different divisions. Their first league meeting was a Second Division match in 1966, following Viking's relegation the year before. By this time Bryne had acquired ambition. The chairman Reidar B. Thu announced proudly before the derby match at Bryne in 1967 that Viking belonged to the past and that the future was Bryne's (Askeland and Olsson, Bergesen, 1999). However, Viking wiped the floor with their new rival, winning 5–0, and gaining promotion later that year.

Before 1975, Bryne were generally perceived as being in a different football universe to Viking, such was the latter's domination. Viking used to sign the best players at Bryne, including Johannes Vold, the all-time top scorer for Bryne who went on to enjoy successful years with Viking in the early 1970s. Many people from Bryne and the neighbouring villages would support Viking as their major team and Bryne as their local one. This is in sharp contrast to the usual case in more urban settings in most football nations.

Up until the 1950s Bryne did not even dominate the Jæren football scene. Before the Second World War, Klepp FK were the best club in the district, and another village team, Nærbø, achieved more success than Bryne in the local leagues. For a few years after the war, Ålgård were the better side, and joined Viking in what was called the Main League for two seasons. When Bryne grew to become the biggest Jæren club from the late 1950s onwards, these three clubs were true local rivals. Viking were literally in a different league when the Norwegian Football Association introduced the original nationwide First Division in 1962. These local teams have continued to be Bryne's rivals, and animosities are manifested particularly when Bryne attempt to sign their best players. Many people from neighbouring villages have continued to support Viking as the 'big club', *especially* after Bryne were promoted. Conversely, people from Stavanger's suburbs adopted Bryne as their team on the principle of opposing domination by one's nearest neighbour. This complicates the picture of what the prime rivalry in the area is. And yet, a sense of loathing based on perceptions of disrespect and contempt in the more general relationship between townies and countrymen may be traced back to before the war. Reidar B. Thu states that:

> When Viking came out to play at Bryne before the war they didn't even bother sending the Reserves, but rather sides which appeared more like Reserve Reserves. They had no respect for us and playing football in a peasant field at Jæren was not likely to be considered attractive for their star players. Even during games with their subordinates there were regular remarks of 'cowsmell' emanating from the Viking contingent. After the War, Bryne improved and soon established themselves as the best team at Jæren. Things started to get more serious and Viking fielded a stronger side, but still not a full first eleven. They demonstrated a remarkably arrogant attitude towards us well into the 1960s. In fact when we were promoted to the Second Division in 1965 and played two seasons in league competition with Viking, it was still not in doubt that Viking were the big brothers. They would not take us seriously, not even when we were promoted to Division One in 1975.

In 1962 Bryne finally beat Viking for the first time in a competitive match, a third round Cup replay before nearly 10,000 fans, a staggering attendance at Bryne in those days. The game was played under conditions quite different to current ones and depended on the aid of local farmers, which the following account by former club chairman and school teacher, Kjell Olav Stangeland, articulates:

> I was only a kid and since the game had to be played on the unterraced ground beside the main ground at Bryne, we had to build the terraces! I helped out and I remember we went to Stavanger to collect a few benches from the town's Park and Sports Unit. At this time an old Viking legend, Reidar Kvammen, was a coach at Bryne. His brother, a great Viking supporter called Arthur, welcomed us at the Park and Sports Unit. When we asked him if we could just keep the benches if Bryne won he rolled over laughing. On the day of the match, the club had also managed to get a lot of farmers to provide tractor trailers for terraces. Around 10,000 people turned up to see us win 2–1. It was unbelievable.

This game proved to be a sign of things to come. Football interest in the district was phenomenal after Bryne's promotion in 1975, and for the first derby match against Viking in the 1976 season the attendance was close to 13,000, an amazing attendance for a village of 5,500 and a ground which holds 10,000. Like the game in 1962, farmers had been asked to provide trailers for the game; the terrace, which was then just a slope, was packed with slightly elevated trailers to form a perfect if, by today's UEFA standards, rather insecure 'terracing'. In 1979, the crowd was officially a record 13,500, but unofficially a suspected 17,000 were there. The gates at Stavanger stadiun were generally a few thousands higher with a record 18,000 at a derby match in 1980.

Loving the enemy: a Norwegian virtue?

For various historical reasons, politeness is a virtue in Norwegian sportsman-ship. In the privileged narratives of Norwegian sports, gloating is out of order, even when expressed from a packed terrace (Goksøyr and Hognestad, 1999). Historically, sports have been a strong pedagogical instrument for promoting reconciliation and friendship, while the expression of passionate antagonisms has been deprecated by various public bodies. There was also a strong social incentive in the way that organized sports were valued for bridging the class divide (Asdal, Goksøyr and Andersen, 1996). Local football and organized sports emerged in Jæren from the 1920s onwards, and they were valued for uniting different classes and enhancing the national policies of social equal-ization (Melkevik Jr., 1994). In this sense, loving your neighbour seems to be pedagogically ingrained in the very foundations of Norwegian sports. Combined with the argument of Norwegian anthropologist Tord Larsen (1984) that impartiality and a deep scepticism towards ritual expressions are key elements in the hegemonic national narratives in Norway, the ideal sports participant in Norway emerges as a sober, modest and polite man.

However, as a cultural practice, football, even in Norway, has never been quite like this. A gap exists between the ideal of privileged politeness and the reality of semi-public, tribalistic gloating between the supporters. Hence, whenever Bryne stadium is informed by an emotionless tannoy announcer that Viking are a goal down in some other game, a jubilant, malicious roar emanates from the terraces. The same scene is regularly re-enacted at Stavanger stadiun. Yet, despite the bitter rivalry that evolved between Bryne and Viking fans, no violent incident was ever reported to police, and verbal support was mostly limited to backing one team and not abusively denigrating the rival. If a Viking player was lying injured on the pitch, individual Bryne fans could sometimes shout 'Send him to Grødaland', referring to a factory at which they 'recycle' deceased animals into cosmetic products. Conversely, Viking fans would chant the occasional, farm-related denigration towards Bryne fans.

Oral testimonies elicited via interviews illuminate that there were club men at Bryne who loathed the big brother in Stavanger even in the 1950s and 1960s. One of them was Kjell Olav Stangeland, later founder of Bryne supporters club in 1977 and chairman between 1980 and 1987. Stangeland states how:

> As a boy I used to get the train into town to watch Viking games. But I always supported the away team. I'm not sure why, but I always refused to accept that there was a team in Stavanger better than Bryne. I had no problems accepting that teams from the big cities were better than us, but not a team from Stavanger.

Similarly, Gabriel Høyland, who played for Bryne between 1970 and 1986, was known as someone who had 'always' disliked Viking. Høyland was capped twenty-three times for Norway and had been an exceptional talent from the age of fifteen when he made his debut for the senior side. Along with other top clubs in Norway, Viking tried to sign Høyland several times while Bryne were in the Second Division. He remained a one-club type of footballer, which had much to do with his duties on the family farm, and became something of an icon for the club's progress over the next decade. In the press and in the national football vernacular he is still simply referred to as 'Mr Bryne'. As a young player he declared to the local media that he would never join Viking. Høyland also had a regular column in the biggest regional paper, in which he was often accused of being blatantly prejudiced against Viking. After the first league win for Bryne over Viking, he hinted that Viking supporters at local workplaces would probably get a hard time in the week to come (*Stavanger*

Aftenblad, 27 May 1980). He consequently became a particularly hated player in Stavanger circles, and was attacked in letters to the local papers for what was perceived as impoliteness and disgraceful local patriotism.

Farmers turning into protagonists

After narrowingly surviving their first year in the top flight in 1976, Bryne soon became protagonists in the gradual professionalization of coaching methods and tactics in Norway. While all the players of the 1976 team had been locals, the club started to sign players from other parts of Norway. Scottish player Peter Dunne, formerly of St Mirren, became the first foreigner to join the club in 1978. One cause of this development was the new coach, the late Kjell Schou Andreassen. 'Schouen', as he was known, was a former Viking coach who also coached the national team with the current Rosenborg coach Nils Arne Eggen between 1974–7.[6] Schouen was one of the first Norwegians to combine a previous career as a footballer with a pedagogical education as a coach. His football philosophy, built on principles of interaction and organization, might be seen as an early version of 'the Norwegian way' developed so successfully in the 1990s by Eggen at Rosenborg and Egil Olsen as the national team coach for 1990–8. Combined with the professionalization of club management as a whole, this process gave Bryne a pioneering status in Norwegian football in the late 1970s. At a time when a few clubs were about to turn semi-professional, almost overnight Bryne became one of the most attractive clubs to play for. At this time, money earned from outside attendances was becoming an issue in Norwegian football. Hence, developing a successful club still depended principally upon leadership, talent networking and substantial support. The fact that Bryne rapidly started to mount a serious challenge to the dominance of Viking marked an historic turning point as the relationship between the two clubs grew gradually more strained. Much rested on the fact that Andreassen had turned down an offer to rejoin Viking to join Bryne. Arne Johannessen, a former player, coach and chairman at Viking, argues that:

> Bryne were a good local number two in the 1950s and 1960s, but it wasn't until 1976, their first year in the First Division, that we started to look upon them as a challenge. When the season finished, 'Schouen' chose Bryne ahead of us. This irritated us enormously. As a consequence Okland and Ottesen[7] signed for Bryne rather than us after 'Schouen' had

6. The current Rosenborg coach, Nils Arne Eggen, has repeatedly stressed the influence Andreassen's ideas have had on the way that Rosenborg has been run over the last decade (Eggen, 1999).

7. Okland and Ottesen were two of the most talented players in the district who went on to play for Norway.

convinced them that the future was brighter at Bryne. Bryne was suddenly a competitor in a way we had never encountered before and we simply didn't like the new situation.

In the national media Bryne was regularly presented from the late 1970s onwards as the model for clubs with limited resources because efficiency and professionalism dominated their profile. Gone was their previous image as backward peasants. The fact that the board of directors at Bryne in 1987 decided that the club's ambition was to reach at least the quarter-finals of a European tournament in the near future, demonstrated their ambition a decade before Norwegian teams managed to compete on a European level. Meanwhile the more cynical, big brother in Stavanger was laughing, as Johannessen indicates:

We were fighting with Bryne about players and sponsors and as a club we were struggling at the time. In this situation Bryne liked to present themselves as the 'Model Club'. And of course, people like Kjell Olav Stangeland [former chairman] and Reidar Omdal [former director] were central figures in those days, both of whom blatantly hated us. We all felt that Bryne appeared a bit too polished and straight. We laughed at their ambition to play in a European Cup Final some time in the future. Rune Hauge was at Bryne then as well and . . . well we all felt that they were a bit too slick.

Bryne players and officials on the other hand disliked what was perceived as an arrogant attitude and a pompous self-image among their Viking counterparts. Throughout the 1970s and 1980s they were often referred to simply as 'byasar' (townies), a term perceived to represent a strong contrast to the more down to earth, sober attitude believed to be the mark of villagers in the Bryne area. Arne Johannessen in particular was singled out as something of an archetypical carrier of the perceived attitudes of 'townies'. Høyland, the former Bryne player, says that:

We did think of Arne Johannessen as a gangster-type because his whole appearance provoked us. Who did he think he was? He was wearing a leather jacket and dark shades. We just found that a bit stupid and remote from the more sober and honest spirit we were used to at Jæren. Generally you will find that 'jærbuer' [people from Jæren] do not like exaggerations like that.

Johannessen was for a long time married to a Bryne woman and knew many people there, but that did not diminish his status as 'a poseur from the town'. Furthermore, among club officials and others involved with Bryne, there was a general belief that some local media favoured Viking in profiling the two clubs. Apart from a minor and very local newspaper, all the local and regional newspapers were located in Stavanger. Reidar B. Thu regards the media's role as part of a more general conspiracy:

> When it became clear that we intended to establish ourselves in the top flight, Viking had to take us seriously – and they did. They applied all their skills to try and keep us down. Viking were much more clever than us when it came to public relations and even appointed a committee of elder members to work out strategies of how to keep us down. As a result, they basically ended up getting their people stationed in some of the local media.

Within the social context and ethos of amateur football, some local media started to question the ethical standards of Bryne's methods, particularly in connection with two transfers from Bryne to Viking. There had been several uncontroversial cases of low profile players moving between the two clubs. However, when Viking wanted to sign the quick winger, Magnus Flatastøl in January 1978, Bryne demanded NOK 35,000 (£3,000) in transfer money, at a time when money was only just becoming an issue in transfers between domestic clubs that were still operating on an amateur basis. This caused uproar at Viking and their supporters wrote angry letters to the press, one of whom claimed (*Stavanger Aftenblad,* 24 January 1978) that Bryne's demand was an example of 'greediness and reckless trading with human beings'. After the Norwegian FA supported Bryne's demand, the chairman at Viking, Arne Johannessen, was quoted in the local press, stating that:

> It is an insane amount of money. We have only paid for one player previously when we bought Trygve Johannessen from Florvåg [a lower division club based near Bergen], for a much lower fee. There is only one clear outcome of this case: the relationship between Bryne and Viking is destroyed for years. We do not wish to have anything more to do with this club. (*Stavanger Aftenblad,* 17 January 1978)

In the following derby match later that year, Flatastøl equalized for Viking three minutes into injury time, with a brilliant 30-yard shot into the top left-hand corner. In a gloating fashion Flatastøl stated that 'a goal had never felt that good' (*Stavanger Aftenblad,* 23 June 1978).

In 1980, Nils Ove Hellvik, a talented 18-year-old Norwegian international, was signed by Viking in 1981 whilst still under contract with Bryne, a year after he had scored the winner in Bryne's first-ever league win over Viking. The peculiar point with this transfer was that Hellvik was always known as a Viking fan. One of his teachers at school had been Kjell Olav Stangeland, chairman at Bryne in 1981. Stangeland and the Bryne board made this case a matter of principle. They demanded NOK 100,000 in transfer money and refused Hellvik permission to play for Viking during the entire 1982 season, when Viking won the league and Bryne were runners-up. Viking brought the case before a court of law, but lost. Hellvik considers Bryne's reluctance to release him was due to his likely destination:

> Viking had promised to sign me no matter what the demands of Bryne were, but Bryne clearly wished to make this a matter of principle. Kjell Olav [Stangeland] was known as something of an anti-Viking man and he had been my teacher before I went to Bryne as a 15-year-old, so we always used to exchange some banter. I believe that the case would have been solved more smoothly if I had gone to another club. They didn't like to see their most talented players going to the town. (Nils Ove Hellvik, former Bryne and Viking player)

Both transfer cases intensified an escalating reciprocal contempt between the two clubs at all levels; supporters, officials and players. A profound lack of trust between the clubs evolved, reinforced by a few bizarre signings which to the other appeared as sabotage:

> It was no secret, particularly when Bjarne Berntsen[8] was their coach, that they would sign players, not because they needed them, but because someone tipped them off that we were after these particular players. There were 'stråmenn'[9] everywhere; local referees, ex- players etc. who would gossip non-stop. (Gabriel Høyland, former Bryne player)

The close, but not very friendly contacts between the clubs also resulted in some amusing incidents. One particular story indicates how the psychological, if rather amateur, strategies between the teams could evolve, as Høyland explains:

> It was before the derby match at Bryne in 1977 and one of our star players, Magnus Flatastøl, had been injured for a while. The club announced to the press that he wasn't match fit even though he was. Keeping the secret of fielding him in the first eleven was meant to be a psychological device for destabilising Viking's tactics on the day of the match. Flatastøl was even sent somewhere else to warm up, in Arne Larsen Økland's[10] garden in fact! However as it turned out, Viking knew that Flatastøl was playing days before the match, as one of our former players who had later joined Viking, had picked up the information from someone at Bryne and been on the phone to Viking.

8. Berntsen is a former Viking player and Norway international. He coached Bryne in 1987–8 only to leave the club in turmoil. Between 1992 and 1995 he was coach at Viking.

9. A Norwegian term referring to a person with contacts in different camps. Their supposed supplying of information and gossip to rivals or enemies is generally perceived to be treacherous.

10. A Bryne forward and Norway international at the time who went on to play with West German club Bayer Leverkusen between 1980–4. He returned to Bryne and ended his playing career by winning the Cup with them in 1987. Since then he has coached both Bryne and Viking for short and unsuccessful spells and has also been the assistant coach of Norway.

While Bryne established themselves as a mid-table First Division club in the late 1970s, Viking won or drew all of the first eight league derbies. When Bryne eventually beat Viking for the first time in a league match in 1980, Reidar B. Thu, the Bryne chairman, expressed his joy in the dressing room after the game by stating that he wished to be buried at the spot where the ball had gone into the net. Five months later, in the final game of the 1980 season, Bryne lost the league championship on goal difference to Start. Start's decisive winner in a 4–3 thriller against Rosenborg came seven minutes before the end. Arne Johannessen tells of his experience of *schadenfreude*, at a time when Viking witnessed how Bryne were about to pass them in terms of success, in the following way:

> Bryne had gradually established themselves in the top division and after a while passed us in terms of success on the pitch. We never wept when Bryne lost and our main ambition became more and more to just get better than Bryne. I remember when Bryne lost the league championship to Start on goal difference in 1980. Bryne relied on help from Rosenborg who were playing away to Start in the last match that season. It was 3–3 with seven minutes to go and I was listening to the drama on the radio in my car. The thought of Bryne winning the league was unbearable. Then Steinar Aase scored for Start and I drove straight into a hedge! Two years later we won the league and Bryne were runners up once again. We congratulated them on winning the silver medals, but no congratulations were returned [laughs].

This final remark is illustrative of the reciprocal sense of joy at the expense of the others' failure, a quality that dominated the postwar relations between the clubs. After the 1985 season Viking collapsed, were relegated to the Second Division in 1986 and nearly relegated to the Third Division in 1987, a year in which Bryne won the Cup and would have clinched a double but for a poor finish to their league campaign. These two years were the only ones in which Bryne were definitely the most powerful of the two in terms of success, finance and support. In 1988, however, Bryne were relegated from the top division while Viking were promoted from the second. Suddenly the roles were reversed to a pre-1975 scenario again, and one which lasted eleven years, when Bryne finally won promotion in October 1999. During this period, expressions of animosity between the clubs flared only occasionally, in connection with a couple of Cup ties.

Conclusion

In a society still strongly influenced by hegemonic rural narratives and virtues it might appear odd that 'farmer' is generally taken as an insult on the contemporary football scene in Norway. This may be explained with reference to the influence of the dominant urban international ethos of football. Football in Norway lacks the potential to carry national virtues in the way that Nordic winter sports do (Goksøyr and Hognestad, 1999). As a sport it is in this sense partly liberated from the privileged images and narratives of Norwegian national identity. Norwegian football, particularly at club level, forms a semi-public space in which hostilities may be expressed in ways that do not subscribe to the dominant national narratives regarding sport's role in reconciliation and national unification. Nevertheless, the expression of hostilities has remained relatively innocent, reflecting a reality which is far from the more escalated and violent rituals witnessed in the leagues of football's traditional strongholds. The recent emergence of partisan fan groups in Norway does bear testimony to a development which is more in line with international practices, demonstrating that history is in the making in Norwegian football. Furthermore, the fact that gloating and the mocking of rural life appear as dominant features in this process, reflects Norwegian football's sub-cultural edge. It has become an arena for expressing opinions and forging identities which do not conform to the politically-correct national virtues in Norwegian society. With Bryne back in the top flight of Norwegian football, it will be interesting to see how their new generation of fans will react to anti-farmer chants from opposing fans, and whether it will be possible to recreate and maintain an identity as a club of and for 'farmers'.

11

Competition and Cooperation: Football Rivalries in Yemen

Thomas B. Stevenson and Abdul Karim Alaug

The sports world was surprised by Saudi Arabia's advance to the second round of the 1994 World Cup. Just as startling was the sight of traditionally robed fans, waving flags and cheering wildly for their side. Such passionate support reflects the importance of football in the Middle East[1] whose best-known football culture is Egypt's. The Cairo clubs, al-Ahli and Zamalek, are long-standing rivals. Their fixtures, nicknamed 'the summit', are the high points of league play, draw over 80,000 fans and so capture popular attention that they empty the city's normally bustling streets. The victors set off fireworks, ebullient supporters dance in the streets and rampaging fans leave a trail of destruction (Middle East Times, 1998a, b; Wagg, 1995: 164).

Similarly, in Yemen fixtures between rival clubs attract the greatest interest, with several interconnected forms. Rivalries are enacted on the pitch, in derby matches and fixtures between the capital's dominant teams and those from other regions; and in private, between club officials. The first two rivalries derive from citizens' parochialism and the country's history as a divided state, reflecting identity-based oppositions located within Yemeni society. The third, a consequence of the others, represents competitive patterns of leadership and influence characteristic in the Middle East. Despite different guises, central to each is the hope for one team's victory and defeat for the other.

Yemen: Background and History

In global terms the Republic of Yemen is a remote, largely unknown place. The republic was formed in 1990 when the People's Democratic Republic of Yemen (PDRY – South Yemen)[2] and the Yemen Arab Republic (YAR – North

---

1. Murray (1996: 146) notes the 'region's fanaticism for soccer', but Sugden and Tomlinson (1998: 166) suggest some 'interest' is manufactured.

2. Following Britain's withdrawal in 1967, the People's Republic of South Yemen was declared. In 1970, the designation People's Democratic Republic of Yemen was adopted.

Yemen)[3] united. This national reconciliation ended roughly twenty years of political competition and occasional wars between the Soviet-bloc allied PDRY and the West-leaning YAR. The two republics were independent for only a quarter century, but their separation dates from Britain's colonization of South Arabia (eventually South Yemen) in 1839 and the second Ottoman occupation of the Kingdom of Yemen (North Yemen) in 1849.[4]

Beyond history and politics, Yemen's topography maintained its cultural heterogeneity. The littoral and interiors are extremely arid, but rugged, monsoon-watered mountains bisect the northern and central areas and extensive wadis dominate parts of the eastern region. With temperate climate and arable soils, these districts are home to most Yemeni. Urbanization, public education, telecommunications and highway systems have moderated parochialism, but kinship and regional ties remain significant. Despite a brief civil war (1994), since unification most Yemeni have begun to apprehend their social and historical differences as the foundation of their new national identity.

Football in Yemen

Organizational aspects

The first all-Yemeni sports club dates from the beginning of the twentieth century but modern sports organizations were not established until the mid-1950s in South Yemen and the late-1960s in North Yemen. The two republics followed different political models and occasionally used football matches to highlight national achievements, but their sports systems were structured similarly (Stevenson and Alaug, 1999).[5] At unification, the two sports ministries were merged.

In 1998, Yemen had 233 sports clubs classified into Premier, First and Second divisions.[6] Clubs are organized by communities but their administration and activities are regulated by the Ministry of Youth and Sport (MOYS) which provides modest financial support. Some clubs field teams in many sports; all clubs have football teams. The 40 per cent plus rise in clubs since unification indicates football's popularity, signifies the civic pride attached to clubs, and, we believe, accompanies the penetration of government authority and hegemony (Stevenson, 1989b; Stevenson and Alaug, 1997).

---

3. The 1962 coup d'état replaced the imamate with a republican regime.

4. The official demarcation was the 1904 Anglo-Ottoman Line (Burrowes, 1995: 260).

5. Besides sports, the Yemens had some parallel civil institutions such as the workers' and women's unions. Compared to the north, those in the south were subject to stronger government or party controls. However, it was not structural similarities but a strong popular ideology of 'oneness' that underlay unification.

6. The PDRY had two divisions and the YAR had three. Unification resulted in four divisions: premier, first, second and third. The latter two discussions were merged around 1997.

The 200 second division clubs are located primarily in rural towns and compete only within their regions. The nineteen first division clubs also compete principally on the provincial level. Most lower division clubs field young, inexperienced teams supported by small, local followings. The fourteen premier division clubs, all from principal cities, attract the most media and fan attention. These teams are composed of older, seasoned competitors some of whom have advanced from the lower divisions, others from their clubs' junior teams. Players are amateurs but may receive cash or benefits. Depending on match results, clubs reward teams with bonuses which are viewed as incentives for determined play and compensation for lost wages. A few, high-calibre athletes may receive monthly stipends of varying amounts to avoid appearing as salaries. Players recruited from other clubs may be given jobs they do not attend, treatment abroad for serious injuries, or free housing.[7]

The football scene

Yemeni football has not reached a competitive world level[8] but this does not diminish fans' interest. Knowing match results, following league standings, and supporting one's club are important elements of men's daily lives. Televised World Cup, Olympic and Yemeni national team fixtures attract large audiences.[9] Few domestic matches are carried on radio or television, but print and broadcast media provide scores, standings and match details. Yemeni fans are knowledgeable and passionate. Team nicknames are used in conversations and chants. While there are few nationally recognized stars, most fans know the names of some players. Football's importance in enthusiasts' lives is apparent at crucial matches when emotions run high and some loyalists, overcome with anxiety, cannot bring themselves to attend.

The 50,000-seat Revolution Sports Center in Sana'a is used only for special competitions. Routine fixtures are held in municipal stadiums the largest of which seats 10,000 spectators. Attendance frequently approaches capacity; often fans sit atop perimeter walls or stand on rooftops overlooking the field.[10] Many men talk about football, but it is the younger cohort, aged from mid-teens to early thirties, that attends fixtures regularly.[11] Their youth and

7. There are no formal procedures, but the recruiting club is supposed to compensate the 'selling' club. Transactions tend to be secret.

8. In May 1999, Yemen ranked 147 but fell to 150 following four defeats in the Asian Olympic Qualifiers (*Asian Football Confederation News*, 1999a, b).

9. Based on Stevenson's observations in 1982 and Alaug's experiences for subsequent years. The Ministry of Communication does not measure audience sizes. Satellite receivers provide access to Middle Eastern and other international fixtures.

10. Attendance figures are not reported.

11. Sexual segregation precludes women's attendance.

exuberance explain the frenzied action at ticket windows and entrance gates. The MOYS sets a single national ticket price, which in 1998–9 doubled to YR40 ($0.28),[12] about half the cost of a restaurant breakfast. Low admission costs and open seating illustrate that Yemeni football does not have the class associations found elsewhere.[13]

Fans are attentive – rising in unison with shots on goal – and are vociferous – shouting encouragement, cheering aggressive tackles or skilful play, deriding lacklustre efforts, or criticizing unpenalized fouls or the disciplining of players. Because stadiums are shared, a team's supporters have established or assigned seating areas. Several clubs have organized cheering sections of flag-waving, headband-wearing supporters who are directed by cheerleaders;[14] other clubs have similarly equipped, informal groups. Spontaneous cheering erupts from ground sections to taunt opposing players and deride opponents' injuries, and these actions heighten the always latent potential for disturbances.[15]

Fencing separates the stands from the pitch and security forces armed with clubs and rifles patrol this perimeter. Although they are checked for weapons on entering the stadium,[16] fans sometimes throw fireworks, empty plastic water bottles, rocks or other debris on the field. Security forces escort referees. At matches, fan behaviour exhibits elements common to football matches in Europe or South America, but it would be misleading to see these as indicative of the globalization of fan styles. While the recent proliferation of satellite receivers has increased exposure to fan practices elsewhere, if the Yemeni model any behaviour, they copy that of the fans they see on television. However, fan cultures constructed through speech, clothing or music styles (cf. Armstrong, 1998) are not found in Yemen.

The Football Rivalries

Fixtures between rival clubs, primarily those premier division teams located in the same city,[17] generate the most popular interest and media coverage.[18]

12. With unemployment at 35 per cent, tickets are a luxury for many.

13. Stadiums have sections for dignitaries – ministry officials, government and business figures and honoured guests – but these barely differ from those for ordinary fans.

14. While reminiscent of Japanese baseball cheering sections (Whiting, 1989: 111–22), the style derives from traditional Yemeni dancing.

15. Despite strong emotions, owing to shared venues, fans exhibit none of the territoriality described by Bairner and Shirlow (1999a) for club-owned stadiums in Northern Ireland.

16. Traditionally-attired men wear a large dagger as a symbol of masculinity and adulthood. These weapons are prohibited in stadia.

17. Owing to MOYS limits on clubs, only the five largest cities have well-known, established intra-urban rivalries.

18. Hobsbawm (1968: 264) suggests intra-urban derbies in England and Scotland developed to make matches accessible and ultimately to control the working class. While the former explanation may apply to Yemen, the latter does not.

Guided by location, history and support, we focus on three rivalries: al-Tilal and al-Wahda of 'Aden; al-Sha'b and al-Ittihad of Ibb; and al-Ahli and al-Wahda of Sana'a.[19] A brief survey presents these.

The 'Aden Rivalry[20]

Introduced by British soldiers and merchant seamen, football has been played in parts of South Yemen since the 1880s (Stevenson, 1989a; Stevenson and Alaug, 1997). 'Aden, seat of PDRY government and Yemen's economic capital, is a sprawling city whose neighbourhoods spawned many football teams. For political and competitive reasons 'Aden clubs were consolidated three times. The al-Tilal vs al-Wahda rivalry dates from the 1975 merger that left one club in each quarter. Al-Tilal, located in Crater, traces its roots to the first all-Yemeni club,[21] Muhammadan's Union, founded about 1905. Despite its history, the club has a modest club-house with adjacent grounds. The Shaykh 'Uthman-based al-Wahda, founded in 1939, has a very large club-house with volleyball, basketball and tennis courts. Practice football fields are located elsewhere.[22] Although the football rivalry originated in neighbourhoods, it gained national prominence because the teams dominated PDRY football. Al-Wahda won the championship three times and al-Tilal captured the cup six times. Their fixtures, nicknamed 'the summit',[23] received extensive media coverage and were showpieces at which the government hosted visiting dignitaries. Loyal fans decorated their houses, businesses or cars with their team's colours. Meetings between the protagonists always attract special attention. For example, a non-league match played during Ramadan 1998 filled the stadium and remained a conversation topic for several weeks. Location and success account for the clubs' large memberships.

Prior to and immediately following unification both clubs enjoyed solid fan support, matches drew full houses and some contests were televised. Al-Tilal won the first Unity Cup[24] in 1990, but no southern team has won the title since. After union, government financial and logistical support declined

19. Club names have the following meanings: al-Ahli (National); al-Shab (People); al-Tilal (Hills); al-Ittihad (Union); and al-Wahda (Unity).

20. 'Aden fixtures are held in al-Hubayshi stadium. The British-built, former PDRY national stadium is located in Crater district. The pitch is surrounded by stands seating about 8,000. During rival fixtures, about 70 per cent of seats are reserved for fans of these clubs.

21. There were expatriate, Indian and mixed clubs in South Yemen in the late 19th century.

22. The PDRY confiscated properties, some of which were given to sports clubs. Since union the original owners have demanded restitution.

23. After unification the sobriquet changed to the ''Aden summit'.

24. Originated in 1990, the Unity Cup was awarded to the champion of the first unified season. Now the victor in a special, by-invitation, tournament held in conjunction with the 22 May unification anniversary, wins the Cup.

making it difficult for the teams to maintain their dominance. Today, clubs lack the resources to attract and retain the best players, some of whom have been lured away by competitors, or even to maintain club facilities or repair damages from the civil war. Following other clubs, al-Tilal and al-Wahda officials have begun to implement new income-generating strategies.

The Ibb Rivalry[25]

Football spread through North Yemen's southern uplands during the first quarter of the twentieth century with migrants returning from 'Aden or abroad. In Ibb, a city midway between Sana'a and 'Aden, football and other sports gained popularity partly because young people regarded them as evidence of national modernization. Before the 1962 revolution established the YAR, Ibb and several other cities had sports clubs. These remained autonomous until the YAR sports system was created in 1969. The Ibb rivalry dates from the beginning of the republic. Al-Sha'b was formed around 1964, and in the 1970s and 1980s the club attracted most of its members from the less-educated, apolitical 'children of the market',[26] but now all classes are represented. Founded in the late 1960s, in the 1970s and 1980s al-Fatuah became strongly associated with politically-inclined students. Unlike al-Sha'b, many al-Fatuah members and players relocated to Sana'a to attend university, so their club had neither a solid financial nor membership base, hence the team was relegated and promoted several times. In 1995, financial problems led to al-Fatuah merging with al-Salam, a first division club.[27] Named al-Ittihad, the new club assumed the mantle of al-Sha'b's rival.

The al-Sha'b and al-Ittihad club-houses are located a short distance from al-Kibsi Stadium. Al-Sha'b has several buildings with adjacent basketball and volleyball courts and plans to expand. Practice pitches are located elsewhere. Even though al-Sha'b has dominated the rivalry, the matches are hard fought and emotionally charged. The club's first president reported that before derbies he lectured his team on the importance of friendly competition and avoidance of violence. Al-Sha'b's supporters are probably the most fanatical and faithful in Yemen, but al-Ittihad's fans are not far behind.[28]

---

25. Ibb fixtures are played in al-Kibsi stadium located near the main market. This old facility, with seating on three sides, has a capacity of 5–6,000. Non-paying fans watch through a fence at the open end. Al-Ittihad and al-Sha'b fans sit on either side of the officials' box.

26. Yemeni society was divided into ascribed, ranked occupational groups. Marketeers were in the lowest stratum. However, this designation refers to modern attitudes and aspirations, not traditional statuses.

27. Officials predict financial difficulties will force more mergers and several are under discussion.

28. Ibb is sometimes referred to as the Napoli of Yemen.

and other expatriates taught boys and
950s there were a number of Yemeni
...hers associated with secondary schools
...t club, dates from 1937 and draws most
...ana'a residents. Club records list over
...utside a gate to the old city, al-Ahli has
...luding basketball and volleyball courts,
...The club has a full-time staff and is
...club, the Union of al-Ahli, that travels
...a, formed officially in 1962, probably
...nbers, numbering as many as al-Ahli's,
...ocated to the capital. The club-house,
including volley... courts, adjoins al-Dharafi stadium; the
practice pitch is in a suburb where a new club-house is planned.

The al-Ahli vs al-Wahda rivalry, also dubbed 'the Summit', is Yemen's best-known and most widely followed. Both clubs count among their past and present members government ministers, business leaders and military officers whose affiliations are widely known and add to the aura surrounding matches. Being in the capital, the media gives these clubs and their fixtures special attention. Both teams have strong records; in the 1990s each club won the championship three times.

Rivalries, Variations and Fan Loyalties

Regardless of league standing, fixtures between rivals are the season's high points. Newspapers provide extra coverage, fans become emotionally charged and players feel tremendous pressure. Play is often defensive resulting in low scores or draws. Violence during or after matches was not unusual in the 1970s and seems to be returning. With supporters present in large numbers, rival matches pose the greatest risk of disturbances. While cheering and jeering characterize fan behaviour, players and fans are sometimes pelted with stones and fights break out on the pitch and in the stands. In recent seasons, referees have stopped some matches because on-field fights spread into the stands, and police have been called in to prevent the disturbances continuing outside the grounds. Ministry and club officials blame these incidents on the intensity

29. Sana'a fixtures are played in al-Dharafi Stadium, a 10,000-seat facility near Liberation Square and the Republican Palace, built about 1962. Al-Ahli supporters congregate at the north end; Al-Wahda fans sit at the southern ends of the east and west stands.

30. The club was originally named Red Star.

of the rivalries.[31] The ministry encourages player and fan restraint, promoting cooperation between clubs.

Fan involvement extends to matches played by their rivals. For example, al-Tilal supporters might attend the al-Wahda ('Aden) vs Hassan match to cheer their rival's opponent, and occasionally such provocations turn ugly. For example, when Al-Sha'b hosted al-Sho'lah, al-Ittihad supporters sided with the latter team. Late in the game with the visitors leading 1–0, the al-Ittihad fans, hoping to be taken for al-Sha'b supporters, tried to force an early end to the contest by whistling, yelling and throwing stones. Security was increased and play continued. Al-Sha'b scored and the match ended in a draw. Afterwards, al-Sha'b fans stoned al-Ittihad's club-house and bus. While club loyalties are paramount, fans hold strong regional affiliations.[32] As the seat of ministries, businesses and a university, Sana'a attracts internal and repatriated migrants (Stevenson, 1993), and relocated football fans support any team from their birthplace especially when that club plays al-Ahli or al-Wahda (Sana'a). Ordinarily the home team has the advantage, but in Sana'a visiting teams often find the stands filled with supporters.

Regionalism is evident when al-Ahli or al-Wahda (Sana'a) play away matches because all spectators want to see them defeated (cf. Alabarces, 1999). In 'Aden, victories over Sana'a clubs carry special significance and violent episodes that suggest an inter-urban rivalry, reminiscent of pre-unification matches, are emerging. In 1992, fighting interrupted the al-Tilal vs al-Ahli match prompting the Yemen Football Association (YFA) to move al-Tilal's home fixtures to another city. In 1995, during the al-Wahda ('Aden) vs al-Wahda (Sana'a) match, rifle shots fired in the stands halted play. Such incidents stem from the shift in power since unification – the Sana'a clubs' dominance and the 'Aden clubs' decline – and, especially, southerners' opposition to northern control and anger over the destruction inflicted during civil war. While this may suggest 'ideological resistance', it would be premature to conclude that football has become a forum for political disturbances (cf. Stevenson, and Alaug, 1997; Tuastad, 1997).

Intra-urban derbies such as Celtic vs Rangers (Murray, 1984; Finn, 1994), Hearts vs Hibs (Hognestad, 1995), Flamengo vs Fluminese (Lever, 1983) or FC Barcelona vs Español (Colomé, 1997) are often 'underpinned by deeper historical and cultural divisions' (Giulianotti, 1999: 10). Despite superficial

31. To date, there is no connection between violence in stadiums and demonstrations and protests outside.

32. A number of studies illustrate football's connection to identity formation in culturally distinct regions (Gehrmann, 1997; Duke and Crolley, 1996; Lever, 1983). While less dramatic than European ethnic divisions, Yemeni regionalism is significant.

similarities, Yemen's rivalries are not sectarian, class or ethnically-based. Club loyalties are expressed fervently in the stadium, but usually remain within its walls; chants routinely celebrate a team, while those attacking a rival are not vituperative.[33] In the absence of jackets, hats or other emblems, team affiliation is not advertised, and members of rival clubs are welcome in each other's club-houses. Match-day opponents socialize off the pitch; and brothers or fathers and sons, including many from prominent families, belong to rival clubs.[34] When disturbances occur they appear to be situational and opportunistic rather than planned or arising from long-standing animosities. This suggests that an intense 'we–they' opposition, such as the 'radically negative' images of opponents constructed by Argentinian fans (Alabarces, 1999), is not part of Yemen's intra-urban football. Regional sentiments are more deeply rooted. Binary oppositions are present in these rivalries where teams symbolize cultural differences or evoke memories of real or perceived inequities, which is most evident in the growing Sana'a vs 'Aden enmity provoked by political, military and social factors.

Hidden, Political Rivalries

To devotees and casual fans, rivalries are contested on the pitch, but, as is generally true of Yemeni sports, these competitions have political dimensions. Pre-independence South Yemen clubs were linked to liberation groups; after independence most officials were members of the Socialist Party. While political parties were prohibited in North Yemen, since the 1950s club leaders have included modernists who favoured progressive policies. After unification, parties were legalized and club elections were politicized. This changed as Yemen's president's party gained ascendancy and most clubs elected officers affiliated with it believing this might facilitate new or stronger links.

Clubs compete for control of sports policy, political influence and access to financial support. These practices are not new, but acquire greater prominence as private support replaces government subsidy. We refer to these as 'hidden' rivalries because, like hidden or informal economies where transactions are known but not reported in official records, club officials' activities often extend beyond the normal sports sphere or circumvent established lines

---

33. An example is this al-Sha'b chant taunting its rival, 'Hurricane, hurricane and in your eyes there is only envy' (meaning that its team is like a hurricane and al-Ittihad can only be jealous). This pales in comparison to the enmity of Rangers or Celtic songs (Bradley, 1998).

34. Yemeni President Ibrahim al-Hamdi (1974–7) was a member of al-Ahli while his brother 'Abd Allah was a member of al-Wahda; the current YFA President played for al-Wahda (Sana'a) and his brother for al-Ahli; and a former Minister of Youth and Sport was President of al-Ahli while his son played for al-Wahda (Sana'a). Lever (1983) reports similar patterns in Brazil.

of authority. Fans know of these dealings, although not necessarily the specifics, but do not believe they determine or undermine match outcomes. Hidden rivalries are enacted in several ways as discussed below.

Ministry of Youth and Sport and Yemen Football Association Offices

Clubs compete to place their representatives in important offices. MOYS and YFA officials determine sports policies and, while unproven, the popular perception is that club affiliation influences decisions. The recent success of al-Wahda (Sana'a), for example, is attributed to its control of the 'Ministry of al-Wahda'. MOYS officials, especially al-Wahda members, deny preferential treatment, and argue that al-Ahli controls more important posts and assert that contests are played on the field not in the ministry.

The situation is clearer with the YFA whose decisions about season structure, match schedules and referee assignments may affect results. Owing to a tight budget, prior to the 1998–9 season the YFA considered splitting the premier division. Rumours placed al-Ahli in the weaker group to insure it reaching the finals.[35] This illustrates the YFA officials' power. Since each of the 233 clubs has one vote in YFA elections, candidates' club affiliations cannot guarantee selection. To be successful, a nominee must be well-known and respected and either he or his club must have links to other clubs. Al-Ahli sent its team to Hadhramawt province to practice with and conduct clinics for some lower division clubs. This forged ties between the clubs and, in elections, al-Ahli's candidates may receive support from these new allies. If this happens, the Hadhramawt clubs' rivals will support other challengers.

Club Alliances

As the foregoing shows, some clubs may become allies. Some premier division clubs are suspected of being allies on the pitch and in official business but their relationships are not discussed openly. For example, during the late 1980s, al-Sha'b felt some animosity towards al-Ahli, apparently due to the latter's dominance, but had good relations with al-Wahda (Sana'a), one of whose players had joined al-Sha'b. Near the season's end, al-Sha'b agreed to lose to al-Wahda so that the club might wrest the championship from al-Ahli. Despite al-Sha'b fans' charges that their players had been bought, al-Wahda won the match. In late 1998, an al-Ahli officer was rumoured to have offered a weak Sana'a premier division club a large sum of money. While we suspect an

---

35. Yemen Times (1998) identified the proposed alignment but neither group was markedly weaker. This structure takes effect in the 1999–2000 season.

alliance was being attempted, apart from electoral support its benefits are not apparent.

Money and Influence

Maintaining facilities and fielding teams are expensive but clubs do not bear these costs alone. Premier division clubs receive YR80,000 ($570) from the Ministry, support comparable to that in the YAR, but lower than subsidies in the PDRY. Since 1996, the MOYS Youth Fund has provided grants. In 1998, each club received YR500,000 ($3,500). The YFA provides modest travel expenses, and clubs receive 35 per cent of ticket receipts that average about YR25,000 ($175) per match.

The costs of recruiting or keeping players, expenses for training and travel, and rewards to players have increased while subsidies have held steady and inflation eroded their purchasing power. Many clubs are experiencing financial problems. While money does not buy success, clubs with the deepest pockets usually have the strongest teams.[36] There are two ways to supplement funds: rents and donations. Rents are a common income source and al-Ahli's preeminent position is partially explained by the revenue its twelve, centrally-located stores have generated over the last thirty years. In 1998, monthly rents yielded YR350,000 ($2,625), about half the club's expenses for the period. Al-Sha'b also earns income from its well-placed shops.

In 1984, the YAR ministry encouraged other clubs to follow al-Ahli's example and provided each club with land on which they can build stores. In the PDRY, clubs derived income from leasing shops and renting premises for social events. Since unification, some effort has been made to equalize club resources but land is only a start. Clubs must finance construction work. Clubs solicit gifts from businessmen or corporations,[37] or use connections to get special ministerial assistance. In a society where the politics of personal connection prevails, clubs with prominent members are more successful in gaining favours or securing contributions for equipment, travel or construction.

Since prestigious members are essential, clubs compete to enrol them. Some clubs have made organizational changes to reward influential figures with titled positions. Most clubs have a president[38] responsible for daily affairs, and an honorary president[39] obligated to use his position and associations to obtain

---

36. There are exceptions. Al-Ittihad, financially the weakest of the clubs discussed, won the 1998 President's Cup and played respectably in the 1999 Arab Champions' Cup.

37. Sponsorship is essential on the national level as well. Corporations underwrite the President's Cup and contributions partially support the football league.

38. This sometimes onerous position is filled by a volunteer.

39. Unlike presidents in early-twentieth century Lima (Stein, 1988), Yemeni officials' actions are not intended to ingratiate them to their members.

monies from his business, the ministry or other agency, to arrange corporate sponsorship or recruit respected men on the club's behalf. Each of the six clubs discussed has many economically or politically influential men on their rosters. Before unification both Sana'a and 'Aden clubs were renowned for counting many high-ranking government officials among their members. The 'Aden clubs' decline in the number of prominent members corresponds with the socialist party's loss of power and the relocation of ministries to Sana'a. Now, like Ibb clubs, they often enlist officials from outside their area.

To increase fund raising, al-Ahli and al-Wahda (Sana'a) created honorary councils, a strategy copied by some other clubs. Like honorary presidents, members of council[40] are expected to use personal and professional networks to the clubs' benefit. In mid-1998, al-Wahda (Sana'a) converted the presidency to a hands-on position.[41] The club filled the post with a long-term backer, a relative of Yemen's President and chairman of a cement corporation who contributed money and drew support from his associates. Seeing the benefits of this new position, al-Ahli replied in kind, selecting another relative of Yemen's President who chairs the national drug company.[42]

Given these machinations, what can officials accomplish? Three recent cases are suggestive: (1) Al-Ahli played training matches in Eritrea, and the 'new' president used his networks to pay for travel and team expenses. (2) Arguing that training on grass would improve the national team, Yemen's President ordered irrigation pumps for al-Ahli's practice fields. Kinship ties explain al-Ahli's good fortune. Al-Wahda's connections were mobilised to obtain pumps from the Youth Fund. (3) Most clubs need money to build rental properties, but the Youth Fund supported al-Ahli's application to build ten additional shops, a decision suggesting the importance of contacts.

Hidden rivalries appear divorced from the playing field but victories in fund-raising and influence-wielding are linked to the pitch. A 'new' president met with a prominent member of a contending club, offered YR2,500,000 ($17,600) for capital improvements and suggested that team lose so the President's club would win the championship. The proffer, if serious, was declined. Honorary council and 'new' presidents may use their positions to benefit other clubs. The honorary president of a Ta'izz club is from a wealthy family that owns Yemen's largest corporation. He hired Iraqi coaches for his side and for a rival club.[43] A recently promoted premier division Sana'a club

---

40. Al-Ahli's honorary council members serve three-year terms.

41. Management of daily affairs remains in the hands of a volunteer whose position was renamed.

42. When selected, the official was serving as president of al-Sha'b's honorary council, a position he continued to hold.

43. This practice of supporting rival clubs is common. The Minister of Local Administration supports both Ibb clubs. Like formal leaders, these actions help gain control of networks.

is reported to have asked the 'new' al-Ahli president for money; he responded by raising YR100,000 ($705) which he distributed between the requesting club, al-Wahda (Sana'a), and al-Ahli.[44] When al-Wahda travelled to Saudi Arabia for a match,[45] the club president and al-Ahli's president, who allegedly provided YR600,000 ($4225) towards expenses, accompanied the team. The leaders stated their cooperative effort was intended to help reduce tensions between their clubs. While these manoeuvres bear a superficial resemblance to those described by Portelli (1993) for Napoli's power-brokers and owners, Yemeni club officials are not perceived as self-interested, are not thought to have different goals and motivations than fans, and their actions are not defined as corrupt (cf. Giulianotti, 1999).

In their hidden competitions, club officials' actions include: (1) helping competitors to preserve rivalries; (2) assisting other clubs to reinforce and maintain the sport system; (3) avoiding the appearance of self-interest to increase prestige; (4) demonstrating connections to substantiate power and influence; and (5) giving precedence to the public good to express civic responsibility. While these actions appear sports-specific and lack a common, self-serving purpose, we speculate that (1) the officials' styles follow traditional leadership patterns, and that (2) as heads of voluntary associations, officials are poised to be leaders of emerging civil society institutions.

Azoy (1982) describes how Afghani khans are more concerned with successfully organizing buzkashi contests than how their teams perform. The games are a metaphor for a political process characterized by competition and cooperation; leaders use buzkashi to enhance their reputations and public profiles. Parkes (1996) illustrates how Pakistani polo became the basis for long-term, status-crossing alliances in which matches created confederations. Like the paradoxical goals of Afghani or Pakistani leaders, Yemeni club officials cooperate and compete with each other, using their positions to establish personal networks and to build and maintain their reputations. Even though the 'new' presidents are kin from a powerful family we think they follow similar patterns. Leadership positions afford them opportunities for public recognition, to polish their skills, and through club successes to demonstrate personal attributes. They are prepared to mobilize their membership during elections or political unrest and, as Yemen democratizes, work to maintain the regime and its control of public organizations. While personal advantage seems to take precedence over team performance, victories remain important to club officials.

44. The sums were respectively: YR30,000 ($210); YR30,000 ($210); and YR40,000 ($285).

45. This case also shows the role played by presidents. The head of Yemen's airline was solicited to provide the team with reduced airfares.

The decisions of officials reflect the dyadic nature of Yemeni and Middle Eastern leadership. Men validate their positions as patrons by fulfilling obligations to their clients in formally-defined vertical networks, and as mediators by utilizing connections to others to expand horizontal networks (cf. Fernea and Fernea 1987: 330–2). In the former case, preserving the status quo is central; in the latter instance, accumulating social capital (Bourdieu, 1983) is the goal. Achieving these ends requires leaders to alternate between competition and cooperation, so permanent enmities are prevented.

Yemen has a long history of civil activism built upon such groups as syndicates, self-help organizations and, since unification, political parties. Despite attempted co-option and repression by the government, these civil-society institutions have maintained their independence and helped to shape the contemporary socio-economic and political milieu (Carapico, 1998). As voluntary associations in rural areas, sports clubs contributed to this process through links with local development associations. The situation appears to have been different in cities where premier division clubs were not tied to local institutions. Because they were subject more directly to ministerial control upon whose support they depended, urban clubs were co-opted by the state. The move toward privatization, however, opens the door for these clubs to emerge as significant civil institutions. We agree with Allison (1998) that sports clubs may be important components of civil society, but as Putnam (1993: 245) suggests for Italy, in Yemen this role is not linked to sporting values but political power. We suggest that prominent men are attracted to club service not merely for reasons of titular status or prestige aggrandisement but because of the growing influence these positions may wield.

To conclude, Yemen's rivalries are waged in private and on the pitch. The hidden machinations conducted in offices provide some clubs with fiscal, material and player advantages – all of which might make clubs dominant. But neither money, equipment nor coaches prevent player mistakes or teams playing poorly, so match results remain the most transparent measure of success. The essence of rivalry is found on the pitch and trophies on the shelf. In late 1998, the al-Ahli's 'new' president, whose rival won the preceding three championships, remarked privately that he would do anything to end al-Wahda's reign. When the 1998–9 season ended, al-Ahli claimed the title.

12

'The Colours Make Me Sick': America FC and Upward Mobility in Mexico

Roger Magazine*

Larissa Lomnitz is an anthropologist known for her writings on both marginal and elite communities in urban Latin America. In an influential article on the social structure of urban Mexico, Lomnitz derives an explanatory model from local actors and their self-conceptions of their experiences. In doing so, Lomnitz (1982: 52) frames her discussion of 'the process by which actors get matched to positions within the existing power structure'. Her model likens the urban Mexican social structure to a set of pyramids, with each containing a stack of horizontal layers. Actors in each layer mediate between a single patron above them and various clients below, creating a series of smaller pyramids within larger ones. These mediators represent the interests of their clients to the layers above, providing clients with services and jobs in exchange for loyalty and support. Successful performance, as a mediator in these 'vertical' relations, often depends on access to resources provided by 'horizontal' relations to friends and kin. According to Lomnitz, the four main pyramids or sectors of urban Mexico's social structure are: the public sector or state apparatus, the organized labour sector, the private sector, and the informal labour sector. Lomnitz posits that this pyramid model, with its incorporation of vertical and horizontal relations, is useful for understanding social processes and political stability in urban Mexico because it is a self-fulfilling prophecy. While it models, it also informs and elicits action for those seeking upward mobility (ibid.: 52).

This chapter describes a different but complementary local model of social structure and action to that of Lomnitz. The model presented here is depicted by my informants as an idiom of football fandom, and contributes

* The Wenner–Gren Foundation for Anthropological Research funded the research in Mexico on which this chapter is based. Portions of this chapter were written while I was a Fulbright scholar in Norway, where the Department and Museum of Anthropology, University of Oslo, was my generous host institution.

to understanding social relations in urban Mexico. This other Mexican (or perhaps Latin American) model divides social relations into two incompatible types: horizontal or egalitarian relations characterized by solidarity, and vertical or hierarchical relations characterized by competition for upward mobility. Furthermore, it divides people into those attracted by the former or the latter type of relation. I do not contradict Lomnitz's argument that horizontal relations, such as kinship or friendship, facilitate upward mobility. I believe that even people who classify themselves as solidarity-minded recognize and practice this upwardly-directed use of 'horizontal' relations. Rather, I want to suggest that not everyone in Mexico is constantly interested in upward mobility and that actors may recognize the potential for tensions between relations of solidarity and those linked to political or economic upward mobility.

Solidarity versus Upward Mobility in Latin America

Scholars concerned with local understandings of social relations in Mexico and elsewhere in Latin America have frequently noted the solidarity-upward mobility dichotomy. The late anthropologist Eric Wolf's (1955, 1957, 1986) writings on types of peasant communities in Mesoamerica, the cultural region reaching from Honduras to the highlands of central Mexico, are probably the best-known illustrations. Wolf revolutionized thinking about Meso-american communities by demonstrating how anthropological tendencies to focus on bounded, traditional cultures obscure the fact that supposedly isolated and timeless 'Indians' can be more fruitfully understood as peasants, integrated into regional, national and global economies in historically-determined manners. He suggests that communities tend towards a closed corporate form and cultural orientation, whilst the Spanish colonial government developed a system of indirect rule through an organized communal structure between peasants and the outside world. On the other hand, communities with an open cultural orientation (in which the peasants' direct contact with the outside world is unmediated by communal structures) arose 'in response to the rising demand for cash crops which accompanied the development of capitalism in Europe' (1955: 462). Wolff's characterization of the cultural orientations of the two types of communities clearly indicates which type I see as related to solidarity and which one I connect to upward mobility:

> The corporate community frowns on individual accumulation and display of wealth and strives to reduce the effects of such accumulation on the communal structure. It resists reshaping of relationships; it defends the traditional equilibrium. The open-ended community permits and expects individual accumulation and display of wealth during periods of rising outside demand and allows this new wealth much influence in the periodic reshaping of social ties. (ibid.: 462)

More recently, anthropologist James Greenberg (1989), known for his writings on the Chatino peoples of the Mexican state of Oaxaca, located this dichotomy within individual communities where it is manifested through violent political struggle between two factions, each attempting to arrange the community's social relations to its liking.

Lesley Gill (1997) is an anthropologist who has studied the effects of economic change on peasants, miners and domestic workers in Bolivia. She frames the solidarity-upward mobility tension within the recent global political-economic shift from Fordism, with its state-controlled national economies and strong workers' unions, to neo-liberalism, which requires a transnational economy and 'flexible', individualized workers. She shows that neo-liberal reforms closed the large state-run tin mines and fragmented the powerful miners' union. The ex-miners, forced to compete with each other as street vendors, still yearn mostly for the 'solidarity' and 'co-operation' of the mines. In other words, miners conceptualize the change they have experienced in terms of the shift from social relations based on solidarity to those based on individualized upward mobility. In this new situation, people must turn to hierarchical, clientelistic relations to get by, completing the realignment of social relations from egalitarian miners' unions to individualized, vertically-oriented street venders.

In the case presented here, actors conceptualize this dichotomous model of social relations through the idiom of football fandom. This model contributes to understandings of clientelism in Mexico and elsewhere. It suggests a way of thinking about 'the process by which actors get matched to positions within the existing power structure' (Lomnitz, 1982: 52), but in a manner that Lomnitz does not address. That is, how does an actor initiate a patron–client relation from the client position? Or, in other words, how do some people get themselves 'promoted' to higher client positions over others at the same horizontal level? Lomnitz suggests that such promotions have little to do with support from below, and instead occur through exchanges with patrons where the client offers his loyalty, dedication and personal charisma to the patron (ibid.: 55, 59). Hence, we can imagine that promotion must be an extensive, time-consuming process. What I want to suggest here, however, is that the local Mexican model includes the possibility that such relationships can be established more quickly through actions that signal a propensity for or commitment to loyalty and dedication and to upward mobility more generally. If we begin with a local model that divides people into those concerned with horizontal solidarity and those concerned with vertical mobility, then the first signal a want-to-be client must give to a potential patron is one that associates him with the latter category of persons. Many

Mexico City residents, whether or not they are football fans, disparagingly claim that being a fan of the football club known as 'América' is one of these signals.[1]

The Mexican Football League

To discuss how América's fans are portrayed by their rivals we must begin with a contextualization of the clubs within Mexico's professional football league. The majority of the eighteen league teams have a regional fan base. However, most Mexican fans cheer for one of four 'national' teams, defined as such because they have a large, nationwide fan base and because fans do not follow them through their explicit association with a city or region. Instead, fans are supposedly drawn to these teams because of their association with other categories of persons. Three of these teams, América F.C., Cruz Azul and the Pumas of the National Autonomous University of Mexico (UNAM) play their home games in the capital, Mexico City, where about one-fifth of the country's 90 million inhabitants reside.[2] The country's second largest city, Guadalajara, is home to the fourth national team, Las Chivas.[3] Probably because these four teams have larger fan bases than the regional teams and are thus richer, they tend to remain near the top of the league standings year after year.

According to popular wisdom, Las Chivas (the Goats)[4] has the largest following of these four teams. As one Pumas fan explained to me,[5] Chivas fans are from *las clases populares* (the popular classes)[6] and are drawn to the team because of its philosophy of '*puros Mexicanos*' (pure Mexicans): unlike every other league team, Chivas only contract Mexican nationals to play for them. Thus, Chivas fans are supposedly attracted by the team's association with nationalist sentiments. For these fans, a Chivas victory signifies the success

1. In Mexico, as in the rest of Latin America, 'América', considered as team or place, refers to the Americas (North and South) and not to the United States of America.

2. Mexico City hosts two other teams, Atlante and Necaxa, which are not considered 'national'.

3. Guadalajara, with a population of about five million, hosts two other teams, Atlas and los Tecos, which do not have a national fan base.

4. In Mexico, unlike English-speaking countries, to be a 'goat' in a team-sports context does not have any negative implications.

5. Most of the descriptions of teams and their fans in this chapter come from recorded interviews with Pumas fans with whom I conducted extended ethnographic research. However, in casual conversations, fans of other teams and non-fans characterized the teams in the same manner. América fans are somewhat exceptional since they do not explicitly portray their fandom in the same manner as non-América fans.

6. 'The popular classes' is a necessarily vague category used to describe the wide variety of impoverished and oppressed social groups in Mexico and in Latin America more generally. The category 'working class' is too limited to include the many unemployed, street vendors and others who are included in the idea of the popular classes.

of an independent Mexico in the context of a long history of political, economic and football-related submission to, and dependency upon, North America and Europe.

América FC is known as the country's second most popular team, but since its fans are the focus of this chapter, I discuss them later. Cruz Azul (Blue Cross), the third most popular team, is named after the cement company that owns it. Fans of Cruz are supposedly attracted by the team's association with the working class, and in particular with construction workers. The Pumas of UNAM are considered to have the fourth largest following in the country. Pumas fans are supposedly attracted by the team's philosophy of '*puros jóvenes*' (pure youths). Unlike other clubs, Pumas 'give young players a chance' by using players from its *fuerzas básicas* (basic forces) – a youth league – rather than signing proven players from other teams.[7] In the early 1960s, an Argentine coach, Renato Cesarini, introduced this philosophy and the basic forces system to the Pumas and Mexico. Cesarini is a direct link between the Pumas and the Argentine notion of *el pibe*,[8] the young boy whose individualistic, restless and undisciplined football play symbolizes the Argentine football style (Archetti, 1998). Cesarini, himself *un pibe* as a player, thus introduced Mexico to the idea that the best football is not found in mature, older players, but in the undisciplined, creative style of boys.

Among fans of other teams, the *puros jóvenes* philosophy of the Pumas is important because the team is known as the breeding ground for the country's best players. Fans sometimes draw an analogy between UNAM's scientific-bureaucratic training of the country's leaders and the Pumas' training of the country's leading players.[9] However, although the Pumas were the first team in Mexico to have 'basic forces', many other clubs now have their own youth leagues and no longer depend so much upon the Pumas to train young players.

Whereas fans of other teams value the Pumas' philosophy of pure youths because it supplies their teams with players, Pumas fans are drawn to the team because of its young players and its association with youth. They claim that because the players are young, they still play for the love of the game and the team *camiseta* (jersey) and not out of personal interest as do older, jaded professional players. Thus, the fans argue, the players play with more passion and the team plays an aggressive, attacking style of football that favours

7. About one-quarter of the club's players at any one time did not come up through the basic forces. Most of these players still qualify as *jóvenes* (youths) according to fans. Additionally, the team usually includes at least a couple of older players, who may or may not have been trained in the basic forces and who are supposed to guide and teach the younger players.

8. I am grateful to Eduardo Archetti for pointing out this link to me.

9. Most of the recent Mexican presidents have studied at UNAM, before obtaining an economics degree at an Ivy League school in the United States.

excitement over the dull and conservative tactics of other teams. Many Pumas fans view themselves as youths and state that they, in particular, can identify with the players' feelings. They explain that these frustrations and desires arise out of the frequent fact that one needs experience to get a job and one needs a job to get experience – a catch-22 situation which the Pumas' practice of 'giving young players a chance' allows the players to bypass. The Pumas fans claim, however, that the exclusion of youths has positive aspects as well. Exclusion from the patron–client relations of Mexico's economy and polity can allow them to maintain a critical stance towards these exploitative relations, while those who participate in such relations are compliant and uncritical. Therefore, the young Pumas fans also associate their youth and their choice of team with opposition towards the political-economic order. The young fans derive much of the particular content and form of this opposing stance from an institutional trajectory that they are part of, or aspire to join, and with which the team is associated: UNAM,[10] with its Marxist educational inclination and its tradition of student movements in protest against Mexico's undemocratic and clientelistic political and economic systems.[11]

Fans of these three teams generally group themselves on the solidarity side of the upwardly-mobile-solidarity divide. However, each group of fans conceives of this solidarity in different ways. For Chivas fans, solidarity relates to Mexicans; for Cruz Azul fans, it means solidarity among the working classes; and for Pumas fans, it refers to solidarity among youths or among people who take a particular, Marxist-intellectual-urban stance of political opposition. Since each version of solidarity includes people in particular ways, rather than including all people, it also excludes certain categories. For example, Chivas fans' solidarity would likely exclude the Central American migrants passing through and working in Mexico. Cruz Azul's solidarity would exclude the

10. Although the football club continues to use the University's name and facilities, it is no longer administered by UNAM. They first joined the Mexican football league in the early 1960s as an amateur team, drawing players entirely from the student body of UNAM. In the early 1970s, in an effort to compete in the improving league by making the team professional, but at the same time to protect UNAM from financial loss, a group of university alumni formed a non-profit-making corporation separate from UNAM that would sponsor and administer the team. Profits from ticket sales and television contracts would be directed back to the team or to UNAM whereas the alumni on the board of directors would absorb any financial losses incurred by the corporation. No other team in the Mexican First Division football league, not even the other university team, is administered in this non-profit manner. Although the team usually includes one or two players who study at UNAM, it is not obligated to include any UNAM students.

11. UNAM embodies this contradiction between solidarity and upward mobility. Viewed synchronically, UNAM breeds student movements with egalitarian objectives. Viewed diachronically, a degree received from UNAM and, perhaps more importantly, contacts made at UNAM are essential for upward mobility through the state bureaucracy.

street-sellers and peasants who usually earn less than industrial workers. The Pumas fans' solidarity excludes people who do not fit into the Marxist-intellectual mould, including workers in Mexico City and everyone outside of the capital. For example, at games against Cruz Azul, Pumas fans chant that their rivals are drunken, pot-bellied construction workers. When they travel to away games outside Mexico City, they enter the stadium chanting: 'Now civilization has arrived!' Even though Pumas fans do not follow the team because of its capital associations, it is significant that the team makes Mexico City its home. Although Pumas fans may claim that they do not want to rise through the national power structure located in Mexico City, their solidarity is still drawn towards the centre of national power in an effort to oppose the power structure.[12]

Being an Americanista

In contrast to these three representations of fan solidarity, América FC fans are portrayed by their rivals as concerned with upward mobility. They claim that fans are drawn to América because of its association with political and economic power – a power associated not with collective solidarity, but with vertical flows through the clientelist pyramid. In this model, since this power reaches levels of greater and greater concentration in the individuals higher up in the pyramid, people such as América fans who are concerned with upward mobility are drawn not just to the pyramid but to its apex. America is associated with hierarchical power because its owner, the television broadcasting conglomerate Televisa, is commonly depicted as a close ally of the urban elite and of the Institutional Revolutionary Party (PRI) that has controlled the national government for the past eighty years. The national government and the PRI are practically synonymous since no other party besides the PRI has controlled the current government, and the PRI uses its governmental control to win re-election.

Blurred Boundaries: The PRI, Televisa, and América FC

In 1955, the owners of the three television broadcasting companies in Mexico decided to merge in order to share the costs of broadcasting to a wider audience (Jauregui Morales, 1995: 13). After merging, the new conglomerate, Telesistema Mexicano (now named Televisa), had a monopoly on television broadcasting in Mexico. This occurred when the national government was paying little attention to television as an educational and political tool or as a source of tax revenues (Pérez Espino, 1991; Trejo Delarbre, 1992). Following the student movements of 1968, the government faced its first serious legitimation crisis

---

12. See Magazine (1999) for further discussion of Pumas fandom.

since its installation in 1919 following the Revolution;[13] it thus realized the significance of its lack of access to a key component of mass communication that could otherwise help to spread its perspective on social events (Pérez Espino, 1991: 27). Consequently, the government passed a law that would give Televisa a choice between a crippling 25 per cent tax and a 49 per cent government control of its programming content (ibid.: 28–9). But the government's attempt to impose itself on the television industry came too late; the monopoly had grown too strong (Trejo Delarbe, 1992). Televisa, using its access to the communication media, publicly opposed the government's efforts as unconstitutional, and forced the government to repeal the new law (Pérez Espino, 1991: 31). Out of this confrontation grew a symbiotic relationship between Televisa and the government, each recognizing the other's power and interests. In this relationship, the government taxes Televisa at a very low rate considering its high profits, and in return Televisa portrays the government and, during election years, the PRI in a favourable light (Mejía Barquera, 1988). Although the government has periodically attempted to gain direct control over television by establishing state-owned stations, this symbiosis has lasted until this day.

Besides advancing the interests of the government and the PRI, Televisa also uses its control over the production and dissemination of television programming to promote the ideology of Mexico's urban economic elite. For example, in its treatment of labour disputes on news programmes, Televisa has ignored the perspective of workers and has falsely accused them of conspiring with foreign interests to discredit the Mexican nation (Trejo Delarbre, 1992: 47–9). Furthermore, on its commercial-free, educational channel, Televisa reproduces the elite notion that culture refers solely to North American and European culture through the exclusion of any Mexican content (Pérez Espino, 1991: 61). Unsurprisingly, many Mexicans who are critical of the country's undemocratic one-party system and its extremely unequal distribution of wealth do not take Televisa's portrayals as 'the truth', and come to loathe Televisa for its complicity in these injustices. In fact, it seems that Televisa receives disproportionate blame for the country's ills. The example of public opinion regarding Televisa's rivals – state-owned stations and their current, privatized form, TV Azteca – illustrates this point. Although the state-owned stations were even more biased towards the PRI during elections than Televisa, and TV Azteca's political coverage is almost indistinguishable from

13. The Mexican Revolution (1910–19) was a series of conflicts and popular uprisings that brought an end to Porfirio Díaz's 35-year dictatorship and led to the ratification of a new constitution which guaranteed, among other things, the redistribution of land to peasants.

that of Televisa, the latter was and still is much more heavily criticized (Trejo Delarbre, 1992: 46). Perhaps because of its daily presence in people's homes, Televisa, and by association América, has become a lightning rod for criticism of the government, the economic elite and Mexico's hierarchical power structure in general. This association between Televisa- América and hierarch- ical power is so pervasive that among Mexico City residents who claim to be on the solidarity side of the solidarity-upward mobility divide, a common way of accusing someone of pursuing upward mobility is to call them an *Americanista*, whether or not the person is actually an América follower. Further, non-América fans often refer to the club as '*el equipo de los ricos*' (the team of the rich), which refers to the team's association with Mexico's rich and powerful, and not to its fans who mostly come from the *clases populares*.

As noted earlier, Lomnitz (1982) posits that securing a position in the pyramid and moving up through it requires an upward exchange of loyalty, dedication and personal charisma. Non- América fans claim that being an América fan, as an act of conspicuous consumption, can help to secure a 'higher' and more powerful client position. On one occasion, a Pumas fan explained to me that the América fans in her office did not really care about football at all; she explained further that they wear América paraphernalia to work, and watch the team's games and talk about them at work, with the intention of showing off this allegiance to office superiors. Furthermore, she asserted that they did this to demonstrate their dedication to vertical relations with the hope of obtaining promotion. Signalling a dedication to vertical relations also implies a rejection of solidarity relations at the horizontal level. This rejection is important to patrons because solidarity among workers can lead to collective demands that threaten the patron's power by decreasing the individual worker's dependency on him.

If horizontal relations threaten the flows of power in hierarchical relations, then in a similar way vertical relations threaten the integrity of solidarity relations. For example, in the workplace, even the presence of a few *Americanistas* who align themselves with bosses as *consentidos* (favourites; spoiled ones) is enough to threaten workers' ability to make demands as a group. This threat is even greater when the 'favourites' display the dedication and personal charisma necessary to become leaders themselves, by pursuing promotions, and as a consequence re-align some of their fellow workers towards vertical relations. Therefore, since relations of solidarity and patron–client ties are not compatible, it follows that those who favour solidarity feel threatened by and thus despise América, its fans, and all others who could be metaphorically classified as *Americanistas*.

Loathing for América FC: Physical and Verbal Aggression

The loathing that followers of other teams feel for *Americanistas* takes the form of verbal attacks and physical violence at football matches. Pumas fans, for example, gathering outside their stadium before all other home games, ignore fans of the opposing team as they pass by on their way to the ticket booths and entrances. However, before games against América, many Pumas fans direct disparaging comments at their rivals. Perhaps in order to avoid more personal and serious confrontations, the comments are usually aimed at the rival's paraphernalia and choice of team and not at other aspects of his person. For example, Pumas fans often exclaim '*Estos colores me dan asco!*' (those colours make me sick!) when referring to an opposing fan and his canary yellow and sky blue América jersey. The latter comment expresses an important characteristic of Pumas fans' understanding of their loathing for *Americanistas*: it is a deeply engrained bodily revulsion that they cannot control.

Pumas fans' threatening comments outside the stadium escalate to physical attacks inside the stadium, but these are still usually aimed at América paraphernalia and not at the fans themselves. If someone displaying an América jersey or banner walks into the Pumas fans' side of the stadium, he receives verbal abuse until, eventually, a couple of Pumas fans descend upon him and strip him of the shirt or flag. The aggressors then tear their prize into strips to divide it among fellow fans, who burn their share, tie it together with other strips to make a long rope, or take it home as a souvenir. Although Pumas fans verbally abused fans of teams other than América if they entered the Pumas' side of the stadium, I never observed Pumas fans seizing their paraphernalia.

Occasionally, the Pumas fans' attacks escalate to beatings as fans confront one another when leaving the stadium. Often, these beatings occur when an América fan exchanges words with a Pumas fan, perhaps assuming that the equality of the one-to-one match-up will prevent an actual fight from occurring. But he then finds himself surrounded and only then realizes that he has confronted an entire group. The Pumas fans generally let their frightened victim scurry away without serious harm after a few blows.

Although Pumas fans are less aggressive when they visit América's stadium, they, and not América fans, are still the principal aggressors. Yet, whenever they confront the fans of other teams and especially those from outside Mexico City, the Pumas fans are more often than not victims rather than aggressors. Therefore, we must look to the inter-fan relationship and not to any essential characteristics of Pumas fans to explain the opposition's inequality. Pumas fans see América and the hierarchical relations they represents as a direct threat to the solidarity among youths that defines their fandom. Conversely, América fans, concerned with individual upward mobility, view the success of other individuals or individual teams and not the solidarity of Pumas fans as their greatest obstacle. Furthermore, Pumas fans can get away with aggressive acts more often than América fans because their superior numbers give them strength. Here, by 'superior numbers'. I refer not to the total number of fans in attendance, but to the fact that Pumas fans, in putting ideas about egalitarian solidarity into practice, usually attend the games with large groups of friends or with organized cheering groups, whereas América fans attend with their families or with smaller groups of friends. Thus, attention to the solidarity-upward mobility divide suggests why Pumas fans' verbal and physical attacks on América fans are not reciprocated.

América FC According to Americanistas

When América fans give reasons for their support, they do not simply repeat the explanations provided by non- América fans. Rather, they claim to be drawn to the team because of its winning tradition and because the team only signs high-priced superstars. I often heard América fans say that they were devoted to the team because it was the 'best' in the league and had the 'best' and 'most expensive' players. In contrast, Pumas or Chivas fans are proud of the fact that they continue to support their team even when it plays quite badly, since their devotion to the team depends on principles (that is, pure youths and pure Mexicans) that outlast individual seasons and players.

América, like the Pumas or Chivas, occasionally have a bad season, and although they usually reach the eight team play-off at the end of each half-season,[14] they have not won a championship for over ten years. Thus, it would seem that América constantly lose and gain fans depending on their performance. However, América's home attendance figures suggest that this is not the case. Furthermore, América fans continue to claim that their team is the best, even when its record is quite poor, and they continue to speak of its winning tradition despite the recent lack of championships. Rival fans attribute these 'delusions' to the fact that América fans, being uncritical by nature, are easily duped by Televisa's biased promotion of its team. Indeed, I have observed how Televisa sportscasters, whether they are covering an América game or even a game not involving the club,[15] shamelessly and exaggeratedly promote

14. After each half-year regular season, the first and second-placed teams in each of four divisions participate in the play-off. However, if one or two third-placed teams have more points than the one or two second-placed teams with the lowest point totals, then those teams play home-and-away fixtures to decide who will enter the play-off. Once the eight teams have been determined, the team with the most points is matched with the teb,am with the least points, and quarter-finals, semi-finals and a final are played out in a home-and-away series.

15. Televisa has contracts to broadcast the home games of half the teams in the league. TV Azteca, Televisa's rival broadcasting company, owns the rights for the other half.

the quality of their team and its players. However, I do not believe that América fans are passively duped by these promotions; rather, Televisa is providing América fans with what they want: a team associated with winning. The fans depend on Televisa's sportscasters to provide this association when América are playing poorly.

Although América fans do not state that they follow the team to gain promotions in a clientelistic political-economic system, their proclaimed affinity for a winner – that is, a team that values rising above the rest without a commitment to a style of play or a category of players – does not contradict the interpretations of rival fans. For example, a client who claims devotion to a winner, rather than to a group of people such as Mexicans, the working class or youths, might be giving a patron just the signal of commitment that is sought. Following this model of upward mobility to its logical conclusions, it is possible that América fans do not openly admit to this goal because achieving it requires a misrecognition of such intentions among all parties. In other words, part of the charisma that clients must display involves the ability to practice clientelism without openly opposing the values of equality that legitimize the social order. Or, perhaps, América fans do not need to be aware of the connection between upward mobility and América fandom for their choice of team to work as a signal to patrons. That is, perhaps people who desire upward mobility tend to be drawn to América for the same reasons without calculating how to use their fandom for instrumental purposes. As a Puma fan once told me: a distinctive type of person becomes an América fan.

My intention here has not been to model comprehensively how certain clients get promoted over others. This process is much more complex and ambiguous than this model can explain. However, I do want to suggest that, as this model contributes to our understanding of how urban Mexicans conceptualize the social order in which they live their daily lives, it can also help us to grasp one aspect of the process through which patron–client relations are formed. That is, how want-to-be clients can signal to potential patrons their allegiance to clientelism and upward mobility over egalitarian relations of solidarity. Mexicans who claim to value relations of solidarity posit that being an América fan constitutes one of these signals. The connections drawn by other fans between América fandom and a propensity for upward mobility derive from the 'folk' knowledge of Mexico City residents regarding the relations between América, Televisa, the PRI, the Mexican government and the national economic elite. The case presented here demonstrates how football fandom can provide actors with a concrete idiom for modelling society and its contradictions.

13

Three Confrontations and a Coda: Juventus of Turin and Italy

Patrick Hazard and David Gould

Introduction

While it is true that football may well be only a game, it is never *merely* a game. Football is one of societies flights of fancy, one of its adventures of thought. It 'occupies heads and stadiums, panoramas and thoughts, words and gestures (Ormezzano, 1999: 9). Each thought seeming to erupt into new dimensions, until this 'language of the body', this 'extraordinary ballet' (Ferrarotti, 1998), this 'exceptional event in the spectacularisation of social relations' (Bromberger *et al.*, 1993: 100) offers temptingly to fill the entire void of cultural understanding. On the surface, therefore, an examination of 'fear and loathing' among Italian football fans, and all the rituals of identity construction and boundary maintenance that this implies would suggest a classic micro-level study, in which the football fans are heuristically identified as a discrete cultural unit subject to an internal and epiphenomenal coherence. However, such cultural processes need be located within both broad and specific social, political and historical contexts, for what is certain is that within the bounded entity of the football stadium – real or virtual – new cultural units and associations are being forged. It is here, in the clash and recon-figuration of the economic and political spheres, in its realization of the spectacular, that we find social tensions, festering contradictions and contemp-orary mythemes, establishing their representation in *cultural terms*. Somewhere in these confrontations there is a sense in which each encounter is part of a wider assemblage, of which each sign is only one gesture amongst many, and subcultural confrontations reveal deeper social processes.

What follows touches on a number of perspectives commonly adopted in the analysis of sport and suggests that football is almost too redolent of social 'factness', too diagnosable, to the effect that: First, we recognise what is stable rather than what is becoming; second, we tend to focus on football as a series of marginal identities, subcultures, or oppositional cultures, professionalizing our interest in marginal identities until the results are 'reactionary' (Deleuze, 1995), and depoliticized; third, the diagnosis of football as opiate, as an instrument of ideological oppression, is not redundant but in need of a more sophisticated analysis of ideological operations; fourth, the complimentary and sometimes opposing tradition of the sporting occasion as a liberating carnival is equally problematic; as is, fifth, the notion of symbolic appreciation which sees football condensing 'like a philosophical drama, the essential values that model our society' (Bromberger, 1993: 90–1). The trajectory of this chapter is towards some of those significations as they have coalesced about *La Vecchia Signora* (trans. the Old Lady) or Juventus of Turin. In so doing we describe some of the confrontational operations within the Italian social cosmology where the symbolism and centrality of *il calcio* has long been discussed (Dal Lago, 1990; Roversi, 1992; Papa and Panico, 1993; Ferrarotti, 1998; Ormezzano, 1999), and where there is nothing absurd in Eco's comment that

> There is one thing that – even if it were considered essential – no student movement or urban revolt or global protest or what have you would ever be able to do. And that is to occupy the football field on a Sunday. (Eco, 1969)

The Old Lady' its OK to Hate

In the case of Juventus we can establish three main lines or types of contestation: (1) 'local rivalry' with FC Torino (Turin); (2) 'emblematic' or 'structural rivalry' with southern Italian teams, most notably SSC Napoli (Naples); (3) 'campanilistic'[1] or rivalries of local honour. We will conclude with a fourth in which Juventus is only a player among players, and that we identify as a contemporary power nexus of media, politics and football. In the first two examples we encounter various sociostructural aspects that extend beyond the subcultural rivalries of opposing fans. We find confrontations and allegiances that take nourishment from aspects of Italian society quite unrelated to football. The third type of contestation is more generally contingent, fluctuating in its intensity according to recent events. For example the rivalry between Juventus and Fiorentina (Florence) that, while always owing something to *campanilismo*, has during the last twenty years found extra sustenance from events on the field. 'We are friends, we are brothers', as the Torinese

---

1. *Campanilismo* or *localismo* equals 'an excessive attachment to ones place of birth' (Manconi, 1998: 38) that produces identification and differentiation and not infrequently fragmentation and conflict. It finds general expression in the tensions between the periphery and centre, between autonomy and centralized government, and is frequently described as a 'national characteristic of the Italians'. N.B. *amor di campanile* equals *amore del proprio paese* (Tommaseo and Bellini, 1897).

fans now celebrate their Florentine counterparts, thanks to the bitter con-clusion to the 1981–2 season when Fiorentina, who have made only a sporadic impact upon the footballing big-time, seemed about to add that season's *scudetto* (Italian Championship pennant) to their two previous victories of 1956 and 1969. Yet, despite having led the field for most of the season, by the final day Juventus had drawn level. The showdown found Juventus away at Catanzaro and Fiorentina at Cagliari. At half-time both matches were score-less. In the second-half two events occurred which sent the title once more to Turin. A disputed penalty was converted by Juventus, while, in Cagliari, Fiorentina had a goal disallowed. The reaction from Florence was immediate. Levelling accusations of bribery at Juventus, official protests were lodged with the Federazione Italiana Gioco Calcio (the Italian equivalent of the FA), all of which came to nothing. The results stood and Fiorentina continues to smart under the perceived injustice. This bad-blood soured even further when the two clubs met in the 1990 UEFA Cup Final. The first leg played in Turin stimulated so much crowd trouble that UEFA ordered the Italian authorities to choose a neutral venue for the second leg. The site chosen was Avellino, a town in the south of Italy with a loyal Juventus fan base. Protests were again lodged by Fiorentina but to no avail. The second match finished 0–0 and victory again went to Juventus. The antagonism was compounded shortly afterwards when, on the eve of Italia '90, the 'violas' star player Roberto Baggio signed for Juventus for a then world-record sum of £8 million. An act for which neither he nor Juventus have ever been forgiven by the Florentine fans.

But interesting as this is, we intend to concentrate on the embedded rather than the contingent. In other words on the first two types of oppositions that, while not excluding *campanilismo*, see it only in terms, or as a consequence, of other socio-structural relations. At the same time, while it might be argued that football offers the 'quickest entry into most cultures' and 'a prism for both witnessing and interacting with identities and cultures' (Armstrong and Giulianotti, 1999), we are aware that this can in practice amount to no more than treating football fandom as an autonomous micro-culture that, in much the same way that ethnic or archaic social forms are celebrated, be broken down into ritual and symbolic practices that appear able to comment on the cultural world they so colourfully inhabit, but to which they are attached without being additions.

Il Calcio Italiano

There is always a ritualistic element to the discourse of sport, a sort of quasi-political discourse. Even in the recent psychoanlaytical-biographical tradition of Hornby (1992) and Shindler (1998), football is the ritualized pretext for social discourse. And indeed, being a country in which formal institutions exert little influence and national integration is weak, Italy has long been used to unofficial mediums and institutions, such as football, providing the medium for debate and for the creation and discourse on national symbols (Gundle, 1995: 312). The centrality of *il calcio* in Italian social life is irrefutable. Support cuts across gender, class and age. There is extensive coverage in every media of Seria A, the lower and local leagues. Three national daily newspapers are dedicated to sport: *Il Corriere dello Sport*, *La Gazzetta dello Sport*, and *TuttoSport* (based in Turin)[2] – in which sport is almost synonymous with football – as well as many pages in the conventional dailies. Beyond this there exists a corpus of everyday sayings derived from the game, and a cats-cradle of symbols and ludic acts that every city-dweller considers their own and which operate for the most part beyond the reach of official culture.

Yet, in Italy we also find a special characteristic in that, from roughly 1945 to 1980, political conflict has involved all social fields including football (Podaliri and Balestri, 1998: 89), and football 'fandom' involves all social classes unlike, until relatively recently, the United Kingdom (see Dal Lago, 1990). Furthermore, whereas the Italian term *Ultra* is usually translated erroneously as 'hooligan', it is not a simple equivalent. There are differences in derivation and of social practice associated with the term. Most notably, the *Ultras* have been a politicized construct that until recently were commonly affiliated with formal political networks of all persuasions (Podaliri and Balestri, 1998). In the early 1960s for instance, Inter Milan's supporters group was organized by Servello, a representative of the radically conservative Italian Social Movement. At the same time, 1964, a Torino supporters club, *Fedelissimi*, – was a well-disciplined left-wing group capable of taking on the fascists at a political rally in Bergamo (Calligarices, 1965). Up until 1977, according to the four-stage development of the *Ultras*, as outlined by Podaliri and Balestri (1998), it was the norm for *Ultras* to adopt the colours and slogans of political street groups and organizations, to recruit members, and hold mid-week meetings with political content. During the phase of political terrorism (1977–83) there was an increase in the use of *brigades* and *directorates* as group names – a direct reference to the *Red Brigades* and the *directorates*[3] – following which

---

2. Circulation figures for Italian newspapers, excluding sports, political and provincial papers: circa 3,000,000 copies sold daily (source, *La Prima Communicazione*). Sports dailies account for a further 1,000,000 sales per diem. On Mondays this figure doubles. For example, in 1990 the Monday sales of *Il Corriere dello Sport* and *La Gazzetta dello Sport* were respectively 511,000 and 809,000 (Lumley, 1996: 204). In the 1950s there were four daily sports papers.

3. Extreme right and left-wing political groups.

the *Ultra* phenomenon reached the small towns where local definitions corresponded to traditional rivalries. While generally, during the 1980s, the *curva* (curved terraces behind the goals) evolved from a politically 'liberated space' into a small 'mother country'. Contemporaneously, a generational change and novel political-cultural orientations produced a fresh index of group names, for example: 'Wild Kaos' The Sconvolts', 'Verona Alcohols'. In short, the fan base became less political and more purely antagonistic-hedonistic, with an increased incidence of racist and xenophobic outbursts, including, amongst some northern *Ultras*, a pronounced anti-Southern Italian sentiment.

These modifications reflect something of the material and ideational transformations swirling about Italian society during these years. Moreover, they suggest that despite the seemingly homogenous profile of a crowd the confrontations are many. That while all activities actualize notions of identity and relation, these operations are variegated and no total social fact or average man emerges. Having said that, let us put some things in perspective. It is commonly assumed that while Juventus is the most successful club in Italy, having won twenty-five Italian championships and nine Italian cup victories, 'La Vecchia Signora' is notable not only for its success but also for the enmity it arouses. Indeed this article takes this commonly stated 'fact' as a starting point. However, set against this supposed uniformity is the fact that there is not a single province in Italy that lacks a Juventus fan club; that even in 1985 Juventus had 1,166 fan clubs nationally and internationally (Bromberger, 1995: 54), including thirty fan clubs in Campagnia, southern Italy, and two in Naples.[4] While, if we examine the little data relating to fan group alliances we find (as well as noting, with reference to the above comments on *Ultras*, the genealogy of names), that the immediate anecdotal evidence collected either in conversation or via popular media such as newspapers and TV must be carefully contextualized. As becomes rapidly apparent the system of allegiances, whether pro or anti a significant 'other', is more variegated than linear, so that it would appear that supporter groups operate a system of fission and fusion; coming together in strategic alliances with one group under certain conditions, while at other moments severing all ties (see Table 13.1).

Even taking into account the date of these figures (1990)[5] they immediately highlight a number of points: First, although commonly described as the most

4. In Piemonte itself there are 136 fan clubs and in neighbouring Lombardy 278 (three in Milan, and sixty-nine in the Province of Milan). In the mid-1990s one could find fan clubs in eleven countries other than Italy: Great Britain, Germany, France, Belgium, Malta, Switzerland, San Marino, Canada, South Africa, Nigeria and Thailand.

5. See D'Errico (1990) '*Aspetti giuridici e criminologici della cosiddetta 'criminalità degli stadi*', Verona: unpublished manuscript cited in Roversi (1992).

Table 13.1 *Networks of Fear and Loathing in Italian Football*

Team	Principle Fan Groups	Friends	Enemies
Bari	Ultras Curva Nord, Brigate, Stonati, Arditi, Malati.	Lazio, Ascoli, Torino, Inter, Cesna.	Lecce, Roma, Juventus, Foggia, Milan, Pescara.
Bologna	Forever Ultras, Mods, Supporters, Freak Boys.	Milan, Napoli, Genoa, Pescara, Ancon.	Fiorentina, Verona, Cesena, Lazio, Modena.
Cagliari	Ultras Curva Nord, Sconvolts, Eagles.	Lazio, Torino,	Palermo, Roma.
Florentino	Collettivo, Viola, Supporters Ultras.	Verona, Torino, Catanzaro, Modena, Empoli, Sampdoria.	Bologna, Milan, Roma, Genoa, Juventus, Pisa.
Genoa	Fossa dei Grifoni, Skinheads, Vecchia Fossa.	Torino, Napoli, Vicenza, Pisa, Acona.	Sampdoria, Verona, Inter, Juventus, Lazio, Milan.
Inter	Boys, Ultras, Skins, Vikings, Brianza Alcolica.	Verona, Sampdoria, Lazio, Bari, Udinese.	Milan, Juventus, Bologna, Roma, Ascoli.
Juventus	Arancia Meccanica, Drughi, Viking, Area BN.	Avellino	Torino, Milan, Inter, Roma, Lazio.
Lazio	Eagles Supporters. Irriducibili.	Bari, Torino, Ascoli, Inter, Como, Triestina.	Roma, Genoa, Milan, Napoli, Bologna, Sampdoria, Lecce.
Napoli	Commando Ultras Curva B, South Boys, Blue Lions.	Bologna, Bari, Genoa, Ascoli, Avellino, Cesena.	Lazio, Verona, Inter, Atlanta, Lecce, Sampdoria.

Team	Principle Fan Groups	Friends	Enemies
Roma	Commando Ultras Curva Sud, Fedayn.	Bologna.	Lazio, Inter, Juventus, Bari, Milan, Atlanta.
Sampdoria	Ultras, Tito.	Verona, Inter, Atlanta, Cremoneso, Fiorentia.	Genoa, Torino, Bologna, Milan, Pisa, Lazio.
Torino	Leoni della Maratona, Granata Korps, Eagles.	Genoa, Pisa, Lazio, Bari, Fiorentina, Cagliari	Juventus, Milan, Inter, Atlanta, Verona, Roma.
Verona	Brigate Gialloblu, Verona Front, Gioventu, Scaligera, Eagles.	Fiorentina, Inter, Sampdoria, Lecce, Catania.	Milan, Roma, Genoa, Juventus, Napoli, Bologna.

Number of Teams that regard named team as 'enemy'

Milan	11
Lazio	10
Roma	10
Juventus	8
Inter	7
Fiorentina	5
Napoli	5
Torino	4

Number of teams that regard named team as 'friend'

Torino	7
Lazio	6
Inter	6
Fiorentina	6
Milan	5
Napoli	5
Juventus	1
Roma	0

Table 13.1 *Networks of Fear and Loathing in Italian Football (continued)*

Number of Teams that regard named team as 'friend'		*Number of teams that regard named team as 'enemy'*	
Lazio	6	Lazio	7
Fiorentina	6	Fiorentina	6
Napoli	6	Inter	6
Torino	6	Juventus	6
Inter	5	Roma	6
Juventus	1	Torino	6
Milan	no figures	Milan	no figures

hated team in Italy, Juventus is less frequently cited as an 'enemy' than Milan, Lazio and Roma; second, the number of positive identifications as 'friends' sees Inter leading the list with Milan and Lazio close behind, while Juventus can only scramble one 'friend' (the tiny Avellino), and Roma finds itself totally friendless. Juventus is no more hated, but it is less loved than others – or so it would seem until we add to this the fact that there is not a single province in Italy lacking a Juventus supporters club. The situation is far from clear-cut. Juventus it would appear inspires few contingent loves, yet it has many lovers in every port. The so-called enmity therefore would appear to find energies in the common dislike of success and the general distrust of powerful men and their accoutrements, but is tempered by servile respect. This master–slave relationship is taut and uncomfortable. Respect is paid to the power (political, financial and sporting) that the club possesses, but love is less forthcoming, mixed as it is with awe and subservience for the very structures of the unchanging world. In this Juventus is neither unique or particularly revelatory, but it does express the paradox and conviction at the heart of all conceptions of power and ideology, namely, that power does not operate in a one-way street, but is an action of affection proposed by the dominated towards that which dominates.

When we look at Turin itself the demographics of 'fear and loathing' are even less clear cut than popular imagination would have us believe. It is commonly asserted that the fans of Torino represent the native working-class population, and those of Juventus are 'essentially the Fiat workers; immigrants from Southern Italy' (Bromberger, with Hayot and Mariottini, 1993: 109); and according to the Italian sportswriter Gabriele Marcotti, Juventus may be the most popular team in the country but in the city of Turin 70 per cent of the footballing population support Torino (Marcotti, cited in *The Independent*, 27 September 2000). The support profile has always been skewered thus. This view would appear to find some support in the strong concentration of Torino supporters clubs in the city and its surroundings. Of the 222 Torino supporters clubs at the time of Bromberger's writing (1994–5), twenty-four of these were situated in the city itself and sixty-eight in the province of Turin, compared to the five and forty-seven respectively of Juventus. However, when one considers the scale of the migration towards Turin during, and beyond, the period of the so-called 'economic miracle' (1951–70) when of all Italian cities Turin received the highest proportion of southern Italians (mostly from the regions Foggia, Bari and Reggio Calabria), swelling the population from 719,300 to 1,124,714 and causing Turin to be known as the 'third largest southern city' in Italy (Fofi, 1964: 22; Meneghetti, 1971: 174), one might expect to find a much greater concentration of support within the city itself.

It seems reasonable, therefore, to conclude that the support for Torino is not composed entirely of native Torinese but also of those 'southerners' whom it has been noted played a prominent role in the industrial unrest of the 1960s and 1970s. As Michele Dimanico, a worker at Fiat-Spa, told Lanzardo: 'the Piemontese have never had the anger which these uprooted southerners have got' (Lanzardo, 1979: 101). These same workers might be willing to give their labour to 'Mamma Fiat', but not necessarily their leisure time as well.

Each of the fan-couplings previously listed is no doubt worth its own micro-historical study. Some being based on the immutable status of teams and-or cities *vis-à-vis* a particular 'other' in the *campanilistic* sense. Hence we find Fiorentina lists Pisa as an enemy even when the two teams rarely meet in competition, playing as they do in different divisions of the Italian League, but their historic city rivalry still finds expression in footballing terms. Other couplings are purely contingent, but all wax and wane in intensity and the point we wish to extract from this brief summary is that it doesn't do to over-egg the confrontational pudding. Each confrontation is context-dependant which enjoins us to look at the precise socio-historical significations embodied by Juventus which have, in the brief historical span we are looking at, proved more or less impermeable.

La Vecchia Signora

Having long been part of the Agnelli fiefdom, Juventus is in many respects no more than a 'super' works team, although it was founded in 1897, a quarter of a century before the election of Eduardo Agnelli as president. Students of the Massimo d'Azeglio College in Turin contrived the idea of a football club while idling away time on the benches in Corso Umberto. Initially, in common with many others, it was a private social and sporting club, and although they won their first championship in 1905 it can barely be described as a national title with only teams from Piemonte, Lombardia and Liguria participating.[6] Likewise, their second *scudetto* (1926) preceded the creation in 1929 of a nationally unified championship. Shortly after, Juventus embarked on a sequence of five straight *scudetti* (1930–5)[7] losing along the way only twenty-one matches out of 166. By the time of Italy's second World Cup victory of the 1930s, Juventus were established as the most dominant team in

---

6. The first champions of Italy (1898) were Genoa who emerged victorious from a tournament comprising four teams – one from Genoa, and three from Turin. Genoa proceeded to win the next six championships, but thereafter the most successful teams were now forgotten provincial clubs such as La Pro Vercelli and Casale, both of Piemonte.

7. The 'quinquennio' as their five *scudetti* came to be known has only been equalled once – by Torino in the 1940s.

the country and provided the backbone of the national team, contributing, for example, nine players in a 1933 match against Hungary. It was this early pre-eminence that established the club in the minds of the nation and first delineated its particular characteristics: the generous patronage of the Agnelli dynasty; a singular sporting ethos; widespread support and a deterritorialized corporeality (it was known at that time as the 'team of Italy'); and equally prevalent envy.

While it might be said that in the beginning football was just a game, the game hadn't anticipated Eduardo Agnelli. Agnelli represented for his time something new. Five hundred years ago men such as he would have commissioned Raphael, Michelangelo or Brunelleschi to paint frescoes, carve marble from Carrara, or build a cathedral. Today these same men, the Cragnotti's, the Berlusconi's and the Agnelli's – the *New Medici* – create football teams. When, during the early 1920s, the directors of Juventus approached the Agnelli family for financial assistance, it wasn't just a business proposition that insured the family was provided with three-sixteenths of the club's shares and the installation of Eduardo as President, but the enthusiasm of an already devoted fan who then applied to football the philosophy and endeavour previously reserved for industry. Agnelli was the first to stress the importance of recognizing Fifa, and the first to financially reimburse players. When the Argentinean outside-left, Raimundo Orsi, joined the club in 1928 he received a signing-on fee of L.100,000, a guaranteed monthly salary of L.8,000 and the use of a brand new Fiat 509,[8] even though such practices were officially prohibited.[9] By such means he made Juventus into not only Italy's greatest team but its first truly professional club, its motto a perfect axiom for industrialized efficiency: 'Simplicity, Seriousness and Sobriety'. So successful has been this philosophy that when, in 1997, Giovanni Agnelli celebrated his 50th year in charge he was able to point to a victory roll greater than any team in the world, comprising at that point: twenty-four *scudetti* (one to follow later that year), nine Coppe Italia, one Supercoppa Italiana, two Coppe di Campione, two Coppe Intercontinental, one Coppa delle Coppe, three Coppe Uefa, two Supercoppe Europee, one Coppa delle Alpi, one Torneo mundialito.

8. At the same time an Italian elementary school teacher earned approximately L.400 per month, while a magistrate could expect to receive a monthly stipend of no more than L.1,000 (Papa and Panico, 1993:141).

9. It might be argued that the first case of professionalism occurred in 1922 when Virginio 'Viri' Rosetta was 'transferred' from La Pro Vercelli to Juventus with a contract that carried a L.45,000 signing-on fee (Ormezzano, 1999).

The First Confrontation
Il Derby: 'Toro–Juve the ancient fascination' (*La Stampa*, 3 November 1999)

1310 days is a long time to go without anything, let alone a footballing derby, or at least the Agnelli-owned national daily *La Stampa* would have us believe, but on Sunday 7 November 1999 this important relational aspect of the city was restored, prompting one to wonder what was really missing during those 1310 days and how, despite the rhetoric, the city had survived:

> The derby is not a vice like alcohol or cigarettes, that if for three years you stay well away from you are de-intoxicated. On the contrary, the more you miss it the more you think about it . . . It is an unsurpressable obsession. (*La Stampa*, 7 November 1999)

But survive it did, *Il Toro* arising from the purgatorial gloom of Seria B to face once again *La Vecchia Signora* in the 217th Turin derby.

On derby day the stadium is divided into two contrasting universes. *La Maratona* of Torino, and *La Filadelfia* of Juventus, where, roughly speaking, the *tifosi* represent 'grosso modo, two distinct social and cultural universes' (Bromberger with Hayot and Mariottini, 1993: 109). But, what exactly does the confrontation re-established by 'il derby' bring into relief? In order to see if the antagonisms of Derby day (antagonisms that seem, nevertheless, to be on the wane: *'In spite of the hunger for the Derby, it will not be a packed house'* (*La Stampa*, 7 November 1999)) have significance beyond sibling rivalry, jealousy and alternate claims for city-authenticity, we will look at the influential work of Christian Bromberger.

Bromberger's analysis of the Turin derby is determinedly structuralist. That is to say he is interested in culture as an object that is revealed in signs: in a symbolic dimension that is composed of differential relations between things. These relations may be analysed independently of other data as they inhabit an autonomous realm of meaning, independent of individual subjectivities, but to which individuals are subject. In Bromberger's words, football 'symbolises, in its actual organisation, the salient characteristics of industrial society' (Bromberger *et al.*, 1993: 116). His analysis of the symbols surrounding the game is an attempt to uncover the hidden structure of the social order as symbolized in a specific situation. In this respect his approach is similar to Clifford Geertz's (1973) influential analysis of the Balinese Cockfight as society in microcosm. From this perspective football is a total social fact that 'can give imaginary shape to both [society's] unity and its diversity'. That operates within a 'privileged space for the affirmation of a certain number of values' (Bromberger with Hayot and Mariottini, 1993: 112). Bromberger lists these values in a series of universal, and-or contingent, oppositions. The Turin derby reveals the following: the masculine *Il Toro* versus the feminine *La Vecchia Signora*; Torino's nostalgic glance at a glorious past compared to the ever more successful present of Juventus; one team speaks of humility, the other arrogance; one is powerful, the other weak; one breaks all parochial boundaries, the other remains embedded in the local; one is faithful, the other fickle. Ultimately he gathers each opposition under the general headings of the present and future versus the past; the universal versus the local; good fortune versus bad (Bromberger, 1995: 54–6). We can summarize this as in Figure 13.1.

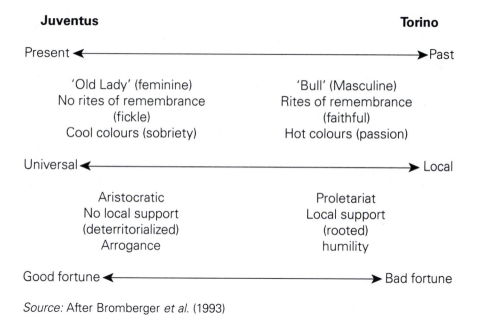

Juventus   **Torino**

Present ◄───► Past

'Old Lady' (feminine)   'Bull' (Masculine)
No rites of remembrance   Rites of remembrance
(fickle)   (faithful)
Cool colours (sobriety)   Hot colours (passion)

Universal ◄───────────────────────────────────────► Local

Aristocratic   Proletariat
No local support   Local support
(deterritorialized)   (rooted)
Arrogance   humility

Good fortune ◄─────────────────────────────────────► Bad fortune

Source: After Bromberger *et al.* (1993)

Figure 13.1 *Bromberger's oppositions*

The usual accusations can be levelled at this sort of approach: for example, how can the hypothesis be falsified? The ethnographers only take account of the successes not the failures of correspondence, and so forth. The question also arises as to what is the relationship between the symbolic dimension and the organization of social systems? In other words, if football is indeed a symbolic language, what does it say and how is what is said related to what is done? How does one prevent the relationships described from remaining singularities and their interpretations merely the conceit of the ethnographer?

Nonetheless, Bromberger stakes out a dual semiological function for football and its signs. First, football expresses all the attributes and values of industrial society; second, football comprises a series of more or less universal opposit-ions. These two approaches are quite different. In fact the difference corresponds to the two varieties of symbolic meaning: syncretic and analytic, where syncretic talks of the world of experience and analytic of the categories of the mind (Sperber, 1975). The syncretic interpretation of symbols produces enormous degrees of banal observations about the natural world, of the order of universes 'loaded with meaning, where images of life and death, warfare, sacrifice and religious ritual jostle with each other' (Bromberger with Hayot and Mariottini, 1993: 112). Observations that seem to fly in the face of the complexity on offer, leaving the gap between the density of a social practice and its meaning unexplained. Analytic meanings, on the other hand, tell us that symbolic thought, rather than utilizing categories to make statements about the world, as in ordinary language, utilizes statements about the world to establish relations between categories (Sperber, 1975). In this case the redundancy is in the repetition of relations between categories.

The syncretic approach posits the existence of an underlying tacit know-ledge. Which is to say that tacit knowledge comprises data that are intuitions, 'they are the judgements that the members of a cultural group systematically express without elaborating on the underlying argument' (Sperber, 1975: xi). In the case to follow, that of Juventus versus Napoli, the expression of this tacit shared knowledge is demonstrated through the creative manipulation of cultural symbols by the Neapolitan fans. In the case of the Turin derby the nature of this knowledge and its relationship to explicitness is more vague. As for the analytic prospect, the knowledge here is of a purely formal logic derived from the interpretation of the analyst. 'The problem of meaning therefore comes down to that of analyticity: This does not in any way lessen the interest of the relationships revealed; only they are not relations of meaning' (ibid.: 12). Lèvi-Strauss himself notes that symbolic relationships can be based on contiguity or resemblance, that they can be sensible or intelligible, static or dynamic. But for these 'concrete logics', 'the existence of some connection is more important than the nature of the connections. On the formal plane, one might say they will make use of anything that comes to hand' (Lèvi-Strauss, 1966: 66). This is exactly the approach also of the ethnographer. There is in essence a total freedom of connection, so that meaning becomes a misleading metaphor rather than a descriptive category. In this respect Bromberger is well and truly Lèvi-Straussian: a symbol is not a symbol because it is interpreted but because it is part of an opposition of another element.

Given that Bromberger argues that the meaning of a social act or cultural product is not only that which is explicit, and that he speaks of football as offering 'an exemplary condensation of the ethos that models the modern, urban and industrial world of which it is, in its actual organisation and codified form, a product' (Bromberger with Hayot and Mariottini, 1993: 116), it is curious that he doesn't explore more fully the relationship between symbols and values. For it is the necessary function of the semiological view to deconstruct sign systems in order to reveal the underlying operations of power. In other words, how ideologies operate though symbolic structures (see Eco, 1968; Althusser, 1971, 1981; Barthes, 1972; Derrida, 1981). He seems unwilling to acknowledge that the 'symbolic field of differential relations is not neutral . . . but invested with all kinds of operations and effects of power' (Goodchild, 1996: 114), and that it is not possible to de-politicize even neatly circumscribed microcultural expressions.

The ambiguities of Bromberger's structuralism opens up the debate by revealing an old tension between the dominant interpretations of sport. For despite insisting that fans are not 'cultural idiots', that they encounter the game in the Bakhtinesque spirit of Carnival, where rejuvenated folkloric activities represent a genuine emancipatory tendency, he cannot ignore the fact that football condenses like a 'philosophical drama, the essential values that model our society' (Bromberger *et al.*, 1993: 90). That it provides in other words a 'stabilising factor for the existing social order . . . a basis for reinforcing the commodity spectacle . . . a basis for regimenting and militarising youth and reproducing a set of hierarchical, elitist, authoritarian values' (Jarvie and Maguire, 1994: 96). In his analysis of the spatial dynamics of the stadium itself he touches more fully on ideas derived from Ehrenberg (1980), who in turn utilizes Foucault's vision of a carceral society where architectural spaces educate and discipline through the bodily appropriation of social divisions.[10] It does, in short, form part of the ideological and repressive state apparatus (Brohm, 1978). Neither position is entirely satisfactory. These two views, the Carnivalesque and the classic Marxist position in which sport is viewed as an obscurant of social reality, as atomistic and the silent avoidance of real issues, are not in themselves mutually exclusive, although Bromberger tends to react to the prospect of any ideological workings among the ritualized paraphernalia as if there is indeed a battle line between two visions of society in which the operations of power are, or not, Manichaeistic. Yet, what he misses is the sense that although the world may be comprised of symbolic oppositions, and that the actors may be aware of these to the extent that they

10. See Bale (1993); Dal Lago (1990).

can use them ironically in the rituals associated with the game, these symbols nevertheless pack an ideological punch.

If, as in the transgressional theory made popular by Bakhtin, carnival is revolution, how are we to explain:

> why power has used *circences* to keep crowds quiet; why the most repressive dictatorships have always censured parodies and satires but not clowneries; why humour is suspect but circus is innocent; why today's mass media, undoubtedly instruments of social control are based mainly upon the funny, the ludicrous, that is upon a continuous carnivalization of life. To support the universe of business, there is not business like showbusiness. (Eco, 1984: 3)

If, as Eco has said elsewhere, 'we must have *circences,* some blood at least should be spilled' (Eco, 1994: 33). There is in fact no transgression at all for, like comedy, we are reminded of the rules and our relationship to them even as we are involved in the process of telling the joke or participating in the carnival. Which brings us to the 'scenic, ludic and festival culture which predisposes Naples to become inflamed by the spectacle of football' (Bromberger *et al.*, 1993: 97).

The Second Confrontation
Italy's 'Questione Meridionale': Naples vs Juventus

When Napoli go north the opposing fans greet the arrivals with slogans that carry historical significance: 'Forza Vesuvio!'; 'Welcome to Italy'. The Neapolitan fans are fully in tune with this dialogue and respond in kind: 'Milan, Turin, Verona is this Italy? It's better being Africans!'; 'Better to win as country bumpkins than lose with Berlusconi'. The exchange is tribute to Italy's enduring *questione meridionale* (Southern Question) and the inter-related problematic of the 'Mediterranean' and its relationship to the concept of 'Europe'. The *questione meridionale* has been a significant component of Italian political social and economic life for roughly one hundred and fifty years, and just as there have been debates as to whether the idea existed before Unification in 1861 or was a subsequent political construct, so there have been two consistent threads to its analytical elaboration. On the one hand, from the biological determinism of Lombroso (1836–1909),[11] through Banfield's 'amoral familism' (1958)[12] and Friedman's *la miseria* (1976), it has

---

11. Born in Verona, Lombroso and others adopted the ideas of the Social Darwinist, Herbert Spencer, and founded the science of criminology. In 1906 Lombroso became Professor of Criminal Anthropology at the University of Turin – see Schneider (1998), Gibson (1998). For Lombroso, see Lombroso (1871, 1898).

12. 'Amoral familism' equals excessive familism that privileges the individual or its immediate family over other forms of social co-operation.

been intimated that, due to a flaw in their essential character, the southern Italian has been unable to organize collectively, or express any of the usual civic attributes, so that the south remains a pre-modernized culture. The key theme associated with 'southerness' is thus backwardness. On the other hand the approach exemplified by Gramsci (1954, 1955, 1975; see also Femia, 1981) and de Martino (1949, 1953), has been to comprehend the problem of the south in material and structural terms. More specifically to see the south in relational terms, as a result of internal colonization by the north. However, it is the former view that dominates the popular and political imagination, so that the *questione meridionale*'s 'dominant representation has been composed of economic, social and political elements measured against broad Enlightenment-inspired criteria of progress or development. The result [being] a series of narratives, at times romantic, at times merely condescending, of failure' (Petrusewicz, 1998: 27–8). This discourse has revolved about a series of well-worn stereotypes which have, in Schneider's evocative phrase, encouraged 'orientalism in one country'. The stereotypical representations of the south – passionate, undisciplined, religious, superstitious, competitive, incapable of generating group solidarity – as opposed to the orderly civic values of the north which have sustained an 'everyday symbolic geography' (Schneider, 1998) of north versus south, in which two conceptions of progress and rationality are opposed.

Although recently re-examined (see Moe, 1992; Petraccone, 1994; Dickie, 1996; Gribaudi, 1996; Schneider, 1998; Patriarca, 1998) the *questione meridionale* remains a virile component of Italian self-consciousness. But whether the interpretations have chosen to stress the politically constructed nature of the divide or have seen its roots in a specific Mediterranean *mentalitè*, certain core ingredients remain unchanged. These are: the south as a place of 'primitiveness', as 'African', as less-civilized. These symbolic and philosophical orthodoxies immediately raise their heads in any north-south confrontation, whether it be Luigi Carlo Farin, a government envoy, writing back to the Prime Minister Cavour in Turin during the 1860s: 'What barbarism! Some Italy! This is Africa: compared to these peasants the Bedouin are the flower of civilised virtues' (Cavour, 1952),[13] or the *tifosi* of Napoli and Juventus exchanging insults: 'Neapolitans, help the environment, have a wash!'; 'No to vivisection, use the Neapolitans'; 'Civilization is not bought with money'; 'Naples champion of football, culture and civilization' (Bromberger, 1995: 24–5). Whatever the century, the conceptual dualism is between Europe and

13. See also the parliamentary deputy Stefano Castagnola speaking in 1863 of Basilicata during a parlimentary discussion on brigandage: 'It's the Middle Ages right under our eyes!' (cited in Villari, 1885: 40).

Africa; Christianity and the Arab world; civilization and barbarism. Even Bromberger wraps some of his analysis in the same language, emphasizing repeatedly the 'extraordinary' Neapolitan passion that seems to possess the fans as if an ineradicable ague. This 'passion' that in 1975 ensures that more than 70,000 season tickets were sold; that for the decisive match against Juventus in Turin 10,000 fans made the long journey north; that for Maradona's debut at the club in 1984–5 67,000 season tickets were sold; and that in the championship years of 1987 and 1990 more than a million souvenir products were sold, with a value of £30,000,000.[14]

Nevertheless, it is surely true that the *questione meridionale*: the long-held view of the south as backward and primitive; finds expression in the conflicts between Napoli and the teams of the north. In relation to Juventus the confrontation is exclusively about the unbalanced structural relationship between north and south Italy. A relationship that contrasts nature and culture; modernity and the past; poverty against wealth; corruption against clean hands; superstition versus rationality. A highly politicized conflict that finds expression in a parodic utilization of ancient and modern symbols amongst the Neapolitans. Additionally, it might be argued that the team style corresponds to a particular mode of collective existence, allowing us to contrast the style of Juventus: simplicity, seriousness and sobriety; with Napoli: complex, cunning and intoxicated; but the fans do not so neatly mirror the symbolic necessity. While confronting the contest in a carnivalesque mode the Neapolitans do not merely serve to reproduce their own symbolic function within the wider Italian cosmology, they also punctuate, however ineffectually, the symbolic gloom with a clear-sighted recognition of the social and economic realities: 'Against Freemasons, cheats, exploiters, mercenaries and racists, the Neapolitans invite the Blues to fight without fear' (in *Napulissimo* the Ultra Commando magazine). Thus the sophisticated and fuzzy demarcation between oppression and resistance is again emphasized.

In the behaviour of the Neapolitan fans there is a relation between expression and experience, and this expression is organized according to a unifying symbolic system that is sedimented in language and culture 'in such a way as to generate historically located habitualities' (Dillon, 1998: xii). Thus, a practical and material logic is revealed that reminds us that while we cannot reduce football just to the symbolic; we cannot at the same time deny its symbolic content. It fluctuates in its social activity between functionality and the symbolic. Symbolic systems are somehow ingredients of the world, they are 'related to it and reflect it though the medium of ideology' (Eco, 1977:

---

14. The exact figures are difficult to quantify as the market for such goods comprises a part of the informal or 'black' economy. Estimates are taken from Ghiocci, cited in Bromberger (1995: 23).

163). But any given society is more than a series of interrelated needs geared towards its own reproduction. Because to what end is this reproduction aimed? It is 'functional' in relation to what? (Castoriadis, 1997: 135) Cultural practices do form 'a symbolic network', but this network, by definition, refers to something other than symbolism.

Conclusion and the Fourth Confrontation

We wish to conclude by proposing a fourth confrontation of which Juventus is only a part, and that refers to current relations of power and consumption. What has so far been discussed reveals something of the contingency of human relations and their historical specificity, it has touched on the ambivalent responses to the issue of ideology in mass culture, and has attempted to produce insights into Italian culture through the eye-piece of anti-Juventus sentiments. We would now suggest that while Juventus represents what was once new, the confrontation that best represents the present is found a little to the north and east of Turin, namely in that nexus of forces that has coalesced about Silvio Berlusconi the owner of AC Milan. A synergy has arisen between the forces of the media, politics and football. Berlusconi not only owns AC Milan, and controls the broadcast rights to Champions League games in Italy, but also cross-fertilizes symbolic elements from football into his political repertoire. He is not a cause but a consequence of a view that places football in a pivotal and metaphorical position *vis-à-vis* society, and he makes hay with the ambiguity that allows football to speak for many. His combining of symbolic elements would have been inconceivable without the rhetoric of community and competition that already existed or the unquestioned spectacularization of life, in which 'one's identity and dreams have been commodified, turned into spectacular, generalised lifestyles and images and sold back to one' (Shields, 1999: 77). The sports landscape has been completely commodified by TV (Raitz, 1995: xi)[15] and so in the process are the social relations amalgamated in the spectacular.

Until the late 1970s Italian TV was comprised of only the state-owned station RAI, but from the late 1970s TV changed from 'paleo-TV' to 'neo-TV' (Eco, 1990), the defining characteristic of which is that it talks less about the external world and more about itself and its public. This movement was driven for the most part by Finivest,[16] the conglomerate of media interests owned by Berlusconi. In 1987 *'Il teleavvocato'* (as Agnelli was dubbed – a

15. See Immen (1990) in Raitz (ed.) (1995).

16. Since 1984, Berlusconi has, through 'his highly ramified holding company Finivest . . . dominated Italian private TV. He controls the three principle private networks: Canale 5, Italia 1 and Rete 4' (Schlesinger, 1990: 270).

reference to his professional status of *avvocato*-lawyer and his involvement in the broadcast media), as if to emphasize the changing face of power and the sense of himself and Juventus belonging to a different order of industrial and social organization, attempted to realize some effect upon this burgeoning industry. In the autumn of 1987, Fiat, through its publishing subsidiary Rizzoli-Gemina,[17] took a 50 per cent option in Tele MonteCarlo (TMC) owned by the multimedia conglomerate of Brazil Globo, but the challenge to *'La Sua Emittenza'* (Berlusconi: a play on words referring to the similarity between *eminenza*-eminence, as in 'his eminence', and *emittenza*-transmission or broadcast) was short-lived. Berlusconi remains preeminent in the field of media and in the overtly political stakes, and has manipulated quite overtly the structural and emotional sympathies between popular sporting culture and national politics, as if confirming the opinion of commentators such as Hoch (1972) and Brohm (1978) that sport was but 'a microcosm of modern capitalist society and an integral facet of cultural domination and exploitation' (Jarvie and Maguire, 1994: 96). When Berlusconi wraps his political party in the colours of the Italian State and names it 'Forza Italia' in a deliberate echo of the tifosi's cry for the national team: 'Forza Italia', the circle is complete. Neo-TV, the commoditization and spectacularization of football, the change in the supporters profile and deterritorialization, all relegate the themes explored by Bromberger to a lesser order of significance: the key function is no longer the rites and oppositional categories associated with the derby, and the localization of 'authentic' subcultures devolved from questions of power, as if mass culture referred to a non-contentious and depoliticized whole; it is no longer sufficient to isolate oppositional cultures whether they be football fans or any other stratum.

Instead, Berlusconi exemplifies that 'economic imperialism', that 'violent conquista of the cultural market' that Certeau (1997: 134) talks of. The primary opposition becomes the struggle between a liberated or colonized dynamic in which the appropriation of the entire cultural field is at stake. Culture itself is 'the colonised of the 20th century', a medium in which 'contemporary technocracies install whole empires . . . in the same way that that European nations occupied disarmed continents in the 19th century. Corporate trusts rationalise and turn the manufacturers of signifiers into a profitable enterprise' (Certeau, 1997: 134). Colonization means that the penetration of contemporary capitalism is total. Every sphere of life, each image and desire is occupied. There is, as Debord would put it (cited in

---

17. Rizzoli-Gemina also owns *La Gazzetta dello Sport*, *La Stampa*, *Stampa Sera* and *Il Corriere della Sera*.

Marcus, 1989: 145), 'an effective third world in the heart of the First'. In general, therefore, we must be careful not to regard football as somehow more privileged than any other cultural effect. The antagonisms that revolve around football are often reactionary and passive, without recognition of the historical totality in which they are caught up, and without a clear-cut positing of one potentiality against another. They are very often civil rather than political actions, by which I mean they are bound always within the discreet subcultural elements that seem to speak of variety and strategies of the weak. This is not to say that between fans there are not inequalities and modalities of power that favour some and not others, but that although football may seem to dramatize all the one-way streets of ideological struggle, it is equally redolent of a shared project in which the totality of the relations involved remain the same because they are underpinned by a non-negotiable dream of the entire population.

In talking, therefore, about 'fans' and their oppositional cultures, it is necessary to be clear that this encompasses a number of socio-economic groupings. For if by 'fan' we mean to stabilize a representation of the 'fan' in a particular sociological dictum, then not only do we misrepresent the 'fan' in a mythologicalized-idealized subset, ignoring the variegated strata on offer, but we, under the heavy cloak of 'authenticity' and cultural purity, deprive those fans of their involvement with a more general network of cultural relations. Once we understand this we do not see oppositions between fixed horizontal cultures, but instead vertical understandings that invade and disrupt, as well as stabilize, horizontal discharges of authoritative representations, structures of ideology and planes of power. The confrontations that do exist take place within an already colonized territory and mental space, so that even if football speaks of stolen subjectivities, at the same time it appears to represent the world to ourselves.

Part IV

The Others Abroad: Modernity and Identity in Club Rivalries

14

Olympic Mvolyé: The Cameroonian Team that Could Not Win

Bea Vidacs*

Anyone looking at Cameroon's squad for the 1994 World Cup would have noticed that some home-based players came from the second division team, Olympic Mvolyé[1] (OM). It is of course highly unusual for lower division players to play in the World Cup, but they were indeed among the best available in Cameroon. Despite their players' qualities, OM remained in the Second Division for five seasons and the Cameroonian public (or at least the people of Yaoundé, the nation's capital and the team's home city) was largely hostile to the club and watched with great pleasure their repeated failures to win promotion. In this chapter, I discuss the widespread dislike of OM in Cameroon, and seek to explain why some people support this club. The issue has to be viewed in the larger context of stereotypes which Cameroonians hold of Western and African types of action.

The Creation of Olympic Mvolyé

Olympic Mvolyé was founded in 1990, bearing the name of one of Yaoundé's neighbourhoods. Many of the key founder members had been part of the leadership of Tonnerre, one of the oldest clubs in Cameroon. Of special importance was Omgba Damase, who had been a Tonnerre sponsor and patron during the 1980s. Following disagreements, Damase and a dissident group of Tonnerre leaders decided to secede and create Olympic. This also meant that despite running a new club, OM's leaders exerted considerable influence in the Cameroonian Football Federation (Fécafoot) – for example the club president was the Federation treasurer.

* Fieldwork for this paper was supported by the Wenner Gren Foundation.

1. The name of the team is spelled differently by different Cameroonian sources (Olympique de Mvolyé, Olympic de Mvolyé, Olympique Mvolyé, Olympic Mvolyé.) For the sake of consistency I have chosen to use the latter form.

Ombga Damase is a millionaire several times over, and one of the most influential people in the entourage of Paul Biya, Cameroon's President (cf. *Le Messager*, 6 July 1998). Though never appearing on the roster of OM's leadership, Damase's involvement is something of an open secret (Nguini, 1996). When OM was founded, it was too late to join the much contested Third Division[2] (*la ligue*) based in the capital. Hence, the team joined the Third Division based in another region (*département*) in which there were only three teams – practically guaranteeing OM's victory. According to Fécafoot rules, a league competition can only proceed with a minimum of four teams, so Olympic's participation allowed the tournament to go ahead! Thus, paradoxically, OM – a Yaoundé team – was created in Mbalmayo a neighbouring town, and rose to the Second Division of the Centre Province from a region outside their home city. These unusual origins later resurfaced in explanations for the team's failure to win further promotion.[3]

Olympic's exceptional wealth ensured the acquisition of the best players in Cameroon, particularly internationals. In the natural order of things, top players would refuse to sign for a club from the Second Division, which is typically described as 'hell' by local journalists. As one would expect, the Second Division has lower prestige and its clubs have fewer resources. In Yaoundé, the Second Division championship is split into two groups; the group winners play '*les barrages*' with the winner then qualifying for the inter-group competition involving the winners of all Second Division tournaments from across Cameroon's ten provinces. The top three clubs are promoted to the First Division, from which the bottom three are relegated.

For the first five years, OM failed to win promotion; and when they did so in 1996 it was considered to be the result of highly irregular circumstances. Up to 1995, OM won the Challenge Cup twice (1992, 1994), proving their talent. Nevertheless, in the league they either lost in the preliminary group stages (three times), or failed to finish in the top three from the inter-group tournament. In 1994, for example, OM lost to Fogape in a crucial match; had they won, they would have qualified for the inter-group tournament. The defeat drew the following comment from a journalist:

> Poor O.M., accursed Olympic Mvolyé, beaten in the home match by Fogape of Yaoundé whose players (mark my words!) were on strike two days before the match, and were not training. In the meanwhile O.M., with its stars, was already in training [en stage]. The opposite was to be seen on the terrain, where the Olympians were given a rough time . . .

2. The Third Division is organized regionally, while the Second Division is provincial. The First Division encompasses all ten provinces and is thus a national competition.

3. OM only managed to rise to the First Division after my departure from the field, in 1996.

Fogape did hold its own on the pitch and did not succumb to attempts at corruption, like those of Bara Abdoulaye of Olympic, who called Essomba of Fogape aside to offer him wads of bank-notes. Needless to say, Essomba delivered an exemplary performance. Olympique will continue to play in second division, despite its means. (Ayinda, 1994)

Attempts at corruption and other irregularities are common in Cameroonian football. This mixture of amazement at OM's lack of success – despite their superior preparation and financial means – combined with a degree of gloating, are typical of any commentary surrounding the team.

Amateurism or Paternalism by Another Name?

By African standards Cameroon is one of the most credible football countries in the international arena, having won three African Nations Cups, and participated in four World Cup Finals, the most memorable of which concerns their qualification for the quarter-finals at Italia '90. Nevertheless, Cameroon football remains essentially amateur, not necessarily in the sense of adhering to the lofty ideals of Pierre de Coubertin, but more so due to local realities. The ideals of amateurism were based on aristocratic principles, and predicated on sportsmen not needing an income from sport as they had independent means (cf. Bourdieu, 1978). In Cameroon, however, the reverse is the case. Although amateurism is codified in Fécafoot regulations, it is in effect enforced by the lack of financial means among clubs and their officials. Former players do recall that many players were 'taken care of' by their club presidents, either by being given a job, having meals paid for regularly, having their rent paid, or by living in the president's household. It is difficult to know how widespread these practices were, as some recollections may be rosier than the reality. On the other hand, the same players state that they played football for the fun of it, without expecting any returns. This is a reference to monetary recompense since in-kind rewards were clearly available. The ex-players thus distinguish themselves from current players, who are thought to expect or at least would like to have monetary rewards. And when current players do not get it – which for many reasons is often the case – they grumble, and when the moment is opportune they go on strike.

To some extent the practice of in-kind recompense for football survives today, but it is becoming rarer; increasingly, players have to fend for themselves. Some players are aware of this: a young goalkeeper explained to me that he had studied catering because, to pursue a football career, he knew he needed a profession with a secure income. Others, however, are less lucky and clear-sighted, and so eke out an existence, often relying on the unreliable bounty of club presidents. Even First Division players lack the luxury of a guaranteed income. The few teams that are sponsored, or owned by state or parastatal companies, constitute an exception.[4] However, in these cases the fortunes of the team and players are closely related to those of the sponsor company. Fogape was such a team, rising to the First Division in 1994, but due to the enterprise's failure, being relegated within a year. Most clubs are run more or less on a voluntary basis and team presidents have great difficulty meeting their financial obligations. The requisite fees such as league affiliation, license fees, fines and the like, plus playing and training equipment, present many problems and are too expensive for most Cameroonian clubs to afford.

Most clubs lack special training equipment, hence obstacle courses at training sessions are created out of discarded tyres, propped up on the uneven terrain by tufts of weeds. The pitch itself has no turf, only dirt and dust. There are only two stadiums in Cameroon with proper turf (Yaoundé and Douala), which of course means that even in the First Division championship only matches played at these two venues will be played on an ideal surface. Many Cameroonians argue that this creates a disadvantage for teams unprepared for grass (cf. Ntonfo, 1994).

Club officials are comprised of volunteers, who more often than not maintain the team out of their own pockets. Even when supporters organize a collection to help towards the costs of an away match, or to assist with bonuses or equipment, their task is difficult and such attempts rarely if ever yield sufficient funds. This is not due to the absence of goodwill – albeit that accusations abound of individuals enriching themselves at the expense of the players because there are many stories of people becoming paupers as a result of having 'loved football too much'. Rather, there is since 1987 an ongoing serious economic crisis in Cameroon and resources are stretched to their limits in all aspects of life, thus the demands on any disposable income come from many directions.[5]

In addition to the economic crisis there is another factor influencing the remuneration of players and officials. Cameroonian life is pervaded by patron–client relationships, and even professional relationships outside football are filled with rituals of respect and an air of paternalism where a clear *quid pro quo* is hidden under expressions of respect and bounty. Although this may

4. Most notable among these are Cotonsport de Garoua and Prévoyance de Yaoundé, both in the First Division, but there are others in the Second and Third Divisions.

5. Until the mid-1980s Cameroon was one of the most economically reliable countries in Africa, with a steady pace of annual economic growth of around 6–7 per cent. This, however, started changing in the mid-1980s, and in 1988 Yaoundé was forced to seek World Bank and IMF assistance, which in turn introduced a Structural Adjustment Plan which meant further hardship for the population. Political upheavals and a general strike in 1991 further deepened the economic crisis. The 1994 devaluation of the CFA franc made matters worse. Mbembe and Roitman (1995) paint a vivid picture of the sense of confusion and despair the economic crisis led to among Cameroonians.

seem traditional, it would be a mistake to see this culture of paternalism as a simple survival of tradition. Patron–client relationships are often seen as associated with ethnicity, but in the case of football these ties often unite people from different ethnic groups.[6] Thus, these patron–client relationships can also be regarded as an adaptation to modern and especially urban situations, where they increase the power of patrons and provide – at least in theory – a modicum of security for clients, often across ethnic lines (cf. Barnes, 1986). Coaches refer to their players as their children, players to coaches as their fathers, a newer team to a better-established team as their big brothers, and so on. But these relationships go beyond rhetoric and mean, among other things, that players and coaches are not paid on a regular, contractual basis. Most players do not have a fixed income from playing; some are paid a 'signature bonus' upon signing for the club, but afterwards they too find that the generosity of the club subsequently dries up and their payments become haphazard.

At a minimum players need to be given transportation (taxi[7]) money, which they usually receive, in order to attend training. In principle players are always promised a match bonus, but whether they get it depends on many possibilities. Very rarely are they paid for training (if they are paid, it is 'bonus' rather than pay). Commenting on this state of affairs, Ntonfo (1994: 77) – a Cameroonian literary historian and author of one of the most important works on Cameroonian football – goes so far as to ask rhetorically whether Cameroonian football players receive alms or a salary. The same is true of coaches. They too only get paid from time to time, depending on the pocket or the whim of the club's president. Hence, there is nothing that either a player or a coach can expect as his dues, everything is at the president's discretion or one of his associates (who is almost invariably accused of pocketing some money.)

Players can try to force team presidents into paying them by other means, and it is not uncommon for them to organize unofficial and unannounced strikes, particularly before important matches, which are the only times the players have any real leverage. This even happens at national team level, as for example in the 1990 and in 1994 World Cups (cf. Nkwi and Vidacs, 1997; Mahjoub, 1990). Such paternalistic relationships can lead to ambiguities. Since dues are not fixed, the players and coaches can never be sure of what form and magnitude their recompense will take and, more importantly, when it will materialize. Another source of ambiguity stems from the skilfull movement

6. Ethnicity did not seem to be an issue in the case of OM. This may have been due to the fact that the teams most wronged by them (in particular, the teams of Mbalmayo, as well as Tonnerre and the other First Division teams from which Olympic recruited its players) were of the same ethnic grouping.

7. Taxis function as public transportation in Yaoundé. The bus company folded in 1995.

of people between acting in the contractual and paternalistic modes. My friends often complained bitterly about these practices, expressing a very clear preference (at least to me) about their wish for things to be more business-like. For example, a highly-qualified coach told me that he was constantly being asked to train various teams, but kept refusing because 'it is not normal' for him to be expected to work for nothing. However, at other times the same individuals would act in the paternalistic mode, of which they had disapproved in other contexts.

Olympic: 'the Child Born with a Silver Spoon in its Mouth'[8]

The appearance of Olympic Mvolyé on the Cameroonian football scene was a novelty in that it was organized in an unusually business-like manner and had much greater resources than any other team. Due to the wealth of its shadowy 'patron', the player salaries far outstripped those of almost any other occupation in Cameroon. It was rumoured that players received monthly incomes of CFA 600,000 francs (roughly $1,200 after the 1994 currency devaluation, and double that before devaluation). This is an astronomical figure by Cameroonian standards. By way of comparison, university professors earned about a quarter of this sum and a taxi driver one-twentieth! OM were the only team in Yaoundé to have established offices, in a modern commercial building in the city-centre. They hired one of Cameroon's most respected coaches (also the trainer of the under-17 national team) who was one of the few coaches to own a stop-watch. The players had proper kit and even for a junior match the team carried their own net, an amazing sight as junior matches are never supplied with such luxuries. Naturally, OM had their own minibus to ferry players to matches. Despite this, not even OM owned their own ground, but instead trained on the pitches of a well-respected secondary school.

Financially, Olympic could afford to corrupt rival players, officials and referees alike. Accusations of corruption are common in Cameroon: in 1998 the nation was cited by Transparency International as the most corrupt in the world, and whilst it is questionable how such a judgement is arrived at, it is no secret that corruption is indeed rife. Naturally, it is very difficult to know anything concrete about such matters as by definition such transactions take place outside of the public eye. It is also clear that rumours of corruption are one of the ways in which a team can be denigrated and its success presented as unjustly gained, therefore one has to exercise caution. However, both insiders and outsiders to Cameroonian football were convinced that OM did not stop

---

8. This is how Nguini (1996) characterizes OM in a metaphorical story explaining that, despite advantages, the 'child' continues to fail at school and is surrounded by hostile 'classmates'.

short of corruption to achieve promotion. There is even some concrete evidence to support such allegations.

In the course of the return leg of the semi-final of the 1993 Challenge Cup there was such blatant referee favouritism towards OM that afterwards the referee was suspended for life. A facsimile of his written confession is reproduced by Nguini (1996: 63), confirming that the referee received CFA 200,000 ($800) from OM. Referees in fact have enormous pressures on them, and given both the generalized poverty and the paternalistic relationships prevalent in Cameroon it may be difficult for them to resist such demands (cf. Ongoum, 1998, for a first-person account of how a referee who had every intention of staying 'clean' had to eventually give up refereeing).

One of my friends was a Second Division referee who had suddenly given up refereeing. When I asked him why he explained that he had been approached by OM before a match at which he was chosen to officiate. He had agreed to favour the team on condition that they paid him eighteen years of his salary as a policeman. His argument was that that was how long remained of his service and once he allowed himself to be bought he would no longer be able to perform his duties as a policeman as he would be compromised. Naturally, OM refused to pay such an outlandish sum, but my friend had deemed it prudent to retire from refereeing after the incident.

People watched with glee OM's unsuccessful struggle for promotion. They seemed to look forward to how the team was going to fail next, considering it highly amusing. Even though this sentiment was common, it was not uniform and there were some who wished the team well. The combination of talent, money and corruption seemed irresistible, thus OM's inability to win promotion was inexplicable, prompting a variety of supernatural explanations.

Explaining the Inexplicable

To explain OM's failure, people often invoked beliefs in the occult and forces beyond the visible, which effectively 'tied' the team and prevented its success. Allegations of the use of magic are not unusual in Africa (cf. Leseth, 1997) and are to be seen as part of the game, although some people debate whether magic is effective in football or not. In discussions, team coaches will usually deny employing magical means when preparing their teams, though such a vehement denial will often be followed by snide remarks by others along the lines of: 'of course he denies it, what coach would admit to using magic?' Since there is a generalized belief in occult powers in Cameroon, admitting to the use of such powers would be tantamount to admitting to cheating. One of the favourite statements of some of the coaches was 'work is my magic'. These coaches tend to be of the opinion, publicly at least, that 'work', namely training hard, is the only thing that leads to results in football. Players seemed less convinced, but they too could be heard discussing the relative merits of magic and training. Some asserted that magic 'played a part' in results, while others expressed cynicism. All agreed, however, that whether magic played a part or not, the psychological effects of such beliefs could be consequential (cf. Leseth, 1997).

Accusations of witchcraft in Cameroon are mainly aimed with the purpose of censoring people who gain wealth and at the same time attempting to force people to redistribute what is seen as ill-gotten wealth. Via this process, ideally social differences will be reduced or the wealth can be channelled back into the community. However, there is a basic ambiguity: wealth, according to this argument, is suspect and has to be checked, but as many authors point out wealth is also a sign of power, therefore it inspires respect (Geschiere, 1997; Bayart, 1993). It would have been logical to accuse OM's patron of witchcraft due to his inordinate wealth, but because his wealth did not translate into football successes (and possibly also because he was not directly involved with the team), this was not at issue. In the case of OM, the commentary went in reverse.

There were several explanations for the absence of success. Many indicated that OM had done harm to others and those sinned against had 'cursed' or 'tied' the club, thereby preventing promotion. The identification of sinner and those sinned against varied with the speaker. Some thought that Mbalmayo clubs, which had been used by Olympic to reach the Second Division, were the ones behind OM's subsequent fate. One person argued that Olympic had failed to appease the ancestors of the land in Mbalmayo when it was formed, and it was their wrath which was pursuing the team. Other explanations centred around the First Division teams from which Olympic had lured their players. This had destabilized the teams and was a cause for resentment. Any conversation regarding OM's performance produced easy references to such allegations; however, as indicated above, there was little consensus as to who exactly was causing bad luck. Significantly, what was common to them all was the absence of criticism expressed towards the perpetrators.

The phrase 'money isn't everything' was offered by observers after OM lost a home match to Union de Douala in the Cameroon Challenge Cup semi-finals in 1994. Such an explanation focused on social justice. Since the kind of wealth at OM is beyond almost everyone's reach, there was consolation in that it, in turn, could not translate into football success. The concept of the level playing field is involved here. Similarly, 'the ball is round', is one of the most common clichés about Cameroon football, meaning that in football people have an equal chance of doing well. Football is one of the few arenas in Cameroon where there is at least the illusion that participants have a 'sporting chance' of appearing as equals, regardless of their external socio-economic and historical circumstances. OM's privileges threatened this precept in trying to 'tilt' the playing field both by having better-equipped players and by corruption; this annoyed many people, and when the team did not succeed people rejoiced.

How Things Should Be in an Ideal World

Amidst the general joy over Olympic Mvolyé's failure there were some dissenting voices. Those who wished OM well did so mostly out of a desire for seeing a team, which had the benefit of proper organization and proper equipment, to succeed. To such people the team represented a more efficient way of doing things than is usual in Cameroon. Cameroonians generally, and especially those involved in football, acknowledge that it is necessary to pay players, and that proper organization and equipment is necessary to get results. At the same time, due to their financial constraints, coaches and presidents of clubs often request that players give their services free.

In public, coaches will exhort players to play for honour, or self-respect, or for the joy of the game or for what their efforts may yield in the future. They might argue that players do not deserve the pay and equipment. In private, however, they acknowledge that players need to be paid their dues. On one occasion a coach I know discretely bought a pair of football boots for a player he deemed worthy. This surreptitious action was necessary because he could not afford a pair for everyone else. Another time, after a training session when one of the players had ruined his training shoes, the coach whispered to me, 'it hurts when you see that and you can't help'.

Thus, people employed in football work in very frustrating circumstances, confronting insurmountable obstacles on a daily basis. They often feel their efforts are wasted due to inadequate material circumstances and poor organization, and in this context we can understand why the people who wished to see OM succeed were drawn from the inner circles of football. Such people are trying to 'create' football with their investment of energy and enthusiasm, against enormous financial and personal sacrifices. They believe that given optimal circumstances they would be able to succeed in realizing their dream of creating great football clubs. Thus, for them Olympic was the experiment that should have proven them right.

The Clash of Stereotypical World Views

Those hoping for OM to succeed grappled with the question of the efficacy of action around how things should be done. They contrasted the way in which things are routinely done in Cameroon with a more professional and business-like approach. This could be constructed as the juxtaposition of African vs European, or traditional vs modern ways of doing things. Cameroonians often explicitly evoke these contrasts.

Of course, as has been argued by anthropologists, historians and political scientists alike, Africa is not by any means pristine and traditional, and has not been so for a long time. Cameroonians, like all Africans, do not live in isolation and their history and present is shaped by outside influences. Piot (1999) even argues that the seemingly traditional Kabre people of Togo in fact live very much in the modern world and have done so for at least 400 years. His point is that the Kabre appropriate the external elements and put them to use in their own culture. Football itself is an obvious import, though Africans have appropriated it in various ways. It has been used as a tool of domination as well as of resistance in both colonial and post-colonial times (cf. Fair, 1997; Farred, 1999; Martin, 1991; Nkwi and Vidacs, 1997). Because the sport is such a symbolically rich field it can fit a variety of ideological moulds; it can galvanize people's ethnic as well as nationalist sentiments, but it can also enable expressions of anti-colonial or pan-Africanist views and, as will be illustrated, can also be the forum for debating the relative merits of different ways of acting in the world.

This latter dimension becomes apparent when we consider the attitudes and debates surrounding OM, which question the relative merits and efficacy of Western and African types of action and the applicability of the former to the latter. In the debates that are heard continually in bars, at corner news-vendors, alongside football pitches, in taxis and anywhere where people come together, Cameroonians construct overstated dichotomies wherein they compare themselves to others along ethnic, national and international lines. They also compare their lives to that of other Africans and, overwhelmingly, to what they know of the 'white man's' world, and in discussing OM's successes or failures.

Such debates contain stereotypical notions of 'whites' in which rationality, efficacy and long-term planning are seen to characterize the Western world, and the opposite of these terms are seen as emblematic of the African. These are deep, hegemonic stereotypes which feed on a long history of Western representation of Africans, perpetuated by Europeans throughout the history of contact and interaction with Africans. These stereotypes are by no means innocent, they were tendentiously introduced and reinforced by the colonial powers, used as a means of subjugation of Africans, and not as a means of their 'elevation', despite much rhetoric about the 'civilizing mission' of colonialism. While hegemony is never complete, these dualistic views have, to a large extent, been internalized by Africans. To understand where they come from we have to look back to colonial times.

Colonialism: the Denigration of the Other

Cameroonians are painfully aware of Europe's advantages over them in terms of material well-being and power. In Cameroonian eyes Western society is successful, certainly in the material and political sense, a fact they attribute to the 'white man's way'. While recognizing that the wealth of Europe (and in the Cameroonian case especially of France) is to a great extent due to the exploitation of Africans, they also attribute these differences in material wealth to a different kind of rationality and organization. The combination of the hegemonic power of these stereotypes and the inadequacies of their lives pervaded by underdevelopment, poverty and the mismanagement of affairs small and large leads to the paradoxical situation that almost forty years after gaining independence, Cameroonians continue to subscribe to these notions.

Despite this 'faith' in the white man's world, Cameroonians have little reason to trust whites, and by extension their ways. I kept being presented with these positive stereotypes of whites and began to wonder whether I was being humoured, so one beer-filled evening I asked one of my closest friends to tell me whether, when I wasn't around, they also spoke of whites in such glowing terms? He side-stepped the issue slightly, but nonetheless his answer was very revealing – as a child he was told never to trust whites.

Faced with local failures, people pin their hopes on the 'other' way of doing things (as another friend was fond of remarking 'if I were in charge of Cameroonian football I would entrust it to a white') yet seriously doubt whether it is meant to or can work for them.[9] It is in light of this that my friend's statement about not trusting whites begins to make sense. Cameroonians are aware that European organization and rationality were not created to benefit them. Whilst they may try to appropriate these Western assets, doubts are still voiced as to whether they can successfully attain and sustain such qualities. Thus, Cameroonians are faced with a paradox, attempting to emulate Western ways whilst questioning their applicability and efficacy for themselves.

People often bring up the 'white man's magic' in conversation. Usually they are referring to technological innovation, and though there is a degree of joking in the term it is also quite serious. For example, travelling in a communal taxi in Cameroon an old man, clearly a cultivator of little wealth and education,

---

9. There are equally strong sentiments going the other way too, thus witness the reaction to the French coach in the 1994 World Cup (Vidacs, 1998).

said to me: 'The good God had given Europeans technology and to Cameroonians [he paused for effect and concluded] Paradise!' Technology, in this formulation, is the 'God-given' natural realm of the European, not something that belongs to Cameroonians. What they have instead is Paradise, and though it is not clear what Paradise is, it is the flip-side of technology and something that is equally good to have.

This statement helps us begin to get a glimpse of one of the possible ways of coping with the untenable situation in which Cameroonians find themselves. Finding refuge in what one has, given by God, is one way of overcoming the tension inherent in the obvious inequality they see between their chances of getting ahead in the world and those of Europeans-whites. One of the recurring clichés that people presented me with about Cameroon and football was that the country is teaming with talent. As many put it in a curiously essentialist statement, which, however, also has parallels in much of the literature on sports (about Africans or even blacks in general), 'Cameroonians are born footballers'. This predilection of Cameroonians to attribute innate talent in football to themselves, belongs to the same type of argument where the superior organization of whites is countered by claims of superior innate abilities on the part of Africans.

There is, however, an equally important strand in people's discourses. It involves a questioning of Western ways of acting and thinking, wondering aloud whether the Western way is the only one that leads to desired results or whether the African way may not in some cases be more efficacious. This is patently so in discussions of witchcraft in relation to football and other aspects of life. I have mentioned above that players and coaches openly debate whether magic is efficacious or not in football. Most Cameroonians are convinced that there are other factors at work, darker occult forces in the background which can change results. By attributing superior force to magic they argue that there are things that are beyond the reach of white man's rationalism, which cannot be explained by rationalistic means and which are stronger than he is.

Cameroonians do not reject Western rationality, either for the West or for themselves. They, however, know better than to think that it is meant to work for them, or to think that that is the only kind of logic around. One evening I was sitting with my friends and they were telling stories of the kinds of damage that witchcraft can bring to people. After listening for a while I hazarded the statement that 'where I come from' we don't believe in witchcraft anymore. One of my interlocutors, a young economics student, then asked me if we had lightning where I came from. I said yes. He continued asking if it ever happened that lightning struck and killed someone. Upon hearing my affirmative answer, he threw his hands up and said to all and sundry 'you see, they have it, but refuse it'.

Witchcraft accusations in Cameroon and elsewhere in Africa are frightening in their implications. They lead to accusations against innocent people, allowing unscrupulous individuals to take advantage of these fears. Fear of accusation acts as a levelling mechanism, actively discouraging 'rational' 'market-oriented' behaviour (cf. Geschiere, 1997). At least in this context they are also a source of power because they represent a plus, something that whites have not been able to master, no matter how much they have interfered with African minds. Thus witchcraft is something proper to Africans, an inalienable knowledge that is their own and nobody else's.

As opposed to this specifically African form of knowledge, there is Western knowledge, which is an everyday one by comparison. It is foreign to Africans and as I have argued it is also a duplicitous one, not quite to be trusted. Yet, as it seems that is how Europeans and whites have got ahead, it is also attractive and thus it is that there were some people who – despite the majority's dislike of OM – were rooting for the club, wanting to see these practices put to the test on the football field. So why did OM fail to join the First Division for five years? I have to admit to not knowing the answer, just as my informants did not know. The very variety of the explanations put forth by people seems to indicate that they were shooting arrows in the dark. It seems likely that the players of OM themselves were labouring under the weight of the many contradictions and paradoxes outlined above, themselves doubting whether indeed the 'white man's magic' was superior to that of the Africans. Under the circumstances this weight was too much for them.

15

Treacheries and Traditions in Argentinian Football Styles: The Story of Estudiantes de La Plata

Pablo Alabarces, Ramiro Coelho and Juan Sanguinetti*

When Argentinian football was formally institutionalized, with player professionalism in 1931 and the foundation of the football association (AFA) in 1934, five 'big' clubs were given the greatest political and administrative power: Boca Juniors, River Plate, Independiente, Racing Club and San Lorenzo of Almagro (Scher and Palomino, 1988). Their privileged position reflected their successes during amateur days, and their hegemony over Argentinian fan loyalties. In opposition, all other domestic clubs were 'small'. The big five's power was demonstrated economically through the purchase of exceptional players from smaller clubs. When a small team offered a serious championship challenge, politics would replace sport in terms of match officiating.[1] Consequently, the big five won all championships between 1931 and 1967, leading to a historical alternation of hegemonies, such as Racing (1949 to 1951) and River (1952 to 1957). Small, epic parts were played by small teams in temporarily (but fruitlessly) threatening this order of power.[2]

This process coincided with Argentinian football's 'golden age'. A proliferation of excellent players, some of them successful in Europe, allowed Argentinian football to consider itself as the world's best. This view was further nourished by the intervention of the Second World War, and Argentina's chosen isolation from the 1950 and 1954 World Cups, which curtailed the wider 'testing' of

* This research was financed by UBACyT and CONICET.

1. For example, in the first professional tournament in 1931, match refereeing in the final rounds badly affected the Estudiantes team, known as 'The Professors' for their quality of play.

2. The most famous case involved Banfield in a championship final against Racing in 1951. The media still interpret this match according to the alleged preference of Perón's wife, the famous Eva Perón, for Banfield, so that the small team's victory could reflect the political empowerment of the lower classes in the context of Peronism. See Alabarces (1996) for an early treatment of this topic in connection with films of the time.

Argentina's sense of superiority. Competition was restricted to South America, occasional European tours, or the 1953 exhibition match against England in Buenos Aires. Football successes consolidated the victorious image, in accordance with the prevailing Peronist discourse that presented Argentina as among the world's leading nations (Rodríguez, 1996; Alabarces and Rodríguez, 2000).

After Perón's fall in 1955, this world-view was transformed, leading to a period of great discursive uncertainty in all fields of Argentinian society. In sport, de-Peronization was officially judged to be indispensable, but resulted in a de-politicization in the most drastic and deplorable way: the disappearance of public sport policies.[3] Second, within football, Argentina resumed international competition in 1957, winning the South American championship with a brilliant performance. But at the 1958 World Cup in Sweden, after 24 years of isolation,[4] Argentina lost 6–1 to Czechoslovakia, thus fracturing the old myths of superiority (Archetti, 1999). The media's response to the 'Disaster of Malmö' may be interpreted as a discursive world-view. Argentina, in all fields, had to be modernized (Di Giano, 1998): politically, the anachronisms of Peronism had to be suppressed; economically, developmental doctrines appeared;[5] culturally, consumption was transformed, for example through television and the multinational cultural industry.

Modernization also engendered what was called a 'football-show' by River Plate president, Antonio Liberti. Investments in players were made to increase attendances which had declined continuously after Perón's fall (Scher and Palomino, 1988: 46–50), and European tactics and training were introduced to discipline the perceived Creole indolence of Argentinians.[6] Two coaches were paradigmatic: Helenio Herrera, a naturalized Italian from Argentina who built the highly successful, defensive, *catenaccio* system at Internazionale in

---

3. We are in uncharted territory. Rein (1998) shows that a very early measure of the anti-Peronist Aramburu dictatorship during the mid-1950s involved the break-up of public organizations. The new government took control of private associations (such as the AFA and the Argentinian Olympic Committee) to eradicate the Peronists' influence, and then 'normalize' these bodies through controlling the electoral process. The participation of Argentinian teams in international competition became a separate issue.

4. Argentina participated in the 1930 tournament and lost in the final to the hosts, Uruguay. In 1934, an amateur team was sent to Italy and was knocked out in the first game.

5. The development doctrines (*desarrollismo*) were a series of economic, political and social programmes that were fashionable in the 1950s and 1960s throughout Latin America, and which began with the creation of CEPAL (Economic Council for Latin America), an institution controlled by the United Nations. CEPAL defended Latin America's modernization through the introduction of foreign capital (ultimately North American), and changes to sociability, communication and consumption, in order to overcome the subcontinent's structural underdevelopment.

6. Ford (1994) demonstrates that this popular opposition of European and Creole precedes the 1950s by a long way.

the early 1960s; and Juan Carlos Lorenzo, who learned to coach in Italy to the admiration and envy of his Creole peers. In the spirit of this modernity, Lorenzo was appointed Argentina coach for the failed World Cup campaigns of 1962 and 1966. But, the primarily economic impetus of the football-show was reflected in the clubs' purchase of foreign players, mainly Brazilian after Brazil's victories at the 1958 and 1962 World Cups, yet the clubs also failed in the Copa Libertadores (which was dominated in the early 1960s by Santos and Peñarol). Beyond this, the football-show contained a double movement: of continuity, by confirming the power of 'big' clubs; and of change, by substituting romantic narratives on the golden age for a new discourse, in which victory could be achieved by any means. This latter, essentially mercantile logic, came to supersede the symbolic logic of style (to play beautifully). Victory now meant profit; defeat was not only humiliating, but was also seen as financially threatening.

Paranoid Identities

Participation in the 1966 World Cup, in England, was a crucial moment in this process. Argentina played stylishly in the opening games and qualified for their fourth-ever match against England in the quarter-finals.[7] But in this match Argentina's captain, Rattin, was sent off, the team lost, and the German referee's performance was questioned amidst suspicion of an anti-South American plot (an Englishman had refereed the Germany match against Uruguay). All of these elements contributed strongly to the creation of an imaginary epic around the match. Two facts are axiomatic: first, England coach Alf Ramsay described the Argentinians as 'animals'; second, upon their return, the Argentinian team were received as the moral victors by the new president, the dictator Onganía, at Government House in Buenos Aires.[8] Ramsay's comment must be understood within the context of a radically paranoid identity.[9] Argentina's uncertainty was resolved defensively: the Other, those

---

7. Comparative research indicates that Argentina and England viewed these matches with the same narrative themes: football isolation, 'moral superiority', conspiracy theories, the insular situation of each continent, the influence of heroes, and so on (Alabarces, Taylor and Tomlinson, 2000).

8. The Onganía coup occurred during the championship.

9. The omnipresent, paranoid views in Argentinian football culture deserve interpretation. We are drawn to Jameson's position: 'Fully as striking on another level is the omnipresence of the theme of paranoia as it expresses itself in a seemingly inexhaustible production of conspiracy plots of the most elaborate kinds. Conspiracy, one is tempted to say, is the poor person's cognitive mapping in the postmodern age; it is a degraded figure of the total logic of late capital, a desperate attempt to represent the latter's system, whose failure is marked by its slippage into sheer theme and content' (Jameson, 1988: 356). Despite Jameson's reference to a 'postmodern age', we believe he describes accurately the condition of the popular imaginary after the fall of Peronism. We owe the reference to Jameson to Jeffrey Tobin.

beyond the Empire, were defined negatively, allowing for value reversal: from animals to heroes. Moreover, all of these statements seem to confirm the conspiracy theory regarding the strategies of the powerful: England and Germany, plus FIFA (an institution dominated by Anglo-Saxons), against the peripheral countries (Argentina and Uruguay). As 'moral champions', the paranoid enters a political level (legitimizing dictatorial authority),[10] and a moral level (the facts of the match result are superseded by unquestionable ethics). The tournament dominated Argentina's imaginary until the mid-1970s: the moral champions continued to fail, losing to Peru and Bolivia in 1969, and giving a mediocre performance in 1974. However, the club sides dominated South American competitions between 1967 and 1975, winning world club titles in 1967, 1968 and 1973. These successes consolidated an aggressive, paranoid nationalist discourse that saw football as a successful representation of the nation in difficult socio-economic circumstances. Discursively, sport successes represented a victory of the poor over the powerful, using the weapons of the poor: violence, but redefined as physical courage and team solidarity.

Revenge of the Small

The symbol of that process was the small team, Estudiantes de La Plata, which exploited a transformation in club tournaments to introduce a series of victories for themselves and other newcomers. In 1967, the AFA President, Valentin Suárez, who had been appointed by Onganía, redesigned the European-style championship which had included only teams from the richest areas (Buenos Aires, La Plata and Rosario). Suárez created two tournaments: the 'Metropolitan' championship was played with two groups of teams (mainly from Buenos Aires), leading to the finals involving the top four; the 'National' championship incorporated provincial teams for the first time. The new competition demonstrated that the poorest, provincial teams, as in industry, continued to lose their elite to the capital, and so suffered heavy defeats,[11] with the exception of some teams from Cordoba, the nation's 'third city'. However, shorter tournaments gave smaller clubs a better chance of success.

Accordingly, Estudiantes's victory in the 1967 Metropolitan championship was continued by other clubs: Vélez Sarsfield won the 1968 National championship; Chacarita Juniors won the 1969 Metropolitan; Rosario Central conquered the National in 1971 and 1973; Huracan won the 1973 Metropolitan, followed by Newell's Old Boys of Rosario in 1974. Thus, small clubs

---

10. Argentinian football people (players, journalists and officials) had few scruples in dealing with dictatorships.

11. In 1967, River beat San Martin of Mendoza 8–0; Vélez lost to San Lorenzo 8–1. The following year, Vélez defeated little Huracan of Bahía Blanca 11–0.

broke the 36-year hegemony of the big clubs. But Estudiantes were especially significant. After local success (not repeated until 1982), they won the Copa Libertadores in 1968, 1969 and 1970. They defeated Manchester United for the 1968 European–South American Cup, but lost in 1969 to Milan and in 1970 to Feyenoord. This successful run was exceptional, and generated an intense debate. To illustrate this, we have examined the coverage of Estudiantes by the sport magazine *El Gráfico* from 1967–71, and other press articles of the time. *El Gráfico* played a central role in constructing the Argentinian football imaginary from 1919, featuring the most literate and respected sport journalists (Archetti, 1999). Additionally, the magazine's two star journalists – Juvenal and Osvaldo Ardizzone – had embraced the modernizing discourses after the 1958 World Cup. However, and contradicting the schematic interpretation of Di Giano (1998), the magazine did not maintain a singular position. During this period of deep discursive uncertainty, ambiguity prevailed. Hence, when Estudiantes's successes began in 1967, Jorge Ventura could praise:

> A football that is elaborated over a hard week of laboratory work, and explodes on the seventh day with an effectiveness that consecrates the table of positions. Because Estudiantes continue to manufacture points just as it manufactures its football: with more work than talent . . . Estudiantes keep winning. Their games do not delight, but do have intensity. Their style does not convince, but their campaign is convincing. They are not a 'luxury' team, but a good team. With the conviction of a winning unit, with the work of a modern team and with the strength of a big club. (*El Gráfico*, 3 May 1967)

Two weeks later, a loss to the Lanus club was described as a 'homage to football'; Estudiantes were 'a praiseworthy combatant', but 'lacking in the talent to change a system that doesn't function' (*El Gráfico*, 17 May 1967). Hence, the ambivalence between talent and system begins to frame the field of possibilities. The schema points to other associations, of system-effectiveness, of the modern laboratory. The coach responsible was Osvaldo Zubeldía, who was profusely eulogized, being acclaimed both as a future coach for the national side, and as an exponent of modern values: work, discipline, physical preparation.

Significantly, a later report stated that 'the humility' of the players was the 'most remarkable thing' in the Estudiantes make-up (*El Gráfico*, 21 June 1967). In other words, Estudiantes's key property is not their small condition, but their humble nature, which is recommended for all of Argentinian football. On 4 November 1967, Racing defeated Glasgow Celtic 1–0 in Montevideo and won the European–South American Cup; the fixture had featured three rough matches involving several injuries and red cards. The violence of these games marked a continuation of the previous year's fixture between England

and Argentina. Celtic's Scottish identity made no difference to the Argentinian imaginary: they were all English.[12] Finally, when Estudiantes won their first championship in 1967, Juvenal wrote:

> Their victory has been a triumph for the new mentality, so many times proclaimed from Sweden until here, but rarely established in facts. A new mentality served by young, strong, disciplined, dynamic, vigorous, spiritual and physically upright people. It is clear that Estudiantes didn't invent anything. They followed the path already traced by Racing the previous year . . . Estudiantes won after the 36 year 'ban' of championships on ambitious 'small' teams. Estudiantes defeated their convictions and their limitations as an ultra-defensive-biting-destructive team. Estudiantes defeated the intoxication of a unique week in their club history, claiming the most exemplary of their attributes in the hour of victory: humility. (20 July 1967)

Here, the new mentality designates a claim upon modernity, constituting a series of positive terms that also represent those opposing qualities that are to be banished. And these terms can be placed in a more political context. Estudiantes's values were identical to those claimed by the dictatorship for all Argentinians. Onganía's military government was an alliance of conservative and ultra-catholic sectors, with fascistic temptations, and was militantly anti-Communist. It was framed by the Cold War and the Doctrine of National Security, a policy imposed by the USA throughout the Americas to combat internal leftist groups.

Anti-football and National Representation

During the 1968 Copa Libertadores which Estudiantes won, a pejorative, new adjective appeared in relation to their play: anti-football. Its origin were clear: the tendency towards violence in Copa matches, with injuries and red cards in evidence, added to the rough, fighting style of Estudiantes. *El Gráfico* denied this accusation; when Estudiantes won the Copa against Palmeiras of Brazil, the editorial (21 May 1968) stated:

> Some fashionable talk refers to 'anti-football', by way of qualifying the destructive style of Estudiantes; of this Estudiantes which has won perhaps the highest praises ever given by the foreign press to an Argentinian team. Man-marking with all their men across the entire pitch cannot be called 'anti-football'. Their game is more solid than beautiful, but that's not enough for it to be called 'anti-football', this authentic football created by Estudiantes, of mass production and convincing results.

---

12. The Scotsman Alexander Watson Hutton, founding father of Argentinian football, was always considered an Englishman by the football mythology (Alabarces, 1999a).

Another notable ingredient appears: Estudiantes are eulogized by the foreign media. The mirror speaks. The saga of the team is not debated here; instead, discussion centres on all of Argentinian football, so long as Estudiantes are seen as representing the nation in international competition. It is simpler to build inclusive generalizations around small teams than with big teams. The 'others' of Estudiantes, their classic rivals, are Gimnasia y Esgrima (Gymnastics and Fencing), also from La Plata, and another small team. Hence, there is little that stands between the tranformation of Estudiantes from a locally specific club, into a fuller and more national representative.

That symbolism reaches its zenith against Manchester United for the 1968 European–South American Cup. The matches were played, first on 26 September in Buenos Aires in the presence of Onganía;[13] and then on 21 October in Manchester. Media coverage was intensely chauvinistic in both nations.[14] The Buenos Aires match was covered extensively by *El Gráfico*. The game was hard and tense, with one player sent-off; Estudiantes won 1–0. The *Daily Mirror*'s headline stated, 'The night they spat on sportsmanship' (27 September), and Alex Stepney, United's goalkeeper, stated: 'The Estudiantes players are dirty, they are animals' (*El Gráfico*, 26 September). Brian Glanville, of the *Sunday Times*, wrote a special column:

> Some of their tactics . . . drew us again to question how football, at the highest level, can survive as sport. Tactical fouls as practiced tonight by Estudiantes, by Racing last year and by Argentina in 1966 at Wembley, simply make it impossible to practice the game. Every sport, especially when corporeal contact is unavoidable, should depend on mutual respect between rivals. If a man dodges the other and is clinically fouled, then it is better to leave the game and to enter the pitch with a bomb in the pocket and a stick in the hand.

For the English press, an obvious continuity exists between the three fixtures, and that continuity is violence, methodically applied. For *El Gráfico*, continuity exists, but in the form of a plot. At the Buenos Aires game, the English journalists were identified as responsible; a brief note criticized the 'infantile flippancy' with which they had reported the 'climate of violence' before discussing the game itself. Coverage of the second game was more explicit. The special correspondent, Osvaldo Ardizzone, focused on the violence of English fans, as an examination to be passed by heroes:

13. The match was played in Boca Juniors' stadium: the Bombonera, located in Buenos Aires Estudiantes' ground in La Plata was too small for such an event. The move was also indicative of the political policy of centralization being promoted at the time wherein Buenos Aires was regarded as the window to the country.

14. We have analyzed the English newspapers *The Times*, the *Guardian*, the *Sun* and *Daily Mirror* for both games.

Atmosphere. Climate. Ground. Hostility. Intrigue . . . Estudiantes defeated everything. Was there football in Manchester? Perhaps not. But, anyway, in Manchester it mattered little . . . what really mattered was this: running a lap of honour in front of stands that kept shouting 'animals . . .animals . . .' (22 October)

Estudiantes drew 1–1, thereby winning the Cup 2–1 on aggregate. George Best attacked Estudiantes's Medina and both were sent-off: *El Gráfico*'s photograph showed both players heading for the tunnel, under a rain of missiles, with the caption, 'Those "animals" are protected by those "gentlemen" . . .'. Later, Ardizzone commented:

'Fair Play' is a lie. Yes, I assure you, a lie . . . That well dressed man to my side, looking at me with a fixed expression, did not applaud the winners . . . It is the same in Mataderos, the same as in Avellaneda . . .[15] (Ibid.)

If the English identify themselves according to fair play and sportsmanship, Ardizzone denies any distinction: fans are all equal. Further, in the same issue's editorial, written somewhat exceptionally by the publisher, Constancio Vigil, the Englishmen are described as traitors for rejecting the typical Argentinian cordiality:

Estudiantes's leaders maintained their class until departure, until the airplane left Ezeiza for England, ignoring the resentful, hysterical, exaggerated and lying English journalism that spread throughout the world . . . A journalism whose representatives we received and treated with gentlemanly hospitality, for stupefying them as to our animal condition, according to the stigma that Alf Ramsey brought upon us in 1966 . . .

And they are the gentlemen and we the animals . . . our capacity for indignation was already exhausted. But not our capacity to measure, objectively and without exaggeration, the abysmal difference that exists between the gentlemen and the animals . . . to be gentlemen like them we prefer to be animals in our simple, open, human and frank Argentinian way . . . (Ibid.)

The construction of this we-they opposition demonstrates how Estudiantes triggered national representations. Soon after, the film director Federico Padilla created the movie *We are the Best* in which a group of 'neighbourhood boys' accompany Estudiantes to Manchester for the final game and celebrate their victory with immense joy. 'We' designates the Nation, bravely represented by Veron's goal, the play of Bilardo or Manera, and the celebrations of those humble Argentinian boys after crossing the seas to create a forceful patriotism.

---

15. Mataderos and Avellaneda are working-class suburbs of Buenos Aires.

The Fall

If victory in Manchester was Estudiantes's greatest epic, the match a year later against Milan signalled a fall. By now Estudiantes were no longer the 'small' team that scaled unexpected heights, but the worthy representative of the Nation which had responded to the Wembley defeat. The metonymic victories of Racing and Estudiantes replaced indolence with work, disorder with discipline, underdevelopment with development. As Juvenal said:

> Racing organize and consummate the first great revolution . . . that eliminates, or at least reduces underdevelopment before our own eyes . . . Estudiantes continue with the campaign of emancipation, strengthening Racing's first crusade. They won with the same, or at least similar arsenal to that of Racing: defensive structures, dynamics, temperament, sacrifice, aggression in defence, fighting spirit, team thinking, organization. We eliminate improvisation. We improve and evolve into what had caused our inferiority according to the same critics. (7 January 1969).

Emancipation is a term inherited from the nineteenth-century War of Independence against Spain; crusade has obvious religious connotations There were close discursive relationships between sports journalism and the dictatorship's militaristic, Catholic authoritarianism. Success was the strongest form of political legitimation. After winning the second Copa Libertadores in 1969, against Nacional of Montevideo, Ardizzone accepted that 'Estudiantes go out to destroy, to dirty, to irritate, to deny the show, to use all the illegal subterfuges in football'. But he concluded, 'I, personally, surrender . . . If it is good to win it must be good' (27 May 1969). However, the ambiguity of the period had not disappeared. In July 1969 Chacarita Juniors, a team from San Martin, a poor Buenos Aires suburb, defeated River Plate 4–1 to win the Metropolitan Championship. Juvenal then revised his defence of Estudiantes, which he had sustained to that point:

> Chacarita's victory validates the values that made Argentinian football big. Exactly when those values seemed to have been forgotten by many teams, players and coaches . . . Because Chacarita is not an 'enlarged small' team that enjoys its greatest historical victories by running and playing roughly, by biting and fighting, by sweating and continuous rough play. Chacarita run, bite, sweat, give, sacrifice, but they also play football. Rather: they want to play, taking care of the ball throughout the park, and they also fight. (8 July 1969)

Ambiguities surrounding the Estudiantes style were confirmed in defeat. In September 1969, Argentina's home draw against Peru ensured their elimination from the 1970 World Cup. *El Gráfico* viewed elimination as a catastrophe;

in their editorial, Estudiantes appeared implicitly as an accomplice to Argentina's humiliation:

> We don't have time to seek those guilty for this new frustration. We don't want to do so because it is useless and indeed negative. When the Swedish disaster struck us with tremendous impact, we chose to seek and identify the guilty parties. We chose everyone: those that direct, those that sustain football with their popular contribution, those that commentate, those that play. Some guilty ones emerged from the witch-hunt, and a great victim too: the school of Argentinian football. From that crucial point, the most important thing was obfuscated: the player's personality, which he best knows and understands. The desire to erase the memory of those six Czechoslovakian goals propelled us towards a defensive game, towards the eternal fear of losing, making us forget the necessity and pleasure of scoring more goals than our opponents to win. The desire to overcome our lack of speed and physical power before the Europeans induced in us an indiscriminate imitation, a contempt for ability and intelligence. Thus, we fall a little more every year, because we did not deceive ourselves with the honourable achievements of the World Cup in England, with a mentality of fear, we arrive at this point today . . . (2 September 1969)

The text is self-critical. Defence of Estudiantes is displaced by a questioning of even the heroic Wembley saga. Elimination from Mexico is equated with Sweden 1958, as a new point of inflection. In this novel series, the article of 23 September 1969 is significant. With the title 'Who would win: The Machine or Estudiantes?', Juvenal contrasted the 1940s River Plate team (nicknamed 'The Machine' and regarded as the best 'Argentinian school' team), with the 'modern' Estudiantes. Against previous expectations, the magazine chose The Machine.

In October, the fall began. Estudiantes played in Milan in the first leg of the European–South American Cup, and lost 3–0. The violent play of Estudiantes was criticized by *El Gráfico*'s editor (14 October 1969). One week later, the coach Zubeldía recognized that his players had struggled under the pressure of being Argentina's saviour after the Mexico debacle (21 October 1969). The return leg was catastrophic: in the Boca Juniors stadium, as against Manchester United, Estudiantes won 2–1, but several players contested the aggregate defeat and attacked the Italians violently. The Milan player Combín (paradoxically, an Argentinian himself) suffered a broken bone in his face, courtesy of the elbow of Aguirre Suárez, while the goalkeeper Poletti savagely kicked the Italian midfielder, Rivera, across the turf. The two Argentinians and another assailant, Manera, were jailed following Onganía's intervention and then suspended from football for one year – except Poletti who was banned *sine die*. After the scandal, the *El Gráfico* editorial declared:

They have just put us across the front pages of the world's newspapers – even the Vatican's *L'Osservatore Romano* – leaving us with an enormous and bitter experience, the reverberations of which we still cannot measure. (28 October 1969)

A year earlier, the English had been viewed as expressing their devastation about an unexpected defeat; but here, there was no way to claim innocence.

The punishment of players can be discussed . . . But it was necessary to make the punishment 'historical' in the same way that the blame and damage were historical. It is damaging to the country, let's not forget . . . We played ourselves – as a people and country – before the world, and it was necessary to respond in this way; somehow it was necessary to confirm that we are not this way. (Ibid.)

The text is crystal-clear: the value of 'we' is put at stake. As noted earlier, the *We are the Best* film of 1968 situated the saga of Estudiantes in terms of the Nation. After the disaster, it was essential to adjust the picture to one which could be read as 'we are not this way'. The year's end served only to rationalize the interpretation for *El Gráfico*:

Television took the deformed image of a match and transformed it into urban guerrilla warfare all over the world . . . The Estudiantes that we admired, applauded and defended, were a very different thing. When they won their first finals, their play was not anti-football, but authentic football suffused with effort, vitality and sacrifice. That sad night at the Bombonera damaged our deteriorating international prestige a little bit more. (17 December 1969)

Although the transfer from local to national representation was assumed ('it damaged our deteriorating prestige'), the scandal's metaphorical form was at least suggestive: 'a match transformed into urban guerrilla warfare'. The displacement is radical: Estudiantes now occupy the enemy of the state's place par excellence, that of the leftist urban guerrillas who had already begun their operations in Argentina. Starting from there, despite winning another Copa Libertadores in 1970 and playing a fourth consecutive final in 1971 (losing to Nacional), Estudiantes disappeared almost completely from *El Gráfico*. On the night of their last defeat, Osvaldo Ardizzone closed the tale with a farewell note. A return to mythical origins was due: in 1973, Huracan won the Metropolitan championship under a young coach, long-haired and vaguely politically leftist, named César Luis Menotti.[16] Huracan, another small team,

16. Menotti's membership of the Communist Party was rumoured then and confirmed after the dictatorship.

played in a classical style, respectful of Argentinian football traditions.[17] From then until the 1978 World Cup, Argentina followed another path.

Conclusions

We conclude with three arguments: the first relates specifically to sport practice; the second is political; the third is more suggestive. First, we may ask, how exactly did Estudiantes play? Beyond the enormous archival problems for this type of research – it is almost impossible to access complete recordings of their games – the question is not too pertinent. The testimonies, both then and now, agree that Estudiantes stretched both the rules of the game and the discretion of referees to the limits. There are certain disputes about detail: one legend is that the players used pins to harass opponents, a claim denied emphatically by those involved. But clearly, Estudiantes practiced a strongly defensive style that paid homage to the Italian way, with the use of physical force, tactical discipline, an absence of improvization – and roughness, a lot of roughness. Hence, the agreement even of Estudiantes's defenders here, allows us to say that there is little difference between what is said now and what was done then. On the other hand, in discussing styles, the practice that supports them is less important than the myths that they produce. And the myth of the 1960s Estudiantes team is very effective: it represents a landmark in the Argentinian football imaginary.

Second, political references are unavoidable. A strong homology existed between the new values developed by Estudiantes, profusely eulogized by *El Gráfico* and praised by the Onganía dictatorship. The development doctrine of the late 1950s and early 1960s were introduced by unstable democratic governments (because Peronism was forbidden), but after the 1966 coup it became an authoritarian policy that was coercively imposed. The State's resources were employed repressively: political parties, strikes and unions were banned; art was censored, academics expelled and dissidents persecuted, even murdered.[18] The Estudiantes story unfolded in that context, and its crisis coincided with the dictatorship's end. In May 1969, before the Milan scandal, the 'Cordobazo' occurred: a popular rebellion seized the city of Cordoba for two days until the Army intervened to restore order. From that point we may trace the demise of Onganía. One year later, the Montoneros reemerged to kidnap and execute General Aramburu, who had been responsible for the 1955 coup against Perón and subsequent repression. Onganía fell, to be

---

17. The youthful image of the team and coach, symbolizing the spirit of the times, was accompanied by their fans' sympathy for the Leftist Montoneros guerillas (see Archetti and Romero, 1994).

18. Onganía's fascism saw the modernization of customs and civil society, through the original development doctrines, being replaced by a reactionary and deeply conservative Catholicism.

replaced successively by the dictators Levingston and Lanusse, culminating in the democratic elections of 1973. From that point, the political climate was radically different: repressive dictatorships were followed by Perón's populist return, with left-wing influence the most dominant alongside the enormous influence of guerilla organizations. The slightly cynical discourse of success generated by Estudiantes was replaced by a leftist populism: the return to 'the essence of style'. In politics, and in football, the strategy of authoritarian development had failed.

Third, we can argue that the saga of Estudiantes has not really ended. If the main protagonist was the coach Zubeldía, the press were unanimous that Carlos Bilardo, the right-sided midfielder, was his on-field representative. Bilardo was a cynical spokesman, defending unreservedly the team's instrumental, law-bending approach.[19] After retiring in 1970, Bilardo returned a few years later as coach, leading Estudiantes to the new local title in 1982. That same year, after Menotti's failure in the Spanish World Cup, Bilardo was named national team coach, winning the 1986 World Cup and finishing second in 1990. Bilardo looms larger than Zubeldía and Estudiantes in the football imaginary. He stands juxtaposed against Menotti, in one binary opposition that defines Argentinian football (Archetti, 1999). At Italia '90, an awful Argentinian team was sustained by the few scraps of creativity by an injured Maradona. Bilardo arrived in the final against Germany, bestriding two strands of continuity: illegal practices (on-field violence and gamesmanship),[20] and a paranoid discourse (about the world conspiracy identified and denounced by Maradona). A discontinuity existed only in politics: from authoritarian development policies, Argentina had moved to democratic, neoconservative populism. Bilardo was the constant element that united them.

19. For example, Bilardo stated in May 1969: 'it is essential to win and nothing else'.

20. It was suggested that, during a break in play against Brazil, the Argentinian masseur offered water to the Brazilian Branco; the liquid contained an emetic drug.

16

Ferencváros, Hungary and the European Champions League: The Symbolic Construction of Marginality and Exclusion

János Bali*

International matches involving Hungarian football sides – at national or club level – often acquire an extra-sports, occasionally political, overtone in Hungary. In the Soviet-type party state era, for example, especially in the early 1950s, the national team's successes often appeared in the media as signifying the political system's superiority. In the 1990s, Hungarian results abroad are interpreted differently, often in relation to 'European-ness'. Hungary's geographical position relative to Europe is a deep-rooted motif of national identity and historical memory; geographical marginality has always been linked to socio-cultural marginality.[1] Hungarian historiography often analyses different national epochs in terms of lagging behind Western Europe. Thus, for example, Hungarian national consciousness conceives of the 150-year Ottoman Turkish rule (which followed the 'glorious era', fifteenth-century reign of King Matthias) as the beginning of this lag and one of its main symbols. Besides the concept of periphery, the idea that 'we are indispensable, rightful members of Europe' is also present. Sometimes it appears as Hungary, 'bastion of Europe' (in the course of history warlike non-Christian peoples coming from the East such as the Tartars or the Turks were stopped by Hungarians, or they stopped in Hungary). Alternatively, the notion appears through the 'talented nation', beginning with 'it is no accident that this small nation has survived for more than a thousand years', through the commonly held view that, relative to its population, Hungary gave the world the highest

---

* I dedicate this paper to Tamás Hofer.
1. See also Hofer (1991, 1994) and Niedermüller (1989).

number of Olympic champions and Nobel-prize winners, even though the latter won scientific fame when living abroad.

Through these notions, the definition of the country's geography, society and culture is based on this peculiar duality. Where do we belong in Europe? The question has become topical once again in the 1990s. Previously, in the context of the two political systems (socialism, capitalism) in Europe, Hungarians were labelled East European by the West but considered themselves to be in Central Europe – as it appeared in contemporary text-books also – or, as interpreted by public opinion, felt that they were 'the western-most non-capitalist country'. In tandem with the disintegration of the socialist regime, a feeling of marginality has revived in Hungarian public thinking. The slogans that we should 'join Europe', or 'learn to behave, work, earn, think etc. in the European way' were heard increasingly in different settings. In the 1990s, Hungary's integration to the European Union took the form of a specific political programme. Under the circumstances, in Hungary, sports, and especially football, became a symbolic field displaying and expressing, in an amplified way (occasionally in extreme forms and at times over-sensitively) the efforts (sometimes successful, sometimes not) of a nation's European integration.

Sports Events and the Value System of 'European-ness'

In the 1990s, owing to the defeats of the national football team,[2] public interest has gradually shifted towards international matches involving the Budapest club FTC (Ferencvárosi Torna Club – Ferencváros Gymnastics Club, popularly known as Fradi). Fradi are the only Hungarian club to have qualified for the Champions League; and, for socio-historical reasons they are by far the most popular Hungarian club nationwide. Fradi's image was created first by its petty bourgeois and working-class supporter base (as opposed to teams supported by the rich upper-middle class), but after the Second World War they were seen as opposed to the Communist state-backed teams (the police and the military), acquiring the image of being the most authentic representatives of the Hungarian nation. Fradi thus represented the positive values that other teams had lost through their prior contamination by powerful social groups. In the contemporary Hungarian media, Fradi is the team most often referred to as the 'flag-bearer of the nation'. Many phrases equate the Fradi–Europe relationship with that between Hungary and Europe. 'Ferencváros: the first to start out for Europe' was the headline of one news item, announcing that Fradi – a pioneer in this respect among Hungarian football teams – was

---

2. Hungary has not qualified for World Cup or European Championship finals since 1986.

planning to sign a player from the German Bundesliga.[3] Sports public opinion believes that the name 'Fradi' still has credibility in Western Europe, therefore it was clear to every player that they could transfer to reputable foreign teams exclusively from Ferencváros. The most important consequence of a major Fradi success is that 'Europe speaks of Ferencváros once again'.[4]

The motivation to meet the expectations of foreigners, of Europe, is an organic and essential part of not only the self-image of Fradi fans, but also of Hungarian national identity. Prior to the 1995 visit of Real Madrid to Üllöi út (the Ferencváros ground and headquarters), Fradi's managers launched an appeal for 'fair' support, 'lest half of Europe should speak of us'.[5] In the same year, Fradi's women's handball team played a Champions Cup match against Bremen. Fans embittered by the narrow defeat of their team threw missiles onto the court, leading the press to complain that 'Fradi fans made a "fine" exhibition of themselves in front of the whole of Europe'.[6] Fuelled by an inferiority complex and sense of peripheral status nationally, media interpretation of Hungarian sports (especially football) is usually full of symbolic comparisons between events on the pitch – such as playing style, physical condition of players or lack of concentration – and national characteristics.

A highly common stereotype applied in football is that Hungarian players are unable to last the full ninety minutes. This view intensified in the 1970s, when absence from two World Cups (in 1970 and 1974) and the ageing of the 'Albert-Mészöly' generation resulted in Hungary's obvious lagging behind Europe. Fans recalled several important internationals when Hungary lost goals at the very end of the match.[7] The general opinion was that '90 minute performance is a must to belong to European football'.[8] One recurrent theme in evaluations of Fradi was defeatism, juxtaposed in every case to the values of 'courage' and 'self-confidence' associated with European-ness. Fiascos are seldom attributed to lack of capabilities; given the notion of 'talented people (nation)' as an essential organizing element of Hungarian national identity this makes sense. If Fradi lose to a European rival, it is because they play in a

3. *Nemzeti Sport*, 25 April 1995.

4. Statement of Gyula Rákosi, a prominent Ferencváros player in the 1960s: *Nemzeti Képes Sport*, 26 September 1995.

5. *Nemzeti Sport*, 1 November 1995.

6. *Sport Plusz Foci*, 25 February 1995.

7. Fans recall many games which took a bad turn near the end: the 1973 Hungary-Sweden World Cup qualifying match (3–3); the 1982 Hungary–Belgium World Cup match (1–1); the most recent World Cup qualifying matches Hungary–Turkey (2–2 from 2–0), Hungary–Switzerland (2–2 from 2–0), Norway–Hungary (3–0, with three goals in the last ten minutes); and the Olympic match Hungary–Japan (2–3) where Hungary led until the last minute.

8. *Nemzeti Sport*, 21 December 1995.

defeatist way:[9] the curse of Hungary and Ferencváros. Similarly, a shock victory is typically attributed not to physical or intellectual capabilities, but to overcoming this defeatism. 'What has made Fradi so brave?' – *Nemzeti Sport* inquired on 16 August 1995 after defeating Anderlecht in Belgium. Thanks to that win, Fradi joined the 'millionaires' club', the Champions League. Sporting success is openly interpreted as the success of the entire nation, and according to the commentary on the Fradi–Real Madrid (1–1) Champions League match in the same series ('One point from Europe'), every point scored by Ferencváros is a national feat, one more step towards European integration.[10]

The Frad–Ajax Match: Failure and National Sensitivity in the Hungarian Media

The Budapest fixture between Fradi, freshly victorious over the Swiss champions in their first Champions League appearance and Ajax Amsterdam, reigning European champions and still considered the best team, was awaited most eagerly in Hungary. More than 100,000 requests were received for 20,000 tickets. The Hungarian media labelled the match a battle between West and East, and in the pre-match analysis a sports daily published an article entitled 'Eastern defeats' carrying the positive message that Ajax had lost to several East European teams before, a direct parallel being their loss in 1974 to CSKA of Bulgaria.[11] The match took place on 28 September 1995, with Ajax defeating Fradi 5–1 after a scoreless first half.

Below, I discuss the events in detail because they point well-beyond a specific match, and provide an excellent illustration of how the insult suffered by Fradi grew into a slight upon the nation. Most illustrations originate in the press and present journalist and fan opinion. I do not evaluate the legitimacy and truth content of the ideas in question. Rather, discussion of the 'Ajax Affair' seeks to disclose the social and cultural embeddedness of football in Hungary, the emotional-conceptual meanings that a match can convey, and the media's capacity for 'moulding' events into an 'affair'.

The anguish caused by the result was enhanced at the after-match press conference when Ajax's Dutch coach – in the view of Hungarian broadcasters – commented on Ferencváros's performance in an arrogant and disdainful way. He declared that

> the atmosphere in the stands was hostile from the first moment of the warm-up; spectators emitted monkey-hoots to show scorn for our coloured players who were completely taken

9. Ferencváros coach Novák, *Sport Plusz Foci*, 9 December 1995.
10. *Nemzeti Sport*, 2 November 1995.
11. Ibid., 21 September 1995.

aback: *What kind of nation is this that greets its guests by emitting jungle sounds.*[12] (emphasis added)

The following day's newspapers concentrated on the press conference, expressing shock at the identification of a group of fans with the entire nation, and the Dutch (whose supporters are commonly known as the most prone to vandalism across Europe) labelling of Fradi fans as racist.[13] The papers stressed that UEFA inspectors found no fault with Ferencváros supporters, hence the Dutch agitation (to the extent that their coach contemplated recalling the team from the pitch during the match) was incomprehensible.[14] The bitterness of Hungarian public opinion was reinforced further by reports of the Dutch response. According to *Algemeine Dagblad*, 'Ajax have never played against as weak a team as Ferencváros since the Champions League came into existence'.[15] Danny Blind, the Ajax captain, observed: 'Had we played with all our might throughout the match, we could have scored more than ten goals. But this public does not deserve our entertainment'.[16] The Dutch television commentator dwelt longer on events in the stands than on those on the pitch, calling the public vulgar and primitive 'hooters'.[17] At the press conference following the match, Ajax's fitness coach, of Hungarian origin (!), addressed Hungarian journalists in a censorious tone, declaring that he had thought prior to the match that he was in Europe.[18]

From the start, the conflict reflected a poor but good-hearted, honest and proud nation, conscious of its own worth, versus a haughty, disdainful, wealthy and arrogant Europe, in the final analysis the opposition between East and West Europe. This feeling intensified after another event in the Champions League. In autumn 1995, UEFA expelled Dynamo Kiev after a referee reported that the team managers tried to bribe him before the match against a Greek side. Dynamo protested in vain: the referee's statement was accepted as evidence. Beside the ban, the club and its managers were banned from international football for several years. Hungarian sports circles, Fradi fans included, saw a similarity between the two cases, feeling that the former socialist countries of East Central Europe, which were looking to 'join' Europe, were completely at the mercy of the West, as no one seemed to listen to their protests. One

12. Ibid., 29 September 1995.
13. Ibid. Previously, the Hungarian media had highlighted English fan vandalism on practically every occasion, with little prior mention of Dutch vandalism.
14. Ibid.
15. Ibid.
16. Ibid.
17. Ibid.
18. Ibid.

conclusion drawn by people was that Europe had no need for this region: the West would, whenever possible, obstruct every effort at integration. In other words, it would indirectly deny what these commentators saw as their claim to be considered part of Europe – even if this was done symbolically, in the language of sports.

The Ajax match clearly touched a neurosis in Hungarian national identity. At first the press did not reject the Dutch charges unanimously. The charges reflected European values, and so 'hooting' was condemned as an expression of un-European, racist conduct, which the press interpreted as an unfortunate fad among some fans. Initially, fan opinion varied on whether Fradi deserved this Dutch antipathy; some even asked, 'How can we get into Europe with behaviour like this?'[19]

Nevertheless, public opinion could not digest the events leading to the conflict, or take the blame so easily. The media and supporters questioned the Dutch right to judge. The first 'counter-charge' focused on the Dutch coach's style of critique; at the press conference he had reacted in 'a haughty, arrogant, disdainful and utterly primitive way', inexplicable even by the rules of '*Vae Victis*'.[20] Second, in the West, much more brutal and extreme fan behaviour occurred which often culminated in violence; hence, it was commendable that fans did not use anti-Semitic slogans and posters despite the famously strong ties of Ajax to the Dutch Jewish community.[21] Third, it was wrong to make a summary negative judgement on an entire nation on the basis of a few hundred or thousand people: especially not if the 'accuser nation', such as the Netherlands, have, for centuries, as colonialists, 'held in disdain, humiliated and exploited blacks'.[22] The storm would probably have subsided quickly except for the open letter of two Dutch football heroes, Johann Cruyff (then coach of Barcelona) and Frank Rijkaard (a former Ajax player), published in the Spanish paper *Marca* three weeks after the Fradi–Ajax match. The letter urged Real Madrid to eliminate Ferencváros from Europe by scoring a victory in the name of the Netherlands at the next Champions League match.

On 25 October 1995, *Sport Plusz Foci* published a compilation entitled 'On what grounds do Ajax scream? Beatings and vandalism are permitted, hooting is forbidden?', showing that

19. Fan's opinion communicated by telephone: *Nemzeti Képes Sport*, 3 October 1995.
20. *Nemzeti Képes Sport*, 3 October 1995.
21. *Nemzeti Képes Sport* published a history of Ajax on 23 May 1995.
22. *Nemzeti Képes, Sport*: 3 October 1995.

the conduct of the Dutch club is all the more difficult to understand since their own fans have in the past 15 years become one of the most feared in Europe. They wreaked havoc wherever they appeared. Apparently, this does not trouble Ajax's chiefs-of-staff in the least.[23]

The same issue also reported that, despite the ban, fan groups and travel agencies were busy organizing trips to the return match in Holland. The title of the article, 'They will not mess with us . . . Fradi fans will be there in The Netherlands!', indicates that this was already considered a national issue – it was imperative to show that Hungarians could not be dealt with so easily. On 26 October, *Nemzeti Sport* answered the presumed insults in a sarcastic article entitled 'Some thoughts on Frank Rijkaard's spits':

There must be a mistake here. Mr Jos van der Vegt was either tipsy (let's say he swallowed a pint or two of 'Amstel-dam' lager . . .), or else . . . But I really write this with diffidence: he does not like Ajax. How else could the manager of the Feyenoord establishment have mustered the courage to categorise the fans of the Amsterdam team as vandals? I repeat, there must be a mistake here, for we Hungarians (especially Hungarians living at home) know very well that the managers, players and even fans of Ajax have risen almost to the level of Desmond Tutu, or even perhaps Martin Luther King in terms of 'fighting for human rights'. The brave men of Amsterdam have taken a strong line against racism, fascism, idiocy and who knows what other extreme manifestations. And they have done so after the Fradi–Ajax match, in the name of all mankind. Later on, they even found the time and energy to call the attention of the Spanish public to Ferencváros, Public Enemy No. 1 of Europe (all right – of European football). However, before we Hungarians start to repent and to dissuade in the future from hooting not only our fellow human beings, but also a few owls here and there, let's recall a few little things. Let's remember Frank Rijkaard, for instance, who has not always been such a positive hero, spokesman for all mankind. Many will remember the Dutch–German match played at the 1990 World Cup where . . . let's not be euphemistic, Frank Rijkaard spat at Rudi Völler on the nape of the neck so hard that the German forward nearly fell over . . ."[24]

On 28 October, mainly under pressure from fans and sports public opinion, *Sport Plusz Foci* continued to deal with the Dutch charges. This was the first time the full translation of the open letter was published.[25] The article reviewed reactions to the Dutch appeal, primarily interviewing Hungarian sports officials, players, and the FTC coach and businessmen. Some thought that the Dutch could stir up such passions 'because we are still treated as being

23. *Sport Plusz Foci*, 25 October 1995.
24. *Nemzeti Sport*, 26 October 1995.
25. A glance at the original Spanish version shows that the manifesto was not only signed by the two renowned footballer experts mentioned above, but signatories included actors, directors, singers and even world-famous Dutch chess player, Jan Timman.

from the East',[26] and the majority of interviewees believed the Dutch charges had to be answered. In the Hungarian Parliament, an MP addressed the Foreign Affairs Minister and called for government action on the grounds that the 'open letter caused incalculable harm to Hungary's good reputation, to how the country will be viewed internationally, and gravely damaged its image'.[27] By then the general opinion was that there were among Ferencváros fans – just as among fans of any other European team – extremist elements and groups. Other fans should disassociate themselves and teach the offenders more sportsmanlike behaviour. Meanwhile, it was thought that racism and vandalism among Hungary's extremist fans was far smaller than in Germany, England or the Netherlands. In public opinion, the conflict went beyond the football match, and was transformed into a quixotic quest for justice by the small East European nation. The general mood was captured by a journalist's comment:

> To date, the self-appointed spokesmen of Western Europe subject us by and large to the same treatment as those few silly fans did the black stars. The prejudices of the trouble-makers who mingled with Fradi's fans are, of course, not even worthy of the name, they are not worth the disdain . . . It looks very much as if we, former socialist countries, are to become Europe's new blacks. We would take the place of the traditional scapegoats, the blacks and the Jews, while those looking down on us and trying to ban us from joining the circle of decent and distinguished European clubs will defend, with all their might, their own former scapegoats *from us*. (emphasis added) We cannot prevent ourselves becoming scapegoats, but we could perhaps avoid becoming guilty."[28]

From this point on, the 'Ajax affair' proceeded along two lines. First, the stadium events led to national self-examination; the question was 'to what extent are we European and what does our value system look like?' Second, an 'all-national' consensus emerged pointing well beyond Ferencváros, and which manifested itself in occasional counter-moves. The 28 October issue of *Nemzeti Sport* printed in full the three letters in Hungarian, two of which were addressed by László Benkö, President of the Hungarian Football Association, to the presidents of UEFA and the German Football Association, respectively, and one signed by members of the Hungarian 'Golden Team' of the 1950s (headed by Ferenc Puskás) and addressed as an open response to the Spanish paper *Marca*. All promised to do their utmost to end the repre-hensible behaviour of fans, while affirming that this was not a specific Hungarian

---

26. Statement by FTC coach Dezsö Novák (*Sport Plusz Foci*, 28 October 1995).
27. *Nemzeti Képes Sport*: 7 November 1995 (quoted from 'Let's take care of football').
28. László Szále's column: 'Europe's new Negroes': *Sport Plusz Foci*, 28 October 1995.

problem, but one present throughout the football world. They rejected the smear-campaign which cast aspersions on the entirety of Hungarian sports and the whole country, and which aimed at 'removing Ferencváros and Hungarian football from the arena of European football', but whose aggressive tone replicated the mentality to which it objected. This official stand was taken to a great extent due to fan pressures.

While part of the official sports management weighed the pros and cons of a letter of protest for diplomatic reasons, the majority of fans expressed informally their desire 'to tell the world that we shall not put up with this, that this nation is not racist, and has nothing to do with fascist manifestations'. People were unanimous in thinking that

> European football and within it the Champions League is an outstanding opportunity to raise money. Big clubs are reluctant to share profits with small ones. Wonder teams from the East are an irritant to them. These teams have a smaller capacity for publicity, they are less able to lure spectators into the stadium. Therefore, if possible, out with them from 'Europe'.[29]

Hungarian sports opinion analysed those elements of the Dutch accusations and of the smear-campaign which could be answered in an 'unbiased, objective' way, in order to defend the nation. One of these was the motif of scorn and disdain evident in the Dutch attacks, something that Hungarian teams had never made others feel, not even when, thanks to the successes of Hungarian football, they ranked among the top football nations of the world. In the follow-up to the Ajax affair, in addition to defence, the Hungarian media had turned increasingly to counter-attacks, striving primarily to question the 'European-ness', democratic nature and sense of moral superiority of 'the Dutch' as a whole. The Dutch were described as racists, or belittled in comparison with the British, who were of impeccable morality and indubitably European in the media's eyes. Sharp-eyed journalists noticed that when Ajax visited Hungary, at team meals, white and non-white players ate at separate tables. 'So much for unbounded Dutch democracy',[30] was the rather sarcastic comment of journalists.

In the following months, the Hungarian sports press gave priority to news indicative of racial discrimination in Dutch teams (Ajax, the Dutch national team), so much so that many Fradi fans, for example, knew exactly that at the 1996 European Championship white and non-white Holland players had such a public quarrel that, according to news reports, on the pitch they preferred to pass to members of their own cliques and they did not speak to

29. *Nemzeti Képes Sport*, 31 October 1995 : 'Fradicalism'.
30. Ibid.

each other off the pitch. Hungarian fans saw these events as evidence that the very same Dutch who were appealing to European-ness, democracy and racial tolerance, were also likely to violate these principles. On 31 October, *Nemzeti Képes Sport* reviewed expressions referring to the Dutch in the English language, portraying them as a rather flawed, somewhat despised and ridiculed nation of simpletons, in justification, as it were, of the sound morality of Hungarian counter-attacks:

> It is not my intention to maltreat the Dutch, because I find them a most sympathetic people. I have visited there on several occasions and always had a good time. Nevertheless, some civilised nations do not like them. The English, for one. On the other side of the Channel, a prostitute is called a 'Dutch widow', and a cushion-like foot-holder a 'Dutch wife'. Drunken bluster is 'Dutch courage'. And frogs croak like a 'Dutch nightingale'. 'Dutch courage' is the equivalent of cowardice. And, *non plus ultra* of insolence, the comically protruding front teeth of an English child are nicknamed 'Dutch teeth'. The only reason why I write this is that the brave Dutch should not be all that proud of themselves if the English gentlemen refer to them like this."[31]

Previously, the Dutch attack was read as an 'all-European' stand, but these articles clearly showed that Europe lacked homogeneity, while some 'civilized nations', such as the English, disparaged the Dutch and did not entirely identify with them. Experience has taught several European countries to receive Dutch fans by putting the police in a state of emergency.[32] Fans mentioned several incidents to highlight the vandalism of Dutch fans.[33]

Hungarian views, regarding 'hooters' and flags with swastikas in the stadium, were ambivalent at this time. Some – mainly non-Fradi fans and those who did not attend football matches – rejected the Dutch generalizations about Hungary, but agreed with the charges themselves: these kinds of fans, the trouble-makers parading with fascist symbols, could impair Hungary's image in Europe. Others, however, rejected every feature of the accusations, considering the symbols in question to be Hungarian offshoots of a European fashion, symbolizing strength and boundless love for Fradi, and were not essentially fascist given the value system of the fans using them.

In mid-November, the Ajax affair took a new turn. Hungarian public opinion was about to forget the press conference and the open letter published in *Marca*, when Ajax addressed a letter to UEFA indicating that, contrary to custom, they would not provide tickets to Ferencváros fans for the Champions

31. *Nemzeti Képes Sport*, 31 October 1995.
32. *Nemzeti Sport*, 4 November 1995.
33. Such as the Ajax–Austria Wien match, where the local fans hit Wohlfart, the visiting goal-keeper, on the head.

League return match scheduled for early December. Fans first reacted with surprise, disbelief and doubts as to whether Ajax's decision was legal. Even if they did, what would happen to Hungarians who travelled to see Fradi despite everything? After their earlier caution, Fradi's management expressed indignation in the clearest terms and joined those urging diplomatic action, given the fact that 'fans have proven in the meantime that we do belong in Europe'.[34] The Fradi family proved their unity in practice also. Conflicts between different fan groups and fans and managers were relegated to the background. Fradi fans considered it a national mission to fight the Dutch both on and off the pitch, and thought it was once again their turn to save the honour of the nation while still demonstrating its European-ness. Journalists and fans both considered this last move by the Dutch an act of expulsion, 'so, even white men are undesirable in Europe'.[35]

After UEFA's official notice informing Ferencváros of the Dutch decision, the club management issued a communiqué declaring that Ajax's statements and actions were outrageous. Meanwhile, they requested Ferencváros fans not to travel to Holland, to prevent fans or the club being the subject of provocation. The management lodged a complaint with UEFA, and the match was arranged so that in Amsterdam the team and officials would stay away from the protocol events or press conferences in protest at the Dutch sanctions. The moral base for national indignation was strengthened by the news that the Dutch had adopted a haughty, bad mannered and disdainful attitude to Ferencváros prior to the ominous September game in Hungary, and before any 'hooting' had taken place:

> An unprecedented event took place at Vadrózsa restaurant. After dinner, the representatives of Ajax gave no gift to the Fradi representatives. They accepted the package (including Herendi china) offered by the Hungarians and left, sated and laden with gifts. In international football, this qualifies as an embarrassing and even offensive gesture. This happened one day before the game. That is, when no mention had been made yet of racism, fascism, hooting and the 'ruthless' behaviour of the Fradi public."[36]

By this time, the moral justification for nationwide opposition to the Dutch had become rooted in the same European system of standards to which the Dutch themselves had appealed in their condemnation of the Hungarian people. The effects of the Ajax affair were felt in politics as well, and forced

34. Statement of FTC President Dr István Szívós: *Nemzeti Sport*, 18 November 1995.

35. *Nemzeti Képes Sport*, 21 November 1995.

36. *Nemzeti Sport*, 25 November 1995. It is worth noting the date of the article. This incident reached the press two months (!) after the ominous events – clearly, as part of the press campaign against Ajax.

the ambassadors of the two countries to take a stand. The Dutch ambassador
to Hungary, for example, advised Fradi fans not to go to Amsterdam in view
of the negative shift in the Dutch public perception of Hungary. He declared
that he himself would only attend the match at the invitation of the Fradi
management.[37] An 'anti-Ajax front' was formed among fans, joined by
supporters of Újpest despite their otherwise strong rivalry with Fradi. News
received from The Netherlands indicated that Groningen and Feyenoord fans
opposed to Ajax were already waiting eagerly for Fradi fans to take joint action
against Ajax supporters.[38]

The Ajax coach Van Gaal personified the whole attack, hence he received
the Fradi fans' annual Lemon Prize by a massive margin.[39] While Hungarian
public opinion seemed unified in its anti-Ajax stand and even found allies in
Holland, rumour had it that conciliatory overtures had been made to the
Dutch and personally to the Dutch physiotherapist who was of Hungarian
origin. *Sport Plusz Foci* investigated the affair and revealed that indeed the
Hungarian Ajax Fan Club had written a letter, asking him to pass on their
views to the club president, the players and the coach. The letter condemned
the fans' racism, and stated:

> Let us assure you that the **Hungarian Ajax Fan Club <u>has never tolerated and will not
> tolerate</u> among its members people who discriminate by age, colour of skin, language,
> religion or ethnic origin!** We sincerely hope that despite this sad experience, you will not
> identify the Hungarian public with those vulgar persons who completely forgot themselves
> on Wednesday. [original emphasis reproduced][40]

In an interview, the group's leader stated: 'I am not in the least ashamed of
not having rooted for Fradi: this was not a match of the national team, but
one between clubs, and hence the slogan that 'every Hungarian should root
for Fradi' was demagoguery to say the least. Our group includes Fradi, UTE,
Kispest, MTK and Vasas fans also, not to mention those in the countryside.
If their favourite Hungarian side plays against Ajax, fans of the given club
will root for the Hungarians and the rest for the Dutch.'[41] A letter to *Sport
Plusz Foci* (23 December 1995) quotes another example. The reader noticed
and regretted that, after the Ferencváros–Ajax (1–5) match, Újpest fans put
up a 'Thank you, Ajax' banner on the stands. The letter-writer asks 'whether
such people consider themselves Hungarian fans at all'.

37. *Nemzeti Képes Sport*, 28 November 1995.
38. Ibid., *Sport*, 28 November 1995.
39. Cf. *Sport Plusz Foci*, 25 November 1995.
40. Ibid., 2 December 1995.
41. Ibid., 2 December 1995.

The return match between Ajax and Ferencváros took place on 6 December 1995. Prior to the match, Ferencváros fans addressed a communiqué to the nation:

> Hungarians!!! Ferencváros fans hereby declare that they are not kept away from Amsterdam by fear of the Ajax fans or the ban of the Dutch authorities, but by their boundless and inextinguishable love for Ferencváros. Therefore, we call on every Ferencváros fan to come to Üllöi út at the time of the match and protest, through their personal appearance, against the assault on Ferencváros Gymnastic Club. Let's prove that we are capable of supporting our beloved team even from a distance of 1600 km. Therefore, we ask you to create such an atmosphere at the time of the encounter (with posters, flags, scarves) as if the match took place at Üllöi út. 2nd sector, Aryan Army, Cannibals, Green Monsters [fan groups signing the communiqué – J.B.].[42]

This reaction of the most radical fan groups was a symbolic gesture, meant to prove that the frequent attacks upon them, in the interests of the team, and the criticisms blaming them for lack of disciplined behaviour, were unfounded. They would make any sacrifice for the club, to the point, in this specific case, of not being present personally at the match and not getting even with the Dutch side. No incident occurred at the Amsterdam match, which also meant that the Ajax affair came to an end. As the storm subsided, the event was remembered by a few readers' letters only. The letters – as well as press reaction to the return match – tended to return to football (in the strict sense) and the expression of less extreme views, with only a few more nuanced references to the relationship of Hungarians and Europe. According to these views, the traditions and history of Fradi are too deeply rooted to question their *raison d'être* on the European football scene:

> I find the servile humility manifested in the treatment of Ajax by the Hungarian press a tiny bit repulsive. As we know, this is really an excellent team, full of brilliant Nigerian, Surinamese, Finnish and of course a few Dutch stars. We know they have already won the Champions Cup a few times, that Cruyff, Neeskens & Co. had earlier won a smashing victory over Beckenbauer's Bayern (5–0), and were the backbone of the Dutch national team that twice could have become world champions had it not rejected with two hands and arrogant Netherlander pride the Jules Rimet trophy. That is, they can play football and to date they have more goals – eight of them – than Fradi. However – and I send this fax precisely because of this 'however' – neither have Ferencváros come out of nowhere. This club already had a Schlosser, a Pataky, a Turay, a Sárosi, a Lázár, a Kocsis and a Golden Ball winner Albert; they won Central European Cups at a time when the Dutch still had difficulties distinguishing a ball from an Eidamer. Up to the beginning of the 1970s, the world had no

---

42. *Nemzeti Képes Sport*, 5 December 1995.

idea football was played at all in Holland, by which time Fradi had some 50 wonderful and highly successful years behind them . . . Let's not have the papers say and make it appear that the nearly 25-year results of the 'big Ajax' faded the patina of Fradi. Or else, Géza Toldi [a legendary forward in the 1930s] will have to be resurrected and told that Fradi are being hurt again. And then the good Dutch would learn what Attila's scourge looks like.[43]

Anthropologically, the phenomena associated with the Fradi–Ajax match can be interpreted as follows. In the first half of the 1990s, in line with certain nationally articulated political goals, the 'European-ness' of Hungarians and the need to integrate into Europe moved into the foreground of Hungarian patriotic public thinking. Certain areas, such as sport and especially the international results of Fradi, were seen as excellent occasions to provide symbolic proof that present results and past traditions made Hungarians eligible to be part of the 'new Europe'. Fradi's 1995 football victories, their entry to the Champions League and victory over the Belgian and Swiss champions not only suggested that Hungarians were already 'in Europe', but also that they could contribute new and fresh values to its culture. This reading, of the successes of Fradi as 'the national team', explains the great expectations before the Ajax match. The Amsterdam team symbolized the *crème de la crème* of Europe, represented European performance at its highest level, and the match provided an excellent opportunity for Fradi, and hence the Hungarian nation as well, to measure itself against the best. Public opinion awaited the match with such excessive optimism that the majority of those betting expected a draw or a Hungarian victory. The final score itself intensified fears that Fradi, as representative of the Hungarians, was very far from the European élite, and could relapse to the level of a few years earlier when catching up with Europe seemed very distant indeed. National anguish over the defeat was enhanced by the statements of Ajax's coach after the game and by later Dutch charges directly challenging the 'European-ness' of the Hungarian nation, expressed through the Dutch demand, in the name of European-ness, to remove Ferencváros from the (football) map of Europe.

The events strengthened – as is typical of national-level fiascos – the power of football to build solidarity both in the case of the club and the nation. A symbolic battle ensued, in the form of reaction to Ajax charges based on the opposition of West and East Europe. The argument set out to prove that it was precisely the *Dutch*, apparently the champions of European values, who adopted an exclusive attitude, while Hungarians truly belonged to Europe in spite of their undoubtedly peripheral economic and geographical position,

43. Quoted from a fan's letter published in *Sport Plusz Foci*, 16 December 1995, written by a Fradi fan of Hungarian origin living abroad.

on the basis of the traditions and the values of their national past. A game of football and its aftermath hence provided an opportunity for the revival, through Fradi, of the peculiar ambiguity of Hungarian national identity based on the concepts of core and periphery; for an examination of such issues as national fate, national values, the place of Hungarians in Europe, the national feeling of being threatened, and so on.

The Ajax affair would not have developed into a national issue had the Dutch faced a team other than Fradi, traditionally the most popular club in Hungary. External and internal events related to Fradi have a much greater propensity for turning into public affairs than similar events involving other club teams, a circumstance that has probably contributed to the extent of the publicity and interest, and also the passions and emotions, triggered by the Ajax affair. The converse, however, is also true: should Fradi suffer atrocities of any kind in the international football arena – whether a (grave) defeat suffered in the field or something like the Ajax affair analysed here – that will activate instantly the nation's sense of danger concerning the issue of belonging to Europe.

Afterword Constructing Social Identities: Exploring the Structured Relations of Football Rivalries

Richard Giulianotti and Gary Armstrong

Sometimes, unfortunately, the sporting world is hit by episodes that damage the real significance of competition. In particular, passionate support for a team must never reach the point of insulting people and damaging the collective well-being.

(His Holiness, Pope John Paul II, 28 October 2000, quoted in *The Independent*)

The 'Middle-Range' Structure of Oppositions

How can we begin to explain, in more theoretical terms, the underlying social nature of football rivalries? One strategy is to begin by seeing how football rivalries relate to social identities. In the book *Football: A Sociology of the Global Game*, Giulianotti (1999) indicates that social identities, including football ones, may be seen as taking semantic and syntactic forms. Semantic-centred identities emerge through how people define themselves, either individually or collectively, in terms of *what they are*. More syntactic identities emerge through how people define themselves through understandings of *what they are not*. Succinctly stated, the semantic is rooted in inner self-affirmations, while the syntactic is defined by external opposition. The underlying logic of football as a cultural form tends to privilege the syntactic over the semantic, through the creation of oppositions at all levels. Players, teams, supporters, managerial staff, directors and team officials all have social identities that are rooted in rivalry with their 'opposing numbers'. One essentially semantic category may be reserved for the match officials and football authorities who would claim to stand above such competitive rivalries through their roles as accredited, disinterested custodians of the game. Yet this elevated status may itself be interpreted as crystallizing syntactically, through the strict self-definition of football officials against the interested, competitively committed position of football's other participants.

This binary cognition of social life is most obviously located within the structuralist school of anthropology as led by Claude Lévi-Strauss (1968). Structuralists argue that cultural beliefs underpin our understanding of the world, and that this 'knowledge' of our surroundings is organized through our systems of classification, especially those founded upon forms of binary or triangular opposition. Food, for example, may be classified as 'raw', 'cooked' or 'rotten'. Some sub-classifications may be appended to fill out the model, such as food that is 'altered' (cooked and rotten) or 'unaltered' (raw) (Lévi-Strauss, 1978).[1] Crucially, Lévi-Strauss draws a sharp distinction between the 'surface' relations of things, and the deep structural relations that may be common to all cultures and which reflect a 'universal mind'. Surface relations may be recorded easily enough, but the objective, deep structures are latent and may only be disclosed by the social researcher. For Lévi-Strauss, the researcher should consider the logic of social patterns in a synchronic sense (within a specific temporal moment) rather than diachronically (as an unfolding historical process).

To explore football rivalries across the world, we would advocate an engagement of the structuralist approach, but in a qualified form at which we arrive through three general caveats. First, the structuralist antagonism towards a diachronic approach is both self-limiting and implausible. Here, it would not allow us to consider the cultural life of a sports-related rivalry or opposition from its origins through to its various manifestations and its conclusion, if such a point were reached. We require particular awareness of the power inequalities that situate and strongly influence the relationships between people over time. Second, Lévi-Strauss's sharp distinction between surface and objective structures is analytically useful, but weak in terms of its privileged epistemology. In other words, we consider that it is a little extreme in allowing the social researcher to decipher the 'objective' structural patterns of a society, while none of the social actors within the society are considered capable of such insights. Third, Lévi-Strauss asks us to submit to an article of faith, rather than yield to verifiable argument, when advancing his claims regarding a 'universal mind'. Even if we did accept this proposition, it would still encourage us to pass over the complexity of data in favour of finding only confirming evidence that would fit within an objective, underlying model.

---

1. For an application of Lévi-Strauss's culinary commentary, see Archetti (1997).

Nevertheless, we may still applaud Lévi-Strauss's motives here, in trying to consider how research findings from different cultures can be compiled to identify underlying, cultural continuities. In the contemporary academic world, cross-cultural comparisons are far more viable than ever before, if only because of the greater geographical movement of researchers between international research groups, conferences and publications (as this book demonstrates). Moreover, in the late modern era of intensified globalization, we find that different societies are increasingly united through the sharing of social practices (such as the shared, transnational aesthetics of spectator styles) and cultural forms (such as football itself, the 'global game'). We would therefore argue for a more 'middle-range' approach towards researching clusters of social relations, such as in football culture.[2] We do require to be highly cognizant of the classificatory practices and binary oppositions that shape football rivalries; but we need to allow for the possibilities that these oppositions contain relatively unique cultural properties, and are understood in complex terms by the social actors themselves. Moreover, we need to consider the underlying power inequalities that also shape the structure of oppositions and social identities.

Seven Structured Relations of Football Opposition

These questions become more relevant as we turn to examine the themes that emerge from our case studies. We identify seven specific themes, or structured relations, that relate to the production and reproduction of football-centred oppositions. The themes should be seen as reflecting the 'middle range' structured relations that exist beneath the surface rivalries and opposing identities within the case studies. Yet in contrast to the more adventurous elements of structuralist thinking, these structured relations are typically known to the social actors as well as to the social researcher. There is also no insistence

2. In employing the term 'middle-range', we are, of course, borrowing from Merton (1968), and his modification of Parsons. Merton did not share Parsons's *a priori* conviction that all social practices must be functional to the reproduction of the social system. Instead, Merton (1968: 39–72) advanced a less-ambitious claim, arguing that research into specific social structures should be undertaken to determine their degree of functionality or otherwise to the maintenance of the wider social system. We use the term 'middle-range' in two senses. First, for Merton, the term 'middle-range' had a strong methodological meaning in bridging the practical thinking behind daily research and the unlikely ideal of a grand, unifying social theory. In some contrast, we employ the term to link the epistemological practices of the researcher and his or her research group; otherwise stated, a middle-range approach emphasizes the common frameworks of knowledge that exist between those caught up in observable social relations and those outside specialists who are charged with their interpretation. Nevertheless, and second, we share Merton's concern to produce a less-ambitious, but more testable, flexible set of theoretical statements on a specific realm of social life. In our case, this involves the use of a critical, comparative approach to identify the continuities and differences between various sports cultures in specific settings.

here that these structured relations are universal in their manifestation or intrinsic to the human mind. Such a broad claim would underplay the cultural complexity and diversity of human societies that are dramatized, in part, through football.

1 The Construction of Conflicting Identities: Legitimizing, Resistance, Project

First, and most generally, the articles serve to discuss how specific, conflicting social identities are constructed through football. We have already noted the primarily binary basis of these identities which may be disclosed through adopting a modified structuralist approach. Yet how do power inequalities also shape the interaction of these social identities? Castells (1996: 8–10) provides a useful three-fold typology to explain how power shapes the interplay of social identities:

- 'Legitimizing identity' is constructed through the dominant institutions of society. This helps to generate a 'civil society' of institutions and organizations in which such domination is reproduced and, potentially, challenged. For example, predominant forms of nationalist identity would certainly fit here, and would be produced and reproduced through the national football associations as part of the broader 'civil society'. Bali's article on Ferencváros, and the club's representation of a dominant Hungarian identity, illustrates this process. Other power resources may come into play here as well, notably material wealth or cultures of patronage. The articles on Juventus in Italy and América FC in Mexico are instructive.
- 'Resistance identity' is constructed by those individuals and groups who are at the wrong end of social domination, in the sense that they are socially excluded or stigmatized within the existing power framework. This identity gives rise to 'communes' or 'communities' that can enable a collective resistance, often defensive, to the forces of social domination. For example, smaller football clubs (such as Millwall in England or Bryne in Norway) may husband this sense of 'resistance identity' through appeals to a strong sense of community representation, or the emphasizing of ethnic differences.
- 'Project identity' is constructed by social collectives that are committed to the creation of a different life. This identity generates 'subjects' whose project points towards the transformation of society. A project identity may be found in fan or club cultures that explicitly envisage projects of broader, collective empowerment. For example, in the UK we may point to independent supporters' associations that seek to transform the power relationships within football. In Europe, we may point to those popular

270

cultures surrounding clubs such as Barcelona, which foster a nationalist identity that may envisage a separate nation-state. The article on Croatian teams in Australia demonstrates this point with equal facility. Equally, in the developing world, the new 'project' identities may concern an attempt to Westernize the local, traditional culture. The articles on football in Argentina and in Cameroon demonstrate the kinds of conflict that may subsequently arise.

As the reader will discern, social actors are not fixed into one of these three identity categories. Movement between categories will depend upon historical and contextual factors, such as the distribution of resources, levels of social exclusion within the society, and the collective self-identification of social actors at specific junctures. This becomes most obvious if we recall the study of Croatian clubs in Australia; more specifically, we may turn to consider the imagined 'home' of these clubs, Croatia, and the complex recent history of Dynamo Zagreb, Croatia's most famous club. During the postwar period in Yugoslavia, until the civil war, Dynamo Zagreb were the most popular club among those of Croatian extraction. In that sense, Dynamo Zagreb were primarily associated with a 'resistance' identity, symbolizing Croatian difference to the 'legitimizing', national identity that the Serb-dominated state sought to inculcate through the Yugoslav national football team.

In the build-up to civil war, Dynamo Zagreb's 'resistance' identity began to acquire an increasingly 'project' form, as a vehicle through which broader social transformation might occur, such as the realization of a separate Croatian state. Indeed, one obvious trigger for the outbreak of civil war was a major riot involving fans, players and the police at a match between Dynamo and the Serb side, Red Star Belgrade in 1990. After military conflict, the Croatian state was established in 1991, President Tudjmann was sworn in, and a nationalist government was elected. Dynamo Zagreb changed their name to Croatia Zagreb to symbolize a break with the Yugoslav, Communist past, and to advance the 'legitimizing' of a post-Communist, Croatian identity. The reincarnation of the club was strongly supported by the pro-government directors, but 'resisted' by a small community of fans known as the BBB. The opponents quickly acquired a collective, project identity, ranged across the new civil society, to demand a return to the original name. Explicit support was expressed by other fan groups across Croatia. The BBB were violently excluded from the club's matches and dismissed critically by Croatia's political elite. However, the fans' project eventually succeeded with a return to the original name of Dynamo Zagreb. The result seemed to legitimize both the club's long history and its degree of autonomy from the new state in Croatia;

but it also reflected wider social changes, as the President died and his government was voted out of office.[3]

The recent history of Dynamo Zagreb illustrates how a sports institution may traverse different identity statuses. More significantly, perhaps, the story indicates that, at any one juncture, groups of social actors may coalesce or fragment to produce new identities; for example, the BBB fans elect to depart from the 'legitimizing identity' of the new Croatia to produce a resistance identity, then a project identity, that finally succeeds by legitimizing Dynamo's old identity once more. In this sense, we do not have reified and unchanging conceptions of communities or power relations, but dynamic ones that unfold in time–space terms. More generally, Castell's categories are very useful for mapping the underlying power relations in identity construction. Therefore, we would interpret the remaining six themes within the chapters of this book as ways of organizing our understanding of this interplay of 'legitimizing', 'resistance' and 'project' identities.

2   The Drama of Power Inequalities

Our second theme concerns the way in which football dramatizes relationships between the rich and politically powerful elites, and the others. In other words, we have an underlying contest, rooted in political and economic inequalities, between the powerful 'legitimizing' identities and those that adopt 'resistance' or even 'project' identities towards unseating these elites. The world's richest and most popular club, Manchester United, with an annual turnover of £111 million in 1998-9, are at the apex of this hierarchy both in England and in global terms. At the national levels, there are comparable cases involving Glasgow Rangers in Scotland (especially during the 1990s), América of Mexico, and Juventus in Italy. All of these clubs have enjoyed long periods of football dominance and economic superiority over their rivals that may be assisted to varying degrees by political patronage or through the representation of powerful elites. In cases such as Linfield (Northern Ireland) and Olympic (Cameroon), economic and political power has assisted without delivering an equivalent level of success. Nevertheless, the broader recognition of these clubs as putatively dominant, leads to supporters of many other clubs strongly defining themselves in resistance to such monolithic structures. In most instances (notably in Mexico, Scotland and England), temporary communities are constructed against the superclubs by fans of different, rival clubs. In Manchester United's case, for example, English fans at England internationals will collapse their club differences to chant about their common identity

---

3. For a full description of this story and a Habermasian analysis of its meaning within the public sphere, see Vrcan (2000).

through an anti-United stance: 'Stand Up If You Hate Man U'. In Cameroon, the defeat of OM respectively might take on some project properties, by symbolizing for political subjects the possibility of wider social transformation. Yet in Scotland, Mexico, Italy and England, the national and indeed global supporter base of these superclubs can be symbolically contrasted with the more stratified, internally cohesive identities of smaller, rival clubs, such as Aberdeen, Cruz Azul, Torino and Manchester City respectively.

Meanwhile, within these superclubs, we find struggles between supporters to control the definition of the 'legitimate' club identity. On one hand, there tend to be the less-committed and more distant fans who are drawn to the club so long as it is successful; their role is increasingly legitimized by club marketing strategies that seek to win the 'middle ground' of floating football consumers. Conversely, the more traditionalist, longer-term fans will turn increasingly to a resistance identity towards market-centred changes to the club, perhaps resulting in a project identity that draws other fan groups into a cross-club 'popular front' against their disenfranchisement. Nevertheless, the more traditionalist fans of superclubs might struggle to authenticate their 'true support' in the eyes of these other club fans, and thus may be at the receiving end of a cross-club popular front which seems to acquire a 'project identity'. Consider the anti-Manchester United songs at England internationals.

3 Submerged Nationhoods

Our third theme concerns football's role in the construction or maintenance of 'submerged nationhood', to borrow Benedict Anderson's (1983) term. In this sense, we are interested in how football clubs not only reproduce more prosaic senses of community solidarity, but reflect more specific, resistant national identities that are otherwise suppressed or relatively dormant. The articles on Croatian football clubs in Australia, and Basque clubs in Spain, are obvious examples of this process, whereby 'the people' employ football clubs to represent a stateless, national community. 'Ethno-religious' identities are also relevant here. In Northern Ireland and Scotland, we find strong elements of a Protestant, Unionist and (in Linfield's case) staunchly Loyalist identity that imagines specific national communities to the exclusion of other peoples (notably Irish-Catholics). Rangers fans, for example, move discursively between 'legitimizing' and 'project' identities: first, through clear acknowledgement of their majority Protestant status, their songs about British imperialism at home and abroad, and their claims to be 'chosen' (through chants like 'We are the People'); second, through playing upon their perceived ties with Ulster Protestants and aspects of Englishness, in an era when the United Kingdom appears to be fragmenting. In India, communal politics finds its football manifestation in the rivalry between the 'legitimate' Hindu side of East Bengal, and the resistant, minority Muslim institution, the Mohammedan Sporting Club. In Mauritius, perhaps most violently, the communal violence between ethnically-based football clubs highlights forms of popular resistance to the national 'legitimizing' identity, of a 'rainbow nation'.

These case studies highlight the fact that the apparently straightforward nexus of these clubs with submerged nationhood is far more complex and contradictory than the surface appearances denote. We need to recognize the extent to which these resistant clubs can contain diverging, conflicting or even minority visions of community identity. In Northern Ireland, Linfield's Loyalist traditions are a rather more extreme strand of Orange politics compared to other Unionist clubs and have themselves been ameliorated, such as through lifting the ban on signing Catholic players. In Scotland, the traditional anti-Catholic values of Rangers represent one of many strands of Scottish Unionism. In India, the East Bengal club's Hindu identity is complicated by its original association with exiled groups from Bangladesh. In Mauritius, many fans have weakened their support for non-Creole clubs due to a perceived weakening of community ties, through the hiring of Creole players. In Australia, Croatian football clubs were certainly a cultural medium through which immigrants arriving from the former Yugoslavia could gradually integrate in all ways within the broader society while sustaining traditional cultural practices that related to the homeland. Yet, latterly, these community clubs have struggled to survive as the second and third generation of Croatian Australians have become assimilated to engage in other, 'legitimate' Australian pastimes. Perhaps most strikingly, we may note the historical divisions that exist between Basque clubs, the intensity of which calls into question the tendency of European intellectuals to conceive routinely of Basque identity as a relatively uncomplicated, homogeneous and teleological project.

In general, this discussion of football's 'submerged nationalities' points us towards two conclusions. First, we need to adopt a more critical reading of wider political and cultural assumptions. For example, in Europe since the late 1980s, there has been a tendency to generalize freely upon the strong regionalist, separatist and sub-nationalist political tendencies in central Europe, Scotland, Ireland, the various regions of Spain. Conversely, the papers here suggest that the sport of football may highlight how such 'sub-national' identities contain a breadth of internal rivalries and resistant identities. Second, football clubs with a sub-national or strong regionalist dimension are not simply dependent upon these sources of social identity, but stand in a 'relatively autonomous' relationship, and thus possess their own specific histories and identities. This at least has become most apparent to those club chairmen who have sought to amalgamate local clubs to create a regional super-force, only to have the media, supporters, players and coaches assail such a contempt-uous dismissal of football history.

4   Minority Identity and Local Difference

That conclusion draws us into our fourth theme, specifically football's role in underpinning minority identities and local differences. This is most obvious when we consider football rivalries within relatively peripheral settings. In Malta, for example, a relatively strong degree of homogeneity exists in religious and ethnic terms. Hence, senses of difference need to be constructed within this legitimizing identity in more localized and practical ways, some of them class-based, others rooted in party affiliation, and others still in terms of diverg-ing membership of brass-band associations. In Yemen, interurban rivalries have emerged between clubs, while political competition is also apparent in the recruitment of dignitaries to clubs. Local rivalries may take the form of an imagined, cultural opposition between civility and backwardness. In Norway, for example, the strong opposition between Viking Stavanger (who consider themselves more sophisticated) and the rural club from Byrne (defined by opponents as premodern) reflects deeper cultural antagonisms that are tied to the Western regions of the nation, some distance from the capital, Oslo. In contrast, in Scotland, it has been the relatively peripheral club of Aberdeen which defined itself, in resistance terms, as more cultured in opposition to Glasgow's teams, whose 'sectarianism' and domination of the game seemed to provide the 'legitimate' model for Scottish club identity.

5   The Symbolic Violence of Exclusion

In cases where these divisions are strong, we encounter material expressions of marked social exclusion. These divisions are often played out through violent incidents and stereotyping, and this constitutes our fifth theme. The Millwall club in England has a particularly violent reputation that tends to belie its close community identity. It stands in symbolic resistance to soccer's financial boom from which small clubs like Millwall, with their strong roots in working-class locales, are obviously excluded. Among Mauritian and Croatian-Australian clubs, some similar tales unfold of violent reputation, community identity and degrees of social exclusion. The popular antipathy that América attract in Mexico is certainly influenced by a sense of political and cultural exclusion among their opponents. Yet we should also note that supporters of relatively large clubs have been publicly notorious for their violent propensities, particularly at times when these sides' power has not been 'legitimized' through victories on the park. In England, the Manchester United 'Red Army' received intensive media criticism during the 1970s as the team fell into decline and relegation. In Scotland, Rangers' fan notoriety was its most extensive during the 1970s when the club struggled to compete against Celtic and remained virulently anti-Catholic in its recruitment of players. At Linfield, a staunchly Loyalist and Unionist 'legitimizing' identity underpins the violence of fans in opposition to any perceived 'project identities' that might appear to weaken this power.

6 *Aesthetic Codes, Tradition and Modernity*

Our sixth theme examines the rivalries that surround the football aesthetics within specific societies. These oppositions become most obvious through the interplay of traditional and modernizing forces in shaping 'national' playing styles, which are in turn viewed as representations of a national identity. Typically, the apparently more 'modern' styles are viewed as offering a project identity within football that threatens to unseat the legitimate, traditional styles. For example, in Argentina during the 1950s and 1960s, the traditional, 'legitimate' playing style (of Latin expressivity and technical skills) had come under threat from an apparently more successful, European and modern model (of physical power and defensive tactics). This latter model acquired a confrontational, project identity when the Argentinian club side Estudiantes de La Plata employed instrumental, extremely tough tactics in 1968 to win across South America and then to defeat Manchester United for the European–South American Cup. The debate over Latin or European playing styles continues in Argentina today, with most coaches pointing towards a hybrid model. In places such as the Basque country and Hungary, 'honest' and highly committed playing styles are viewed as more legitimate and reflective of national, masculine identity, in contrast to the more rationalized, professional styles that prove to be successful projects if comparatively unpopular ones among most fans. A comparable binary opposition exists in Mexico between América and other, less powerful, but more entertaining sides. Of course, football aesthetics extend beyond playing styles hence a further critique of América concerns the unduly sedate 'atmosphere' among their fans.

7 *Disorganized Capitalism and the Transformation of Rivalry*

Our seventh, final theme centres on how 'disorganized capitalism' is rewriting the framework of football oppositions. Since the late 1980s, world professional football has undergone a fundamental economic restructuring and expansion. The main sources of this boom are income from satellite or subscription television stations, and merchandising revenues from kit and other product sales. The other, notable structural change has been through the *Bosman* ruling that opened up a free market in European transfers. As we write, further transformations may be introduced through regulations that allow players to quit European clubs freely, with only a few weeks' notice. Collectively, these changes have exaggerated the financial and competitive differences between club sides. At the new millennium, the most successful club sides are at a crossroads, whereby the old, 'legitimized' rivalries with smaller domestic rivals are no longer so rewarding. Instead, a corporate resistance is expressed towards the constrictions placed on financial growth by this national competition. Top clubs turn instead to more rewarding, continental or global projects, such as an enlarged European Champions' League or a world club league, to match the international way in which their 'brand-names' have come to be marketed.

Hence, we find clubs like Rangers and Celtic in Scotland, or Manchester United in England, dominating more than even before in domestic terms, and losing interest in weaker club tournaments (including the FA Cup) to pursue new global projects. These changes will reduce the international rivalries involving clubs from less-powerful European nations, such as Malta, Hungary, Poland, Northern Ireland and even Norway. Where once these smaller nations entered several sides into European competition to compete against the most illustrious names, now they must battle against each other in many preliminary ties before advancing into proper European draws. Latin America has endured further, more problematic experiences of mass media corporate interests in shaping tournaments and rivalries. The numerous South American club tournaments pull in very low attendances but relatively good viewing figures; and tournaments such as the world club championship offer small competitive openings to the very best clubs from peripheral football and financial regions, such as Australia, Africa, the Middle East and Asia. The problem with all this concerns the extent to which the project of the television and football authorities seeks to legitimize the new, international rivalries. Juventus versus Athletic Bilbao may appeal in terms of playing aesthetics, but can it rival the nation-centred atmosphere of Juventus–Fiorentina or Athletic Bilbao–Racing Santander? As Giulianotti and Gerrard point out in their chapter, television is a 'cool medium', given to low intensities and affects; the resulting football rivalries will have a similarly sterile texture, at least in their early years. One radical conclusion here might be that the underlying format of football rivalries will be changed forever. These top clubs will no longer harbour the potential for a community or subject identity among fans. Instead, the rivalry could take an Americanized format, centring on the technical execution of game-plans by players and coaches, before a relatively cool television audience that exchanges sides just as it switches soap operas or channels.

According to some social theorists we are currently living through an era of 'disorganized' capitalism. This constitutes a new epoch in which 'culture, consumption, the global, the local, and concern for the environment' predominate (Lash and Urry, 1994: 258). The globalization of economic and cultural practices is particularly influential, as 'the flows of subjects and objects are progressively less synchronized within national boundaries' (ibid.: 10). The old institutions and organizations, that had arisen under 'organized capitalism' to regulate and control economic and cultural procedures, embark upon an often terminal decline in the late-twentieth century and new millennium (Lash, 1994: 213–4).

Inevitably, this process is itself dominated by new forms of political and economic conflict. In world professional football, there are clear signs of this 'disorganizing' process, manifested through the proliferation of rivalries and conflicts between specific institutional actors, each of which pursues its own project identity, thereby destabilizing the old, legitimizing identities within the game. Football's old organizational pyramid imagined a civil society in which FIFA stood at the apex, followed by the continental associations, the national associations, the clubs, the players and the fans (literally, 'the supporters' at the base) in a neatly administered hierarchy. Economic, legal, political and symbolic changes in world football have shaken that arrangement to the very foundations. FIFA, the continental and the national associations encounter greater clashes of interest, such as the legal and financial control over the world game's congested calendar of fixtures. UEFA's 'legitimizing' identity was first resisted by individual clubs, and is now challenged by the exclusive G-14 group of top European clubs which, as an established legal 'subject', is advancing its own vision of fundamental reform. Meanwhile, the clubs enter into fundamental conflicts with the national associations over payment of players and distribution of television revenues. Major non-football transnational corporations, such as Nike, Adidas and BSkyB television, exercise a growing influence over the game's strongest symbolic assets, the star players and top clubs. These companies are caught up in stronger internal competitions, such as through the Nike–Adidas battle to win club contracts, or BSkyB's battle with ON-digital and other satellite companies to earn television contracts.

To a large extent, football's history has been studded with surface outbreaks of institutional rivalries. In England until the First World War, the more aristocratic, amateurist southern clubs and the FA were in constant disagreement with northern, entrepreneurial clubs that pushed for professionalism and a Football League. Internationally, the Francophone FIFA and the patrician philosophy of the UK's four football associations were regularly at loggerheads.

Yet, we would argue that these conflicts are now much more widespread. There is a far greater range of institutional 'subjects' within football, all with their various personal 'projects' towards shaping the game in their economic and normative favour. The new intensity of business-centred competition under-pins such oppositions. Given the possible arrival of 'cool rivalries' involving top teams on global television networks, the hot rivalries will be much more apparent off the field between these institutional subjects.

Bibliography

Alabarces, P. (1996) 'Épicas chiquitas: apuntes sobre fútbol y peronismo en el Hincha (1951)', in Alabarces, P. and M.G. Rodríguez, *Cuestión de pelotas. Fútbol, deporte, sociedad, cultura*, Buenos Aires: Atuel.

Alabarces, P. (1999a) 'Argentine National Identity and Football: The Creole English Adventures of a Scot in the River Plate', paper to the XVIII British Society of Sports History Conference, Sport and Leisure Cultures, Chelsea School Research Centre, University of Brighton, 31 March–1 April.

Alabarces, P. (1999b) 'Post-Modern Times: Identities and Violence in Argentine Football', in G. Armstrong and R. Giulianotti (eds) (1999).

Alabarces, P. and Rodríguez, M.G. (2000) 'Football and Fatherland: The Crisis of National Representation in the Argentinian Football', in G. Finn and R. Giulianotti (eds), *Football Culture: Local Contests and Global Visions*, London: Frank Cass.

Alabarces, P., Taylor, C. and Tomlinson, A. (2000) 'National Narratives: England–Argentina', unpublished paper.

Alagich, R. (1995) *Soccer: Winning through Technique and Tactics,* Sydney: McGraw-Hill.

Albrow, M. (1996) *The Global Age: State and Society Beyond Modernity*, Cambridge: Polity Press.

Aldridge, J. with Jawad, H. (1999) *My Story*, London: Hodder and Stoughton.

Allan, J. (1989) *Bloody Casuals: Diary of a Football Hooligan*, Glasgow: Famedram.

Allison, L. (1998) 'Sport and Civil Society', in L. Allison (ed.), *Taking Sport Seriously*, Aachen: Meyer and Meyer Sport.

Alonso, J.M. (1998) *Athletic for ever! 1898–1998*, Bilbao: Coronet.

Althusser, L. (1971) *Lenin and Philosophy and other Essays*, London: New Left Books.

Althusser, L. (1981) 'Force and Signification', in *Dissemination*, London: Athlone.

Anderson, B. (1983) *Imagined Communities*, London: Verso.

Anonymous (1998) 'La gouvernance du Cameroun: le pouvoir ethnico-tribal de Biya mis à nu', *Le Messager*, 6 July.

Appadurai, A. (1990) 'Disjuncture and Difference in the Global Cultural Economy', in M. Featherstone (ed.), *Global Culture*, London: Sage.

Archetti, E. (1997) *Guinea-Pigs: Food, Symbol and Conflict of Knowledge in Ecuador*, Oxford: Berg.

Archetti, E. (1998) '*The Potrero* and the *Pibe*: Territory and Belonging in the Mythical Account of Argentinian Football' in N. Lovell (ed.), *Locality and Belonging*, London: Routledge.

Archetti, E. (1999) *Masculinities: Football, Polo and the Tango in Argentina*, London: Berg.

Archetti, E. and Romero, A. (1994) 'Death and Violence in Argentinian Football', in R. Giulianotti, N. Bonney and M. Hepworth (eds), *Football, Violence and Social Identity*, London: Routledge.

Armstrong, G. and Mitchell, J.P. (1999) 'Making the Maltese Cross: Football on a Small Island' in G. Armstrong and R. Giulianotti (eds).

Armstrong, G. and Young, M. (1999) 'Fanatical Football Chants: Creating and Controlling the Carnival' in G. Finn and R. Giulianotti (eds).

Armstrong, G. (1998) *Football Hooligans: Knowing the Score,* Oxford: Berg.

Armstrong, G. and Giulianotti, R. (eds) (1997) *Entering the Field: New Perspectives on World Football*, Oxford: Berg.

Armstrong, G., and Giulianotti. R. (eds) (1999) *Football Cultures and Identities*, Basingstoke: Macmillan.

Ash, M. (1971) *A Guide to the Structure of London*, Bath: Adams & Dart.

Asian Football Confederation News (1999a) 'Asians Continue to Slip', July: 35.

Asian Football Confederation News (1999b) 'Iran: Asia's Only Risers', August: 39.

Askeland, O. J., Olsson, A. I. and Bergesen, H. O. (1999) *Drømmen om de mørkeblå – Fotballklubben Viking gjennom 100 år*, Stavanger: Stavanger Aftenblad.

Ayinda, C.T. (1994) 'Fogape et ASPTT de Mfou en finale', *Challenge Sports*, 16 August.

Azoy, G.W. (1982) *Buzkashi: Game and Power in Afghanistan*, Philadelphia: University of Pennsylvania Press.

Back, L., Crabbe, T. and Solomos, J. (1996) *Alive and Still Kicking: An Overview Evaluation of Anti-Racist Campaigns in Football*, London: Commission for Racial Equality.

Bairner, A. (1997) '"Up to Their Knees"? Football, Sectarianism, Masculinity and Protestant Working-Class Identity', in P. Shirlow and M. McGovern (eds), *Who Are 'The People'? Unionism, Protestantism and Loyalism in Northern Ireland*, London: Pluto Press.

Bairner, A. (1999) 'Soccer, Masculinity and Violence in Northern Ireland: Between Hooliganism and Terrorism', *Men and Maculinities*, 1(3): 284–301.

Bairner, A. and Shirlow, P. (1999a) 'The Territorial Politics of Soccer in Northern Ireland', in G. Armstrong and R. Giulianotti (eds) (1999).

Bairner, A. and Shirlow, P. (1999b) 'Loyalism, Linfield and the Territorial Politics of Soccer Fandom in Northern Ireland', *Space and Polity*, 2(2): 163–77.

Baldacchino, C. (1989) *Goals, Cups and Tears: A History of Maltese Football,* Malta: Bugelli.

Baldacchino, C. (1995) 'The Wandering Blues', *The Times of Malta,* 21 September.

Bale, J. (1982) *Sport and Place: A Geography of Sport in England, Scotland and Wales*, London: Hurst.

Bale, J. (1993) *Sport, Space and the City*, London: Routledge.

Ball, P. (1986) 'Postscript' to E. Dunphy, *Only a Game?: The Diary of a Professional Footballer,* Harmondsworth: Penguin.

Banfield, E.C. (1958) *The Moral Basis of a Backward Society*, Chicago: The Free Press.

Barnes, S.T. (1986) *Patrons and Power: Creating a Political Community in Metropolitan Lagos* Bloomington: Indiana University Press.

Barthes, R. (1972, 1964) *Critical Essays*, Evanston, IL: Northwestern University Press.

Baumann, G. (1992) 'Ritual Implicates "Others": Rereading Durkheim in a Plural Society', in D. de Coppet (ed.), *Understanding Rituals,* London: Routledge.

Bayart, J.-F. (1993) *The State in Africa: The Politics of the Belly*, London: Longman.

Burns, J. (1999) *Barca*, London: Trafalgar Square.

Boissevain, J. (1977) 'When the Saints Go Marching Out: Reflections on the Decline of Patronage in Malta', in E. Gellner and J. Waterbury (eds), *Patrons and Clients in Mediterranean Societies,* London: Duckworth.

Boissevain, J. (1994) 'A Politician and His Audience: Malta's Dom Mintoff', in R.G. Sultana and G. Baldacchino (eds), *Maltese Society: A Sociological Inquiry,* Malta: Mireva.

Boissevain, J. (1995) [1965] *Saints and Fireworks: Religion and Politics in Rural Malta*, 2nd edn, Malta: Progress Press.

Bose, P.K. (1997) 'Partition-Memory Begins where History Ends', in R. Samaddar (ed.), *Reflections on Partition in the East*, New Delhi: Vikas.

Bourdieu, P. (1978) 'Sport and Social Class', *Social Science Information*, 17(6): 819–40.

Bourdieu, P. (1986) 'The Forms of Capital', in J.G. Richardson (ed.), *Handbook of Theory and Research for the Sociology of Education,* Westport, CT: Greenwood Press.

Boyle, R. (1994) '"We Are Celtic Supporters": Questions of Football and Identity in Modern Scotland', in R. Giulianotti and J. Williams (eds), *Game Without Frontiers: Football, Identity and Modernity,* Aldershot: Arena.

Bradley, J.M. (1998) 'We Shall Not Be Moved'! Mere Sport, Mere Songs? A Tale of Scottish Football', in A. Brown (ed.), *Fanatics!,* London: Routledge.

Brick, C. (1997) 'We're Not Singing Anymore', *90 Minutes*, 26 April: 30–1.

Brick, C. (2000) 'Taking Offence: Modern Moralities and the Perception of the Football Fan', in J. Garland, D. Malcolm and M. Rowe (eds), *The Future of Football,* London: Frank Cass.

Brodie, M. (1980) *100 Years of Irish Football*, Belfast: Irish Football Association.

Brodie, M. (1985) *Linfield 100 Years*, Belfast: Linfield Football and Athletic Club.

Brohm, J-M. (1978) *Sport, a Prison of Measured Time*, London: Ink Links Ltd.

Bromberger, C. (1993) '"Allez l'O.M., Forza Juve": The Passion for Football in Marseille and Turin', in S. Redhead (ed.), *The Passion and the Fashion: Football Fandom in the New Europe*, Aldershot: Arena.

Bromberger, C. (1995) 'La Revanche du Sud: la Partissima Napoli-Juventus de Turin (25 mars 1990)', in C. Bromberger, *Le Match de Football: Ethnologie d'un passion partisane a Marseille, Naples et Turin*, Paris, Collection Ethnologie de la France Regards sur L'Europe, Editions de la Maison des Sciences de l'homme.

Bromberger, C. et al. (1993) 'Fireworks and the Ass', in S. Redhead (ed.), *The Passion and the Fashion*, Aldershot: Avebury.

Bromberger, C. with A. Hayot and J.M. Mariottini (1993) 'Allez l'O.M., forza Juve': The Passion for Football in Marseille and Turin', in S. Redhead (ed.), *The Passion and the Fashion*, Aldershot: Avebury.

Bruce, S. (1985) *No Pope of Rome: Anti-Catholicism in Modern Scotland*, Edinburgh: Mainstream.

Bruce, S. (2000) 'Comparing Scotland and Northern Ireland', in T.M. Devine (ed.), *Scotland's Shame? Bigotry and Sectarianism in Modern Scotland*, Edinburgh: Mainstream.

Budd, M.A. (1997) *The Sculpture Machine: Physical Culture and Body Politics in the Age of Empire*, New York: New York University Press.

Bunwaree, S. (forthcoming) 'The Marginal in the Miracle: Human Capital in Mauritius', *International Journal for Educational Development*.

Burrowes, R.D. (1995) *Historical Dictionary of Yemen*, Lanham, MD: Scarecrow Press.

Cain, F. (1994) *The Australian Security Intelligence Organisation: An Unofficial History*, Ilford: Frank Cass.

Calhoun, C. (1997) *Nationalism*, Buckingham: Open University.

Calligarices, G. (1965) *Vie Nuove*, 15 April.

Campbell, D. and Shields, A. (1993) *Soccer City: The Future of Football in London*, London: Mandarin.

Carapico, S. (1998) *Civil Society in Yemen: The Political Economy of Activism in Modern Arabia*, Cambridge: Cambridge University Press.

Castells, M. (1996) *The Power of Identity*, Oxford, Blackwell.

Castells, L. and J.K. Walton (1998) 'Contrasting Identities: North-West England and the Basque Country 1840–1936', in E. Royle (ed.), *Issues of Regional Identity*, Manchester: Manchester University Press.

Castoriadis, C. (1997, 1975) *The Imaginary Institution of Society*, Cambridge: Polity Press

Cavour, C. (1952) *Carteggi: la liberazione del e la formazione del Regno d'Italia*, iii. (Oct.–Nov. 1860) Bologna.

Certeau, M. de. (1997, 1974) *Culture in the Plural*, Minnesota: University of Minnesota Press.

Chircop, S. (1994) 'As We Sit Together, Should We Use The Phone? A Research Agenda for the Study of Media in Malta', in R.G. Sultana and G. Baldacchino (eds), *Maltese Society: A Sociological Inquiry*, Malta: Mireva.

Coelho, J,N. (1998) 'Football and National Identity in Portugal', in A. Brown (ed.), *Fanatics!*, London: Routledge.

Colomé, G. (1997) 'Football and National Identity in Catalonia: FC Barcelona and Español', in S. Gehrmann (ed.), *Football and Regional Identity in Europe*, Münster: Lit.

Colome, G. (1999a) 'Conflictos e Identidades en Cataluna', in S. Segurola (ed.), *Futbol y Pasiones Politicas*, Madrid Debate.

Colome, G. (1999b) 'Dossier: futbol, historia i societat', *L'Avenc*, vol. 238.

Conn, D. (1997) *The Football Business*, Edinburgh: Mainstream.

Connerton, P. (1989) *How Societies Remember,* Cambridge, Cambridge University Press.

Coxsedge, J. K. Coldicutt G. and Harant (1982) *Rooted in Secrecy: The Clandestine Element in Australian Politics,* North Balwyn, Vic.: Committee for the Abolition of Political Police.

Coyle, P. (1999) *Paradise Lost and Found: The Story of Belfast Celtic,* Edinburgh: Mainstream.

Crampsey, B. (1990) *Aberdeen: Final Edition,* Aberdeen: KMP.

Critcher, C. (1979) 'Football Since the War', in J. Clarke, C. Critcher and R. Johnson (eds), *Working Class Culture: Studies in History and Theory,* London: Hutchinson.

Crown, J. (1986) *Australia: The Terrorist Connection,* South Melbourne: Sun Books Macmillan.

Cuvalo, A. (1990) *The Croatian National Movement, 1966–1972,* New York: Columbia University Press.

D'Errico, A, 1990, 'Aspetti giuridici e criminologici della cosiddetta 'criminalita degli stadi', Verona: unpublished manuscript.

Da Lima Leitao, N. (1997) 'Indian Football: Yesterday's Promise, Tomorrow's Glory', webpage: http:—goacom.com-goatoday-97-aug-noel.html.

Dal Lago, A. (1990) *Descrizione di una battaglia,* Bologna: Il Mulino.

Das, S. (1993) *Communal Riots in Bengal, 1905–1947,* Delhi: Oxford University Press.

Davies, A. (1992) *Leisure, Gender and Poverty: Working-Class Culture in Salford and Manchester 1900–1939,* Buckingham: Open University Press.

Davies, H. (1990) *My Life in Football,* Edinburgh: Mainstream.

De Martino, E. (1949) 'Intorno a una storia del mondo popolare subalterno', in *Società,* no. 5.

De Martino, E. (1953) 'Etnologia e cultura nazionale negli ultimi 10 anni', in *Società,* no. 9.

De Mello, A. (1959) *Portrait of Indian Sport,* London: Macmillan.

Deleuze, G. (1995) 'Le 'je me souviens' de Gilles Deleuze', in *Le Nouvel observateur,* no. 1619, 16–22 Nov.

Derrida, J. (1976, 1967) *of Grammatology,* Baltimore: John Hopkins University Press.

Di Giano, M. (1998) 'Avatares de la modernización en el fútbol argentino', in P. Alabarces et al. (eds), *Deporte y sociedad,* Buenos Aires: Eudeba.

Dickens, C. (1985 [1837]) *Oliver Twist,* Harmondsworth: Penguin.

Dickie, J. (1996) 'Imagined Italies', in D. Forgas and R. Lumley (eds), *Italian Cultural Studies,* Oxford: Oxford University Press.

Dillon, M.C. (1998) *Merleau-Ponty's Ontology,* Indiana: Indiana University Press.

Duke, V. and Crolley, L. (1996) *Football, Nationality and the State,* Essex: Addison Wesley Longman.

Dunning, E.,P.M. and Williams, J. (1988) *The Roots of Football Hooliganism,* London: Routledge.

Eco, E. (1984) 'Frames of Comic Freedom', in U. Eco, V. Ivanov and M. Rector, (Ed. T.A. Sebeok) *Carnival,* Berlin: Monton.

Eco, U. (1968) *La Struttura Assente*, Milan: Bompiani.

Eco, U. (1977,1964) *Apocalittic and integrati*, Milan: Bompiani.

Eco, U. (1986, 1969) 'Sports Chatter', in *Travels in Hyper-Reality*, London: Picador.

Eco, U. (1990) 'A Guide to the Neo-Televsion of the 1980's', in Z. Baranski and R. Lumley (eds), *Culture and Conflict in Post-War Italy*, London: Macmillan.

Eco, U. (1994) 'How Not to Talk about Soccer', in U. Eco, *How to Travel with a Salmon and Other Essays*, London:Secker and Warburg.

Eggen, N.A. (1999) *Godfoten: samhandling – veien til suksess*, Oslo: Aschehoug forlag.

Ehrenberg, A. (1980) 'Aimez-vous les stades? Architecture de masse et mobilisation', *Recherches*, no. 43. April.

Eriksen, T. (1998) *Common Denominators: Ethnicity, Nation-Building and Compromise in Mauritius*, Oxford: Berg.

Eriksen, T.H. (1993) *Ethnicity and Nationalism: Anthropological Perspectives,* London: Pluto.

Evans, A. (1999) 'The Potential of Sport for Reducing Racism and Xenophobia', paper to the conference, *How You Play the Game: The Contribution of Sport to the Promotion of Human Rights*, Sydney, Australia, 1–3 September.

Fair, L. (1997) 'Kickin It: Leisure, Politics and Football in Colonial Zanzibar, 1900s–1950s', *Africa*, 67: 224–51.

Farred, G. (1999) '"Theatre of Dreams": Mimicry and Difference in Cape Flats Township Football,' *Polygraph* 11: 65–88.

Femia, J.V. (1981) *Gramsci's Political Thought: Hegemony, Consciousness and the Revolutionary Process*, Oxford: Clarendon Press.

Fernea, E.W. and Fernea, R.A. (1987) *The Arab World: Personal Encounters*, Garden City: Anchor Press.

Ferrarotti, F. (1998) 'Calcio', in G. Calcagno (ed), *L'Identità degli italiani*, Roma-Bari: Gius. Laterza and Figli.

Finn, G. (1999) 'Scottish Myopia and Global Prejudices', *Culture, Sport and Society*, 2 (3): 54–99.

Finn, G.P.T. and R. Giulianotti, (eds) (1999) *Football Culture: Local Contests, Global Visions*, London: Frank Cass.

Finn, G.P.T. and R. Giulianotti (1999) 'Local Contests and Global Visions – Sporting Difference and International Change', in G.P.T. Finn and R. Giulianotti (eds), (1999).

Finn, G.P.T. (1991) 'Racism, Religion and Social Prejudice: Irish Catholic Clubs, Soccer and Scottish Society. I – The Historical Roots of Prejudice', *International Journal of the History of Sport*, 8: 70–93.

Finn, G.P.T. (1994a) 'Faith, Hope and Bigotry: Case Studies of Anti-Catholic Prejudice in Scottish Soccer and Society', in G. Jarvie and G. Walker (eds), *Sport in the Making of the Nation: Ninety Minute Patriots?*, Leicester: Leicester University Press.

Finn, G.P.T. (1994b) 'Sporting Symbols, Sporting Identities: Soccer and Intergroup Conflict in Scotland and Northern Ireland', in I.S Wood (ed.), *Scotland and Ulster*, Edinburgh: Mercat Press.

Finn, G.P.T. (1997) 'Scotland, Soccer, Society: Global Perspectives, Parochial Myopia', Paper to the *NASSS Annual Conference: Crossing Borders*, Canada: University of Toronto, 5–8 November.

Finn, G.P.T. (1999) 'Scottish Myopia and Global Prejudices', *Culture Sport Society*, 2 (3): 54–99.

Fofi, G. (1964) *L'immigrazione meridionale a Torino*, Milano.

Ford, A. (1994) *Navegaciones. Comunicación, cultura y crisis*, Buenos Aires, Amorrortu.

Francis, M. and Walsh, P. (1997) *Guvnors*, Bury: Milo Books.

Fraser, F. (1994) *Mad Frank: Memoirs of a Life of Crime*, London: Warner.

Frendo, H. (1979) *Party Politics in a Fortress Colony: the Maltese Experience,* Malta: Midsea Books.

Frendo, H. (1989) *Malta's Quest for Independence,* Malta: Valletta Publishing.

Friedman, J. (1976, 1957) in P. Clemente, M. L. Meoni and P. Squillacciotti (eds), (1976), *Il dibattito sul folklore in Italia.*

Garnham, N. (ed.) (1999) *The Origins and Development of Football in Ireland,* Belfast: Ulster Historical Foundation.

Geertz, C. (1973) *The Interpretation of Cultures*, London: Fontana Press.

Gehrmann, S. (ed.) (1997) *Football and Regional Identity in Europe*, Münster: Lit.

Gellner, E. (1983) *Nations and Nationalism,* Oxford: Blackwell

Geschiere, P. (1997) *The Modernity of Witchcraft: Politics and the Occult in Postcolonial Africa*, Charlottesville: University Press of Virginia.

Gibson, M. (1998) 'Biology or Environment? Race and Southern "Deviancy" in the writing of Italian Criminologists, 1880–1920', in J. Schneider (ed.), *Italy's Southern Question: Orientalism in One Country*, Oxford: Berg.

Gill, L. (1997) 'Relocating Class: Ex-Miners and Neoliberalism in Bolivia', *Critique of Anthropology*, 17 (3): 293–312.

Giulianotti, R. (1999). *Football: A Sociology of the Global Came*, Cambridge: Polity.

Giulianotti, R., Bonney, N. and Hepworth, M. (eds) (1994) *Football, Violence and Social Identity,* London: Routledge.

Goksøyr, M. and Hognestad, H. (1999) 'No Longer Worlds Apart? British Influences in Norwegian Football', in G. Armstrong and R. Giulianotti (eds) (1999).

Goksøyr, M., Andersen, E. and Asdal, K. (1996) *Kropp, kultur og tippekamp: Statens idrettskontor, STUI og Idrettsavdelingen 1946–96,* Oslo: Universitetsforlaget.

Goodchild, P. (1996) *Deleuze and Guattari: An Introduction to the Politics of Desire*, London: Sage.

Gramsci, A. (1954) *L'Ordine Nuovo, 1919–20,* Turin: Einaudi.

Gransci, A. (1955) *Lettere dal carcere*, Turin: Einaudi.

Gransci, A. (1975) *Quaderni dal carcere*, Turin: Einaudi.

Greenberg, J.B. (1989) *Blood Ties: Life and Violence in Rural Mexico*, Tucson: University of Arizona Press.

Gregory, D. (1994) *Geographical Imaginations*, Oxfor:, Blackwell.

Gribaudi, G. (1996) 'Images of the South', in D. Forgas and R. Lumley (eds), *Italian Cultural Studies*, Oxford: Oxford University Press.

Gundle, R. (ed.) (1995) *The New Italian Republic*, London: Routledge.

Hall, R. (1978) *The Secret State: Australia's Spy Industry*, Stanmore, NSW: Cassell Australia.

Hall, S. (1986) 'Media Power and Class Power', in J. Curran et al. (eds), *Bending Reality: the State of the Media,* London: Pluto.

Hay, R. (1992) 'Violence by Players', in Wray Vamplew et al. (eds), *Oxford Companion to Australian Sport*, Melbourne: Oxford University Press.

Hay, R. (1994) 'British Football, Wogball or the World Game? Towards a Social History of Victorian Soccer', in O'Hara, J. (ed.), *Ethnicity and Soccer in Australia*, ASSH Studies in Sports History Number 10, Campelltown, NSW: Australian Society for Sports History.

Hay, R. (1996) 'Football in Europe', *Bulletin of Sport and Culture*, 8: September, 10–2.

Hay, R. (1998a) 'A New Look at Soccer Violence', in Hemphill, D. (ed.), *All Part of the Game: Violence and Australian Sport,* Sydney: Walla Walla Press.

Hay, R. (1998b) 'Croatia: Community, Conflict and Culture: The Role of Soccer Clubs in Migrant Identity', in D. Mayall and M. Cronin (eds), *Sporting Nationalisms*, London: Frank Cass.

Hay, R. (forthcoming) *The Croatia Story*.

Hoberman, J. (1984) *Sport and Political Ideology*, London: Heinemann.

Hobsbawm, E. (1968) *Industry and Empire*, New York: Pantheon Books.

Hobsbawm, E. (1990) *Nations and Nationalism Since 1780: Programme, Myth, Reality,* Cambridge: Cambridge University Press.

Hoch, P. (1972) *Rip off the Big Game*, New York: Doubleday.

Hocking, J. (1997) *Lionel Murphy: A Political Biography*, Cambridge: Cambridge University Press.

Hofer, T. (1991) 'Construction of the "Folk Cultural Heritage" in Hungary and Rival Versions of National Identity', *Ethnologia Europaea*, 21.

Hofer, T. (1994), 'Introduction' in T. Hofer (ed.), *Hungarians Between 'East' and 'West'*, Budapest: Museum of Ethnography.

Hogg, A, J. McDougall and R. Morgan (1988) *Bullion: Brinks-Mat. The Story of Britain's Biggest Gold Robbery*, London: Penguin.

Hognestad, H. and Goksøyr, M. (1999) 'No Longer Worlds Apart? British Influences in Norwegian Football', in G. Armstrong and R. Giulianotti (eds) (1999).

Hognestad, H. (1995) *The Jambo Experience*, dissertation, Department and Museum of Anthropology, University of Oslo.

Holt, R. (1989) *Sport and the British*, Oxford: Oxford University Press.

Hornby, N. (1992) *Fever Pitch*, London: Orion Books.

Hughson, J. (1996) 'A Feel for the Game: An Ethnographic Study of Soccer Support and Social Identity', PhD thesis, Sydney: University of New South Wales.

Hughson, J. (1997) 'The Bad Blue Boys and the "Magical Recovery" of John Clarke', in G. Armstrong and R Giulianotti (eds), *Entering the Field: New Perspectives on World Football*, London: Berg.

Hughson, J. (1999) 'A Tale of Two Tribes: Expressive Fandom in Australian Soccer's A-League', *Culture, Sport and Society*, 2 (3): 10–30.

Hull, G. (1993) *The Malta Language Question: A Case Study in Cultural Imperialism*, Malta: Said International.

Jamieson, S. (1997) *Graeme Souness: The Iron Lady's Man*, Edinburgh: Mainstream.

Jarvie, G. and Maguire, J. (1994) *Sport and Leisure in Social Thought*, London: Routledge.

Jary, D., Horne, J. and Bucke, T. (1991) 'Football "Fanzines" and Football Culture: A Successful Case of "Cultural Contestation"', *Sociological Review*, 39 (3): 581–98.

Jauregui M.M. (1995) *Televisa*, unpublished undergraduate thesis, Mexico City, Mexico: Universidad Iberoamericana.

Johnson, C. (1999) *We Fear No Foe: A Decade of Millwall Fandom*, Dumfries: Terrace Banter.

Johnson, D. (1968) *Southwark and the City*, London: Oxford University Press.

Jones, R. and Moore, P. (1994) 'He Only Has Eyes for Poms', in J. O'Hara (ed.), *Ethnicity and Soccer in Australia*, ASSH Studies in Sports History, Number 10, Campbelltown, NSW: Australian Society for Sports History.

Josemaritarra (1980) *Txuri Urdin*, San Sebastian: Real Sociedad.

Jupp, J. (ed.) (1988) *The Australian People: An Encyclopedia of the Nation, Its People and Their Origins*, North Ryde, NSW: Angus and Robertson.

Juaristi, J. (1987) *El Linaje de Aitor: la invencion de la tradicion vasca*, Madrid: Alianza.

Juaristi, J. (1994) *El Chimbo Expiatorio*, Bilbao,?.

Kapusinski, R. (1992) *The Soccer War*, New York: Vintage International.

Kelland, G. (1993) *Crime in London*, London: Harper and Collins.

Kennedy, J. (1989) *Belfast Celtic*, Belfast: Pretani Press.

Kertzer, D. (1988) *Ritual, Politics and Power*, New Haven, Yale University Press.

King, A. (1998) 'Football Fandom and Post-National Identity in the New Europe', Paper to the 'Football 2000' Conference, University of Leicester, 9-11 September.

King, J. (1996) *The Football Factory*, London: Jonathan Cape.

Koster, A. (1984) *Prelates and Politicians in Malta*, Assen: Van Gorcum.

Kozanoglu, C. (1999) 'Beyond Edirne: Football and the National Identity Crisis in Turkey', in G. Armstrong and R. Giulianotti (eds) (1999).

Kuper, S. (1994) *Football Against the Enemy*, London: Orion.

Lane, C. (1981) *The Rites of Rulers: Ritual in Industrial Society: The Soviet Case*, Cambridge: Cambridge University Press.

Lanzardo, D. (1979) *La rivolta di Piazza Statuto*, Milano.

Larsen, T. (1984) 'Bønder i by'n', in Klausen, A. M. *Den norske væremåten – antropologisk søkelys på norsk kultur*, Oslo: Cappelen.

Lash, S. (1994) 'Expert-Systems or Situated Interpretation?', in U. Beck, A. Giddens and S. Lash, *Reflexive Modernization*, Cambridge: Polity.

Lash, S., and Urry, J. (1987) *The End of Organized Capitalism*, Cambridge: Polity.

Lash, S., and Urry, J. (1994) *Economies of Signs and Space*, London: Sage.

Le Mauricien, 24 May 1999.

Leguineche, M., P. Unzueta and S. Segurola (1998) *Athletic 100: conversciones en La Catedral*, Madrid: El Pais-Aguilar.

Leseth, A. (1997) 'The Use of *Juju* in Football: Sport and Witchcraft in Tanzania', in G. Armstrong and R. Giulianotti (eds) (1997).

Lever, J. (1983) *Soccer Madness*, Chicago: University of Chicago Press.

Lèvi-Strauss, C. (1966, 1962) *The Savage Mind*, London: Weidenfeld and Nicolson.

Lèvi-Strauss, C. (1968) *Structural Anthropology*, London, Allen Lane.

Lèvi-Strauss, C. (1978) *The Origin of Table Manners*, London: Jonathan Cape.

Lombroso, C. (1871) *L'uomo bianco e l'uomo di colore: Lettere sull'origine a la varietà delle razze umane*, Padova: Sacchetto.

Lombroso, C. (1898) *In Calabria (1862–1897)* Catania: Niccolò Giannotta.

Lomnitz, L.A. (1982) 'Horizontal and Vertical Relations and the Social Structure of Urban Mexico', *Latin American Research Review*, 17: 51–74.

Lumley, R. (1996) 'The Peculiarities of the Italian Newspapers', in D. Forgas and R. Lumley (eds), *Italian Cultural Studies*, Oxford: Oxford University Press.

MacClancy, J. (1996) 'Nationalism at Play: The Basques of Vizcaya and Athletic Club de Bilbao', in J. MacClancy (ed.), *Sport, Identity and Ethnicity*, Oxford: Berg.

Magazine, R. (1999). *Stateless Contexts: Street Children and Soccer Fans in Mexico City*, unpublished Ph.D, Baltimore, MD: Johns Hopkins University.

Magoun, F.P. Jr. (1938) *History of Football: From the Beginnings to 1871*, Bochum-Langendreer: Verlag Heinrich Pöppinghaus.

Maguire, J. (1999) *Global Sport*, Cambridge: Polity.

Mahjoub, F. (1990) '"Jo" Bell: comment j'ai conduit la révolte des Lions', *Jeune Afrique* 1–7 August: 73-6.

Manconi, L. (1998) 'Campanilismo', in G. Calcagno (ed.), *L'identita degli italiani*, Roma-Bari: Gius, Laterza and Figli.

Mangan, J.A. (1986) *The Games Ethic and Imperialism*, Harmondsworth: Viking.

Martin, P. (1991) 'Colonialism, Youth and Football in French Equatorial Africa', *International Journal for the History of Sports*, 8: 56–71.

Mason, A. (1980) *Association Football and English Society 1863–1915*, Brighton: Harvester.

Mason, T. (1990) 'Football on the Maidan', *International Journal of the History of Sport.* 7 (1): 85–96.

Mateos, J.M. (1921) 'La Historia del Athletic Club', *Hermes* 71.

Mbembe, A. and J. Roitman (1995) 'Figures of the Subject in Times of Crisis,' *Public Culture*, 7: 323–52.

McCrone, D. (1998) *The Sociology of Nationalism*, London: Routledge.

McMullan, J.L. (1984) *The Canting Crew: London's Criminal Underworld 1550–1700*, New Brunswick: Rutgers University Press.

Mees, L. (1992) *Nacionalismo Vasco, Movimiento Obrero y Cuestion Social (1903–1923)*, Bilbao: Fundacion Sabino, Argua.

Mejía Barquera, F. (1988) 'Impuestos y tarifas, los recursos de la nación a bajo precio', in R. Trejo Delarbe (ed.), *Las redes de Televisa*, Mexico City: Claves Latinoamericanas.

Melkevik J. Jr. (1994) *Idrettens historie i Rogaland 1919–1994*, Stavanger: Rogaland idrettskrets.

Meneghetti, L. (1971) *Aspetti di geografia della popolazione. Italia 1951–67*, Milano

Merton, R.K. (1968) *Social Theory and Social Structure*, New York: Free Press.

Middle East Times (1998a) 'Ahli gives Zamalek a devil of a time', 24 May 1998.

Middle East Times (1998b) 'Summit clash causes chaos in Cairo', 15 November 1998.

Mitchell, J.P. (1996) 'Gender, Politics and Ritual in the Construction of Social Identities: The Case of *San Pawl*, Valletta, Malta' unpublished PhD thesis, Edinburgh: University of Edinburgh.

Mitchell, J.P. (1998a) 'Performances of Masculinity in a Maltese *Festa*', in F. Hughes-Freeland and M. Crain (eds), *Recasting Ritual: Performance, Media, Identity*, London: Routledge.

Mitchell, J.P. (1998b) 'The Nostalgic Construction of Community: Memory and Social Identity in Urban Malta', *Ethnos* 63 (1): 81–101

Mitchell, J.P. (forthcoming) *Ambivalent Europeans: Ritual, Memory and the Public Sphere in Malta*, Reading: Harwood.

Moe, N. (1992) "Altro che Italia!'. Il Sud dei piemontesi (1860–1)', in *Meridiana*; Revista di storia e scienze sociali no. 15

Mookerjee, S. (1989) 'Early Decades of Calcutta Football', *Economic Times: Calcutta 300*, September: 146–57.

Moore, A. (1995) *The Right Road: A History of Right-Wing Politics in Australia*, Melbourne: Oxford University Press.

Moorhouse, G. (1998) *Calcutta*, London: Pheonix.

Morton, J. (1994) *Gangland: London's Uunderworld*, London: Warner.

Mosely, P. (1994a) 'Balkan Politics in Australian Soccer', in J. O'Hara (ed.), *Ethnicity and Soccer in Australia*, ASSH Studies in Sports History, no 10, Campbelltown, NSW: Australian Society for Sports History.

Mosely, P. (1994b) 'European Immigrants and Soccer Violence in New South Wales, 1949–59', *Journal of Australian Studies*, (40), March: 14–26.

Mosely, P. (1995) *Ethnic Involvement in Australian Soccer: A History, 1950–1990*, Report to Australian Sports Commission, , Canberra: National Sports Research Centre.

Mosely, P. (1997) 'Soccer', in P.A. Mosely, R. Cashman, J. O'Hara and H. Weatherburn (eds), *Sporting Immigrants*, Crows Nest, NSW: Walla Walla Press.

Murphy, B. (1993) *The Other Australia: Experiences of Migration*, Melbourne: Cambridge University Press.

Murray, B. (1984) *The Old Firm: Sectarianism, Sport and Society in Scotland*, Edinburgh: John Donald.

Murray, B. (1996) *The World's Game: A History of Soccer*, Urbana: University of Illinois Press.

Murray, B. (1998) *The Old Firm in a New Age*, Edinburgh: Mainstream.

Murray, J. (1988) *Millwall: Lions of the South*, London: Indispensable Books.

Nairn, T. (2000) *After Britain*, London: Granta.

Nandy, M. (1990) 'Calcutta Soccer', in S. Chaudhuri (ed.), *Calcutta: the Living City, vol. II: the Present and Future,* Calcutta: Oxford University Press.

Nguini, C. (1996) *Le Footoir Camerounais,* Capel, Yaoundé.

Niedermüller, P. (1989) 'National Culture: Symbols and Reality', *Ethnologia Europaea,* 19.

Nkwi, P.N. and Vidacs, B. (1997) 'Football: Politics and Power in Cameroon', in G. Armstrong and R. Giulianotti (eds) (1997).

Ntonfo, A. (1994) *Football et politique du football au Cameroun,* Editions du Crac, Yaoundé.

O'Hanlon, C. (1997) *The Politics of Football in Northern Ireland: the Case of Cliftonville Football Club,* Unpublished BA (Hons) dissertation, University of Ulster at Jordanstown.

O'Rourke, P.J. (1989) *Holidays at Home,* London: Picador.

Ongoum, L.-M. (1998) 'Etre arbitre de football au Cameroun: une expérience douloureuse', *Mots Pluriels,* (electronic journal).

Ormezzano, G.P. (1999) 'Introduction: Il Calcio in Italia: un modo di vivere', in M. Pennacchia, *Il Calcio in Italia,* Torino: Unione Tipografico-Editrice Torinese (UTET).

Papa, A. and Panico, G. (1993) *Storia Sociale del Calcio in Italia,* Bologna.

Parkes, P. (1996) 'Indigenous Polo and the Politics of Regional Identity in Northern Pakistan', in J. MacClancy (ed.), *Sport, Identity and Ethnicity,* Oxford: Berg.

Paterson, I.R. (2000a) *Sectarianism in Scotland,* unpublished PhD thesis, University of Aberdeen, Scotland.

Paterson, I.R. (2000b) 'The Pulpit and the Ballot Box: Catholic Assimilation and the Decline of Church Influence', in T.M. Devine (ed.), *Scotland's Shame? Bigotry and Sectarianism in Modern Scotland,* Edinburgh: Mainstream.

Patriarca, S. (1998) How Many Italies? Representing the South in Official Statistics', in J. Schneider (ed.), *Italy's Southern Question,* Oxford: Berg.

Pawson, T. (1973) *The Football Managers,* Newton Abbot: Readers' Union.

Pearson, G. (1983) *Hooligan: A History of Respectable Fears,* London:

Pennacchia, M. (1999) *Il Calcio in Italia,* Torino: Unione Tipografico-Editrice Torinese (UTET).

Pérez Espino, E. (1991) *Los Motivos de Televisa: el proyecto cultural de XEQ Canal 9,* Mexico City: Instituto de Investigaciones Sociales, National Autonomous University of Mexico.

Petraccone, C. (1994) 'Nord e Sud: le due civiltà', *Studi storici,* no. 35.

Petrusewicz, M. (1998) *Come il Meridione divenne una questione,* Rubbettino.

Piot, C. (1999) *Remotely Global: Village Modernity in West Africa,* Chicago: The University of Chicago Press.

Pitt-Rivers, J. (1961) *People of the Sierra,* Chicago: Phoenix Books.

Podaliri, C. and Balestri, C. (eds.) (1998) 'The *Ultras*: Racism and Football Culture in Italy', in A. Brown (ed.), *Fanatics!* London: Routledge.

Pollard, J. (n.d.) *Ampol's Australian Sporting Records,* comp. Sid Grant, North Sydney: Jack Pollard.

Polley, M. (1998) *Moving the Goalposts: A History of Sport and Society Since 1945*, London: Routledge.

Portelli, A. (1993) 'The Rich and Poor in the Culture of Football', in S. Redhead (ed.), *The Passion and the Fashion: Football Fandom in the New Europe*, Aldershot: Avebury.

Procter, N. and Lynch, R. (1995) 'The Uses of Soccer by Serbian Australians in the Expression of Cultural Identity', in C. Simpson and B. Gidlow (eds), *Proceedings of ANZALS Conference 1995*, ANZALS, Canterbury, New Zealand: Lincoln University.

Putnam, R.D. (1993) *Making Democracy Work: Civic Traditions in Modern Italy*, Princeton: Princeton University Press.

Raitz, K.B. (ed.) (1995) *The Theatre of Sport*, Baltimore: Johns Hopkins University Press.

Redhead, S. (1991) *Football with Attitude*, Manchester: Wordsmith.

Rein, R. (1998) 'Peronismo, Populismo y Política: Argentina, 1943–1955', Buenos Aires: Universidad de Belgrano.

Richardson, C. (1992) *My Manor*, London: Pan.

Robertson, R. (1990) 'After Nostalgia? Wilful Nostalgia and the Phase of Globalization', in B.S. Turner (ed.), *Theories of Modernity and Postmodernity*, London: Sage.

Robertson, R. (1992) *Globalization*, London: Sage.

Robins, K. (1991) 'Tradition and Translation: National Culture in its Global Context', in J Corner, S Harvey (eds), *Enterprise and Heritage*, London: Routledge.

Robson, G. (1999) 'Football, Working Class Masculinity and the Boundaries of Identity', in S. Munt (ed.), *Cultural Studies and the Working Class: Subject to Change*, London: Cassell.

Robson, G. (2000) *No One Likes Us, We Don't Care: The Myth and Reality of Millwall Fandom*, Oxford: Berg.

Robson,G. (1997) *Class, Criminality and Embodied Consciousness: Charlie Richardson and a South East London Habitus*, London: Goldsmiths College, Centre for Urban and Community Research Working Paper.

Rock, P. (1973) 'News as Eternal Recurrence', in S. Cohen and J. Young (eds), *The Manufacture of News*, London: Constable.

Rodríguez, M.G. (1996) 'Pan, circo y algo más', in P. Alabarces and M.G. Rodríguez (1996).

Rook, C. (1899) *The Hooligan Nights*, London: Grant Richards.

Roversi, A. (1992) *Calcio, Tifo e Violenza*, Bologna: Il Mulino.

Russell, D. (1997) *Association Football and the English*, Preston: Carnegie.

Saiz Valdivielso, A.C. et al. (1998) *Athletic Club (1898–1998): cronica de una leyenda*, Leon?.

Samaddar, R. (1999) *The Marginal Nation*, Delhi: Sage.

Sarcar, S. (1971) *The Bleeding Humanity:Poignant Story of Refugees from East Bengal Rendered by an Eye-Witness*, Bangalore: Ecumenical Christian Centre.

Scher, A. and Palomino, H. (1988) *Fútbol: pasión de multitudes y de elites*, Buenos Aires: CISEA.

Schlesinger, P. (1990) 'The Berlusconi Phenomena', in Z. Baranski and R. Lumley (eds), *Culture and Conflict in Post-War Italy*, London: Macmillan.

Schneider, J. (1998) 'The Dynamics of Neo-Orientalism in Italy (1848–1995)', in J. Schneider (ed.), *Italy's Southern Question*, Oxford: Berg.

Seith, A. (1986) *The Terrorist Threat to Diplomacy: an Australian Perspective*, Canberra: ANU Press.

Sennett, R. (1994) *Flesh and Stone: The Body and the City in Western Civilisation*, London: W.W. Norton.

Shields, R. (1999) *Lefebvre, Love & Struggle*, London: Routledge.

Shindler, C. (1998) *Manchester United Ruined My Life*, London: Headline.

Smout, T.C. (1986) *A Century of the Scottish People 1830–1950*, London: Collins.

Sperber, D. (1975, 1974) *Rethinking Symbolism*, Cambridge: Cambridge University Press.

Stauth, G. and Turner, B.S. (1988) 'Nostalgia, Postmodernism and the Critique of Mass Culture', *Theory Culture and Society*, 5 (2–3): 509–26.

Stein, S. (1988) 'The Case of Soccer in Early Twentieth-Century Lima', in J.L. Arbena (ed.), *Sport and Society in Latin America*, New York: Greenwood Press.

Stevenson, T.B. (1989a) 'Sport in the Yemen Arab Republic', in E.A. Wagner (ed.), *Sports in Asia and Africa*, Westport, CT: Greenwood Press.

Stevenson, T.B. (1989b) 'Sports Clubs and Political Integration in the Yemen Arab Republic', *International Review for the Sociology of Sport*, 24 (4): 299–313.

Stevenson, T.B. (1993) 'Yemeni Workers Come Home: Reabsorbing One Million Migrants', *Middle East Report*, no. 181 (Mar.–Apr.) [23(2)]: 15–20.

Stevenson, T.B. and Abdul Karim Alaug (1997) 'Football in Yemen: Rituals of Resistance, Integration and Identity', *International Review for the Sociology of Sport*, 32 (3): 251–65.

Stevenson, T.B. and Abdul Karim Alaug (1999) 'Football in the Yemens: Integration, Identity, and Nationalism in a Divided Nation', in J. Sugden and A. Bairner (eds), *Sport in Divided Societies*, Aachen: Meyer & Meyer Sport.

Sugden, J. and Bairner, A. (1993) *Sport, Sectarianism and Society in a Divided Ireland*, Leicester: Leicester University Press.

Sugden, J. and A. Bairner (eds) (1999) *Sport in Divided Societies*, Aachen: Meyer and Meyer.

Sugden, J. and Tomlinson, A. (1998) *FIFA and the Contest for World Football*, Cambridge: Polity Press.

Sutalo, I. (1999a) *Croatian Settlement in Victoria: The Untold Story*, Brochure accompanying an exhibition at the Schiavello Access Gallery, September–November, Melbourne.

Sutalo, I. (1999b) 'Croatian Pioneers of Victoria', *Matica*, 8: August.

Tanner, M. (1997) *Croatia: a Nation Forged in War*, New Haven, CT: Yale University Press.

Taylor, I. (1971) 'Football Mad: A Speculative Sociology of Football Hooliganism', in E. Dunning (ed.), *The Sociology of Sport: A Collection of Readings*, London: Frank Cass.

Taylor, I. (1971) 'Soccer Consciousness and Soccer Hooliganism' in S. Cohen (ed.), *Images of Deviance*, Harmondsworth: Penguin.

The Un-official Beginners Guide to the History of the Australian National Soccer League, (n.d. ?1999) Bentleigh, Vic.: Studs Up.

Terrachet, E. (1998) *100 anos de historia del Athletic de Bilbao*, Gran Enciclopeadia Varca, 5th Edition, Bilbao.

Tkalcevic, M. (1988) *Croats in Australia: An Information and Resource Guide*, Burwood, Vic.: Victoria College Press.

Trejo Delarbre, R. (1992) *La sociedad ausente: Comunicación, democracia y modernidad*. Mexico City: Cal y Arena.

Tuastad, D. (1997) 'The Political Role of Football for Palestinians in Jordan', in G. Armstrong and R. Giulianotti (eds) (1997).

Tuohy, M. (1978) *Belfast Celtic*, Belfast: Blackstaff Press.

Turner, B.S. (2000) 'The Possibility of Primitiveness', in M. Featherstone (ed.), *Body Modification*, London: Sage.

Turner, V. (1967) 'Symbols in Ndembu Ritual', in *The Forest of Symbols*, Ithaca: Cornell University Press.

Unzueta, P. (1999) 'Futbol y Nacionaliso Vasco', in S. Segurola (ed.), *Futbal y Pasiones Politicas*, Madrid Debate.

Victorian Amateur Soccer Federation Handbook (1958)

Vidacs, B. (1998) 'Football and Anti-Colonial Sentiment in Cameroon,' *Mots Pluriels*, no. 6. (electronic journal).

Villari, P. (1885) *Le lettere meridionale ed altri scritti sulla questione sociale in Italia*, Turin: Fratelli Bocca.

Vrcan, S. (2000) 'A Curious Drama: The President of a Republic Versus a Football Fan Tribe', unpublished paper, Croatia: Department of Sociology, University of Split.

Wagg, S. (1995) *Giving the Game Away*, London: Leicester University Press.

Walker, G. (1990) '"There's No Team Like the Glasgow Rangers": Football and Religious Identity in Scotland', in G. Walker and T. Gallagher (eds), *Sermons and Battle Hymns: Protestant Popular Culture in Modern Scotland*, Edinburgh: Edinburgh University Press.

Walkowitz, J. (1992) *City of Dreadful Delight: Narratives of Sexual Danger in Late Victorian London*, Chicago: University of Chicago Press.

Walvin, J. (1975) *The Peoples Game: A Social History of British Football*, London: Allen Lane.

Walton, J.K. (1998) 'Reconstructing Crowds: The Rise of Association Football as a Spectator Sport in San Sebastian, 1915–1932', *International Journal of the History of Sport*, 15: 27–53.

Walton, J.K. (1999) 'Football and Basque Identity: Real Sociedad of San Sebastian, 1909–1932', *Memoria y Civilizacion* (Universidad de Navarra) 2: 261–89.

Walton, J.K. (2000) 'Tradition and Tourism: Representing Basque Identities in Guipuzcoa and San Sebastian, 1848–1936', in N. Kirk (ed.), *Northern Identities*, pp. 87–108, Aldershot: Ashgate.

Ward, C (1992) *Steaming In: Journal of a Football Fan*, London: Sportspages.

Warren, I. (1995) 'Soccer Subcultures in Australia', in C. Guerra and R. White (eds), *Ethnic Minority Youth in Australia: Challenges and Myths*, Hobart: National Clearinghouse for Youth Studies.

Whiting, R. (1989) *You Gotta Have Wa*, New York: Macmillan.

Williams, J. (1991) 'Having an Away Day: English Football Spectators and the Hooligan Debate', in J. Williams and S. Wagg (eds), *British Football and Social Change: Getting into Europe*, Leicester: Leicester University Press.

Williams, J. (2000) 'The Changing Face of Football: A Case for National Regulation?', in S. Hamil, J. Michie, C. Oughton, and S. Warby (eds), *Football in the Digital Age*, Edinburgh: Mainstream.

Wolf, E.R. (1955) 'The Types of Latin American Peasantry', *American Anthropologist*, 57 (3): 452–71.

Wolf, E.R. (1957) 'Closed Corporate Communities in Mesoamerica and Java', *Southwestern Journal of Anthropology*, 13 (1): 1–18.

Wolf, E.R. (1986) 'The Vicissitudes of the Closed Corporate Peasant Community', *American Ethnologist*, 13 (2): 325–9.

Wolpert, S. (1997) *A New History of India*, Fifth Edition, Oxford: Oxford University Press.

Yemen Times (1998) 'Excellent-Division Football Tournament Next Month', 19 October.

Zavala, V. (1990) *Sociedad Cultural Deportivo de Durango (1919–1949)*, Durango: Ayuntamiento de Durango.

Index